PEN
POC
2(

WORLD ECONOMICS

IN ASSOCIATION WITH

AON

Empower Results®

PENSIONS POCKET BOOK
2019 EDITION

ISBN: 978-0-9567104-9-9

Produced and published by:

World Economics Ltd • 1, Ivory Square
• Plantation Wharf • London SW11 3UE • United Kingdom
Tel: (020) 7326 8350 • Fax: (020) 7326 8351

Comments and suggestions for future editions of this pocket book are welcomed. Please contact: Editor, Pensions Pocket Book, World Economics Ltd at the above address.

Printed and bound in Great Britain by Orchard Press Cheltenham Ltd
www.orchardpress.net

NOTES

(i) Symbols used:
'–' *or* 'n/a' = data not available or not available on a comparable basis.
(ii) Constituent figures in the tables may not add up to the totals, due to rounding.
(iii) For full definitions readers are referred to the sources given at the foot of the tables.
(iv) Some topics are mentioned in more than one place but the information is not necessarily from the same source. Any differences are likely to be due to difference in definition, method of calculation or periods covered.

ACKNOWLEDGEMENTS

The publishers would like to thank all those who have contributed to this compilation of pensions data, in particular Aon – co-producers of the book – whose contribution and support have been invaluable.

Other contributors, including government departments, whose help is gratefully acknowledged, include:

Association of Consulting Actuaries

Barclays plc

General Register Office for Scotland

Government Actuary's Department

Northern Ireland Statistics and Research Agency

Office for National Statistics (ONS)

The Pension Protection Fund

The Pensions and Lifetime Savings Association Ltd

The Pensions Management Institute

The Pensions Regulator

Wilmington plc

CONTENTS

Section 9: PENSIONS TAXATION – REGISTERED PENSION SCHEMES *(cont.)*

Section 10: THE LIFETIME ISA

Section 11: NON-REGISTERED SCHEMES

Section 12: LEAVING SERVICE BENEFITS

Reference Section 4: SOCIAL SECURITY BENEFITS AND TAX RATES

Reference Section 5: CONTRACTING OUT

APPENDICES

FOREWORD

The pensions developments in 2018 have been set against a backdrop of the UK's intention to withdraw from the EU and continued negotiations over the terms of its exit *(see following section)*. This wider political climate has increased the level of uncertainty over the future direction of pensions legislation and regulation.

A White Paper on protecting Defined Benefit (DB) pensions was published in March, proposing more powers for the Pensions Regulator, allowing it to be more proactive at gathering information and to punish employers who put their scheme at risk. This followed a number of inquiries into specific schemes and sponsors in financial difficulties, in which the actions taken by the Regulator were criticised by parliamentary committees. Consultation has subsequently taken place on some of the details of these proposed new powers. In the meantime, the Regulator has stated that it is adopting a 'clearer, quicker and tougher' approach and shown an increased enthusiasm to use its existing powers *(see Section 8)*.

The paper also signalled future changes on DB scheme funding, with a new 'enforceable' Code of Practice expected to add to the level of prescription in the near future, and increased disclosure of risk management and other actions via a chair's statement. Trustees and employers are increasingly looking to reduce risk, using liability management solutions and 'buy-ins' *(see Sections 21 and 24)*.

The White Paper also promises measures to improve the scope for consolidation of schemes, with a planned consultation on an appropriate regulatory regime for 'commercial consolidators', which also would allow an employer to end its obligation to fund a scheme *(see Section 24)*. Higher scheme governance requirements are likely to make some trustees and scheme sponsors think about options to consolidate in new pensions vehicles and the regulatory regime is being revised to ensure it is fit for purpose against this background. A new regime for the authorisation of Master Trusts came into force in October *(see Section 6)*.

Another high-level development is the re-consideration of collective DC schemes. The general legislative framework for 'defined ambition' schemes, which would enable risks to be shared between sponsors and scheme members, is outlined in the Pension Schemes Act 2015 but further regulations were required to facilitate such schemes. A Work and Pensions Committee inquiry has called for the Government to legislate for collective DC schemes.

Looking further ahead, the Government has set out its intention to make changes to the automatic enrolment legislation in the mid-2020s. These include reducing the lower age limit from 22 to 18 and calculating minimum contributions from the first pound earned. The Government will also work with the industry 'to build a sense of personal ownership of workplace pension saving amongst individuals'.

The latest developments are all set out the *Pensions Pocket Book*. We are sure you will find it to be a useful source of reference material.

Michael Clare
UK Director, Aon

BREXIT: THE IMPLICATIONS FOR UK PENSIONS

The UK's decision to leave the European Union (EU) will have wide implications, but many of these will depend on what will replace EU membership and the terms that the UK is able to negotiate. The UK is expected to leave the EU on 29 March 2019; transitional arrangements may be negotiated under which the UK would continue to abide by EU laws until the end of a transitional period, but at the time of writing plans are also being formulated in case there is a 'no-deal' Brexit with a cliff edge at 29 March 2019. This section considers some of the potential pensions implications of Brexit.

Statements from the Pensions Regulator

Following the referendum result, the Pensions Regulator published a guidance statement urging trustees and sponsors to remain vigilant and review their circumstances in light of the economic uncertainty. The Regulator expected trustees to have open and collaborative discussion with their sponsor about the possible effects on the business.

For Defined Benefit schemes, the statement highlighted:

- *covenant issues* – these will be sector- and employer-specific; trustees should consider how exposed their employer is to the risks and opportunities
- *investment and funding volatility* – this will depend on the extent of any hedging; trustees should consider the extent to which volatility and changing market conditions affect the longer-term view of expected risk and returns; scenario planning may help; where the scheme is exposed to an inappropriate level of risk action may be needed, *and*
- *schemes currently carrying out a valuation* – there are no changes to the requirements or deadlines but the statement sets out 'some things [trustees] may want to consider'.

For Defined Contribution schemes, the statement highlighted:

- *investment performance* – it remains important to consider how fund performance affects different groups of members; the impact will depend on age; as the implications become clearer trustees may consider it appropriate to make changes to default arrangements, *and*
- *member communications* – members may be nervous about the impact of the leave vote; trustees should be prepared to explain to members the approach they plan to take.

The statement was issued before actual exit timescales were planned, but the comments on possible market uncertainties in the run-up to the exit and beyond and the possible impact on individual companies and business sectors still apply. The longer-term consequences will depend on what replaces EU membership.

The Regulator's 2018 annual funding statement stated an expectation that trustees and sponsors would have open and collaborative discussions about how Brexit might affect a sponsor's business and its ability to provide support. Where sponsors are reasonably holding back cash from the scheme because of Brexit uncertainty, the Regulator states that trustees should make sure that shareholders are also sharing the burden proportionately.

Legislative change

Many of the EU requirements that are most significant for pensions do not apply directly and needed to be reflected in UK legislation. The Pensions (IORP) Directive *(see Section 8)* and EU anti-discrimination requirements *(see Section 16)*, for example, have been incorporated into UK Acts of Parliament, and the requirements of the new pensions directive are transposed into UK legislation with effect from the 13 January 2019 deadline for member states. This legislation is expected to remain in place after 29 March 2019. Of course, over time, there is likely to be some divergence.

In contrast, the requirements of the EU's General Data Protection Regulation *(GDPR, see Section 7)* apply directly to the UK and technically could fall away if the UK is no longer a member. However, when the UK leaves the EU the GDPR will be incorporated into UK law (alongside the UK's new Data Protection Act) under the European Union (Withdrawal) Act *(see below)*.

Adjustments are already being planned to UK pension legislation to remove references to EU non-UK schemes and in most cases treat all non-UK schemes the same, in the event of 'no deal'.

If the UK negotiated to join the European Economic Area (EEA) and the European Free Trade Association, then although it would not have a say in creating EU legislation, it would have to comply with certain EU regulations – possibly including much of EU-derived employment law. However, this would mean that the cross-border pension scheme provisions would still apply.

The European Union (Withdrawal) Act 2018 will repeal the European Communities Act 1972 on the day the UK leaves the EU, but convert EU law into domestic law. However, after exit, the UK Parliament would be able to make amendments to the details of this legislation.

Reliance on European Court judgments

The European Union (Withdrawal) Act 2018 gives pre-exit case law of the Court of Justice of the European Union (CJEU) the same binding status in UK courts as decisions of the Supreme Court; decisions of the CJEU made after exit day will not be binding on UK courts. However, after exit, legislation can be changed by the UK Parliament, and the Supreme Court would be able to depart from CJEU rulings if appropriate.

SECTION 1

THE UK STATE PENSION SCHEME

The new State Pension applies for those reaching State Pension Age from 6 April 2016. For those who reached State Pension Age up to 5 April 2016, there are two tiers of state pension provision: the Basic State Pension and the Additional Pension (State Second Pension and its predecessor, State Earnings Related Pension).

STATE PENSION AGE

State Pension Age (SPA) is now equal for males and females and is being gradually increased from 65 to 66 between November 2018 and October 2020. It is then to gradually increase to 67 between 2026 and 2028. SPA varies by month of birth; SPAs for sample dates of birth are set out in the table below:

<table>
<tr><th rowspan="2">Date of birth in tax month commencing</th><th colspan="2">State Pension Date</th></tr>
<tr><th>Female</th><th>Male</th></tr>
<tr><td>6 March 1950 or earlier</td><td>60th birthday</td><td rowspan="9">65th birthday</td></tr>
<tr><td>6 September 1950</td><td>6 March 2011</td></tr>
<tr><td>6 March 1951</td><td>6 March 2012</td></tr>
<tr><td>6 September 1951</td><td>6 March 2013</td></tr>
<tr><td>6 March 1952</td><td>6 March 2014</td></tr>
<tr><td>6 September 1952</td><td>6 March 2015</td></tr>
<tr><td>6 March 1953</td><td>6 March 2016</td></tr>
<tr><td>6 July 1953</td><td>6 July 2017</td></tr>
<tr><td>6 November 1953</td><td>6 November 2018</td></tr>
<tr><td>6 December 1953</td><td colspan="2">6 March 2019</td></tr>
<tr><td>6 April 1954</td><td colspan="2">6 November 2019</td></tr>
<tr><td>6 August 1954</td><td colspan="2">6 July 2020</td></tr>
<tr><td>From 6 October 1954 to 5 April 1960</td><td colspan="2">66th birthday</td></tr>
<tr><td>6 April 1960</td><td colspan="2">Age 66 years 1 month</td></tr>
<tr><td>6 October 1960</td><td colspan="2">Age 66 years 7 months</td></tr>
<tr><td>From 6 April 1961</td><td colspan="2">67th birthday</td></tr>
</table>

The Pensions Act 2014 provides for a regular review of SPA to take into account factors such as increases in longevity – it requires a report to be published at least every six years. These reviews (which will seek to give individuals affected by changes to their SPA at least ten years' notice) will be based around the idea that people should spend a certain proportion of their adult life drawing the State Pension. The Government Actuary must report on longevity, and a person independent of government will be commissioned to lead a report on other factors relevant to setting SPA. In March 2016, the first such independent review was launched, and in July 2017 the DWP published a report on that review, proposing a new timetable for rises in SPA to 68 (in line with the review's recommendations). Under the proposed timetable, SPA will increase from 67 to 68 between 2037 and 2039, seven years earlier than under the current legislation: this affects those born between 6 April 1970 and 5 April 1978 (those born after 5 April 1978 were already expecting a SPA of 68). However, before legislation implementing the change is laid before Parliament, a further review will be carried out to consider the latest life expectancy projections.

STATE PENSION FROM 6 APRIL 2016

The new State Pension applies to those who reach SPA on or after 6 April 2016. *See below for transitional arrangements.*

The full rate of State Pension is payable to individuals with 35 or more 'qualifying years'. Qualifying years are years in which the individual has received earnings at least equal to the Lower Earnings Limit (LEL), or is credited as earning the LEL because, for example, they receive certain benefits, or because they care, or receive child benefit, for a child under 12. Those who have fewer than 35 but at least 10 qualifying years receive a pension of less than the full amount; 1/35th of the full rate for each qualifying year. Those with fewer than 10 years receive no pension. Those working overseas may be covered by a reciprocal social security agreement between their host country and the UK, whereby social security contributions in the host country count towards the UK State Pension minimum qualifying years.

The facility to pay voluntary Class 3 National Insurance (NI) contributions enables those with fewer than 35 qualifying years to increase entitlement to State Pension.

The full rate of new State Pension for 2018/19 is £164.35 per week.

Entitlement to State Pension

Unless both members of a couple reached SPA before 6 April 2016, entitlement to the new State Pension is based only on the individual's own NI record, with two exceptions: someone who married or entered a civil partnership before April 2016 and some women who elected (before 6 April 1977) to pay reduced-rate NI contributions.

STATE PENSION SYSTEM TO 5 APRIL 2016

The system applicable to those who reached SPA before 6 April 2016 is described below:

Basic State Pension

The Basic State Pension (BSP) is a flat-rate pension that is payable to any individual who has sufficient 'qualifying years' (defined as above for the new State Pension). The number of qualifying years needed for a full BSP is 30 for both men and women. Individuals without sufficient qualifying years (either from earnings or credits) receive a proportion of the full amount. The 2018/19 rate of BSP for a single person is £125.95.

Subject to certain conditions, it is possible to pay voluntary Class 3 NI contributions to make up qualifying years and increase entitlement to BSP.

State Earnings Related Pension

The State Earnings Related Pension Scheme (SERPS) accrued between 1978 and 2002 and is paid in addition to the BSP. It is based on a person's earnings throughout their career. When it was replaced in 2002, SERPS was targeting a pension at SPA of approximately 20% of the employee's earnings between the Lower and Upper Earnings Limits.

State Second Pension

The State Second Pension (S2P) came into effect on 6 April 2002 to replace SERPS. Any SERPS entitlement earned up until April 2002 remained. S2P had salary bands that built up benefits at different rates *(see below)*. Certain non-earners (or low earners), such as those caring for the sick or disabled, also built up a S2P entitlement.

The salary bands used to calculate S2P took into account the Low Earnings Threshold (LET) and initially also a figure which approximated to 3 × LET – 2 × LEL. This figure is referred to below as the Middle Earnings Threshold (MET).

There were originally three bands:

Band 1 – LEL to LET:	Target pension 40% of earnings
Band 2 – LET to MET:	Target pension 10% of earnings
Band 3 – MET to UAP:*	Target pension 20% of earnings

(* Up to 5 April 2009 this upper limit was the Upper Earnings Limit (UEL). The Upper Accrual Point (UAP) was introduced at 6 April 2009, at a fixed amount equal to the 2008/09 UEL.)

Bands 2 and 3 merged from 6 April 2010 and from that date accrued pension at a target rate of 10% of earnings.

From 2012, the lower band was replaced by a flat rate per year for each year of accrual. From the same date, the Band 2 and 3 accrual was also changed from a target rate of 10% over an individual's working life to 1/440th for each year.

Contracting out

The ability to contract out of SERPS or S2P on a salary-related basis *(see Reference Section 5)* was introduced in 1978. Between 1988 and 2012, it was also possible to contract out on a money purchase basis. The introduction of the new State Pension means that contracting out was abolished completely from 6 April 2016.

TRANSITIONAL ARRANGEMENTS

For those with qualifying years before 6 April 2016, the combined BSP and S2P entitlement earned up to that date is compared to the State Pension accrued by then on the new rules. There is a complex deduction from the pension under each of the old and new rules in order to reflect periods of contracted-out employment – *see Reference Section 5*. The government estimated in 2014 that, for an individual retiring at that time, the maximum amount payable by way of SERPS plus S2P combined was around £160 per week (this was the maximum that could have been attained by a man who had never been contracted out and whose earnings since 1978 had always been above the relevant upper limit), payable on top of the Basic State Pension of some £110.

The greater of the amount under the old and new rules is used as the 'starting amount'. If the starting amount is lower than the full rate of State Pension, the individual can use further qualifying years to add to their entitlement up to the level of the full rate of State Pension. If the starting amount exceeds the full rate of State Pension the excess is protected, although it is not increased in the same way as the rest of the State Pension *(see below)*; the legislation provides for increases only in line with prices.

PAYMENT AND DEFERRAL OF STATE PENSION

State pensions are payable from SPA. They are not paid automatically, and must generally be claimed.

Those who reach SPA from 6 April 2016 can defer their State Pension in exchange for an increased pension (providing they have deferred for at least nine weeks).

Those who reached SPA before 6 April 2016 could defer their State Pension in return for either a lump sum based on pension foregone plus interest or an increased pension.

INCREASES TO STATE PENSION

State pensions are increased in April each year.

For those reaching SPA before 6 April 2016, legislation provides for increases to the BSP in line with earnings, but from April 2012 government policy has been to give annual increases in line with the triple lock – the higher of earnings increases, price increases (based on the Consumer Prices Index measure) and 2.5%. S2P and SERPS are increased in line with prices (based on the Consumer Prices Index measure). Where a worker had been contracted out of the State Additional Pension *(see Reference Section 5)*, the pension increase system effectively 'tops up' increases on the Guaranteed Minimum Pension (GMP) deemed payable by their pension scheme.

Legislation similarly provides for the new State Pension to be increased in line with earnings, although again government policy has been to increase it in line with the triple lock. However the State top-up of increases on the GMP does not apply under the new State Pension. Whether or not the triple lock will continue to be used for increasing State pensions has been a matter of some debate, but Government indications are that it will be retained.

STATE PENSION CREDITS

State pension credits are tax-free weekly entitlements for individuals aged 60 and over and resident in Great Britain, and are targeted at pensioners on low and modest incomes. They can be claimed by one member of a couple, but not both.

The guarantee credit brings recipients' incomes (taking into account notional income from capital) to a guaranteed level and is payable to both men and women at or over the current minimum qualifying age for women to receive the State Pension. For those reaching SPA after 5 April 2016, the guarantee credit is relevant only for those who do not have the full level of State Pension. For those who reached SPA before 6 April 2016 there is also a savings credit for lower earners – this gives a cash addition for income above a certain threshold, which tapers off where income exceeds the guarantee credit amount. For 2018/19, the maximum amount of savings credit to a single person is £13.40 per week. Savings credit is payable to claimants over age 65, or if a spouse or civil partner is over age 65.

With some exceptions savings credit is not available to those reaching SPA after 5 April 2016.

INFORMATION ON STATE PENSION

Individuals are able to obtain a statement of their new State Pension entitlement from *www.gov.uk/government/publications/application-for-a-state-pension-statement*. The State Pension statement gives an estimate of the starting amount of pension based on the NI record as it stands when the statement is produced and a forecast of the State Pension if NI contributions continue up to SPA, and also sets out the contracted-out pension equivalent, which has been reflected in the starting amount. Individuals can also obtain an online estimate and forecast of the State Pension from *www.tax.service.gov.uk/check-your-state-pension*. Once it is released, the 'pensions dashboard' project *(see Section 14)* will allow an individual to see details of their State Pension alongside other pensions.

SECTION 2

SCHEME DESIGN AND BENEFITS

This section gives a brief explanation of the different types of benefit commonly provided by occupational pension schemes in the UK, and some of the factors that affect the design of those benefits.

Pension schemes are often classified as defined benefit (DB) or money purchase (MP). MP benefits are also known as defined contribution or DC. Over recent years, many employers have closed traditional DB final salary pension schemes because of the significant risks, and associated costs, that they have to bear. In many cases employers have replaced these with MP schemes where individual members bear most of the risks.

However, some employers are looking for other solutions that fall somewhere between these two extremes, retaining the risks they want to manage, whilst providing benefits which are still attractive to employees from a recruitment and retention perspective.

Hybrid schemes also exist which provide different types of benefit in different circumstances.

The key characteristics of the various scheme designs are covered below.

TYPES OF PENSION BENEFIT – MONEY PURCHASE

MP schemes provide benefits which depend on the amount of the contributions paid into the scheme, the investment return credited to those contributions, any expenses deducted and the financial conditions at the time benefits are converted into a future retirement income. There are a number of types of arrangement that can be used to provide MP benefits *which are described below.*

Trust-based occupational pension schemes

Employer-sponsored occupational MP pension schemes and master trusts including NEST *(see Section 6)* are operated as trusts *(see Section 7)*. In many cases the scheme may contain separate MP and DB sections within the same trust. Many DB schemes offer Additional Voluntary Contributions on a MP basis and many that accept transfers into the scheme will offer MP benefits in respect of the transfer payment received even if other benefits are accruing on a DB basis.

Personal pensions and retirement annuity contracts

All personal pensions are MP and are provided as a contract with an insurer or other provider, rather than being trust-based. Personal pensions replaced retirement annuity contracts (RACs), often referred to as s226 contracts. Those who already had RACs prior to July 1988 were allowed to continue to contribute to them.

Group personal pensions

Group personal pensions (GPPs) are personal pensions arranged by an employer for the benefit of its employees. Employers often see these as a low-cost alternative to a trust-based, occupational MP scheme, as most administration is handled by the insurance company running the GPP and is usually included in the annual management charge deducted from the members' funds.

Self-invested personal pensions
A self-invested personal pension (SIPP) is an arrangement under a personal pension scheme which allows the member to choose the investments. As the members may select the investments, SIPPs are classed as 'investment-regulated pension schemes', and are therefore subject to prohibitive tax charges if they invest in residential property or most tangible moveable assets.

Stakeholder pensions

Stakeholder pension schemes were introduced in 2001 as a way of encouraging private pension provision. Employers had to provide access to a stakeholder scheme for employees not already covered by a suitable pension scheme, but this requirement was removed from 1 October 2012, to coincide with the introduction of automatic enrolment *(see Sections 3 to 5)*.

TYPES OF PENSION BENEFIT – DEFINED BENEFIT

Final salary

The traditional form of DB scheme was the final salary scheme, under which the pension paid is equal to the number of years worked, multiplied by the member's pensionable salary (as defined under the scheme rules) at or near to retirement, multiplied by a factor known as the accrual rate (commonly 1/80 or 1/60). After a career of 40 years, this would give a pension of one-half or two-thirds of the member's 'final pensionable salary'. Pensionable salary may exclude certain items, or even be capped in some schemes, in order to control costs.

Members generally pay a fixed rate of contributions (or no contributions in some cases), with the employer funding the balance of the costs – and therefore bearing all the funding risks.

CARE

Career Average Revalued Earnings (CARE) schemes are DB in nature, but are a variation on the traditional final salary design. Rather than the pension at retirement being based on earnings close to retirement, it is based on the average earnings throughout the member's entire career. These earnings are usually revalued up to retirement in line with price inflation.

If the revaluation rate is lower than the average earnings increases received by the member, then the pension at retirement will be less than for an otherwise identical final salary scheme. From an employer's perspective, this means that a CARE scheme would usually cost less to fund.

Cash balance and retirement balance

Under these arrangements, members build up a defined lump sum on either a final salary or a CARE basis. For example, the lump sum accrual rate could be

20% of salary per annum, giving a lump sum after 40 years of 8 times either final or career average earnings. Another way of thinking of these schemes is as a MP benefit with the investment return guaranteed at the outset. For example, the return could be defined as the increase in RPI plus 2% per annum.

At retirement, the benefits are classed as 'flexible benefits' and enjoy the same flexibilities as MP retirement funds *(see 'Options at retirement' below)*. Benefits can be converted to pension by purchasing an annuity with an insurance company, in the same way as for MP benefits, although in some cases preferential conversion terms are offered through the scheme itself. However, in order to be designated as flexi-access drawdown funds, cash balance and retirement balance funds must be converted to MP benefits. For funding purposes, the scheme is considered as DB.

TYPES OF PENSION BENEFIT – OTHER

Hybrid schemes

There are many forms of hybrid scheme which incorporate features of the above designs. The two most common types are:

- a better of two (or more) different types of benefit, for example a DB scheme with a minimum level of benefit calculated on a MP basis (under the legislation, such a benefit is considered defined benefit unless the MP benefit bites), *and*
- a combination of different types of benefit, for example benefits might accrue on a final salary basis up to a certain level of earnings, but on a MP basis above that level.

Shared risk and collective benefits

The Pension Schemes Act 2015 set the framework for new models of scheme that would allow greater risk sharing. However, additional legislation would be required to implement the new designs and any such legislation has been put on hold. The Act would have redefined UK pension schemes (both occupational and contract-based arrangements) into three categories based on the extent of the pension promise made to members during the accrual stage and when benefits are taken:

- Defined benefits schemes give a full promise around the level of benefits at all times before retirement.
- Shared risk schemes (also referred to as defined ambition) give, at some time before retirement, a promise about the level of at least some of the benefits. The underlying guarantor could be the employer, an insurance company or the scheme itself.
- Defined contributions schemes give no promise about the level of benefits. Benefits provided include individual MP and cash balance benefits.

Schemes that do not fit within one of the above categories would be treated as two or more separate schemes, each of which fits within one of the categories.

The Act also introduced the concept of collective benefits, where risks are shared between members, in order to allow collective defined contribution schemes or collective shared risk schemes to be set up. Collective defined contribution is fully defined contribution and therefore no benefits are guaranteed, only targeted. As a result, if the scheme assets perform well then above-target benefits would be paid, but if scheme assets perform poorly then below-target benefits would be paid, with the potential for cuts to benefits in extreme circumstances. Collective shared risk would comprise some element of benefits with guarantees acting on an individual member basis together with a collective element without guarantees involving risk sharing across a group of members. The government is considering whether existing legislation can be amended to enable collective defined contribution schemes to be introduced relatively quickly.

OTHER ISSUES AFFECTING SCHEME DESIGN

Automatic enrolment

From 2012 onwards employers have been required to automatically enrol eligible jobholders into a qualifying pension scheme and to make minimum contributions on behalf of their workers *(see Sections 3 to 5)*. The employer may use its own scheme if that meets minimum quality requirements, or a master trust arrangement *(see Section 6)*.

Registered pension schemes

To obtain tax concessions, the majority of UK pension schemes are registered with HMRC. Registered schemes are subject to requirements that impact on the type and level of benefits that they can provide. *These requirements are described in Section 9. Section 11 describes arrangements outside the tax-privileged environment.*

Options at retirement

Members can usually choose to take some of their benefits as a lump sum, currently tax free within certain limits *(see Section 9)*. In a DB scheme this is usually achieved by the member giving up some of their pension, although some schemes provide a lump sum as a separate benefit.

In addition to the standard options, other forms of 'at retirement options' are increasingly being used in DB schemes, typically introduced by employers in an effort to manage their liabilities. These include pension increase conversion exercises (subject to the requirements below for increases in payment) and flexible retirement offers *(see Section 21 for further details)*.

Members of MP and cash balance schemes can take 25% of their fund as a tax free lump sum and have full access to the remainder – as lump sums, unrestricted drawdown, or as an annuity – all subject to their marginal rate of income tax. A legislative override makes it easier for schemes to offer this flexibility even if scheme rules do not permit it, or scheme rules may be changed by resolution. *See Section 9 for further details on all the types of pension and lump sum benefits payable from registered pension schemes, and Section 14 for details of retirement options in MP schemes.* DB members must first transfer to a MP scheme in order to take advantage of the flexibilities (although there is a ban on such transfers from unfunded public sector schemes), and advice requirements apply *(see Section 13 for further details).*

Normal minimum pension age

It is expected that the minimum pension age will increase from 55 to 57 in 2028 (when State Pension Age increases to 67 – *see Section 1 for further details*), and will be maintained at ten years below State Pension Age thereafter. The new minimum age will apply to all registered pension schemes, although existing protections are expected to remain and further protection may be available.

Interaction with State benefits

Many schemes are designed to target an overall level of pension at retirement, including State pensions. Until April 2016, DB schemes were able to contract out of the State Second Pension (S2P), and previously SERPS. However, contracting out for DB schemes was abolished from April 2016, to coincide with the introduction of the new State Pension *(see Section 1).* Contracting out on a MP basis was abolished from April 2012. *For information on contracting out, see Reference Section 5.*

Many schemes therefore reviewed their design to reflect the changes in the State system and the end of contracting out. Regulations give employers overriding powers – for a period of five years from April 2016 – to amend the rules of contracted-out schemes to increase member contributions or alter future accrual of benefits (or a combination of the two), although the quality requirements for automatic enrolment still apply if relevant (*see Section 4 for details*), as does the requirement for consultation *(see 'Consultation by employers' below).*

Some schemes also provide bridging pensions between retirement and subsequent State Pension Age to smooth the change in a member's total income from State and scheme combined. Increases in State Pension Age and changes to the State system *(see Section 1)* have impacted such arrangements and options.

AVCs

Some occupational pension schemes offer a facility for members to make Additional Voluntary Contributions (AVCs), although the requirement to do so was removed from 2006.

Death benefits

Occupational pension schemes can also provide death benefits. The form of benefits may depend on the retirement benefits provided, but may include lump sum benefits and pension *(see Section 9 for further details)*.

'Excepted Group Life Policies' *(see Section 11)* provide lump sum death benefits outside the tax-advantaged registered pension scheme regime *(see Section 9)*. However, they may be useful to those who have insufficient remaining lifetime allowance, or those with certain types of protection against the lifetime allowance (where joining a new arrangement may cause protection to be lost).

Pension increases in payment

Registered occupational pension schemes must provide at least Limited Price Indexation (LPI) on DB pensions accrued after 5 April 1997 once in payment.

The minimum annual increase required is the lower of price inflation and 5% for service between 6 April 1997 and 5 April 2005, and the lower of price inflation and 2.5% for service after 5 April 2005.

The basis for determining price inflation for future statutory minimum increases to pensions in payment and revaluations in deferment changed from RPI to CPI in 2010. The Pensions Act 2011 included provisions to allow schemes to continue to use RPI as the basis for such increases, in certain circumstances – for example where scheme rules require RPI to be used.

Pension salary sacrifice

Pension salary sacrifice is an arrangement whereby an employee waives entitlement to part of their salary (or bonus), in exchange for the employer paying a pension contribution of an equivalent amount.

An advantage of salary sacrifice is that savings in National Insurance contributions (NICs) can be generated. Employee contributions are paid out of salary which is subject to NICs (both employer and employee), whereas employer contributions are not.

Historically, salary sacrifice was used almost exclusively for higher earners. However, the concept is now commonplace through the growth of flexible remuneration plans, under which employees have a flex fund which they can use to select from a range of benefits, and receive the remaining money as salary. The Government's review of salary sacrifice arrangements resulted in changes for certain benefits from April 2017; affected benefits include some life cover arrangements, but pension salary sacrifice is not affected.

Scheme modifications

Overriding legislation may be introduced, to allow changes to be made to scheme rules by resolution in certain circumstances (for example to reflect legislative changes). In all other cases, the conditions for making 'regulated modifications' are set out in legislation. Essentially, modifications of an occupational pension scheme are 'voidable' unless for each member or survivor:

- *either* informed consent has been given in writing by the member or survivor *or* (where permitted) the actuarial equivalence requirements, involving certification by the scheme actuary, have been met, *and*
- the trustees have formally determined to make (or have consented to) the modification and, before it takes effect, have notified the affected members and survivors.

Informed consent is always required in relation to a special category of major changes called protected modifications. Members must be given a reasonable opportunity to make representations, and the modification must take effect within a reasonable period of the consent being given.

The Pensions Regulator may make an order declaring the modification void if the requirements have not been met. It also has the power to levy fines on trustees and others exercising a power to modify a scheme, where voidable modifications have been made or the requirements specified in an order by the Regulator have not been met. The Regulator has issued a Code of Practice to help trustees comply with the legislation and to provide guidance on what the Regulator considers to be reasonable periods for the various stages of the process.

Consultation by employers

Where changes are to be made to general employment conditions, legislation (applying to businesses that employ 50 or more staff) gives employees the right – in certain circumstances – to be informed and consulted about the business they work for, including:

- the prospects for employment, *and*
- substantial changes in work organisation (e.g. proposed redundancies or changes in working hours) or contractual relationships.

The requirement for employers to have an agreement to inform and consult is not automatic but can be triggered in various ways, for example by a formal request from a minimum number of employees. If an employer fails to initiate negotiations for an agreement to inform and consult employees when required to do so, or when negotiations fail, 'standard provisions' apply.

In addition, the Pensions Act 2004 also requires employers to consult with members before they can make certain listed changes to a pension scheme for future service. Listed changes include increasing normal pension age, closing a scheme, changing from DB to MP, ceasing or reducing DB accrual, changing what elements of pay constitute pensionable earnings, reducing an employer's contribution to a MP scheme or changing the rates of indexation to pensions in payment or revaluation of pensions in deferment where that change would be less generous. The Department for Work and Pensions published guidance on the regulations, in order to help employers comply with the legislation.

Consultations must be carried out in an open and transparent manner; failure to do so may result in a breach of the implied contractual duty of trust and confidence between employer and employee. Employers should also carefully consider the messages given to members and ensure that these do not engender expectations which might not be met as a result of subsequent changes – this would be considered a breach of the duty of good faith (or *Imperial* duty). Amendments may be challenged if either the contractual or *Imperial* duty is breached. These issues were highlighted in the *IBM* case *(see Section 30 for details)* although in this case the original challenge has since been overturned on appeal.

Inalienability of occupational pension

With certain exceptions, entitlements or rights under occupational pension schemes may not be forfeited, assigned, surrendered, subjected to a charge or lien, or set off, and an agreement to do any of these things is unenforceable. These exceptions include allowing trustees to reduce future benefits to recover a previous payment made in error or as a result of fraud, or to meet the annual allowance charge from scheme benefits *(see Section 9)*. Pension increase conversion exercises are not considered to involve benefit surrender as, although members give up (non-statutory) pension increases, they receive a higher starting pension in return (*see Section 21 for further details*).

Cross-border activities

The Pensions Act 2004 introduced a number of provisions relating to cross-border activities under the EU Pensions Directive. A UK scheme that wishes to accept contributions from employers elsewhere in the EEA (which employ scheme members working elsewhere in the EEA) must receive a general authorisation from the Pensions Regulator. It must also apply for and receive approval from the Regulator in respect of each EEA employer. Based on information passed on about the social and labour laws of the host member state (i.e. the other EEA country), the UK scheme has the responsibility for ensuring compliance, with the Regulator being able to monitor such compliance and impose sanctions for non-compliance. Where the cross-border activity is the other way round (i.e. the UK is the host state and the scheme is established elsewhere), the Regulator has the role of notifying the other country's authority of relevant UK law and monitoring compliance with it.

The revised EU Directive aims to make it easier for cross-border pension schemes to be set up. 'Cross-border activity' is defined as operating a pension scheme where the relationship between the sponsor and the members is governed by the social and labour law relevant to occupational pension schemes of a Member State other than the home Member State. The present EU Directive requires cross-border schemes to be fully funded at all times. UK law currently interprets this as meeting the statutory funding objective introduced by the Pensions Act 2004 *(see Section 18)*. In addition, in order to be authorised, cross-border schemes must obtain annual actuarial valuations, with any deficit against the statutory funding objective being removed within 24 months of the valuation's effective date. Under the revised Directive, if a cross-border scheme is not fully funded, the regulator will intervene to ensure appropriate measures are drawn up and implemented without delay so that members and beneficiaries are adequately protected.

EU Member States must implement the provisions of the revised Directive by 13 January 2019, but its impact for UK-based schemes may depend on the terms of the UK's exit from the EU – *see Introduction*.

SECTION 3

AUTOMATIC ENROLMENT – EMPLOYERS' OBLIGATIONS

Automatic enrolment was introduced in 2012 and requires employers to automatically enrol workers into a pension scheme. The Pensions Act 2008 and subsequent regulations set out the detailed requirements. Employers' duties vary according to factors such as the earnings and age of workers and the type of pension scheme. Employers must automatically re-enrol certain workers approximately every three years where they have left active membership.

The pension scheme into which workers are automatically (re-)enrolled must meet minimum requirements, *as set out in Section 4*. There are detailed requirements for employers to provide information to workers and the scheme, *which are set out in Section 5*. The scheme can be the employer's own scheme or an alternative arrangement such as NEST *(see Section 6)*.

In December 2017, the Government published a review of automatic enrolment. The review made a number of proposals, including reducing the age for an eligible jobholder *(see 'Workforce Categorisation' below)* from 22 to 18 and requiring minimum contributions *(see 'Earnings Definitions' below)* to be calculated from the first pound of earnings. The Government's ambition is to implement these changes from the mid-2020s.

WHEN DO THE OBLIGATIONS START?

Employers in existence before October 2017 had a prescribed 'staging date' when the obligations first applied. New employers setting up from October 2017 are subject to the requirements from the date their first worker *(see below)* is employed.

However, an employer can postpone automatic enrolment of a worker for up to three months if it so chooses, and if it provides the appropriate notification to the worker. *(See below for more on postponement.)*

WHO DO THE DUTIES APPLY TO?

The duties apply to employers in respect of 'workers'. A worker is an individual who has a contract of employment with the employer, or who has a contract to do work or perform services personally and not as part of their own business. The distinction between personal service workers and those who provide services as part of their own business may be hard to determine, and the Regulator includes a list of considerations in its Detailed Guidance no. 1.

The duties apply in respect of individuals working in the UK or ordinarily working in the UK. This is another aspect that may be hard to determine, and the Regulator provides examples in its Detailed Guidance no. 3.

WORKFORCE CATEGORISATION

Employer duties vary according to a worker's age and earnings. The level of earnings is determined for a 'pay reference period'. The employer can choose to determine the pay reference period of a worker as either the period over which the worker is paid (e.g. monthly, weekly) or using 'tax months' (or 'tax weeks'). The table below sets out the different categories of worker.

Earnings (2018/19)	Age		
	16–21	22–State Pension Age	State Pension Age–74
Up to £6,032 *(lower threshold)*	**Entitled worker** (has the right to join a scheme)		
Between £6,032 and £10,000 *(earnings trigger for automatic enrolment)*	**Non-eligible jobholder** (can choose to opt into a qualifying scheme)		
Over £10,000	**Non-eligible jobholder**	**Eligible jobholder** (must be auto-enrolled into a qualifying scheme)	**Non-eligible jobholder**

The earnings levels shown in the table above are those that apply for a worker who is paid annually. The corresponding levels for pay reference periods of different lengths are set out in the table below.

EARNINGS DEFINITIONS

As well as the two earnings thresholds above, an 'upper limit' is also defined. 'Qualifying earnings' – those between the lower threshold and the upper limit – are used to determine the minimum benefit or contribution requirements for 'qualifying schemes' used for automatic (re-)enrolment *(see Section 4)*. For workforce categorisation and the determination of qualifying earnings, 'earnings' are defined as gross earnings, including sick pay and statutory maternity, paternity and adoption pay – regardless of whether an employer is using its own occupational pension scheme with its own definition of pensionable earnings.

These earnings thresholds are defined for pay reference periods of different lengths as follows:

Earnings (2018/19)	Pay reference period						
	1 week	2 weeks	4 weeks	1 month	3 months	6 months	12 months
Earnings trigger	£192	£384	£768	£833	£2,499	£4,998	£10,000
Lower threshold	£116	£232	£464	£503	£1,508	£3,016	£6,032
Upper limit	£892	£1,783	£3,566	£3,863	£11,558	£23,175	£46,350

These thresholds are reviewed annually by the government.

AUTOMATIC ENROLMENT PROCESS

From the date the obligations apply to an employer, it is required to automatically enrol eligible jobholders into an automatic enrolment scheme. Existing members of a qualifying scheme of the employer do not need to be automatically enrolled. The requirement to automatically enrol a worker into a pension scheme normally applies from the first day the worker becomes an eligible jobholder (unless the employer is operating postponement; *see below*). Scheme membership must begin on this 'automatic enrolment date' although the employer has six weeks to complete the necessary processes. The employer needs to assess new workers and monitor existing workers on an ongoing basis for changes in status in order to automatically enrol those who become eligible jobholders.

A number of exceptions apply to the requirement to automatically enrol workers. Broadly, employers do not have to enrol workers who have any form of tax protection for existing pension savings *(see Section 9)*, those who have left a qualifying scheme in the last twelve months, those under notice to leave employment and those who are company directors or members of limited liability partnerships.

For individuals who are enrolled, contributions must be deducted in line with the scheme rules. All contributions deducted by the employer during the first three months of membership must reach the scheme by the 22nd of the fourth month, where paid electronically (or by the 19th if paid by another means). This contribution payment deadline for new joiners is intended to allow employers to hold the money until such time as it is known whether or not the jobholder has opted out. It applies to all jobholders as well as to entitled workers who exercise their right to join a registered pension scheme.

The employer must provide the scheme with specified 'jobholder information' no later than six weeks after the automatic enrolment date. Specified 'enrolment information' must be provided by the employer to the jobholder, also no later than six weeks after the automatic enrolment date. For workplace personal pension schemes, 'terms and conditions' information must be provided by the scheme provider to the jobholder. *Further detail on information requirements is set out in Section 5.*

Postponement

Employers are able to postpone the automatic enrolment date by up to three months – from staging date, the date on which a worker is employed or the date on which an existing worker becomes an eligible jobholder. The employer must notify the worker within six weeks of when they would otherwise have been automatically enrolled that their enrolment has been postponed. *The requirements for 'postponement notices' are covered in Section 5.*

Transitional arrangements for defined benefit and hybrid schemes

Employers providing qualifying defined benefits (including in a hybrid scheme) were able to defer automatic enrolment for certain existing employees who continued to be eligible to join the scheme for defined benefit accrual, until 1 October 2017, provided those employees could opt in during the period between the employer's staging date and 30 September 2017. During this period, any new employees who satisfied the eligibility criteria had to be automatically enrolled in the normal way.

Corporate restructuring

Where the employer of a worker changes as a result of a corporate restructure, the automatic enrolment duties apply afresh to the new employer, even if the old and new employers belong to the same group of companies. The new employer must satisfy its obligations in respect of the employee in the same way as for any other new employee.

OPTING OUT

An employee who has been automatically (re-)enrolled can subsequently opt out by giving notice within a one-month period, in which case any member and employer contributions paid must be returned. The opt-out period starts from the later of the following dates for an occupational pension scheme:

- the date the jobholder is given the enrolment information *(see Section 5) and*
- the date on which the employer made arrangements for the jobholder to become an active member.

For a personal pension, it commences on the later of:

- the date the jobholder is given the enrolment information *and*
- the date the jobholder is given the terms and conditions information.

In order to opt out, the jobholder must request an opt-out notice, generally from the scheme and not the employer. It is the employer's duty, not the scheme's, to refund any employee contributions that have been made; this is not dependent on the employer recouping the money from the scheme.

The Regulator has powers to issue a compliance notice to any employer that offers a worker an inducement, the main purpose of which is to encourage the worker to opt out of, or cease membership of, a qualifying scheme *(see below)*.

OPTING IN

Jobholders can give their employer an opt-in notice, requiring the employer to arrange for them to be enrolled in an automatic enrolment scheme. An employer is not obliged to act on an opt-in notice if it is less than twelve months since the worker gave a previous opt-in notice.

Entitled workers can give their employer a joining notice, requiring the employer to enter them into a registered pension scheme, which need not be an automatic enrolment scheme. The employer has no obligation to make employer contributions for an entitled worker.

AUTOMATIC RE-ENROLMENT

Automatic re-enrolment is required every three years on a date of the employer's choosing within a six-month window centred on the third anniversary of the date the obligations first applied to the employer, and subsequently the previous re-enrolment date. The Regulator refers to this as cyclical automatic re-enrolment.

The requirements are largely the same as for automatic enrolment. In general, eligible jobholders who are not active members of a qualifying scheme must be automatically re-enrolled with effect from the automatic re-enrolment date, unless they fall within the exceptions *(see above)* or are in a postponement period. Those who are re-enrolled have a right to opt out.

The main difference is that postponement cannot be used for automatic re-enrolment, so pension scheme membership must start from the automatic re-enrolment date. Again, employers have a six-week joining window to complete the automatic re-enrolment process. They do not need to re-send information to members where it has been sent previously and there have not been any changes.

Cyclical automatic re-enrolment should be a simpler process than that required when the automatic enrolment obligations first apply. However, employers need to ensure they have a process in place that meets the detailed requirements of the legislation.

MAINTAINING ACTIVE MEMBERSHIP

In addition to the automatic enrolment requirements, employers must ensure that jobholders remain active members of a qualifying scheme, unless the employee chooses to end their membership. An employer must not stop a scheme from qualifying, eject a jobholder from the qualifying scheme or force an employee to cease active membership of the scheme. For example, where an employer is changing its pension scheme, membership of the new scheme must be arranged within six weeks, and have effect from the day after membership of the old scheme ends. The Regulator refers to this as immediate automatic re-enrolment.

CONTRACTUAL ENROLMENT

Some employers make arrangements for their employees to join their pension scheme upon commencement of employment. They may do this for all workers, not just those who are required to be automatically enrolled under the Pensions Act 2008. This is described as contractual enrolment, as it is usually included in the contract of employment with the worker. Where this is the case, the corresponding opt-out provisions (that apply when a worker is automatically enrolled) are not available. However, a similar opt-out may be possible by cancellation of a personal pension contract, or where an occupational scheme's rules allow for the employee to be treated as never having been a member.

Contractual enrolment can also be used to fulfil automatic re-enrolment duties. In both cases, employers need to ensure that their processes meet or exceed the legislative requirements.

More information about the considerations for employers that are using contractual enrolment is in the Regulator's Detailed Guidance no. 6.

COMPLIANCE BY EMPLOYERS

The monitoring of employers' compliance with the automatic enrolment and contribution requirements is a function of the Regulator. Employers must keep records and provide the Regulator with certain information, which the Regulator refers to as declaration of compliance (although the legislation uses the term registration). Employers are required to declare compliance within five months of the date the automatic enrolment obligations first apply.

Employers are required to keep records relating to the pension arrangements they have made, the enrolment of jobholders, postponement, opt-out and opt-in notices, and the pension contributions they have made. The Regulator can use these records where needed to check that employers have undertaken enrolment and opt-out correctly.

Occupational pension schemes and pension providers are required to keep records of enrolments, opt-ins and opt-outs in respect of each employer. The Regulator will use these records to confirm enrolment and payment of contributions with the pension scheme or provider, and to help identify prohibited behaviour such as employers inducing workers to opt out of pension saving.

Employers are required to re-declare compliance every three years, within five months of the third anniversary of the date on which the automatic enrolment obligations applied to the employer, with subsequent deadlines being five months after the third anniversary of the previous automatic re-enrolment date.

A penalty regime for employers that do not comply with the requirements is administered by the Regulator, which can issue compliance notices and unpaid contributions notices. Employers that contravene the automatic enrolment requirements may be required to take remedial action and fines may be imposed where things are not put right. In particular, workers may have to be put in the same position as if the contravention had not occurred.

A fixed penalty of £400 may be issued to employers that fail to engage with the reforms, or fail to keep records or supply information to the Regulator. Entrenched employer non-compliance may attract further penalties, rising to £10,000 per day for employers with 500 or more workers. Employers that try to screen out job applicants who might want to save in a qualifying scheme may receive a fixed fine, rising to £5,000 for employers with 250 or more workers.

Protection of employment rights

The Pensions Act 2008 includes provision to protect employees who do not opt out after automatic enrolment from suffering detrimental treatment by employers compared with those who do opt out. It includes statutory rights, building on the existing framework of employment rights, so that those individuals who wish to save should be protected from being unfairly dismissed and from other detrimental treatment (including in relation to recruitment).

COMPLIANCE BY TRUSTEES

Automatic enrolment is predominantly an employer's responsibility. However, trustees of money purchase arrangements need to comply with the requirements on charge controls *(see Section 7)* if their arrangement is being used by an employer to comply with its automatic enrolment duties.

The Regulator's scheme return *(see Section 8)* requires trustees to confirm whether the scheme is compliant with these requirements.

SECTION 4

AUTOMATIC ENROLMENT – QUALIFYING SCHEMES

The automatic enrolment regime requires employers to auto-enrol workers who satisfy earnings and age criteria in an 'automatic enrolment scheme'; *see Section 3*. This can be an employer's own pension scheme, a personal pension scheme or a master trust arrangement such as NEST *(see Section 6)*.

An automatic enrolment scheme is a 'qualifying scheme' that contains no provisions that might prevent the employer from making the required arrangements to automatically enrol or re-enrol a jobholder, or enrol one who opts in, and does not require the worker to express a choice or provide any information in order to remain an active member – for example, a money purchase scheme must have a default investment option. Additional criteria apply for non-UK schemes *(see below)*.

A qualifying scheme is an occupational scheme or personal pension scheme that satisfies the 'quality requirement' for that jobholder, and is registered under Finance Act 2004 or is an overseas scheme that satisfies specified requirements. The quality requirement differs for money purchase, defined benefits and hybrid schemes *(see below)*. In addition, a scheme that provides average salary benefits must revalue those benefits during pensionable service at a minimum rate *(see below)*.

Active members of a qualifying scheme do not need to be automatically enrolled, and the scheme does not need to meet the additional requirements to be an automatic enrolment scheme in respect of those members.

MONEY PURCHASE SCHEMES

A money purchase scheme or personal pension scheme will meet the quality requirement if a minimum level of contributions is paid to the scheme for all relevant jobholders.

Subject to transitional provisions *(see below)*, the minimum contributions required are a total of 8% of 'qualifying earnings' *(see Section 3)*, with the employer paying at least 3% and the employee making up any shortfall.

Instead of meeting this quality requirement, schemes can meet the minimum contribution conditions of one of three 'sets' of an 'alternative quality requirement', which are based on different definitions of pensionable pay. This may make it easier for schemes to be used for automatic enrolment where the definition of pensionable pay is not consistent with qualifying earnings. It is not necessary for all jobholders in a scheme to satisfy the same test. Subject to transitional provisions *(see below)* the three sets are as follows:

- Set 1 – 9% total (with 4% employer) where pensionable pay is subject to a minimum of basic pay
- Set 2 – 8% total (with 3% employer) where pensionable pay is subject

to a minimum of basic pay and constitutes at least 85% of total pay across all relevant jobholders, *or*

- Set 3 – 7% total (with 3% employer) where all earnings are pensionable.

(For this purpose basic pay is those elements of pay, before deductions, that do not vary, but excluding certain elements specifically set out in legislation. These exclusions relate to commission, bonuses, overtime, shift premiums, car allowance and certain other allowances.)

There are further requirements for a personal pension scheme to be a qualifying scheme. Broadly, these require agreements to be in place between the provider, employer and employee to ensure that the employer and employee each pay the required contributions, and the provider monitors compliance with the agreed payments. For personal pensions and some master trusts, the 'relief at source' method provides basic rate tax relief, with the relief paid directly into the scheme and counting towards the minimum total contributions. Higher-rate taxpayers need to claim additional relief from HMRC via self-assessment. The employer must deduct any contributions payable by workers from remuneration and pay them to the scheme.

Default fund charges in qualifying schemes providing money purchase benefits cannot be more than 0.75% p.a. *(see Section 7)*.

Contribution requirements during transitional periods

Minimum contributions are being phased in. This is occuring in three steps:

From	**Employer minimum contribution**	**Total minimum contribution** (including tax relief)
1 October 2012	1%	2%
6 April 2018	2%	5%
6 April 2019	Full (as above)	Full (as above)

Higher rates apply under Set 1 of the alternative quality requirements (the above rates apply under Sets 2 and 3):

From	**Employer minimum contribution**	**Total minimum contribution** (including tax relief)
1 October 2012	2%	3%
6 April 2018	3%	6%
6 April 2019	Full (as above)	Full (as above)

DEFINED BENEFITS AND HYBRID SCHEMES

The quality requirements for defined benefits and hybrid pension schemes, which must be met if such a scheme is to be used as a qualifying scheme for automatic enrolment, are set out below.

In addition to the requirements below, a career average scheme cannot be a qualifying scheme unless revaluation of benefits during pensionable service is at least 2.5% p.a. (or price inflation if lower) and is guaranteed and/or funded for.

Defined benefits schemes

A scheme satisfies the quality requirement either by meeting the 'test scheme standard', which considers the level and form of benefits, or by meeting the 'alternative quality requirements', which test the overall cost of benefits accruing.

Test scheme standard for final salary schemes and career average schemes providing a pension at retirement

The test scheme standard requires benefits at least as valuable as a pension paid:

- at an annual rate of 1/120th of average qualifying earnings in the last three tax years prior to exit multiplied by the number of years of pensionable service (up to a maximum of 40)
- commencing at the higher of age 65 and the member's State pension age, and continuing for life, *and*
- including at least the statutory minimum levels of revaluation in deferment (on the final salary method) and of indexation in payment.

Test scheme standard for cash balance schemes, under which a sum of money is made available for the provision of benefits at retirement

The test scheme standard requires benefits at least as valuable as a lump sum:
EITHER

- accrued at an annual rate of 16% of average qualifying earnings in the last three tax years prior to exit multiplied by the number of years of pensionable service (up to a maximum of 40), *and*
- including at least the statutory minimum levels of revaluation in deferment (on the final salary method);

OR

- accrued at an annual rate of 16% of average qualifying earnings multiplied by the number of years of pensionable service (up to a maximum of 40), *and*
- where average qualifying earnings are calculated on the basis that each year's qualifying earnings are revalued during pensionable service by the lower of 2.5% and price inflation each year, *and*
- including at least the statutory minimum levels of revaluation in deferment (on the final salary or average salary method);

OR

- accrued at an annual rate of 8% of average qualifying earnings multiplied by the number of years of pensionable service (up to a maximum of 40), *and*

- where average qualifying earnings are calculated on the basis that each year's qualifying earnings are revalued during pensionable service by 3.5% p.a. plus the lower of 2.5% and price inflation each year, *and*
- including revaluation in deferment of at least 3.5% p.a. above the statutory minimum level (on the final salary or average salary method).

In all cases, the test scheme standard requires the lump sum to be used to provide benefits commencing at the higher of age 65 and the member's State pension age, and continuing for life.

Alternative quality requirements

The alternative quality requirements require a total cost of benefit accrual of at least a prescribed percentage of 'relevant earnings'. In practice, there is a two-stage test to determine (i) whether the pensionable earnings of each jobholder are at least as much as one of the legislative definitions for relevant earnings, and (ii) whether the cost of accrual is at least equal to the corresponding percentage. The earnings definitions and corresponding percentages are as follows:

- qualifying earnings – 10%
- basic pay – 11%
- basic pay, and, taking all relevant members together, their pensionable earnings constitute at least 85% of their total earnings – 10%
- total earnings (where all earnings are pensionable) – 9%, *or*
- basic pay above the LEL or the Basic State Pension – 13%.

All of the above percentages are reduced by 1% where the scheme does not provide pension death benefits.

The cost can be taken from a written report signed by an actuary, which could be a funding valuation report or the schedule of contributions *(see Section 18)*. The methods and assumptions to be used are not prescribed, but it is expected that those adopted for scheme funding will be used in most cases.

Hybrid schemes

The quality test applicable depends on the benefit structure of the scheme.

In general, the scheme needs to satisfy the applicable test scheme standard (or the alternative quality requirements) for members accruing defined benefits and meet the quality requirement (or an alternative quality requirement) for members accruing money purchase benefits.

For a 'combination hybrid' scheme, in which the defined benefits or money purchase quality requirements cannot be satisfied in full, the scheme needs to satisfy a test that modifies and combines those requirements.

CERTIFICATION

Money purchase schemes

Certification can be used to confirm that a money purchase scheme meets the quality requirement. It is required to confirm that a money purchase scheme meets an alternative quality requirement. Certification is the responsibility of the employer, but can be delegated (e.g. to an adviser or another employer), and is carried out in relation to its jobholders and the scheme. Separate tests can be carried out for different groups of jobholders. The key requirement is that either the quality requirement is met or a valid certificate (or certificates) is in place for all relevant jobholders. One certificate can be used for multiple employers.

The certificate can be in force for up to 18 months, although employers may find it convenient to choose a shorter period. It must be reviewed if there is a significant change in circumstances. The review might lead to the certificate being terminated early.

At the end of a certification period, and before a new certificate can be given, the employer must assess whether the quality requirement (or an alternative quality requirement) was met during that period. If an element of the relevant requirement is not met, the employer needs to consider what action is to be taken to rectify this, and then take that action. However, no retrospective calculation of shortfalls in the contributions is required unless the Pensions Regulator determines that the scheme has been mis-certified (i.e. that there were not reasonable grounds for the employer to have certified).

The DWP has issued detailed guidance on certification.

Defined benefits and hybrid schemes

For defined benefits and hybrid schemes, a certification process also exists for the test scheme standard, but the certificate must be given by *either*:

- an actuary, generally the scheme actuary, *or*
- the employer, but only where no actuarial calculations are required.

It is not necessary to re-certify routinely. However, the employer (or, where actuarial calculations were required, the actuary) should keep the scheme's ability to satisfy the test scheme standard under review and, as a minimum, the scheme should be fully reviewed every three years. Significant changes should prompt an early review. The DWP has issued detailed guidance for employers and actuaries on certification.

The DWP has issued separate guidance on the alternative quality requirements. Actuarial certification is not required as employers may be able to rely on work produced for scheme funding purposes.

NON-UK SCHEMES

The implications of Brexit for non-UK schemes in the context of automatic enrolment are unclear. The current, pre-Brexit, position is summarised below.

A pension scheme with its main administration in an EEA state outside the UK can be an automatic enrolment scheme provided it is a qualifying scheme *(see below)* and it is:

- an IORP (institution for occupational retirement provision) as defined in the IORP Directive, or a personal pension scheme that is regulated by the relevant competent authority in its home state and operated by a person authorised by that authority, in relation to that activity, *and*
- subject to the following regulatory requirements:
  - at least 70% of the money purchase benefits (or sum of money available for the provision of benefits under a defined benefits scheme) must be used to provide the jobholder with an income for life *and*
  - benefits must be paid no earlier than age 55 (unless on grounds of ill health).

A pension scheme with its main administration outside the EEA cannot be used for automatic enrolment, although it can be used for eligible jobholders who are existing members at the automatic enrolment date if it is a qualifying scheme.

A non-UK scheme can be a qualifying scheme if it:

- is an occupational or personal pension scheme and, in the country where it has its main administration or is established, there is a body that regulates such schemes and providers, and which regulates that scheme/provider
- is subject to regulatory requirements that provide that some of the benefits may be used to provide the jobholder with an income for life
- is registered with HMRC under Finance Act 2004 for tax purposes as a qualifying overseas pension scheme (or other specified conditions are met), *and*
- meets the quality requirements as outlined for UK schemes (other than in specified circumstances).

SECTION 5

AUTOMATIC ENROLMENT – INFORMATION REQUIREMENTS

Under the automatic enrolment regime the employer is required to provide certain information to its workers and to the pension scheme it has chosen to fulfil its automatic enrolment duties.

The content of the information varies depending on the category of worker and whether the employer is postponing auto-enrolment. *See Section 3 for details*.

This section summarises the main requirements. It does not cover the employer's duty to report and provide information to the Pensions Regulator, nor the need to keep records, *which are summarised in Section 3*. Normal scheme disclosure rules will also apply; *the disclosure requirements for occupational pension schemes are set out in Section 15*.

It is the employer's duty to provide the right information to the right individual at the right time. In all cases, the information must be given in writing. In the Pensions Regulator's view, giving information includes providing a hard copy (by hand, post or internal mail) or sending an email (with the information in the body of the email or as an attachment). It is not sufficient to signpost the employee (by email or otherwise) to a website, intranet site or poster within the workplace. The method used should be appropriate to the workforce and a range of formats may be required. Sufficient time should be allowed for the delivery of the information and addresses should be kept up to date so that information can be successfully delivered.

The Regulator summarises the information requirements and sets out examples in its Detailed guidance no. 10. Its website includes templates and other resources to help employers communicate with workers about automatic enrolment.

INFORMATION TO BE PROVIDED IN RELATION TO ELIGIBLE JOBHOLDERS WHO ARE NOT SCHEME MEMBERS AND TO OPT-INS

Eligible jobholders must be automatically enrolled in a qualifying scheme *(see Sections 3 and 4)*.

As part of the enrolment process, the employer must provide *enrolment information* to the jobholder being automatically enrolled and *jobholder information* to the pension scheme. If a contract-based scheme (e.g. a personal pension) is being used as the automatic enrolment scheme, the provider must also give the jobholder information about the *terms and conditions* of the arrangement.

When the automatic enrolment requirements first apply, there is no need to provide enrolment information to those who are already active members of a qualifying scheme, but they must be given a separate notice about their scheme membership *(see below)*, even if they have been told about the scheme in the past.

Broadly, the same information requirements apply on re-enrolment and when a non-eligible jobholder opts in.

Enrolment information to be provided to the jobholder

Enrolment information must be provided by the employer to the jobholder.

To Be Provided To	Time Frame	Summary Of Information Required
• **Eligible jobholders** who are being automatically enrolled (or re-enrolled). • **Non-eligible jobholders** who opt in. • **Eligible jobholders** who opt in during postponement.	No later than **six weeks** after the jobholder's automatic enrolment date (or re-enrolment date, or opt-in enrolment date).	• That the jobholder has been or will be enrolled into a pension scheme and the automatic enrolment date (or equivalent). • Details of the contributions payable and whether tax relief will be given through net pay or relief at source. • Details about the right to opt out, what it means and when and how to do this. • The right to opt back in. • That a jobholder will normally be automatically re-enrolled by the employer in accordance with regulations. • That any written notice from the jobholder must be signed (or, if given electronically, state that the jobholder personally submitted it).

Terms and conditions information to be provided to the jobholder

The employer must ensure that the provider of the personal pension scheme gives the jobholder information on the terms and conditions of the scheme. This can form part of the key features information that the provider must issue under Financial Conduct Authority rules.

To Be Provided To	Time Frame	Summary Of Information Required
Jobholders who are being provided with **enrolment information** above.	No later than **six weeks** after the jobholder's automatic enrolment date (or equivalent).	• The purpose of the scheme, including information about the default fund(s). • The services to be provided by the provider. • The value of any contributions payable by the jobholder, where the provider has this information. • The charges that may be payable.

Jobholder information to be provided to the pension scheme

Jobholder information must be provided by the employer to the trustees or managers of the occupational or personal pension scheme.

To Be Provided To	Time Frame	Summary Of Information Required
The pension scheme, in relation to **jobholders** who are being provided with **enrolment information** as above. Also applies in relation to **entitled workers** who exercise the right to join *(see below)*.	No later than **six weeks** after the jobholder's automatic enrolment date (or equivalent).	• Jobholder's name, sex, date of birth and postal residential address. • The automatic enrolment date (or equivalent). • National Insurance number (if this is not immediately available, the employer must provide it within six weeks of receiving it). If required, the following must also be provided: • gross earnings in any pay reference period • value of contributions (expressed as a fixed amount or as a percentage of earnings) • postal work address and individual's work email address • personal email address, where the employer holds this information.

INFORMATION ABOUT OPTING IN AND JOINING

Workers who have not been automatically enrolled because they do not meet the eligibility criteria can ask their employer to make them a member of a pension scheme. The employer must inform non-eligible jobholders who are not active members of a qualifying scheme of the right to opt into an automatic enrolment scheme and be eligible for employer contributions. Entitled workers who are not active members of a pension scheme must be informed of the right to join a registered pension scheme.

To Be Provided To	Time Frame	Summary Of Information Required
Non-eligible jobholders. **Entitled workers.**	No later than **six weeks** after the right to opt in or join first applies.	• For the jobholder with a right to opt in: that they may require the employer to make arrangements for them to become an active member of an automatic enrolment scheme and that the jobholder will be entitled to employer's contributions. • For the entitled worker with a right to join: that they may require the employer to make arrangements for them to become an active member of a pension scheme. Alternatively, both types of worker can be given a notice that combines the two statements above. This avoids the need to assess individuals who move between the two categories. In either case, the information must explain that the notice must be in writing and signed by the worker (or, if given electronically, state that the worker personally submitted it).

The employer is only required to provide this information once, per worker, per employment. There is no need to provide this information to a jobholder who has previously opted out under the automatic enrolment legislation, or if it has previously been provided in a postponement notice *(see below)*.

If a joining notice is received from an entitled worker, information about the worker must be provided to the pension scheme. This is the same information that is provided in respect of jobholders *(see 'Jobholder information to be provided to the pension scheme' above)*.

INFORMATION WHEN USING POSTPONEMENT

An employer may postpone automatic enrolment by up to three months for one, some or all of its workers. The employer can use postponement:

- at its staging date
- on the worker's first day of employment, *or*
- when a worker first meets the criteria to become an eligible jobholder.

Postponement is explained further *in Section 3*.

If the employer chooses to use postponement it must provide a notification no later than six weeks after what would have been the automatic enrolment date.

A single postponement notice can be used for all types of worker, or the employer may wish to only give information about the right that is relevant to the worker whose enrolment is being postponed.

Prior to 1 April 2015, there were four types of postponement notice that could be used, with varying levels of detail. Employers with staging dates before April 2015 can continue to use the tailored notices that applied previously.

Each employee must receive their own postponement notice, even if the information on it is generic. All notices must explain:

- that automatic enrolment has been postponed until the deferral date (this is the last day of the postponement period and the date must be given)
- that if on the deferral date they meet the criteria to be an eligible jobholder, and are not already an active member of a qualifying scheme, they will be automatically enrolled, *and*
- that any notice from the worker must be in writing and signed by the worker (or if submitted electronically state that the worker personally submitted it).

Additionally:

- eligible and non-eligible jobholders who are not active members of a qualifying scheme must be told about the right to opt in and receive employer contributions, *and*
- entitled workers must be told about the right to join a pension scheme.

The employer can choose to give information about both of these rights in one notice, or to only provide the relevant information.

OPT-OUT NOTICE

An eligible jobholder who does not wish to become an active member of a pension scheme must provide an opt-out notice to the employer within the opt-out period. The notice must normally be obtained from the scheme, not the employer.

To Be Provided By	Time Frame	Summary Of Information Required
Eligible jobholders who wish to opt out after they have been automatically enrolled or re-enrolled; and **non-eligible jobholders** who wish to opt out having opted into the scheme.	The opt-out period is **one month** from the later of the date the jobholder: • becomes an active member, *or* • is provided with the enrolment information above. It may be extended to six weeks if an invalid opt-out notice is submitted initially.	• Full name of jobholder. • National Insurance number, or date of birth. • That the jobholder wishes to opt out and understands the implications. • Signature or, if submitted electronically, a statement confirming that the jobholder personally submitted it. • Date the jobholder completed the form. • Various statements on what the jobholder needs to know regarding opting out.

SECTION 6

MASTER TRUSTS AND NEST

The automatic enrolment regime *is described in Sections 3 to 5*. Employers are required to auto-enrol employees into a qualifying scheme. The scheme can be the employer's own pension scheme, a personal pension scheme or a master trust. NEST is a master trust set up by the government. Providers have also established master trusts, similar to NEST, to provide further options for employers to meet their automatic enrolment obligations.

MASTER TRUSTS

Under the Pension Schemes Act 2017, a master trust scheme is defined as a multi-employer occupational pension scheme *(see Section 2)* that provides money purchase benefits and is used (or intended to be used) by unconnected employers.

Under regulations on minimum governance standards for work-based money purchase schemes *(see Section 7)*, master trusts are required to meet additional requirements, which recognise that they may face conflicts of interest similar to those under contract-based schemes. The regulations require that:

- master trusts have a minimum of three trustees
- the majority of those trustees be non-affiliated; for these independent members, the appointment process must be open and transparent, and evidenced in the chair's statement
- trustee chairs be consulted on the appointment of other trustees
- individual trustees can be regarded as non-affiliated only for terms of up to five years (and for ten years in total) and they are not then regarded as non-affiliated until five years have elapsed since office, *and*
- master trusts make arrangements to encourage members of the scheme to make their views on scheme matters known to the trustees.

From 1 October 2018, an authorisation regime has applied to master trust schemes, subject to some exemptions, including schemes where the only money purchase benefits provided relate to:

- AVCs made by non-money purchase members
- transfers from other schemes in respect of non-money purchase members, *or*
- pension credit rights.

The regime is administered by the Pensions Regulator, with detailed practical support for schemes provided through operational guidance and a Code of Practice.

To receive authorisation, the scheme must meet five criteria:

- the individuals involved in running the scheme are fit and proper
- the systems and processes used in running the scheme are sufficient to ensure that it is run efficiently and is compliant
- the scheme has an adequate continuity strategy, which must set out how members' interests will be protected should it experience a 'triggering event'
- any scheme funder – a corporate body or partnership that is either responsible for financing the scheme if its member charges cannot meet its running costs or entitled to receive profits where member charges exceed running costs – must only carry out activities relating to the master trust and be able to financially support it, *and*
- the scheme is financially sustainable – a business plan must be submitted, to demonstrate this is the case, and must comply with the Code of Practice.

NEST

The National Employment Savings Trust (NEST) is a trust-based money purchase occupational pension scheme set up by the government to make sure that every employer has access to a workplace pension scheme for automatic enrolment. It is run by a trustee board – the NEST Corporation – which is accountable to Parliament through the DWP but is generally independent of the government in its day-to-day decisions.

Benefits

Members are able to purchase a lifetime annuity under the open market option. NEST also provides members with access to its Retirement Panel, which offers a limited range of annuities from selected providers, at competitive prices, for members unwilling or unable to pursue the open market option. Each provider has given a commitment to provide annuities on pots from £1,500 upwards.

NEST is subject to the same legislative requirements as other registered pension schemes with regard to the payment of benefits. Members can take benefits as an UFPLS *(see Section 9)* – or as a series of UFPLSs. However, in 2017, the Government stated that it does not propose that NEST should offer the full range of decumulation options under the money purchase flexibilities, including drawdown, at this time.

In June 2015, NEST published a retirement income blueprint for its members. It proposed a strategy intended to allow for a regular sustainable retirement income while providing access to lump sums without disturbing the income stream. The blueprint sets out three 'building blocks' – an income drawdown fund, a cash lump sum fund and later life protected income – to cover three phases of retirement (mid-to-late 60s to mid-70s, mid-70s to mid-80s and mid-80s onwards).

Contributions

From 1 April 2017, there is no limit on contributions. Previously, members were subject to an annual contribution limit (£4,900 for 2016/17).

Transfers

From 1 April 2017, NEST can accept any transfer that is consistent with its status as a registered pension scheme, including without-consent bulk transfers *(see Section 25)*.

Also from 1 April 2017, individual transfers out are permitted where the member has a statutory right *(see Section 13)*. NEST has discretion to allow with-consent bulk transfers.

Prior to April 2017, there was a general ban on transfer payments to or from NEST. It could accept cash transfer sums *(see Section 12)*, and transfers out were allowed for members over the normal minimum pension age (55) and members suffering from incapacity.

Transfers out are permitted to comply with a pension sharing order and NEST will accept pension credits on divorce for existing members of the scheme *(see Section 17)*.

Charges

Responsibility for setting the appropriate charges for NEST lies with the NEST Corporation. The government stated that the Corporation is best placed to make decisions relating to the charging structure, the level of charges and any additional charges for particular services. In particular, trust law will provide an incentive for the Corporation to set a charging structure that is fair and to keep charges down.

The intention is that NEST will be self-financing through member charges 'in the long term' and that state support should not provide the scheme with an unfair competitive advantage.

The stated aim is to provide 'a low-cost, good value way to save'. NEST's annual management charge (AMC) is 0.3%. An additional charge is made on contributions going into the scheme of 1.8%, which was intended to continue until initial setting-up costs are recovered. In April 2017, the DWP forecast that NEST would repay its Government loan by 2038.

Investment options

The NEST Corporation is responsible for investment decisions. The NEST Order and Rules *(see below)* provide the trustee with broad powers to invest funds and require the trustee to provide a default investment fund for all members who do not make an active investment choice.

NEST has a published Statement of Investment Principles. NEST's default options are 'Retirement Date Funds' – one for each expected retirement year – invested in a broad and diversified set of asset classes. The investment objectives for these funds include the achievement of performance in excess of inflation, using a benchmark of the CPI.

In addition to the default funds, NEST provides a range of other fund choices:

- Higher Risk Fund – targeting high returns through taking more investment risk
- Lower Growth Fund – taking very little investment risk
- Ethical Fund – investing in companies that meet ethical criteria, and in government bonds
- Sharia Fund – only investing in companies that are compliant with Sharia principles, *and*
- Pre-retirement Fund – for members who wish to buy an annuity in the near future.

Governance

A trustee board – the NEST Corporation – is the governing body, with wide-ranging powers to manage the scheme in the interests of its members. It must comply with general pensions legislation, although regulations modify certain aspects of pension legislation when applied to NEST.

The trustee takes the key strategic decisions, but delegates all executive and operational functions to a management board. It must consult a Members' Panel and an Employers' Panel on key decisions.

The NEST Order, which established the scheme, and the initial Rules of NEST were published in 2010. Changes to the rules may only be made either by the trustee or with the consent of the trustee. Proposed rules must be published in draft for comment by interested persons, and the Members' and Employers' Panels must be consulted. Changes to the Order may only be made by the Secretary of State, with trustee consent and consultation.

SECTION 7

SCHEME GOVERNANCE

This section deals with scheme governance, which encompasses the broad range of functions required to operate a pension scheme. It includes consideration of the role of trustees within the legal framework for pensions in the UK and covers some aspects of managing contract-based schemes. References to the legal system are to the system which in general applies in the UK. However, some differences exist under Scottish law. The existing legal framework includes trust law, tax law, social security law (in particular, specific DWP pensions legislation), financial services legislation and European Union (EU) law.

Trust law is discussed below. Tax law is dealt with in *Section 9*. Various aspects of DWP pensions legislation (including provisions which transpose EU requirements into UK law) are covered in this and other sections. The law relating to the regulation of the financial services market is dealt with in more detail in *Section 27*.

The UK's exit from the EU may impact on certain aspects of UK law, but the longer-term consequences will depend on what replaces EU membership. Many of the EU requirements that are most significant for pensions have been incorporated into UK legislation.

TRUSTS AND TRUSTEES

Trust law

Trust law underpins the governance of private sector occupational pension schemes. The principles of trust law have mainly been established, over the years, by court precedents. However, over time some of these principles have been incorporated in legislation, for example in the Trustee Act 2000.

What is a trust?

One definition is that 'a trust is an equitable obligation binding a person (who is called a trustee) to deal with property over which he has control (which is called the trust property) for the benefit of persons (who are called the beneficiaries) of whom he may himself be one, and any of whom may enforce the obligation'.

In the case of a pension scheme, the trustees hold the pension fund assets for the benefit of the members, and their first duty is to them - not to their employer, their trade union, or any outside body. Members include not just those currently employed and paying into the scheme, but also people with deferred pensions, those who are drawing benefits and those who are potentially eligible for benefits, such as spouses and other dependants.

Why use a trust?

The vast majority of UK occupational pension schemes are set up under trust. The three main reasons why trusts have been used are:

- to provide security for the members by keeping the scheme's assets separate from those of the employer
- to ensure third-party beneficiaries, such as spouses and dependants of members, have legal rights, *and*
- the Pensions Act 2004 requires funded occupational schemes to be established under irrevocable trusts and to have effective written rules specifying the benefits and the conditions on which they are payable. This reflects the requirements of the 2003 EU Pensions Directive.

Historically, schemes were set up under trust to enable them to be approved by the Revenue as exempt approved schemes, and thereby qualify for valuable tax reliefs on contributions, investment income and some of the benefits paid.

Who can be a trustee?

The trustees of a scheme can be either individuals (so long as they are at least 18 years old and are not considered to lack capacity to make decisions under the Mental Capacity Act 2005) or corporations, or a combination of both.

Neither the scheme actuary nor the scheme auditor can be a trustee, and certain people are automatically disqualified (e.g. undischarged bankrupts and people who have been convicted of an offence involving dishonesty). The Pensions Regulator has power to prohibit a person from acting as a trustee of a particular scheme, a particular type of scheme, or schemes in general, where it is satisfied that he or she is not a fit and proper person to be a trustee *(see Section 8)*. It may suspend a person from acting as a trustee where the outcome of legal proceedings is awaited. It may also appoint an independent trustee where an employer becomes insolvent or where it believes the appointment is in the best interest of the members *(see 'Conflicts of interest', below)*.

Legislation requires schemes to have a minimum proportion of one third member-nominated trustees. Such trustees must be nominated as the result of a process involving (as a minimum) all the active and pensioner members of the scheme (or organisations representing them), and then selected as a result of a further process. The Regulator has issued a code of practice on this requirement.

A revised EU Pensions Directive came into force in January 2017. Member states have until 13 January 2019 to incorporate the requirements into their own legislation. As the UK will still be a member of the EU at that time, the Government will be required to implement the Directive into legislation (but there will be no immediate requirements for schemes). This legislation is expected to remain in place after the UK leaves the EU. The changes include extensive governance provisions and a requirement for those who run schemes or have key functions to be 'fit and proper'.

Professional trustees

Some trustee bodies will include professional trustees. In 2017 the Regulator published its policy explaining when it may consider someone to be a professional trustee.

Professional trustees are held to higher standards than other trustees and subject to greater fines for non-compliance.

The Professional Trustee Standards Working Group, established by the pensions industry's trustee bodies following a recommendation by the Regulator, is understood to be developing higher standards, including fit and proper protocols, and accreditation for those who are considered to be professional trustees.

The trust deed and rules

A scheme's definitive documentation usually has two main parts: the trust deed and the rules.

The trust deed defines the powers and duties of the trustees and employer, and the duties of trustees to the members.

The rules generally state who is eligible to be a scheme member and cover details of the benefits promised, and the level of members' contributions.

The trust documents govern the trustees' actions. Generally speaking, only when the trust deed and rules do not deal with a point is it necessary to apply the principles of trust law. It should be noted that Acts of Parliament can override provisions contained in trust deeds, but not all statutory provisions are overriding.

Scheme documentation can be altered in various ways: for example, a supplemental deed extends the definitive documentation, perhaps by introducing new powers. An amending deed changes it. Trustees may have to refer to several different documents, if amendments have not been incorporated into the main deed.

DUTIES, RESPONSIBILITIES AND RIGHTS OF A TRUSTEE

The fundamental duty of a trustee is to give effect to the provisions of the trust deed. A trustee who fails to do this is in breach of trust. Trustees' duties are many and varied, and include:

- paying out the right benefits at the right time
- keeping accurate records of members and their dependants
- keeping proper accounts, *and*
- ensuring that scheme assets are properly and prudently invested.

Under the provisions of the Employment Rights Act 1996, employee trustees (or employee directors of trustee companies) of an occupational scheme of their employer have statutory rights to time off work for the performance of their trustee duties and training, payment for this time off and rights not to suffer detriment or dismissal related principally to the performance of their trustee functions.

Legislation places a number of particular responsibilities on trustees. Exceptions apply in certain cases but, in general, these responsibilities include:

Appointment of professional advisers

The trustees must appoint an individual actuary (except for pure money purchase schemes) and an auditor (known respectively as the scheme actuary and the scheme auditor) and, where investments covered by the Financial Services and Markets Act 2000 are held, a fund manager, to carry out certain specified functions. Another actuary may also be appointed to provide actuarial advice which is not required to be given by the scheme actuary. Any person having custody of scheme assets must be appointed by the trustees, except where they are sub-custodians appointed by a main custodian or other adviser who has been specifically authorised by the trustees. A legal adviser must also be appointed by the trustees if such advice is required.

Investment of the scheme's assets

Trustees have complete power to invest scheme assets as if they were their own, subject to their duty of care, the taking of proper advice from qualified advisers, any scheme restrictions (except that any requirement for the direct or indirect consent of the employer is void) and the statutory restriction that not more than five per cent of the market value of the resources of a scheme may at any time be invested in employer-related investments. Their decision-making powers may be delegated to an external fund manager. The trustees remain responsible for any actions taken, but they are not liable for the fund manager's actions so long as they have taken steps to ensure that he or she has appropriate knowledge and experience, and is acting competently and in accordance with the written statement of investment principles (SIP) *(see below)*.

Regulations introduced to comply with the 2003 EU Pensions Directive require the trustees (amongst other things) to invest predominantly in regulated markets and to ensure proper diversification.

Trustees of occupational schemes providing money purchase benefits (unless these are all AVCs) must ensure the following in relation to any of the schemes' default arrangements:

- assets are invested in the best interests of members
- a SIP is prepared *(see below), and*
- their strategy and the performance of the underlying investments are reviewed at least every three years, or without delay after any significant change in investment policy or scheme membership demographics. Any changes to the strategy will entail amendment to the SIP.

For these purposes, a default arrangement includes not only a traditional default fund into which members' contributions are paid without them making an active investment choice but also any arrangement to which at least 80 per cent of the employer's active members have chosen to contribute.

Statement of investment principles

The trustees must prepare (and maintain) this statement, after taking advice from an experienced investment adviser and after consulting the employer (but without any requirement to agree it with the employer). Amongst other things it must cover:

- the kinds of investment to be held and the balance between them
- risk and expected return
- realisation of assets, *and*
- the trustees' policy (if any) on socially responsible investment, including the exercise of voting rights.

The SIP must be reviewed at least every three years and immediately after any significant change in investment policy.

Certain schemes are exempt from preparing a SIP, including those with fewer than 100 members.

Trustees of occupational schemes providing money purchase benefits must have SIPs in place for default arrangements. This is in addition to the requirement to have a SIP for the scheme as a whole and extends to schemes with fewer than 100 members. The SIP for the default arrangement must set out the 'default strategy' (i.e. the trustees' aims, objectives and investment policies) and an explanation of how this is intended to ensure that assets are invested in the best interests of members and beneficiaries.

Compliance with scheme funding legislation

Scheme-specific funding was introduced under the Pensions Act 2004. Under this regime, trustees are responsible for setting the funding strategy as well as monitoring the funding level and payment of contributions. *See Section 18 for further details.*

Disclosure of pension scheme information

Under UK pensions law, scheme trustees are required to make a substantial range of information available to scheme members and others. *See Section 15 for further details.*

Compliance with data protection legislation

The EU General Data Protection Regulation (GDPR) came into force on 25 May 2018. As well as tighter requirements for obtaining consent to process personal data, the GDPR introduces mandatory breach reporting obligations and places greater emphasis on the documentation that organisations must keep to demonstrate their accountability, policies, registers and controls. The GDPR also imposes stronger sanctions for breaches.

Also on 25 May 2018, the main provisions in the Data Protection Act 2018 came into force. This Act repeals and replaces the Data Protection Act 1998, aiming to keep the UK's existing data protection laws up to date for the digital age and setting new standards for protecting personal data. While the UK remains a member of the EU, it must comply directly with the GDPR. When the UK leaves the EU, the GDPR will be incorporated into UK legislation under the EU (Withdrawal) Act.

Whistle-blowing and notifiable events

Under the Pensions Act 2004, scheme trustees (and others) are responsible for reporting breaches (whistle-blowing), and trustees must notify the Regulator of certain events. *See Section 8 for further details.*

Register of persons with significant control

From 6 April 2016 most unlisted companies – including pension trustee companies – are required to keep a register of people with significant control (PSC), i.e. those people who can influence or control a company. This information must be filed with Companies House where it will be publicly available. Failure to maintain a PSC register is a criminal offence; a company that does not have any PSCs still needs to keep a register.

Trustee Knowledge and Understanding

The Pensions Act 2004 introduced a formal requirement for trustees to have knowledge and understanding about the law relating to pensions and trusts and the principles of funding and investment. In addition, they are required to be conversant with the scheme's trust deed and rules, statements of investment and (where applicable) funding principles and other relevant scheme documents. This means that they are expected to have a working knowledge of the documents, so as to be able to use them effectively.

The Regulator has issued and updated a code of practice and scope guidance on these requirements. The level of knowledge and understanding expected is that necessary for the individual concerned to exercise his or her own trustee function (so more is expected of the chair of the trustee board, or a significant sub-committee). Trustees should carry out a review of their training needs at least annually and when required in response to internal and external scheme changes or new responsibilities. Records should be kept of learning activities undertaken.

Newly appointed trustees generally have a six-month period of grace before the requirements apply to them.

The Regulator maintains an online learning programme called the Trustee Toolkit which trustees are recommended to complete. The Regulator provides updates on specific matters and holds webinars on topical issues.

Internal controls

Legislation requires trustees to have internal controls to ensure compliance with the law and their own rules. The Regulator has issued a code of practice, accompanying guidance and a set of e-learning modules covering internal controls. The code stresses the need for trustees to set up internal controls to enable them to react to significant operational, financial, funding, regulatory and compliance risks. These controls should be proportionate, based on an assessment of the risks to which the scheme is exposed, having regard to its particular circumstances and to their likelihood of materialising and potential impact. Internal controls should be reviewed at least annually and more frequently if substantial changes take place or inadequacies are revealed. It is suggested that a statement confirming that key risks have been considered and effective controls established could be incorporated in the scheme's annual report to demonstrate good practice.

Where trustees delegate their responsibilities (e.g. to third-party administrators or investment managers and custodians), they should take care to examine the internal control assurance reports produced by their agents.

Conflicts of interest

Conflicts of interest can pose a serious risk to good governance and, as such, are subject to some very complex legal considerations. The Regulator's guidance on conflicts of interest covers five broad principles, which relate to: understanding the importance of conflicts of interest; identifying conflicts of interest; evaluation, management or avoidance of conflicts; managing adviser conflicts; and conflicts of interest policy. The principles are supported by practical guidance on matters relating to the governance of each. The Regulator's guidance on internal controls describes behaviours it expects to see in identifying and resolving conflicts of interest.

Conflicts of interest do not generally invalidate trustees' decisions, so long as they are properly managed.

Adviser conflicts

The Regulator has published guidance that sets out some key issues for trustees to consider in their relations with advisers. It covers general issues as well as those specific to the scheme actuary, scheme auditor, legal adviser, administrator, independent financial adviser and benefit consultant. The guidance also raises issues, provides hints on questions that trustees should be asking their advisers and urges trustees to obtain a written statement from the advisers on how conflicts of interest are avoided and/or managed.

Conflicts of interest are covered in Actuarial Profession Standard APS P1, and there is a supporting package of material, including a guide for actuaries and a note for pension scheme trustees. The standard includes a presumption that a scheme actuary who advises the sponsoring employer on the funding of the scheme or on any matter relating to the benefits payable would be faced with an irreconcilable conflict of interest, although in exceptional circumstances the actuary can depart from that presumption provided they record the decision and can justify it.

Preventing financial crime

Trustees are subject to several measures intended to prevent financial crime (specifically bribery, money laundering and tax evasion).

As trustees are exposed to some of the offences under the Bribery Act 2010, they should establish and maintain suitable bribery prevention procedures, guided by six principles:

- *proportionality* – procedures should be proportionate to the risks faced
- *top-level commitment* – a culture should be established in which bribery is unacceptable
- *risk assessment* – exposure to potential external and internal risks of bribery should be assessed, documented and periodically reviewed
- *due diligence* – procedures should be put in place in respect of persons who perform, or will perform, services for or on behalf of the organisation in order to mitigate identified bribery risks
- *communication* – internal and external communication and training should ensure that bribery prevention policies and procedures are embedded and understood throughout the organisation, *and*
- *monitoring and review* – procedures should be monitored and evaluated to ensure that they remain fit for purpose.

The trustees' conflicts of interest policy should also be reviewed in line with these procedures, in order to reduce the risk of corruption.

New money-laundering regulations came into force on 26 June 2017 that introduced record-keeping and disclosure duties. The record-keeping requirements apply to all schemes; the reporting requirements normally only apply to schemes that become liable for certain taxes, such as those arising in connection with a direct investment in property. HMRC has published draft guidance setting out its view of how the legislation applies to pension schemes.

The Criminal Finances Act 2017 introduced new offences in relation to failure to prevent facilitation of tax evasion. These offences apply to the directors of a corporate trustee (but not to individual trustees). The trustee must assess the risks that those who act on its behalf (including service providers, such as the scheme administrator and investment consultants) may criminally facilitate tax evasion, and must put in place reasonable prevention procedures.

Decision making

The *Wednesbury* principles are a set of rules that trustees can apply to decision making in order to minimise the risk of legal challenge:

- the trustees must ask themselves the correct questions
- they must direct themselves correctly in law; in particular, they must adopt a correct construction of the trust deed and rules
- they must not arrive at a perverse decision, i.e. a decision at which no reasonable body of trustees would have arrived, *and*
- they must take into account all relevant and no irrelevant facts.

If the trustees can demonstrate that they followed this process when exercising discretionary powers, it is unlikely that their decision will be overturned by the Pensions Ombudsman or the courts. Ombudsman determinations have highlighted the need for scheme minutes to include a clear record of the steps taken in reaching a decision. However, care should be taken if reasons are given, as these could be reviewed by the court.

Internal dispute resolution procedure

Trustees are required to put in place, and disclose via the scheme's explanatory booklet, an internal dispute resolution procedure under which scheme members may bring written complaints. This may be a two-stage procedure, where an individual rules on behalf of the trustees in the first stage, or a single-stage process under which all decisions are taken by the trustees. If the dispute remains unresolved, at any stage the member may take their complaint to the Pensions Ombudsman.

INDEPENDENT GOVERNANCE COMMITTEES

Contract-based schemes are required to have Independent Governance Committees (IGCs) to oversee quality standards and protect members' interests. The Financial Conduct Authority (FCA) has set out rules for IGCs, imposing similar duties and responsibilities to those of trustees in relation to the governance of money purchase schemes *(see below)*. The key duties of an IGC, as set out in its terms of reference, must include:

- to act solely in the interests of relevant members
- to assess the value for money of the provider's workplace personal pension schemes
- where the IGC has concerns about the value for money, to raise them (as it sees fit) with the provider's board
- to escalate concerns to the FCA, alert relevant members and employers, and make its concerns public, if they are not addressed satisfactorily, *and*
- to produce a publicly available annual report setting out how the IGC has met its duties.

THE PENSIONS REGULATOR'S FOCUS ON GOVERNANCE

For some time the Regulator has been focusing on standards of governance in trust-based schemes as previous research has shown that effective trusteeship and governance are key factors in achieving good member outcomes. The Regulator's experience shows that larger schemes tend to be associated with higher levels of governance activity, whereas there tend to be lower perceived standards of governance in smaller money purchase schemes.

The Regulator has been examining how trustee boards can meet the challenge of scheme governance. Its 21st Century Trusteeship initiative seeks to raise standards of trusteeship by being clearer about what the Regulator expects trustees to do, and being swifter to take action where standards are not met. A dedicated area of the Regulator's website covers topics such as the importance of good governance, clear roles and strategy, trustee training, skills and experience, advisers and service providers, managing risk and managing conflicts of interest. The material highlights various guides and tools that are available to help trustees.

To support scheme governance, the Regulator has released a number of codes of practice, guidance notes and other publications, nearly all of which are directed at trustees. *See Section 8 for further details.*

There are additional requirements and separate standards for money purchase schemes – *see 'Governance of money purchase schemes' below.*

Good scheme administration

The Regulator continuously highlights the importance of administration in enabling good member outcomes from pensions saving. Whilst many aspects of administration may be delegated to third parties, the trustees continue to be legally responsible and accountable for record keeping. As well as the risk to members' benefits, inaccurate and missing data can have serious cost implications for pension schemes.

The Regulator has published guides to help schemes meet their duties, setting out good practice as well as targets for standards of member data. This includes common data (such as a member's name, address, NI number and date of birth) and conditional data (more detailed scheme-specific data such as the employing company and the date of a member leaving the scheme). Trustees are expected to review their data at least once a year, and more often if there is a significant event such as changing the administrator, or winding up.

Trustees must report on record keeping in their scheme returns and the Regulator will be taking a particular interest in those that report persistently low data scores (the percentage of members in the scheme that are assessed to have fully present and accurate data), for both common and conditional data.

Fines for failure to provide information to the Regulator

Since 2017 the Regulator has secured several criminal convictions and fines for failure to provide documents it had requested, demonstrating that it can use its powers to enforce provision of information by relevant parties (even if the parties were not under investigation themselves).

Cyber risk

The Regulator has published cyber security guidance for trustees on the steps they can take to protect scheme members and assets. The Regulator broadly defines cyber risk as the risk of loss, disruption or damage to a scheme or its members as a result of the failure of its IT systems and processes. It includes risks to information (data security) as well as assets, and both internal risks (e.g. from staff) and external risks (such as hacking). The guidance sets out good practice in addressing cyber risk and building cyber resilience – the ability to assess and minimise the risk of a cyber incident occurring, and recover when an incident does take place.

INVESTMENT GOVERNANCE

The Myners Principles set out guidelines for investment governance in pension schemes and cover:

- effective decision making
- clear objectives
- risk and liabilities
- performance assessment
- responsible ownership, *and*
- transparency and reporting.

The principles are voluntary with a comply or explain approach to reporting, although the government has suggested that legislation will be introduced if pension schemes do not comply with the principles.

The government established the Investment Governance Group to oversee the principles and provide further guidance, where necessary. In particular, the Group has published best practice guidance including 'Principles for investment governance of work-based DC pension schemes', which applies to both contract-based and trust-based schemes. The principles are:

- clear roles and responsibilities for investment decision making and governance
- effective decision making
- appropriate investment options
- appropriate default strategy
- effective performance assessment, *and*
- clear and relevant communication with members.

Reporting on these principles is also on a comply or explain basis.

The Financial Reporting Council's (FRC) Stewardship Code sets out guidelines for good practice, which it believes institutional investors should aspire to when engaging with the UK listed companies in which they invest. It is acknowledged that trustees of pension funds may not wish to become directly involved in engagement with companies in which they invest, but they are encouraged to set mandates for their investment managers that require them to act in line with the Code.

Under amended investment regulations, which take effect from October 2019, trustees will have to include in their SIP how they take account of financially material considerations including climate change, their policies on stewardship, engagement and voting rights, and the extent (if at all) to which they take account of members' views. Trustees of 'relevant schemes' (broadly, schemes that offer money purchase benefits other than just AVCs) will also have to prepare an implementation report setting out how they have acted on their SIP and must publish these documents on a publicly accessible website which is signposted from benefit statements.

The Regulator has published investment guidance for trustees of defined benefit schemes and a DC guide to investment governance.

GOVERNANCE OF MONEY PURCHASE SCHEMES

Schemes providing money purchase benefits – both trust-based and contract-based – have become subject to many new requirements in recent years, which apply in addition to those set out above.

Minimum governance standards

Minimum governance standards apply to most work-based money purchase schemes – both trust-based and contract-based. The governance standards for contract-based schemes (such as group personal pension plans) are similar to those for trust-based schemes, and are set out under FCA rules, which include the requirements to operate IGCs *(see above)*.

Measures were also introduced to limit charges in the default arrangements of money purchase schemes used for automatic enrolment purposes; *see 'Charge controls' below*.

The trustees of occupational schemes (and sections of schemes) providing money purchase benefits (unless these are solely in respect of AVCs) are required to:

- have a chair of trustees
- ensure that core financial transactions are processed promptly and accurately
- assess whether the costs and charges borne by members are good value
- ensure that the choice of who can provide administrative, fund management, advisory or other services is not restricted – even under the trust deed and rules, which would be overridden by legislation in this respect, *and*
- meet additional requirements in relation to the scheme's default arrangements *(see 'Investment of the scheme's assets' above)*.

The chair of trustees is responsible for signing off an annual governance statement, which must include explanation of how the scheme has complied with the governance standards and charge controls. It must be produced within seven months of each scheme year end as part of the annual report and accounts, otherwise the trustees face a mandatory fine of between £500 and £2,000. From 6 April 2018, regulations extended the content of the chair's statement *(see 'Disclosure of charges' below)*. The Regulator has published a quick guide to the chair's statement, setting out the legal requirements and clarifying its expectations as to how trustees should meet them.

The Regulator is responsible for ensuring that trustees comply with the requirements and collects information via the scheme return. Where relevant, trustees must confirm whether or not their scheme complies with the new charge cap, provide the name of the scheme's chair of trustees and declare whether or not they have produced a governance statement signed by the chair.

In its compliance and enforcement bulletins, the Regulator has explained that trustees can be fined not only for non-provision of the chair's statement but also for provision of a deficient statement. It publishes quarterly lists of penalties imposed on schemes and employers, which include fines relating to the chair's statement and the scheme return.

Regulating money purchase pension schemes

The Regulator's code of practice on *the governance and administration of occupational trust-based schemes providing money purchase benefits* sets out its view of the actions and behaviours expected of trustee boards to demonstrate compliance with legal requirements. It is accompanied by six supporting guides (corresponding to the main sections within the code) that provide practical guidance on how trustees can meet those standards in practice. The guides aim to help trustees implement the code by providing some examples of approaches that could be taken and factors to consider.

The code applies to all schemes that have two or more members and provide any money purchase benefits. Where a scheme's only money purchase benefits are additional voluntary contributions (AVCs), trustees are expected to take a proportionate approach, having regard to the significance of the value of AVCs relative to members' overall benefits in the scheme.

The Regulator has released a number of other documents intended to support the market in achieving good member outcomes in money purchase schemes, including templates for assessing governance standards. It has also issued a compliance and enforcement policy.

Master trusts

Master trusts are subject to the governance regime for money purchase schemes, but must also meet additional requirements. In addition, from 1 October 2018 a new authorisation and supervisory regime applies to master trust schemes *(see Section 6)*.

Charge controls

From 6 April 2015, an annual charge cap of 0.75% of funds under management applies to default arrangements in most occupational schemes that provide money purchase benefits and that are being used as qualifying schemes (to satisfy an employer's automatic enrolment duties). The cap applies to all management charges, including member-borne deductions relating to scheme or investment administration, but excludes transaction costs. The DWP has produced guidance on the charge cap, including on how to identify which funds are protected by the limits on charges and how to assess charges.

The Government's 2017 review of automatic enrolment *(see Section 3)* decided that there would be no change to the level or scope of the charge cap because evidence suggests that it is working broadly as intended; it will be examined again in 2020.

From April 2016, active member discounts and member-borne commission payments (i.e. charges levied on members to recover the cost of commission payments made to advisers for certain advice or services) are banned in schemes that are being used for automatic enrolment. The DWP has published guidance on the regulations for trustees and service providers.

Early exit charges in occupational schemes are prohibited for members joining a scheme on or after 1 October 2017 (for other members they are capped at 1% of the value of the member's fund). Broadly, an early exit charge is one that is levied on a member if they transfer or take their benefits before normal pension age, if that charge would not apply on or after normal pension age. The FCA has made equivalent rules relating to charges for contract-based schemes.

Disclosure of charges

Since April 2015, trustees (and IGCs) have had a duty to calculate costs and charges borne by members, to make an assessment of value for money and to report on them in the annual chair's statement as far as they are able. However, until recently there was no requirement for asset managers to fully disclose this information. From 3 January 2018 the FCA requires asset managers to disclose transaction costs and administration charges in a standardised form.

The Institutional Disclosure Working Group has been working on industry-agreed templates, to support disclosure to institutional investors (such as pension funds and insurers). The Work and Pensions Committee also launched an inquiry into whether the pensions industry provides sufficient transparency to consumers around charges, investment strategy and performance.

From 6 April 2018, regulations extended the content of the chair's statement to show costs and charges for each default arrangement and each alternative fund option that members can select. The statement must also include an illustration of the cumulative effect of the costs and charges. Schemes must publish this information, together with certain other parts of the chair's statement, on a website that is publicly accessible via search engines, enabling comparison between schemes. This must be done within seven months of the scheme year end, and annual benefit statements must include a statement that this information is available, along with the web address. There is no prescribed form for how the information must be provided, but new statutory guidance covers the production of the illustration and the publication on a website. Certain other information on the underlying funds must be available on request, from April 2019.

THE ROLE OF THE EMPLOYER

The employer is a party to the trust and retains certain duties and powers which may be specified in the trust deed. The employer normally carries a substantial burden of the cost of the scheme benefits, or its administration, or both, and would therefore expect to retain certain powers, especially in areas where there is a cost element, for example the power to augment benefits or to amend the scheme. The employer generally has the ultimate power to cease contributions to the scheme, which will lead to the scheme either winding up or ceasing to provide any further benefit accrual, according to the provisions of the trust deed. In normal circumstances, the employer should act in a reasonable manner to ensure that the trustees can operate the scheme satisfactorily; this includes providing information on members, paying contributions when due, and meeting any obligations imposed on them by the trust deed or by legislation.

Although the Pensions Act 2004 extended the trustees' statutory powers in relation to scheme funding, the method and assumptions, statement of funding principles, any recovery plan and the schedule of contributions are all, generally, subject to the agreement of the employer. *See Section 18 for further details*.

The employer is also required to consult with scheme members about proposed changes to scheme rules, if these fall within prescribed categories. *See Section 2*.

Under the Takeover Code, companies planning a takeover are required to provide information to the trustees of the target's pension scheme, who are then able to express their views about the impact for the scheme *(see Section 25)*.

Schemes must identify the statutory employer(s) on their scheme return and may find supporting information on the Regulator's website helpful. A statutory employer for this purpose is the employer who is responsible for scheme-specific funding, section 75 debts or triggering entry to the Pension Protection Fund. Where trustees conclude that the scheme has no statutory employer, they should contact the Regulator.

Further changes to the employer's role may follow from the 2018 White Paper on protecting defined benefit pension schemes – *see Section 8*.

THE ROLE OF THE ACTUARY

Responsibilities of the scheme actuary

The scheme actuary appointed by the trustees has a number of statutory responsibilities. These include:

- advising the trustees on various aspects of scheme funding, as required by the Pensions Act 2004 *(see Section 18)*
- producing actuarial valuations for funding purposes *(see Section 18)*
- certifying the technical provisions and schedule of contributions as required by the scheme funding legislation *(see Section 18)*
- along with other parties who are involved in running the scheme, reporting material breaches of statutory responsibilities by the employer or trustees to the Regulator (*see Section 8*)
- advising the trustees on various matters in relation to the calculation of individual transfer values *(see Section 13)*
- certifying certain bulk transfers of members' benefits without their consent *(see Section 25), and*
- certifying qualifying schemes for automatic enrolment *(see Section 4)*.

Other actuarial advice

Most schemes require the trustees to take actuarial advice before taking decisions, on such matters as augmentations and bulk transfers, which will affect the finances of the scheme (and this is encouraged by the notifiable events framework – *see Section 8*). Actuaries also provide expert advice in benefit design and implementation, and assist both employers and trustees, subject to any conflict of interest restrictions, in ensuring that the pension provision offered to employees is both appropriate and soundly based.

The abolition of salary-related contracting out gave rise to an increase in National Insurance contributions (NICs) from 6 April 2016 because employer and employee rebates ceased *(see Reference Section 5)*. To help offset this increase in costs, legislation allows employers to amend scheme rules (up to 5 April 2021) to reduce scheme benefits and/or increase member contributions. The changes need to be certified by an actuary as saving no more than the increase in employer NICs.

THE ROLE OF THE AUDITOR

The statutory duties of the scheme auditor include the following:

- producing a report stating whether or not in the auditor's opinion the scheme accounts have been prepared in accordance with regulations
- producing a statement as to whether or not in the auditor's opinion the required contributions have been paid to the scheme
- if the auditor's statement is negative or qualified, giving a statement of the reasons, *and*
- along with other parties who are involved in running the scheme, reporting material breaches of statutory responsibilities by the employer or trustees to the Pensions Regulator (*see Section 8*).

THE ROLE OF THE ADMINISTRATOR

The administrator has many duties. Some of these are imposed by statute and regulations. Others are set out under a contract with the trustees.

Day-to-day administrative responsibilities are very varied, ranging from organising the payment of benefits to individual beneficiaries in accordance with the scheme rules, to tasks such as organising the submission of information required by the Pensions Regulator.

In addition to day-to-day administration, HMRC requires every registered pension scheme to appoint a 'scheme administrator', usually the trustees for occupational pension schemes, to be responsible for providing information including scheme returns and event reports, accounting for tax and monitoring benefits against the lifetime allowance. HMRC may de-register an existing pension scheme or refuse to register a scheme, where it believes that the scheme administrator is not a fit and proper person to fulfil that role – this is aimed at helping to prevent pension scams.

SECTION 8

THE PENSIONS REGULATORY SYSTEM

The Pensions Regulator is the regulator of work-based pension schemes in the UK. This section covers its role, in particular in relation to trust-based schemes. The Financial Conduct Authority (FCA) has a similar role in ensuring that firms providing contract-based schemes treat their customers fairly *(see below)*. The roles of other bodies involved in the regulation of UK pension schemes are also discussed.

THE ROLE OF THE PENSIONS REGULATOR

The Regulator's powers fall into three broad categories: investigating schemes, acting against avoidance and putting things right. It has recently promoted a 'clearer, quicker and tougher' approach to its activities.

The Regulator has statutory objectives to protect members' benefits, to reduce the risk of calls on the Pension Protection Fund (PPF), to promote good administration, to maximise employers' compliance with their duties in relation to automatic enrolment *(see Sections 3 to 5 for details)* and to minimise any adverse impact on employers' sustainable growth in relation to its regulation of scheme funding *(see Section 18)*.

The Regulator also has a role in respect of the governance and administration of public service schemes. It also (from October 2018) supervises the authorisation of master trusts *(see Section 6)*.

In May 2018, the Regulator published its corporate plan setting out its priorities for the next three years (2018–21). These broadly align with those of previous years although there is a new priority on preparing for the impact of Brexit. Its work on improving standards of trusteeship through governance and administration has been given a higher priority and will include a review and consolidation of existing guidance to make its expectations clearer. Its ongoing campaign on 21st-century trusteeship aims to drive up the standards of governance across pension schemes.

Scheme returns

The Regulator requires all schemes to complete a regular scheme return. This provides a wide range of information about schemes, including details of membership, sponsoring employers, trustees, advisers, administration, funding and investment. These returns include the information required by the PPF to determine its annual levies *(see Section 20)*. Most recently, it has included questions on data scores, so that the Regulator can track improvements in record-keeping. A return is required in response to a scheme return notice, which is issued by the Regulator annually for all but the smallest schemes.

It is the trustees' legal duty to complete the scheme return online by the completion date notified on the form, and there is a penalty for non-completion. The online Exchange system also allows trustees and administrators to update scheme details during the year.

Codes of practice, guidance and other material

The Regulator is required to publish codes of practice giving practical guidance on implementing certain parts of the legislation, and setting out the standards of conduct and practice expected. These codes are updated from time to time. The codes are not law but nevertheless would be taken into account by a court in deciding whether or not legislation had been complied with. The following codes are in effect:

- Reporting breaches of the law *(see below)*
- Notifiable events *(see below)*
- Funding defined benefits *(see Section 18)*
- Early leavers – reasonable periods *(see Section 12)*
- Reporting late payment of contributions to occupational schemes *(see below)*
- Reporting late payment of contributions to personal pension schemes *(see below)*
- Trustee knowledge and understanding *(see Section 7)*
- Member-nominated trustees and directors – putting in place and implementing arrangements *(see Section 7)*
- Internal controls *(see Section 7)*
- Modification of subsisting rights *(see Section 2)*
- Dispute resolution – reasonable periods *(see Section 7)*
- Circumstances in relation to the material detriment test *(see below)*
- Governance and administration of occupational trust-based schemes providing money purchase benefits *(see Section 7)*
- Governance and administration of public service pension schemes, *and*
- Authorisation and supervision of master trusts.

In addition to publishing codes of practice (often with related guidance) the Regulator has also issued resources such as ‘essential guides’, quick guides, regulatory guidance, statements and warnings for trustees of defined benefit and money purchase schemes, and for employers. Subjects include automatic enrolment, charges and governance of money purchase schemes, bulk transfers of money purchase benefits, cyber security, managing advisers and pension scams. It has also released a document defining professional trustees and a monetary penalties policy. The Regulator has also published various research documents and survey results.

Notifiable and reportable events

As noted above, the Regulator has issued codes of practice relating to notifiable events and reporting breaches of the law. Trustees and/or employers are required to notify the Regulator in writing of certain notifiable events.

	Notifiable events – all cases
Trustees	A decision by the trustees or managers to grant benefits, or a right to benefits, on more favourable terms than those provided for by the scheme rules, without either seeking advice from the actuary or securing additional funding where such funding was advised by the actuary. A decision to take action that will, or is intended to, result in entering into a scheme apportionment arrangement on or after the employer debt arose. A decision to take action that will, or is intended to, result in a flexible apportionment arrangement taking effect *(see Section 25)*.
Employer	Any decision by the employer to take action that will, or is intended to, result in a debt that is, or may become, due to the scheme not being paid in full. Ceasing to (or deciding to cease to) carry on business in the United Kingdom. Where applicable, receipt by the employer of advice that it is trading wrongfully, or circumstances being reached in which a director or former director of the company knows that there is no reasonable prospect that the company will avoid going into insolvent liquidation. The conviction of an individual for an offence involving dishonesty, if the offence was committed while the individual was a director or partner of the employer.
Additional notifiable events – where scheme was underfunded at last s179 valuation or there has been a reportable breach of the schedule of contributions in previous 12 months	
Trustees	Any decision by the trustees or managers to take action that will, or is intended to, result in any debt (above a *de minimis* threshold) that is, or may become, due to the scheme not being paid in full. Making (or deciding to make) a transfer payment to, or accepting (or deciding to accept) a transfer payment from, another scheme in excess of £1,500,000 (or 5% of scheme assets if lower). Granting (or deciding to grant) benefits, or a right to benefits, to a member in excess of £1,500,000 (or 5% of scheme assets if lower).

Employer	Any breach by the employer of a covenant in an agreement between the employer and a bank or other institution providing banking services, other than where the bank or other institution agrees with the employer not to enforce the covenant. Where the employer is a company, a controlling company relinquishing, or deciding to relinquish, control of the employer company.

Notification is only required for schemes that are eligible for the PPF. The purpose of notification is to reduce the risk of circumstances occurring that might lead to compensation being payable from the PPF, by providing an early warning of possible insolvency or underfunding. The events to be notified, including those under employer debt legislation, are set out below. (Where a withdrawal arrangement or approved withdrawal arrangement *(see Section 25)* is in force, each guarantor must notify the Regulator if it becomes aware that any of the events requiring notification by the employer occur in relation to it, and also if it becomes insolvent.)

Under separate legislation, there is a duty to report significant breaches that are 'likely to be of material significance to the Regulator'. These reportable events are not restricted to schemes eligible for the PPF. The duty to blow the whistle applies to a wide range of people, including trustees, employers, scheme administrators and professional advisers. Criteria for deciding whether or not a breach is likely to be of material significance are set out in the code of practice and guidance and cover the cause and effect of the breach, the reaction to it and any wider implications.

For both notifiable and reportable events, notification should be made in writing and where possible the standard form available from the Regulator's website should be used. The White Paper of March 2018, and subsequent consultation on the Regulator's powers, propose to expand the scope, timing and coverage of the notifiable events framework.

Late payments by employers

The Regulator has issued two codes of practice about the reporting of late payments by employers, one relating to occupational money purchase pension schemes and the other to personal pension schemes. These cover setting up and monitoring payment schedules (for occupational schemes) and direct payment arrangements (for personal pensions), and providing information to members so that they can check what contributions are due. The codes are accompanied by guidance and a separate guide for employers.

The codes set out reasonable periods within which trustees/managers must report material late payments of contributions to the Regulator (within ten working days of identifying that a late payment is material) and to members/employees (no later than 30 days after the report to the Regulator, although trustees/managers are encouraged to do so earlier). The code includes a guide to which circumstances would be considered material, such as where a contribution remains unpaid 90 days after the due date or where the trustees/managers have reasonable cause to believe that the employer is not willing to pay. Requirements regarding late payments to defined benefit schemes are included in the code of practice covering scheme funding *(see Section 18)*.

Acting against avoidance

The Regulator has powers to act where it believes that an employer is attempting to take action that would allow it to avoid its pension obligations (deliberately or otherwise), leaving the PPF to pick up the pension liabilities. These powers are available under what the pensions industry refers to as the 'moral hazard' provisions. They allow the Regulator to issue any of the following:

(a) *Contribution notices*. If the Regulator determines that a company or individual has taken action with the main purpose of avoiding an obligation to meet a debt on the employer under section 75 of the Pensions Act 1995, it may direct that those involved pay a contribution to the scheme.

The Regulator can also issue a contribution notice if the material detriment test is met. This is met if, in the Regulator's opinion, 'the act, or failure to act, has been materially detrimental to the likelihood of accrued scheme benefits being received'. The Regulator has issued a code of practice and guidance relating to the test.

To date, the Regulator has issued only two contribution notices.

(b) *Financial support directions (FSDs)*. These are intended to apply in cases where corporate structures exist for legitimate business reasons but where the effect is that the employer in relation to a scheme is insufficiently resourced to deal with a potential section 75 obligation. Here the Regulator can require the company group to put in place financial support arrangements, and it has the power to issue one or more contribution notices on non-compliance.

To date, the Regulator has issued determination notices in relation to FSDs in respect of four groups of companies, and companies have been threatened with FSDs.

(c) *Restoration orders*. If there has been a transaction at an undervalue involving the scheme's assets, these allow the Regulator to take action to have the assets (or their equivalent value) restored to the scheme.

Companies considering corporate transactions where there is an underfunded defined benefit pension scheme can apply to the Regulator for a clearance statement. This gives assurance that the Regulator will not use its anti-avoidance powers in relation to the transaction once it is completed. The decision is binding on the Regulator unless the circumstances differ materially from what was disclosed in the clearance application. The 2018 White Paper proposes to expand this process, as well as examining the existing anti-avoidance powers. Any enforcement is likely to be retrospective to the date of the White Paper *(for impact on corporate activity see Section 25)*.

The Regulator has also issued reports under section 89 of the Pensions Act 2004, setting out its considerations in relation to some schemes. These reports provide an insight into how the Regulator uses its powers, for example in relation to restructuring, corporate activity, approving Regulated Apportionment Arrangements, scheme funding and automatic enrolment.

Possible developments following from the White Paper

The 2017 Green Paper, *Defined benefit pension schemes: security and sustainability*, noted cases where member protection had been compromised following corporate transactions. The March 2018 White Paper, *Protecting defined benefit pension schemes*, set out the Government's plans, which include supporting a stronger Regulator. The Government aims to clarify rules and expectations but otherwise not make fundamental changes to the existing system. However, it proposes tougher, more proactive intervention powers, and these are explored in a consultation issued in June 2018.

Intervention

When the Regulator decides action must be taken to protect the security of members' benefits, there is a range of options available. These include:

- issuing an improvement notice to one or more persons
- taking action to recover unpaid contributions from the employer
- disqualifying trustees, or issuing prohibition or suspension orders to trustees (the Regulator has used this power to prohibit a number of trustees from acting)
- appointing trustees, including independent trustees in certain circumstances
- voiding rule modifications
- using its 'section 231' powers to direct how a scheme's technical provisions should be calculated and how its deficit should be funded *(see Section 18), and*
- imposing fines (maximum: £5,000 for individuals or £50,000 in other cases). Fines have been imposed for automatic enrolment breaches, failure to complete funding valuations and non-reporting of late contributions. The Regulator has secured criminal convictions and penalties against several parties who failed to provide information it required as part of its investigations. Also, it is now proposing to seize assets to recoup fines and levies, if necessary. It publicises its actions and the schemes involved.

THE ROLE OF THE FINANCIAL CONDUCT AUTHORITY

The FCA is responsible for regulating the standards of conduct in financial markets and for supervising the infrastructure that supports those markets, so that the markets function well *(see Section 27)*. The FCA's remit extends across a wide range of financial services, including personal pension schemes.

The FCA's three operational objectives are:

- to secure an appropriate degree of protection for consumers
- to protect and enhance the integrity of the UK financial system, *and*
- to promote effective competition in the interests of consumers.

A Memorandum of Understanding between the FCA and the Regulator sets out the arrangements for cooperation and coordination between the two in carrying out their respective regulatory responsibilities under the Financial Services and Markets Act 2000, Pensions Acts and other relevant legislation. A joint guide to the regulation of workplace defined contribution pensions, directed particularly at trustees, advisers and pension providers, aims to clarify the regulatory focus and approach of each regulator. The guide sets out how the two regulators interact and how they manage any overlaps and ensure consistency. While they have similar expectations for scheme quality and member outcomes, their regulatory focuses are slightly different – the Regulator oversees the conduct of the trustees, while the FCA works to ensure that firms providing contract-based schemes, and those who give advice in relation to such schemes, treat their customers fairly.

Like the Regulator, the FCA has issued guidance and reports, on subjects such as pension scams, annuity comparison websites and independent governance committees. Its ScamSmart campaign helps consumers avoid investment fraud in general.

In recent years, the FCA has introduced reforms that aim to improve standards of pensions guidance and advice at retirement, and make access to the money purchase flexibilities easier *(see Section 14)*. It has also developed its rules and guidance to reflect recent developments; it has recently consulted on issues such as the quality of transfer advice, and has consulted on proposals as part of the retirement outcomes review *(see Section 14)*. The FCA has completed a study of the asset management market in order to assess competition in that market and to consider what actions are appropriate. This has culminated in the Competition and Markets Authority's investigation into the investment consultants market.

The FCA and the Pensions Regulator have published a joint strategy on regulating the pensions and retirement income sector, setting out how they will work together to tackle the key risks facing the sector over the next five to ten years.

THE ROLE OF THE DWP

The Department for Work & Pensions (DWP) provides the overarching regulatory and legal framework governing the Regulator and the PPF. It has no responsibility for the day-to-day running of the Regulator and the PPF, but expects to be informed by them of potentially significant problems.

A tripartite Memorandum of Understanding between the DWP, the Regulator and the PPF establishes the framework for cooperation between them, including discussion forums, and sets out the role and responsibilities of each body.

THE ROLE OF HMRC

Since pension benefits are often costly, employers (and employees) will generally wish to take advantage of the tax reliefs that are available to schemes that meet certain criteria. This is monitored by Pension Schemes Services (PSS) within HM Revenue & Customs (HMRC). Schemes that wish to benefit from these tax reliefs must be registered *(see Section 9 for details)*.

Following registration, PSS monitors schemes to ensure that they continue to meet their requirements. Scheme administrators are required to supply HMRC with the information necessary to enable its monitoring to be effective. This includes an Event Report, which must be completed annually, giving details of specified events (such as large benefit payments, payment of benefits to members with primary, enhanced, individual or fixed protection, and members' benefits exceeding the annual allowance) that have occurred during the tax year to which the report relates. HMRC also requires quarterly income tax returns to be completed and may require a copy of the audited annual accounts to be submitted. HMRC is moving to an online registration and reporting system. In order to ensure that the requirements are not circumvented by moving pension benefits outside the UK, HMRC also has oversight of recognised overseas pension schemes *(see Section 9)*.

To counter money laundering, occupational schemes have additional record-keeping duties and certain schemes are required to disclose information to HMRC *(see Section 7)*.

THE ROLE OF EU REGULATION

The future role of the European Union (EU) in regulating UK schemes will depend on the terms of the UK's exit from the EU. The summary below sets out the position while the UK remains in the EU.

In the context of EU regulation, UK pension schemes are institutions for occupational retirement provision (IORPs), and therefore subject to EU directives – relating both specifically to pensions (including requirements for supervisory authorities such as the Pensions Regulator) and to employment more generally. UK pensions legislation in many areas has evolved to meet the requirements of these directives.

The European Insurance and Occupational Pensions Authority (EIOPA) is an independent body advising the European Parliament, the Council of the EU and the European Commission. EIOPA's core responsibilities include the protection of insurance policyholders, pension scheme members and beneficiaries. EIOPA will often become involved in developing new directives (for example on governance or pensions portability), and seek evidence from member states including the UK to support this work.

THE PENSIONS ADVISORY SERVICE (TPAS)

TPAS (the Pensions Advisory Service) is a non-profit, independent and voluntary organisation giving free information and guidance concerning State, occupational and personal pensions. It is grant-aided by the DWP. TPAS is also involved in delivery of the Pension Wise guidance service *(see Section 14)*.

The Financial Guidance and Claims Act 2018 will bring the functions of TPAS and Pension Wise together into a single financial guidance body *(see Section 14)*.

THE PENSIONS OMBUDSMAN (TPO)

The Pensions Ombudsman's role is to investigate disputes and complaints concerning occupational and personal pension schemes. Complaints may be made by actual or potential beneficiaries against the trustees, employer or anyone involved in the administration of a scheme. The Ombudsman's jurisdiction also covers complaints made by the trustees against the employer, and vice versa, and disputes between trustees of either the same scheme or different schemes. Since April 2018 TPO has taken over TPAS's role in dispute resolution; members can now access all pension dispute resolution services from TPO, whether before or after they have gone through their scheme's own Internal Dispute Resolution Procedure.

During an investigation, the trustees of the scheme involved, and anyone else against whom a complaint has been made, are given a chance to explain their position, and the Ombudsman can require any necessary information or documentation to be provided to him.

The Pensions Ombudsman has statutory authority with regard to the complaints brought to him. In particular:

- he has the same powers as the court in respect of the examination and attendance of witnesses
- anyone obstructing an investigation, for example by refusing to give certain information, can be taken to court and, following representations by either or both sides, be dealt with as if he or she had been in contempt of that court, *and*
- the Ombudsman's decision, and any directions he gives, are final and binding, and are enforceable in a county court as if they were judgments of that court. An appeal can be made to the High Court on any points of law involved in the case.

The Pensions Ombudsman works closely with the Financial Ombudsman Service (which was set up to resolve individual complaints between consumers and financial businesses more generally) in cases where their remits overlap.

The Pensions Regulator and TPO have released a joint agreement setting out principles of information sharing while each body fulfils its respective functions.

OCCUPATIONAL PENSION SCHEME LEVIES

Occupational pension schemes are generally required to pay the following levies:

- the General Levy (which also applies to personal pension schemes)
- the Fraud Compensation Levy, *and*
- the Financial Reporting Council Levy.

The Regulator or its agents collect these levies. Schemes that are eligible for future entry into the PPF are also required to pay levies to the PPF *(see Section 20)*.

General Levy

The General Levy covers the cost of the Regulator, the Pensions Ombudsman, the PPF Ombudsman and any grants to support TPAS.

The levy rates applying for 2017/18 and 2018/19 are set out below:

		Occupational schemes:		Personal pension schemes:	
Band	Number of members:	General Levy (per member):	Min. payment (per scheme):	General Levy (per member):	Min. payment (per scheme):
1	2–11	–	£29	–	£12
2	12–99	£2.88	–	£1.15	–
3	100–999	£2.08	£290	£0.81	£120
4	1,000–4,999	£1.62	£2,080	£0.69	£810
5	5,000–9,999	£1.23	£8,100	£0.46	£3,450
6	10,000–499,000	£0.86	£12,300	£0.35	£4,600
7	500,000+	£0.65	£430,000	£0.26	£175,000

Fraud Compensation Levy

The PPF is responsible for operating the Fraud Compensation Fund *(see Section 20)*.

This is funded by a Fraud Compensation Levy on all schemes eligible for this compensation at a rate determined by the PPF. Regulations cap the levy at 75 pence per member per year (23 pence prior to 31 March 2011). The levy is only charged as and when needed. Levies were raised in 1997/98, 2004/05 and 2010/11, all at the rate of 23 pence per member, and in 2011/12 and 2012/13 at the rate of 25 pence per member. From 2013/14 to 2016/17 no levy was raised but for 2017/18 and 2018/19, the levy was set at 25 pence per member.

Financial Reporting Council Levy

Since April 2006, the Financial Reporting Council has had responsibility for actuarial standards and regulation. The cost is met by an annual levy, collected separately from the above levies. For 2017/18 the levy in relation to pension schemes (with 5,000 or more members) is £2.75 per 100 members.

SECTION 9

PENSIONS TAXATION – REGISTERED PENSION SCHEMES

The current pension tax regime came into force on 6 April 2006 under the Finance Act 2004, and replaced the previous tax regimes for all types of pension scheme. This regime applies to all members of all arrangements in registered pension schemes. Registered schemes are authorised to make certain specific payments to or in respect of members, or to employers. The making of unauthorised payments results in charges being levied on the recipient and/or the pension scheme. Contributions made to registered schemes by members or employers are eligible for tax relief subject to certain conditions.

The regime was subsequently amended to give more flexibility over the form in which money purchase benefits could be paid out (effectively abolishing the requirement to provide a regular income).

The tax regime for registered schemes can impact certain overseas schemes where the member is deemed to have benefited from UK income tax relief. Retirement and death benefits can also be provided outside a registered scheme by an 'Employer-financed Retirement Benefits Scheme' (EFRBS) and by 'Excepted Group Life Policies' – *see Section 11*.

In this section we outline the tax treatment of contributions to, and payments from, registered pension schemes. We then give an outline of the limits on tax-efficient pension saving. Other issues relevant to the tax regime are covered at the end of the section. This section does not cover DWP legislation or individual schemes' rules, both of which can place additional restrictions on what schemes may provide.

Individuals can receive tax-advantaged benefits subject to two allowances:

- the *annual allowance* – a limit on an individual's retirement savings during the year, *and*
- the *lifetime allowance* – an overall limit on an individual's tax-privileged retirement savings.

CONTRIBUTIONS

Employer contributions

Contributions by employers to a registered scheme will usually be allowed as a deduction in calculating the profits of the employer in the year in which they are paid provided (as is usually the case) that they are paid 'wholly and exclusively for the purposes of the trade'. Generally, no tax charge on the employee (i.e. as a 'benefit in kind') arises from the employer contribution.

Member contributions

Tax relief on member contributions is normally either:

- *net pay* – pay is reduced by the amount of the member contribution so that tax relief is given via payroll at the member's marginal rate; this is the approach used by most occupational pension schemes, *or*
- *relief at source* – the individual pays contributions out of post-tax income, relief at 20% is reclaimed by the pension arrangement and added to the contribution and any further tax relief is then reclaimed under self-assessment; this is mostly used by personal pension schemes.

In any one tax year member contributions of up to 100% of relevant UK earnings (or £3,600 gross if higher where the scheme is operating on a 'relief at source' basis) attract income tax relief. Further contributions may be paid, but attract no tax relief. As well as taxable earnings from employment and benefits in kind, 'relevant UK earnings' includes taxable income arising from share schemes and taxable severance payments. Tax relief is not available on contributions made after age 75.

AUTHORISED PENSIONS PAYABLE TO MEMBERS

For a money purchase arrangement, there are essentially three options as to the type of authorised member pension that may be provided:

- a *drawdown pension*, consisting of income withdrawal and/or a short-term annuity
- a *lifetime annuity, and*
- a *scheme pension* as for defined benefit arrangements *(see below)*, provided the member had been offered a lifetime annuity.

A defined benefit arrangement may pay an authorised member pension only in the form of a *scheme pension*, as *described below*.

All pensions payable from registered schemes are subject to income tax at the recipient's marginal rate and they must be paid under PAYE, where applicable.

Minimum age from which pension may be paid

Member pensions (including drawdown pension) must not commence before *normal minimum pension age*, except on ill-health retirement. Normal minimum pension age is 55; prior to 6 April 2010, it was 50. Under transitional provisions, members may be able to receive an authorised pension before age 55 if such a right existed at 5 April 2006. The Government announced in 2014 that normal minimum pension age would increase to 57 from 2028, and thereafter remain at 10 years below State Pension Age *(see Section 1)*.

Drawdown pension

As an alternative, or in addition, to lump sums (such as an uncrystallised funds pension lump sum or a pension commencement lump sum – *see below*), members can take their benefits in the form of regular or irregular income payments, as income withdrawal and/or a short-term annuity.

Income withdrawal allows a member to gain access to the whole of the drawdown fund in one or more instalments. The benefit is taxed as pension income regardless of the number of instalments. When a member first draws funds from such a 'flexi-access drawdown' fund, this triggers the money purchase annual allowance *(see below)*.

Before 6 April 2015, drawdown pension was normally subject to an annual cap, with an alternative, uncapped, 'flexible drawdown' available to individuals who satisfied a 'minimum income requirement'. Capped drawdown arrangements can continue after 5 April 2015 provided the annual cap is not exceeded. The flexi-access drawdown rules apply where the cap is exceeded, and for former flexible drawdown arrangements.

Drawdown funds can also be used to provide a 'short-term annuity', which is payable by an insurance company and for a term of up to five years.

Lifetime annuity

A lifetime annuity must be payable by an insurance company. Where the member became entitled to the annuity before 6 April 2015 it should normally be non-decreasing, although investment/index-linked variants were permitted.

Scheme pension

Scheme pensions must be payable at least annually and may not be reduced from one 12-month period to the next, except in specified circumstances. These include: the cessation of an ill-health pension; a bridging pension ceasing between ages 60 and 65, or State Pension Age if greater; as a consequence of a pension sharing order; where reductions are applied to all scheme pensions; when a scheme in deficit is winding up; or where the pension scheme has satisfied the individual's liability for an annual allowance charge and a commensurate reduction is made to the scheme pension as a consequence.

Period of payment

Lifetime annuities and scheme pensions must generally be payable for life and may, additionally, carry a guarantee payable (to any person) in the form of continued pension instalments. In the case of scheme pensions, and annuities that commenced before 6 April 2015, the guarantee period cannot exceed ten years.

Pension errors and arrears

Certain payments made in respect of a pensioner are also authorised where it is reasonable for the scheme to make the payment. These can include pensions paid in error to a pensioner or up to six months after the pensioner's death, and arrears of pension from a defined benefit arrangement.

These payments are normally taxable as pension in the tax year of payment.

Other payments that HMRC accept were made in 'genuine error' and are subsequently reclaimed by the scheme can be treated as never having been made.

AUTHORISED LUMP SUMS PAYABLE TO MEMBERS

The main authorised lump sum benefits that may be paid to a member of a registered pension scheme are set out below (amounts taken under drawdown are classed as pension – *see above*).

Pension commencement lump sum

A tax-free pension commencement lump sum (PCLS) of up to 25% of the value of the benefits crystallised (*see 'Lifetime allowance charge' below*) may normally be paid in connection with a member becoming entitled to a 'relevant pension' (a *scheme pension*, a *lifetime annuity* or funds being designated as *drawdown*). Also, the maximum PCLS payable is normally restricted to one-quarter of the unused portion of the standard lifetime allowance. The PCLS normally has to be paid from the same scheme as the associated relevant pension, and not more than six months before, or twelve months after, the entitlement to the relevant pension arises.

The following may also be authorised payments:

- a commencement lump sum based on an incorrect pension figure, annuity or scheme pension purchase price, *and*
- a commencement lump sum paid under a defined benefit arrangement, no more than a year after the scheme administrator first knew (or could reasonably have been expected to know) of the member's death, if entitlement was not established and payment could not reasonably have been expected before the member died.

Uncrystallised funds pension lump sum (UFPLS)

This can be paid in respect of uncrystallised money purchase funds, after *normal minimum pension age* or if the ill-health condition is satisfied. A quarter of each such lump sum is tax free, with the remainder taxed as income. Exclusions apply to certain individuals with protected lump sum rights and where the amount paid would exceed the member's available lifetime allowance. Taking a UFPLS triggers the money purchase annual allowance *(see below)*.

Serious ill-health lump sum

Where a member is expected to live for less than one year, a serious ill-health lump sum may be paid in respect of uncrystallised benefits. Up to the available lifetime allowance, this is tax free if the recipient is under age 75 and taxed as income otherwise.

Short service refund lump sum

A refund of the member's contributions (without interest) may be paid from an occupational pension scheme on leaving service, if the member has no right to preservation. For members joining money purchase schemes from 1 October 2015 this facility is not available to those who have more than 30 days' service.

The scheme administrator is liable for tax on the first £20,000 of such a refund at 20% and on the remainder at 50%.

Interest may be paid in addition to the short service refund lump sum as a 'scheme administration member payment' *(see below)*, taxed as income.

Trivial commutation and other small lump sums

A trivial commutation lump sum in respect of a defined benefit arrangement is permitted only if all of a member's benefits under all pension arrangements are valued in aggregate at no more than £30,000. The commutations must take place within a single 12-month window, chosen by the member, who must have reached *normal minimum pension age* or satisfy the ill-health condition. (Money purchase arrangements can no longer pay trivial commutation lump sums, but are able to use the flexibility provisions instead.)

The range of authorised lump sums includes the following small payments, which must not exceed £10,000 and must extinguish the member's entitlement under the scheme:

- a payment from a public service or occupational pension scheme to a member who has reached *normal minimum pension age* or satisfies the ill-health condition; all benefits including those in related schemes must be within the limit
- a payment by a larger public service or occupational pension scheme (with at least 50 members) to a member who has reached *normal minimum pension age* or satisfies the ill-health condition
- a payment after a 'relevant accretion', such as where a scheme passes on an unexpected additional allocation received after a member has transferred out or purchased an annuity
- a payment made by way of compensation under the Financial Services Compensation Scheme, *and*
- a payment from a personal pension to a member who has reached *normal minimum pension age* or satisfies the ill-health condition; an individual cannot receive more than three such payments.

If the member has uncrystallised rights immediately before the lump sum is paid, 25% of the value of such rights is tax free, with the balance taxed as income.

Winding-up lump sum

A winding-up lump sum, not exceeding £18,000, may be paid, subject to certain conditions, to extinguish the member's entitlement to benefits under the pension scheme. If the member has uncrystallised rights immediately before the lump sum is paid, 25% of the value of such rights is tax free, with the balance taxed as income.

Lifetime allowance excess lump sum

Where none of a member's lifetime allowance is available, any remaining uncrystallised benefits may be taken as a lifetime allowance excess lump sum taxed at 55%. This may not be paid until *normal minimum pension age* unless the member is in ill health. (DWP legislation places a further restriction, that the payment cannot include section 9(2B) rights or GMPs.)

Refund of excess contributions lump sum

Where in any tax year a member's pension contributions exceed the maximum that qualifies for tax relief (relevant UK earnings or, where the scheme is operating on a 'relief at source' basis, £3,600 if greater), a refund of the excess may be paid without giving rise to liability for income tax. Any excess contributions that had been paid net of basic rate income tax under a 'relief at source' arrangement cannot be included in the refund. A 'scheme administration member payment' *(see below)*, taxable as income, may also be made in respect of interest or investment growth.

Scheme administration member payment

A scheme administration member payment is defined as 'a payment by a registered pension scheme to or in respect of... a member of the pension scheme which is made for the purposes of the administration or management of the pension scheme'. The legislation expressly states that scheme administration member payments include the payment of wages, salaries or fees to persons administering the scheme and payments made for the purchase of scheme assets, but not loans to members. A scheme administration member payment may not exceed the amount that might be expected to be paid on arm's length terms. The taxation will vary depending on the nature of the payment.

Pension advice allowance payment

From 6 April 2017, should a scheme allow it, a member with money purchase benefits may take up to £500 tax free, once in any tax year, to redeem against the cost of retirement financial advice. An individual can do this on up to three occasions (so allowing total withdrawals of up to £1,500 in their lifetime). This must be used for regulated advice in respect of the individual's financial position, including their pension arrangements and the use of their pension funds, and is paid directly to the adviser by the scheme. While a self-declaration system is employed, trustees are expected to operate with basic due diligence – e.g. not executing a withdrawal where the allowance has already been used three times under the scheme.

AUTHORISED PENSIONS PAYABLE ON DEATH

In a defined benefit scheme, a *dependant's scheme pension* is a pension payable to an eligible dependant on the death of a member, other than continuing payments of the member's pension for a limited guarantee period. With certain exceptions where the amounts are small, an authorised dependant's scheme pension is restricted to 100% of the member's pension (plus an adjustment for any tax-free lump sum taken) if the member was over 75 years of age at the date of death. Dependants' scheme pensions are subject to income tax at the recipient's marginal rate and must be taxed under PAYE, where applicable.

Eligible 'dependants' are:

- a member's spouse or civil partner at the date of death
- a person who was married to, or a civil partner of, the member when the member first became entitled to the pension
- a child of the member who either has not reached age 23 (extended in some circumstances under transitional provisions) or who, in the opinion of the scheme administrator, was dependent on the member at the date of the member's death because of physical or mental impairment, *and/or*
- any other person who, in the opinion of the scheme administrator, at the date of the member's death:
  - was financially dependent on the member
  - had a financial relationship of mutual dependence with the member, *or*
  - was dependent on the member because of physical or mental impairment.

In a money purchase arrangement, from 6 April 2015, the main pension death benefits other than continuing annuity payments under a guarantee are annuities and income withdrawal payable to an eligible dependant *(defined as above)* or to another individual nominated by the member or scheme administrator. In addition, a recipient of pension death benefit can nominate a successor to receive annuity income or income withdrawal after their death.

Where death (of the member, dependant, nominee or successor) occurs before age 75, the pension death benefit payable from a money purchase arrangement is tax free. Where death occurs at or after age 75, the benefit is taxed as income at the recipient's marginal rate.

AUTHORISED LUMP SUMS PAYABLE ON DEATH

The authorised lump sum death benefits that may be paid by a registered pension scheme are described below. Except where otherwise indicated, the legislation imposes no restrictions on the recipient of the benefit. Amounts taken under drawdown are classed as pension *(see above)*.

Defined benefits lump sum death benefit

On the death of a member of a defined benefits arrangement, a defined benefits lump sum death benefit of unrestricted amount can be paid. This is tax free up to the amount of the member's remaining lifetime allowance if the member died before age 75 and if the payment is made within two years of the day on which the scheme administrator first knew of the member's death (or the first day the scheme administrator could reasonably have been expected to have known of the member's death). From 6 April 2016, if the lump sum is paid in respect of a death that occurred at or after age 75 or paid outside the two-year limit but in respect of a death under age 75, it is normally taxed at the recipient's marginal rate of income tax.

Uncrystallised funds lump sum death benefit

On the death of a member of a money purchase arrangement, a lump sum not exceeding the amount of the uncrystallised funds can be paid. This is tax free up to the amount of the member's remaining lifetime allowance if the member died before age 75 and if the payment is made within two years of the day on which the scheme administrator first knew of the member's death (or the first day the scheme administrator could reasonably have been expected to have known of the member's death). From 6 April 2016, if the lump sum is paid in respect of a death that occurred at or after age 75 or paid outside the two-year limit but in respect of a death under age 75, it is normally taxed at the recipient's marginal rate of tax.

Pension/annuity protection lump sum death benefit

On the death of a member whilst in receipt of a scheme pension or lifetime annuity, a lump sum can be paid. No tax is payable where death occurs before age 75. Where death occurs at or after age 75, the payment is normally taxed at the recipient's marginal rate of income tax. This benefit may not exceed the amount by which the instalments paid up to the date of death fall short of the amount originally crystallised.

Drawdown pension fund/flexi-access drawdown lump sum death benefit

On the death of a member of a money purchase arrangement, or of a dependant/nominee/successor, who was entitled to income withdrawal at the time of death, a lump sum can be paid. If the death occurs at or after age 75 or the payment is made outside the two-year period starting with the day on which the scheme administrator first knew of the member's death (or the first day the scheme administrator could reasonably have been expected to have known of the member's death), the payment is normally taxed at the recipient's marginal rate. Otherwise no tax is payable.

Charity lump sum death benefit

On the death of an individual who was in receipt of a drawdown pension from a money purchase arrangement, where there is no dependant, nominee or successor, a charity lump sum death benefit may be paid to a charity nominated by the member or, if the member made no nomination, by the deceased beneficiary. A charity lump sum death benefit may also be paid on the death of a member who has no dependants, in respect of uncrystallised funds in a money purchase arrangement. No tax is payable.

Trivial commutation lump sum death benefit

In specified circumstances, a lump sum, subject to a limit of £30,000, may be paid to a dependant, taxable as income.

UNAUTHORISED PAYMENTS

If registered schemes make payments that are not specifically authorised, the payments are subject to tax charges applicable to unauthorised payments as discussed below.

Unauthorised payments charge

If a benefit paid from a registered scheme is not authorised *(see above)* the member (or other recipient in the case of a death benefit) is liable for an unauthorised payments charge, at a rate of 40%. A 15% surcharge (resulting in an overall charge of 55%) applies if the unauthorised payment exceeds 25% of the value of the member's benefits. A payment subject to an unauthorised payments charge is, however, exempt from any income tax charge.

Scheme sanction charge

The scheme administrator is potentially subject to a scheme sanction charge at a rate of 40% in respect of most unauthorised payments. If the member has paid an unauthorised payments charge, the scheme sanction charge is reduced by the lesser of 25% and the actual amount of the unauthorised payments charge paid. The scheme administrator can apply to be excused the charge if it could not reasonably have known that the payment was unauthorised at the time it was made.

ANNUAL AND LIFETIME ALLOWANCES

As the table below shows, significant reductions have been made to the annual and lifetime allowances. However, legislation now provides for the lifetime allowance to be increased in line with the CPI, from April 2018.

Tax year	Annual allowance	Lifetime allowance
2006/07	£215,000	£1,500,000
2007/08	£225,000	£1,600,000
2008/09	£235,000	£1,650,000
2009/10	£245,000	£1,750,000
2010/11	£255,000	£1,800,000
2011/12	£50,000	£1,800,000
2012/13	£50,000	£1,500,000
2013/14	£50,000	£1,500,000
2014/15	£40,000	£1,250,000
2015/16	£40,000	£1,250,000
2016/17	£40,000	£1,000,000
2017/18	£40,000	£1,000,000
2018/19	£40,000	£1,030,000

ANNUAL ALLOWANCE CHARGE

Where the 'total pension input amount' – the aggregate of *pension input amounts (see below)* arising under schemes of which the individual is a member – exceeds the annual allowance, the individual is potentially liable for a charge on amounts above the annual allowance. This charge is at the rate(s) of tax that would be charged if the excess pension savings were added to their taxable income. 'Unused annual allowance' can usually be carried forward for up to three years, permitting an annual allowance charge to be reduced or not be payable.

There are exemptions from the charge in the tax year in which a member:

- dies
- has their benefits commuted as a *serious ill-health lump sum (see above), or*
- becomes entitled to an ill-health pension where he/she is unlikely to be able to work in any capacity (other than to an insignificant extent) before reaching pensionable age.

Pension input amount

Under a defined benefit or cash balance arrangement, the pension input amount for the purposes of the annual allowance is the amount of any increase in the value of the member's rights under the arrangement. This is calculated as the difference between the opening and closing values of the member's rights, with an adjustment to the opening value to allow for any increase in the CPI. Under a defined benefit arrangement, accrued pension is valued by multiplying the annual pension by 16.

Under a money purchase arrangement (other than a cash balance arrangement), the pension input amount is the total of the contributions paid by, or in respect of, the individual.

Pension input periods

Pension input amounts are measured over the pension input periods ending in the relevant tax year. From 6 April 2016, pension input periods are aligned with tax years. Before then, pension input periods could vary from arrangement to arrangement and complex transitional measures applied for the 2015/16 tax year.

Scheme pays

Individuals are generally able to require their scheme to pay the annual allowance charge on their behalf. Broadly, where a member's liability to the charge in a particular tax year exceeds £2,000, and their pension input amount in the scheme exceeds the standard annual allowance (before any allowance is made for the taper to the annual allowance for high-income individuals, *see below*), schemes may be required to pay some or all of the charge but must make a corresponding adjustment to the member's benefits. Where this is the case, the legislation sets out deadlines for the scheme and the member to provide information in order to elect for the scheme to pay the charge. In other cases, schemes may agree to pay the charge (with an adjustment to the benefits) on a voluntary basis.

Money purchase annual allowance

An additional annual allowance restriction was introduced from April 2015, in connection with the flexibility provisions for money purchase funds. If an individual takes an 'uncrystallised funds pension lump sum' or draws down payments from 'flexi-access drawdown funds' *(see above)*, any further money purchase contributions are tested against a revised annual allowance each year and are subject to the annual allowance charge above this threshold (if this calculation produces an annual allowance charge that is higher than the standard calculation for the relevant tax year). The money purchase annual allowance was reduced to £4,000 with effect from April 2017 (having been £10,000 for the previous two tax years).

The legislation also includes a number of less common 'triggers'. Individuals will generally be informed by the scheme administrator if the money purchase annual allowance is triggered, and the communication will set out the steps they need to take to ensure that all their pension arrangements are aware that this lower allowance applies to them.

Tapered annual allowance for high-income individuals

From 6 April 2016, the annual allowance for 'high-income individuals' is reduced by £1 for each £2 by which their 'adjusted income' (broadly income – before deduction of employee pension contributions – together with the deemed employer contribution to any pension saving during the year) exceeds £150,000. Individuals whose 'threshold income' (broadly income after deduction of employee pension contributions) does not exceed £110,000 are not classified as high-income individuals for this purpose.

LIFETIME ALLOWANCE CHARGE

The value of benefits must be tested against the lifetime allowance (or the part of it that remains after any previous 'crystallisations') on each occasion that benefits come into payment, or otherwise 'crystallise'.

A single factor (for all ages) of 20:1 is used for valuing *scheme pensions (see above)* on crystallisation. The valuation of annuities provided under money purchase arrangements is based on their cost.

A lifetime allowance charge is payable if the value of the benefits being crystallised exceeds the balance of any lifetime allowance available. The rate is:

- 25% if the benefits being crystallised are taken in the form of pension or through drawdown *(see above)*, or
- 55% (equivalent to the payment of a 25% charge plus income tax at an assumed rate of 40% – irrespective of the individual's actual marginal rate) if taken as a lump sum.

If the charge is met by the scheme administrator (and the member's benefits under the scheme are not reduced to reflect this), the tax payment is itself treated as part of the excess benefit value on which tax is calculated.

TRANSITIONAL PROTECTION AGAINST THE LIFETIME ALLOWANCE CHARGE

Transitional arrangements were put in place at 6 April 2006, 6 April 2012, 6 April 2014 and 6 April 2016 to protect benefits accrued prior to these dates.

Primary protection (6 April 2006)

This applies where total relevant pension rights in approved pension schemes as at 5 April 2006 were valued in excess of £1.5m.

Under primary protection, the individual is granted a personal lifetime allowance, based on the total value calculated as at 5 April 2006, in place of the standard lifetime allowance. The personal lifetime allowance is increased annually in line with the standard lifetime allowance, but taking the latter to be at least equal to £1.8m for tax years following 5 April 2012. It is subject to adjustment if a pension debit arises as a result of a pension sharing order implemented on or after 6 April 2006.

Other than in exceptional circumstances, registration for primary protection was required by 5 April 2009. Any errors in the details registered can be corrected after this date.

Enhanced protection (6 April 2006)

Enhanced protection was available to all individuals with benefits in schemes that became registered pension schemes on 6 April 2006, as an alternative to primary protection. Where this applies, there are no lifetime allowance charges in respect of the individual. This means that, broadly speaking:

- accrued defined benefit rights at 5 April 2006 can continue to be linked to salary (although any pre-6 April 2006 restriction due to the earnings cap will still apply), *and*
- money purchase funds accrued at 5 April 2006 can be increased by the full investment return achieved subsequently.

To retain enhanced protection, no further 'relevant benefit accrual' (which includes money purchase contributions) is permitted under any registered scheme after 5 April 2006.

In a defined benefit arrangement, continuation of contributions or of pensionable service does not in itself count as relevant benefit accrual. Instead, for enhanced protection not to be lost, the resulting benefits must not breach the member's 'appropriate limit' at the first or a subsequent crystallisation date (or where there is a permitted transfer out of the scheme). This, in effect, means that, if the pre-6 April 2006 service benefits turn out to be lower than expected (e.g. because a reduction applies for early retirement), it may be possible to provide post-5 April 2006 service benefits without enhanced protection being lost.

Individuals could apply for both primary and enhanced protection, which allows the individual to rely on primary protection if enhanced protection is lost, either because the conditions for its retention are breached or because it is given up voluntarily. Primary protection cannot be lost or given up.

Other than in exceptional circumstances, registration for enhanced protection was required by 5 April 2009. Any errors in the details registered can be corrected after this date.

Fixed protection (6 April 2012)

Fixed protection was available to all individuals with benefits in registered schemes who did not have primary or enhanced protection. Where this applies, the tax legislation will be applied as if the individual's lifetime allowance is the greater of:

- the standard lifetime allowance, *and*
- £1.8m.

To retain fixed protection, 'benefit accrual' (which includes money purchase contributions) is not permitted under any registered scheme after 5 April 2012. Unlike under enhanced protection, where relevant benefit accrual in a defined benefit scheme can only occur when benefits are crystallised, under fixed protection benefit accrual can occur at any time.

Registration for fixed protection was required by 5 April 2012.

Fixed protection 2014 (6 April 2014)

This is similar to the fixed protection regime introduced from April 2012 but with an underpin of £1.5m applied to the individual's lifetime allowance. As with fixed protection, fixed protection 2014 is lost if 'benefit accrual' occurs after the cut-off date (in this case 5 April 2014).

Fixed protection 2014 is not available to those individuals who retain any of the forms of protection introduced in 2006 or 2012; however it can be used in conjunction with individual protection 2014.

Registration for fixed protection 2014 was required by 5 April 2014.

Individual protection 2014 (6 April 2014)

Where the value of an individual's accrued rights at 5 April 2014 exceeds £1.25m, the individual's lifetime allowance is effectively set equal to this higher amount (but capped at £1.5m).

The value of the accrued rights at 5 April 2014 was determined in a similar manner to values at crystallisation. However, pensions that were already in payment on 5 April 2006 were valued as 25 times the annual rate of pension in payment, to allow for the lump sum that was presumed to have been taken. If the member was taking (capped) drawdown, the maximum possible pension under the relevant drawdown provisions was to be used.

Any benefits that crystallised after 5 April 2006 were taken into account by taking the crystallisation amount and revaluing it to April 2014.

Applications for individual protection 2014 were allowed up to 5 April 2017.

Fixed protection 2016 (6 April 2016)

This is similar to the fixed protection regimes introduced from April 2012 and 2014, but with an underpin of £1.25m applied to the individual's lifetime allowance. As with the other forms of fixed protection, fixed protection 2016 is lost if 'benefit accrual' occurs after the cut-off date (in this case 5 April 2016).

Fixed protection 2016 is not available to those individuals who retain any of the other forms of protection except individual protection 2014 or individual protection 2016.

There is no deadline for applications for fixed protection 2016.

Individual protection 2016 (6 April 2016)

Where the value of an individual's accrued rights at 5 April 2016 exceeds £1m, the individual's lifetime allowance is effectively set equal to this higher amount (but capped at £1.25m). The value of the accrued rights at 5 April 2016 is determined in the same way as for individual protection 2014, with any benefits that have crystallised after 5 April 2006 being revalued to April 2016 rather than April 2014.

There is no deadline for applications for individual protection 2016.

Other transitional protections

Individuals granted a pension credit before 6 April 2006 were able to register for a form of protection that provides an enhanced lifetime allowance in a similar way to primary protection.

Lump sum death benefits that exceed the protected amounts under primary or enhanced protection may be protected.

TRANSITIONAL PROTECTION FROM UNAUTHORISED PAYMENTS CHARGES

When the current tax regime was introduced, transitional protections were included that gave scope to continue paying benefits permitted under the scheme rules as they stood at 5 April 2006 without incurring unauthorised payments charges. These include:

- lump sum rights of more than £375,000 at 5 April 2006 are protected if the individual registered for primary protection or enhanced protection *(see above)*; if an individual with primary or enhanced protection does not have this lump sum protection, the maximum *pension commencement lump sum (see above)* is restricted to 25% of the standard lifetime allowance
- rights to a lump sum of more than 25% at 5 April 2006 can be protected if the individual has not registered for either primary or enhanced protection, or their lump sum rights at 5 April 2006 were valued at less

than £375,000; this is subject to the condition that all pensions under the scheme (that had not already been taken on or before 5 April 2006) are taken on the same date, or within a six-month period if a member has both DB and DC benefits in the scheme, and special provisions apply in some cases where there has been a transfer value paid into or out of the scheme in which the protected entitlement resides

- it is permissible to take benefits as authorised payments before *normal minimum pension age* in certain cases where such a right existed before 6 April 2006
- pensions may in some circumstances be paid to children who are over age 23 and are still in full-time education or vocational training, are suffering from serious physical or mental deterioration, or were financially dependent on the member, *and*
- where at 5 April 2006 a member had an entitlement in a scheme to a lump sum with no associated pension, benefits can be taken as tax-free lump sums provided no 'relevant benefit accrual' (as for enhanced protection) occurs after 5 April 2006.

REGISTRATION AND REPORTING TO HMRC

Registration

'Registration' of a pension scheme replaced the previous 'HMRC approval' as the process by which schemes obtain tax-advantaged status from 6 April 2006. Pension schemes that had HMRC approval prior to 6 April 2006 automatically became 'registered schemes' on 6 April 2006 unless they explicitly opted out.

Reporting

As Section 8 explains, registered pension schemes have to comply with a number of administration requirements, including providing quarterly returns for tax accounting purposes, reports on the occurrence of certain events (including where members have paid contributions in excess of the annual allowance) and, if requested, a *Pension Scheme Return*.

One of the requirements is for registered schemes to report any transfer to a *qualifying recognised overseas pension scheme* (QROPS, *see below*). HMRC can also request information from a QROPS (or certain former QROPS); and on the occurrence of certain events, the managers of a QROPS, or a member who has transferred in from a registered pension scheme, must automatically provide information to HMRC.

OVERSEAS ASPECTS

Scheme membership

There is no restriction on non-UK-resident individuals becoming members of registered pension schemes.

The annual and lifetime allowance charges (including reporting requirements), and unauthorised payments charges, apply whether or not the individual is resident, ordinarily resident or domiciled in the UK. However, the lifetime allowance may be enhanced to allow for overseas periods of membership falling after 5 April 2006 during which contributions to the scheme are not eligible for UK tax relief.

Transfers may be accepted by registered schemes from any overseas pension schemes. The lifetime allowance may be enhanced for transfers from *recognised overseas pension schemes (see Appendix 2, Glossary of Terms).*

Transfers may be made from registered schemes to *qualifying recognised overseas pension schemes*, and count as benefit crystallisation events for lifetime allowance purposes.

Since they were introduced, the requirements relating to transfers to QROPS have been tightened on various occasions with the aim of ensuring better operation of the regime and deterring misuse. In order to be accepted as a QROPS, the overseas arrangement has to satisfy certain criteria and must give HMRC an undertaking to comply with certain reporting requirements *(see above)*. If the scheme does not satisfy the QROPS criteria at the time of the transfer, then the transfer will be unauthorised and the member subject to unauthorised payments charges and surcharges. A transfer to a QROPS requested on or after 9 March 2017 is subject to a 25% overseas transfer charge except in certain circumstances, including where the individual and the QROPS are in the same country (or if not, both are in EEA states) and where the QROPS is an occupational scheme sponsored by the individual's employer.

Following a transfer to a QROPS, various member payment charges could apply in relation to payments made from funds which had their source in a UK registered scheme. These include charges on unauthorised payments, short service refunds and commutation of pensions.

Migrant member relief

Migrant member relief allows UK tax relief on contributions paid to overseas schemes where a 'relevant migrant member' comes to the UK, and was a member of a qualifying tax-relieved overseas pension scheme at any time in the previous ten years. The manager of that scheme must provide HMRC with details of any relevant benefit crystallisation events that occur. Contributions and benefits accruing after 5 April 2006 would normally count towards the annual and lifetime allowances, although this excludes benefits and contributions in respect of earnings that are not subject to UK taxation.

INVESTMENT

There is one set of tax rules covering investments for almost all registered pension schemes. These allow schemes to invest in any type of investment where this is held for the purpose of the scheme, and generally exempt them from income and capital gains tax. However, other non-tax regulations do limit or prohibit certain types of investment. These rules allow 'authorised employer loans' subject to conditions. However, occupational schemes are still prevented from making such loans by the 'employer-related investment' provisions under the Pensions Act 1995 *(see Section 7)*. Special rules apply to schemes where members can direct the investment policy (such as SIPPs and SSASs). In such cases, tax rules make it unattractive to invest in 'taxable property'. This includes tangible moveable property and residential property that is held directly (as opposed to indirectly through for example a Real Estate Investment Trust).

SURPLUS

A repayment of surplus funds to the employer is only authorised in limited circumstances and is taxed at 35%. For instance, a refund cannot reduce the assets of the scheme below the level required to buy out all members' benefits with an insurance company.

PRE-APRIL 2006 TAX REGIMES

Previous tax regimes limited benefits and/or contributions by reference to parameters such as earnings, company service and age in order for schemes to have a tax-advantaged status.

Further detail on the previous tax regimes (including those applicable to personal pensions) is available at *www.pensionspocketbook.com (see Pensions taxation/archive data)*.

SECTION 10

THE LIFETIME ISA

The Lifetime ISA – sometimes referred to as LISA – was introduced in April 2017 and provides an alternative means of saving for retirement for those under age 40.

The introduction of the Lifetime ISA followed a wide-ranging consultation in 2015 on 'Strengthening the incentive to save', which looked at the taxation of retirement savings. The Government did not publish a full response to this consultation when announcing the introduction of the Lifetime ISA, and it had been suggested that it might be the first step in a move to a retirement savings taxation system under which contributions do not receive tax relief but benefits are paid free of tax instead, along with some form of bonus.

Overview

The Lifetime ISA is intended to help young people save flexibly for the long term, without having to choose whether this saving will be used for a first home or for retirement. It is intended to be simple for savers to use, building on the existing ISA (Individual Savings Account) structure, where contributions are paid out of post-tax income but investment growth and future withdrawals are not subject to tax.

Saving

Since 6 April 2017, any adult under 40 (and at least 18) can open a Lifetime ISA. Contributions of up to £4,000 each tax year (post-tax) will receive a government bonus and can continue up to age 50.

In most ways, the rules for opening and saving into a Lifetime ISA are the same as those for a regular ISA:

- it is only possible to pay into one Lifetime ISA in each tax year
- any contributions to a Lifetime ISA count towards the overall ISA contribution limit (£20,000 for 2018/19)
- any contributions in excess of the £4,000 threshold will be removed from the account but will not count as a withdrawal, *and*
- individuals are able to transfer savings from other ISAs as a way of funding their Lifetime ISA. The transferred savings count towards the £4,000 threshold but do not affect the £20,000 annual contribution limit.

Bonus

The Government provides a 25% bonus on contributions up to the £4,000 threshold. Contributions can continue to be made up to the age of 50. Over their lifetime, savers will be able to have contributions of £128,000 matched by a maximum government bonus of £32,000 (i.e. contributions of £4,000 per year and a bonus of £1,000 per year, between the ages of 18 and 50).

The bonus was paid into the Lifetime ISA after the end of the 2017/18 tax year and will be paid on a monthly basis from 2018/19 onwards.

If an individual is buying their first home with someone else they can both use their own Lifetime ISAs and both benefit from the bonus.

Withdrawals

Funds inclusive of the bonus can be used to buy a first home (valued up to £450,000) at any time from 12 months after opening the account, or can be withdrawn from age 60.

Where an individual is terminally ill and has less than 12 months to live, they will be able to withdraw all of the funds (including the bonus), regardless of their age.

On death, the funds will form part of the estate for inheritance tax purposes. The spouse or civil partner gets a one-off increase in their overall ISA allowance, allowing them to invest as much into their own ISA as their spouse used to have, on top of their usual allowance.

Funds can be withdrawn at any other time, but a 25% charge will be applied to the amount of the withdrawal. The Government said it would consider whether funds can be withdrawn without such penalties in other specific circumstances.

The Government indicated that it would explore with the industry whether there should be the flexibility to borrow funds against a Lifetime ISA without incurring a charge if the borrowed funds are fully repaid.

The detailed rules relating to house purchase are based on the Help to Buy: ISA. The withdrawal must be for a deposit on a UK property for the first time buyer to live in as their only residence and not buy-to-let. Funds will be returned to the Lifetime ISA by the conveyancer if the purchase falls through.

Help to Buy: ISAs

Specific rules set out how the Lifetime ISA interacts with the existing Help to Buy: ISA. This will remain open for new savers until 30 November 2019 but savers will only be able to use the bonus from one of their accounts to buy their first home.

SECTION 11

NON-REGISTERED SCHEMES

BACKGROUND

There has for many years been a demand for top-up arrangements of one sort or another outside the 'tax-privileged' pensions savings environment. These have included arrangements that provide only lump sum death benefits (Excepted Group Life Policies), and those whose primary purpose is the provision of retirement benefits (although, similarly to registered pension schemes, death benefits might also be included).

Before April 2006, the main types of top-up vehicles used to provide retirement benefits were Funded Unapproved Retirement Benefit Schemes (FURBS) and Unfunded Unapproved Retirement Benefit Schemes (UURBS). The tax treatment of FURBS was broadly: *t*axed on contributions on the way in, *t*axed on investment returns but *e*xempt from tax on benefits paid out (TTE). There were certain tax and National Insurance advantages on contributions and investment returns, but these were progressively reduced over the years. UURBS were attractive to employers because of cash flow and National Insurance contribution (NIC) considerations. But from the employee's viewpoint, the absence of pre-funding often represented a significant risk. A compromise was the secured UURBS, a benefit promise that was unfunded but where security was given by the employer. Typically, if the employer experiences a change of control or insolvency event, this security is paid into a trust which subsequently pays a benefit to the employee.

From April 2006, FURBS and UURBS became known as Employer-Financed Retirement Benefit Schemes, or EFRBS. The taxation of funded EFRBS was changed from TTE to ETT (relief available on contributions paid in, but benefits ultimately paid out subject to tax – investment returns on the funds are taxed under both regimes). Thus the main attractions of funded EFRBS became the potential exemption from NICs and deferral of income tax. However, since corporation tax relief was also deferred until the benefits were paid, on balance funded EFRBS became unattractive and were rarely used for further contributions after April 2006. Unfunded EFRBS continued to be popular, particularly where security was available.

The Finance Act 2011 introduced measures, effective from December 2010, aimed at reducing the attractiveness of vehicles used to 'disguise remuneration and avoid, reduce or defer payment of tax'. These measures had a significant impact on EFRBS.

EXCEPTED GROUP LIFE POLICIES

An Excepted Group Life Policy is a type of 'relevant life policy' that provides lump sum benefits on death before a specified age (of 75 or less) and which satisfies certain conditions (for example that the benefits are calculated using the same method for each individual included). For some individuals, using such an arrangement might be preferable to providing lump sum death benefits through a registered pension scheme. Examples include individuals with certain types of transitional protection that would be lost if they joined a new registered pension arrangement, and those for whom providing additional death benefits under a registered scheme would breach the lifetime allowance *(see Section 9)*.

EMPLOYER-FINANCED RETIREMENT BENEFIT SCHEMES

Broadly speaking an EFRBS is an arrangement, other than a registered pension scheme or a 's615 scheme', under which an employer provides 'relevant benefits' to employees or former employees. Relevant benefits include payments (not necessarily in cash form) provided on or in anticipation of the retirement or death of an employee or former employee, or after retirement or death in connection with past service. The definition is quite broad, and as a result it is possible that an EFRBS can arise unintentionally.

Taxation of EFRBS

The disguised remuneration provisions contained in Part 7A of the Income Tax (Earnings and Pensions) Act 2003 apply when a 'relevant third person' (meaning broadly someone other than the employer, connected company or employee, but including the employer or employee if they are acting as a trustee) makes provision in connection with the employee's employment. In this case, the money or assets set aside in connection with the benefit promise will be taxed (and NICs due) as employment income. Thus any contributions paid to a funded EFRBS after 5 April 2011 will result in an income tax and NI charge on the employee (although to avoid double counting, there is a deduction from the tax and any NI that would otherwise be due when the benefits are paid out).

The disguised remuneration provisions also apply where an employer earmarks, or starts to hold, assets (or otherwise provides security) in connection with a 'relevant undertaking' to provide retirement benefits to the employee via a relevant third person (such as an insurance company or trust). As a result, except where the benefits payable from a secured unfunded EFRBS will be paid direct by the employer, new security provided after 5 April 2011 can result in an income tax and NI charge on the employee.

Unfunded EFRBS under which there is no undertaking to provide the benefit via a third person are unaffected by the provisions of the Finance Act 2011 as they were originally introduced. However the use of different types of EFRBS is something that the Government is likely to keep under review. HMRC is also understood to view the use of unfunded EFRBS as reportable under the provisions for Disclosure of Tax Avoidance Schemes in certain circumstances.

The other main features of the taxation of EFRBS are as follows:

- benefits accrued under an EFRBS are not to be counted for the annual allowance, nor are they to be tested against the member's lifetime allowance when paid *(see Section 9)*

- the arrangement's investment income and capital gains are subject to tax
- lump sum and pension benefits are subject to income tax when received by the employee, *and*
- employers can deduct the costs of providing the benefits from taxable profits, but only when the benefits are paid from the scheme and chargeable to tax on the employee, or when a charge arises under the disguised remuneration provisions. (So corporation tax relief is not available until then.)

In addition, provided that the payments from the EFRBS meet specific conditions (including that the form of benefits would have been authorised if the scheme had been registered, with the additional restrictions that pension income must be taken in instalments at least annually until the member's death, that employment has ceased and the member is not re-employed by the company), no NICs are payable.

However, if the EFRBS is set up so that provision of the benefits results in a reduction in the benefits payable to or in respect of the employee under a registered pension scheme, or its payment is triggered by a reduction in the benefits payable under a registered pension scheme, then corporation tax relief for the employer will generally not be available, and may be withheld in respect of contributions to the registered scheme.

Anti-avoidance measures

In recent years the government has been concerned by the practice of disguising employees' remuneration in order to avoid tax, sometimes using trusts such as an EFRBS. Finance Acts since 2016 have introduced measures to counter aggressive tax avoidance, such as EFRBS involving 'loans' that are never repaid, although they are not expected to impact significantly on the types of EFRBS typically used for retirement planning.

DWP legislation

The Pension Schemes Act 1993, the Pensions Act 1995 and the Pensions Act 2004 are generally applicable to non-registered arrangements, although there are a large number of provisions from which such arrangements are exempt. For example, the protections against forfeiture of benefits do apply, but the scheme funding provisions do not and the disclosure requirements are limited.

Preservation and EFRBS

Preservation rights for early leavers apply to funded EFRBS as to registered schemes. However, preservation does not apply to unfunded EFRBS unless it is explicitly written into the scheme documentation. Where preservation applies, the following will also apply:

- the normal revaluation requirements
- right to a CETV (including where the EFRBS is unfunded)
- pension sharing on divorce.

Tax treatment of EFRBS

A brief summary comparing the tax treatment of registered pension schemes and EFRBS is set out in this table.

	Registered Pension Scheme	EFRBS[1] Disguised remuneration provisions: Do not apply	EFRBS[1] Disguised remuneration provisions: Apply
Employer's contributions/ allocations to reserves:			
– corporation tax relief for employer	yes	no[2]	yes
– employer's NICs payable	no	no	yes
– income tax charge on employee	no[3]	no	yes
– employee's NICs payable	no	no	yes
Member's contributions:			
– income tax relief for employee	yes[3]	no	no
Investment returns/ growth in reserves:	no income tax or capital gains tax payable	income and capital gains taxable at trust rates	income and capital gains taxable at trust rates
Tax paid by beneficiary[4] on:			
– pension	income tax payable[5] (but no NICs)	income tax payable[5,8] (but no NICs)[6]	income tax payable[5,8,9] (but no NICs)[6]
– lump sum	tax-free (lump sum generally limited to 25%)	income tax payable[7,8] (but no NICs)[6]	income tax payable[7,8,9] (but no NICs)[6]

Notes:

1 The EFRBS is assumed to be established as an 'accumulation trust' with UK-resident trustees.

2 CT relief may generally be claimed when benefits are paid and chargeable to tax on the employee.

3 However, any 'pension input' in excess of the annual allowance may be subject to a tax charge – *see Section 9.*

4 The Finance Act 2007 amended ITEPA 2003 to include a power to make retrospective regulations extending the definition of benefits from an EFRBS that are excluded from taxation.

5 All pensions, regardless of the type of arrangement, are taxed at source via the PAYE system.

6 Provided that the payments from the EFRBS meet specific conditions, no NICs are payable.

7 The amount of the lump sum that is taxable is reduced by the amount of any contributions paid by the employee towards its provision. In addition, part of the lump sum will be tax-free if contributions, on which the employee was taxed, were paid to the FURBS before 6 April 2006; if no contributions have been made since then, the whole of the lump sum will be tax-free.

8 There is no exemption from inheritance tax for benefits payable from an EFRBS, except to the extent that they arose from contributions made to a FURBS before 6 April 2006.

9 The income tax charge will be reduced by the amount of the charge paid by the employee at the time the employer contributions were made.

SECTION 12

LEAVING SERVICE BENEFITS

PRESERVATION

Since 1975, the preservation legislation has provided members of an occupational pension scheme with a legal right to short service benefit (SSB) if they leave pensionable service before normal pension age (NPA). The essential principle is that an early leaver's benefits should be calculated on a consistent basis with those of a member who remains in service until NPA.

Entitlement to SSB is dependent *(but see below)* upon the member either having at least a minimum period of 'qualifying service' or having transferred benefits from a personal pension into the scheme. This minimum period was reduced in 1988 from five to two years. For members entitled only to money purchase benefits, it was reduced further from two years to thirty days, with effect from 1 October 2015.

'Qualifying service' is the sum of all actual pensionable service under the scheme plus pensionable service in any scheme from which a transfer payment has been received. Members who do not satisfy the preservation conditions may nevertheless be granted deferred benefits if scheme rules so provide. Alternatively, the scheme may provide for them to receive a refund of their own contributions, if any, less tax and (until 6 April 2019, for a former COSR) less their share of any Contributions Equivalent Premium required to reinstate contracted-out service back into the State scheme.

Different provisions apply where a member is automatically enrolled before opting out under the Pensions Act 2008 *(see Section 3)*.

Payment of short service benefits

Preserved benefits must normally be available not later than the member's NPA. The preservation legislation defines NPA as the earliest age at which a member is entitled to receive benefits on retirement from the relevant employment, disregarding any special provisions for early retirement. Therefore, even if scheme rules define normal retirement age as (say) 63, NPA could be earlier if members have an unqualified right to retire on an unreduced pension from an earlier age.

However, if NPA is lower than 65, to satisfy the preservation requirements SSB need only be payable from age 65.

The Court of Appeal ruled in both *Cripps v TSL* and *Foster Wheeler v Hanley* that a member can have more than one normal retirement age (for example to comply with the *Barber* judgment). The question of whether a member can have more than one NPA for the purposes of the preservation and revaluation legislation has not been considered by the courts.

Cash transfer sums

Leavers with non-money purchase benefits who do not have the right to preserved benefits but have completed at least three months' pensionable service must be given the option of a transfer value (the 'cash transfer sum') of their full accrued benefits.

Trustees must notify the member of this option, as an alternative to a refund of just the member's own contributions, if applicable, within a 'reasonable period' of leaving pensionable service. The Pensions Regulator's Code of Practice defines a reasonable period as normally within three months for this purpose. If the member does not reply within a further 'reasonable period' (which must have been specified and should normally be at least three months) a refund of contributions may be paid by default (but not before a further month has elapsed). Where the member opts for a cash transfer sum, this must be calculated in the same way as a cash equivalent transfer value under the scheme and paid 'without unjustifiable delay' (in any event, normally within three months). In former COSRs, the overall timetable may have needed to be compressed to meet the normal six-month deadline for payment of a Contributions Equivalent Premium.

REVALUATION

Different types of occupational pension scheme benefit are subject to different statutory minimum requirements for preserved benefits to be increased ('revalued') during the period of deferment (i.e. the period between leaving pensionable service and the date benefits come into payment).

Money purchase benefits must be revalued in deferment in the same way as during pensionable service, i.e. generally in line with the investment return on the member's fund.

Average salary benefits and cash balance benefits are revalued in deferment in generally the same way as increases are applied during pensionable service. However, for average salary benefits, if the trustees do not think that this approach is appropriate, the approach for final salary benefits must be used.

The requirements for revaluing final salary benefits are more complicated. The position of early leavers from final salary schemes improved significantly from 1986. Before then, with the exception of Guaranteed Minimum Pensions (GMPs), there was no legal requirement for preserved benefits to be revalued during deferment. The Social Security Act 1985 introduced the requirement to increase in deferment the preserved pension in excess of GMP by at least the specified revaluation percentage. This requirement applied initially only to service completed on or after 1 January 1985, but was further extended to cover the whole of the member's pension in excess of GMP for members leaving pensionable service on or after 1 January 1991. The revaluation percentage *(see table on next page)* was the *lesser* of the increase in the general level of prices and 5% per annum compound over the whole period of deferment. The revaluation cap for pensionable service after 5 April 2009 was reduced from 5% p.a. to 2.5% p.a.

The increase in the general level of prices is based on the opinion of the Secretary of State. From September 2010 onwards, the increase in prices has been assessed using the Consumer Prices Index (CPI) instead of the Retail Prices Index (RPI) – periods of deferment which straddle 2010 are therefore revalued with a combination of RPI and CPI.

GMPs

In addition to the revaluation requirements on the excess of the member's pension over any GMP, members of former COSRs must also have their GMP revalued between leaving service and age 65 for men and age 60 for women, either:

(1) in line with Average Earnings (Section 148 orders, *see Reference Section 5*), *or*

(2) by fixed rate revaluation at the following rate per annum:

– leavers after 5 April 2017	3.5%
– leavers after 5 April 2012, but before 6 April 2017	4.75%
– leavers after 5 April 2007, but before 6 April 2012	4.0%
– leavers after 5 April 2002, but before 6 April 2007	4.5%
– leavers after 5 April 1997, but before 6 April 2002	6.25%
– leavers after 5 April 1993, but before 6 April 1997	7.0%
– leavers after 5 April 1988, but before 6 April 1993	7.5%
– leavers before 6 April 1988	8.5%

For leavers before 6 April 1997, schemes could choose to apply limited revaluation, which provided the lesser of Section 148 orders and 5% p.a. revaluation. A Limited Revaluation Premium was payable to the State. This option was withdrawn from 6 April 1997.

For members who left pensionable service after 31 December 1984, 'anti-franking' rules prevent the revaluations on the GMP being met by reducing the excess pension over the GMP, or by reducing revaluations on the excess. GMP accrual ceased from April 1997, but GMPs earned prior to this date continue to be revalued as above. For the purpose of revaluing GMPs, members who were still in contracted-out service on 5 April 2016, when contracting out was abolished *(see Reference Section 5)*, are treated as remaining so until their pensionable service ends, and leaving service revaluation applies from that time. (However, scheme rules may have needed to be amended to reflect this.)

Deferred Pension Revaluation Percentages

Complete years since leaving	Calendar year of Normal Pension Age 2018 (%)	2017 (%)	2016 (%)	Complete years since leaving	Calendar year of Normal Pension Age 2018 (%)	2017 (%)	2016 (%)
Applied to pension relating to service before 6 April 2009							
1	3.0	1.0	0.0	17	50.2	50.6	50.8
2	4.0	0.9	1.1	18	55.2	52.3	55.6
3	3.9	2.1	3.8	19	56.9	57.2	61.2
4	5.2	4.9	6.1	20	61.9	62.8	64.6
5	8.0	7.2	11.6	21	67.7	66.3	71.0
6	10.4	12.7	15.1	22	71.2	72.7	74.8
7	16.1	16.2	13.5	23	77.9	76.5	77.9
8	19.7	14.6	19.2	24	81.8	79.7	84.3
9	18.1	20.3	23.8	25	85.1	86.2	91.9
10	24.0	25.0	28.3	26	91.8	93.8	112.8
11	28.8	29.5	31.7	27	99.6	115.0	129.0
12	33.4	33.0	35.8	28	121.4	131.3	142.1
13	37.0	37.2	39.6	29	138.2	144.5	152.2
14	41.3	41.0	42.0	30	151.8	154.7	160.0
15	45.2	43.4	44.4	31	162.4	162.6	
16	47.7	45.8	49.2	32	170.5		
Applied to pension relating to service after 5 April 2009							
1	2.5	1.0	0.0	5	8.0	7.2	11.6
2	4.0	0.9	1.1	6	10.4	12.7	15.1
3	3.9	2.1	3.8	7	16.1	16.2	13.5
4	5.2	4.9	6.1	8	19.7	14.6	
				9	18.1		

TRANSFER VALUES

Members of registered occupational pension schemes who have preserved benefits have the right to the cash equivalent of all or, in particular circumstances, part of their benefits to be paid as a transfer value to another registered scheme *(see Section 13 for further details of transfer values, including transfers of contracted-out benefits; tax considerations; and overseas transfers)*.

SECTION 13

TRANSFERS

Pension scheme leavers have since 1986 had the statutory right to a cash equivalent as an alternative to deferred benefits under a scheme – *see Section 12*. Trustees are responsible for setting assumptions for the calculation of cash equivalent transfer values and may also need to consider whether it is appropriate to offer members more than the minimum required by legislation.

Individual transfers are considered in this Section; *Section 25 covers bulk transfer arrangements and TUPE.*

The Pension Schemes Act 2015 introduced two new terms relevant to transfer provisions from 6 April 2015:

- *flexible benefits* are money purchase or cash balance benefits, or other benefits calculated by reference to an amount available for the provision of benefits to or in respect of the member, *and*
- *safeguarded benefits* are benefits other than cash balance or money purchase benefits.

Since 6 April 2015, there has been a ban on transfers from unfunded public service defined benefit schemes to other pension schemes in which the member can obtain flexible benefits.

The options available from April 2015 for flexible benefit arrangements and increased scope for inheritance tax planning have increased the number of transfers from defined benefit schemes, particularly where schemes allow non-statutory transfers *(see below)*, such as transfers immediately before retirement and/or partial transfers.

Advice requirement

Since April 2015, there has been a statutory requirement on transferring schemes to ensure that members take advice, from an independent adviser authorised by the Financial Conduct Authority, before transferring safeguarded benefits with a view to acquiring flexible benefits. This applies unless the total value of the individual's safeguarded benefits under the pension scheme before any adjustment (*see 'Paying more or less' below*) is £30,000 or less. This advice requirement also applies to conversions or 'internal transfers' within schemes.

In most cases, the member will need to pay for the advice. However, where an employer provides communication to two or more members that 'encourages, persuades or induces' a request to transfer, the employer must arrange for independent advice or otherwise bear the cost of the advice. This does not include routine communications from trustees that simply explain members' options regarding their benefits.

Where advice is required, the individual must be notified of this within one month of requesting information on the transfer, and the transfer cannot proceed until the administrators have received confirmation that appropriate independent advice has been obtained. This must be received in a standard form, within three months of the trustees' notification. The trustees should check that the adviser is appropriately authorised by the Financial Conduct Authority. They are not responsible for checking what advice or recommendation was given or confirming whether the member is following the recommendation. *(Section 14 covers retirement options and advice in more detail.)*

Right to a cash equivalent

Generally, members of occupational pension schemes whose pensionable service ended on or after 1 January 1986 have the right to the cash equivalent of all or, in particular circumstances, part of their benefits to be paid as a transfer value to another registered pension scheme. From 6 April 1997, this right was extended to most members whose pensionable service ended before 1 January 1986. From 6 April 2015, the right applies separately to each category of benefit (money purchase, other flexible benefits and non-flexible benefits) that an individual has in a scheme.

A member can only make one application for a 'statement of entitlement' to a guaranteed cash equivalent transfer value in a 12-month period, unless the scheme rules or the trustees allow more frequent applications. A member must transfer all of the benefits within a particular category; only in limited circumstances do they have a statutory right to a 'partial cash equivalent' of benefits within a category *(see below)*. For non-flexible benefits, the transfer right is subject to there being a period of at least one year between the termination of the member's pensionable service and normal pension age (NPA), although, where NPA is earlier than 60, the right arises on termination of service at any time before NPA. For flexible benefits, the right applies up to the point at which the benefits are crystallised.

Members who opt out of pension schemes without leaving their jobs also have the right to transfer their benefits.

For defined benefit transfer values there is a three-month window from the date of calculation in which the cash equivalent is guaranteed and may be taken without being subject to recalculation; the member must apply to take the transfer value at least one year before NPA, or by age 59 if later. There are other time limits and disclosure requirements *(see Section 15)* imposed on the process of making a transfer.

Non-statutory transfers

Non-statutory transfers may be provided under scheme rules. Such an option may be particularly helpful where a member would not have a statutory right to a transfer, such as a partial transfer or a transfer in the period immediately preceding NPA for defined benefit arrangements. Scheme rules may allow trustees to offer members the ability to transfer either all or part of their benefits out of the scheme shortly before the point of retirement, therefore allowing them to benefit from the April 2015 flexibilities.

Calculation of transfer values – the initial cash equivalent

The trustees have responsibility for setting the basis for the calculation of defined benefit transfer values. The fundamental principle is that the initial cash equivalent transfer value (before any adjustment – *see below*) should be broadly equal to the expected cost of providing the benefit within the scheme. Trustees are required to set financial and demographic assumptions on a 'best estimate' basis, having regard to the scheme's investment strategy and having obtained advice from the actuary. (This contrasts with the scheme funding requirement to use 'prudent' assumptions.) The Regulator's guidance outlines the advice on assumptions that the trustees must seek from their actuary. Nevertheless, the trustees are responsible for determining, amongst other things, the interest rate used for discounting future benefit payments and the expected longevity of members. Trustees also need to determine an appropriate allowance for member options and discretionary benefits. The Regulator's guidance makes it clear that only those options that increase the value of a member's benefits should be taken into account, although allowance can be made for the proportion of members likely to exercise such options. In deciding whether to make allowance for discretionary benefits, the guidance suggests that trustees should usually consult any person whose consent is needed, and consider past history and any allowance in scheme funding, amongst other things.

For money purchase benefits (and cash balance benefits not related to final salary), the cash equivalent transfer value is the realisable value at the date of calculation of any benefits to which the member is entitled. Special provisions also apply to the calculation of cash equivalent transfer values for cash balance benefits that are not linked to final salary.

The Regulator's guidance indicates that normally the same approach would be expected for statutory and non-statutory transfers.

Paying more or less

For underfunded defined benefit schemes, which would not have enough money to pay full transfer values for all members, the legislation permits the initial cash equivalent to be reduced in line with the extent of underfunding shown in an 'Insufficiency Report' commissioned from the actuary. The Regulator's guidance suggests that trustees should not normally make such a reduction where an employer's covenant is judged to be strong and any funding shortfall is being remedied over a reasonably short period.

The legislation also allows the trustees to pay transfer values at a level higher than best estimate. This may be appropriate if the scheme rules require it or where simpler calculations would make it cost-effective. Alternatively, the trustees may simply decide that it is appropriate to pay higher transfer values than the minimum required (perhaps following a request by, or in consultation with, the employer). Higher transfer values might encourage take-up, which, if transfer values remained below the prudent reserves required for funding the members' liabilities, could reduce a scheme's deficit (or increase its surplus). Indeed, a transfer incentive exercise may be undertaken *(see Section 21)*.

Transfers of contracted-out benefits

Transfers of contracted-out benefits can be made between most former contracted-out salary-related (COSR) schemes *(see Reference Section 5)*. GMPs remain as GMPs and post-97 COSR rights remain as post-97 COSR rights.

From 6 April 2012 it became possible to transfer GMPs and post-97 COSR rights to a scheme that was not a COSR or former COSR, provided:

- the member consents in writing
- the transfer payment in respect of any GMP is at least equal to the cash equivalent of the member's GMP
- the transfer payment in respect of any post-97 COSR rights is at least equal to the cash equivalent of the member's post-97 COSR rights, *and*
- the member has acknowledged in writing to the transferring scheme that they have received a statement from the receiving scheme showing the benefits to be awarded in respect of the transfer payment, and they accept that:
    - the benefits in the receiving scheme may be different in form and amount to those payable by the transferring scheme, *and*
    - there is no statutory requirement for the receiving scheme to provide survivors' benefits out of the transfer payment.

In these circumstances, transferred benefits cease to be treated as contracted-out rights in the receiving scheme, if it was not a COSR scheme, although scheme rules may impose special provisions.

Any GMPs or post-97 COSR rights that are already in payment can generally only be transferred to a former COSR scheme.

Disclosure, payment and information

Disclosure requirements, including those in respect of transfer values, *are described in Section 15*. A guaranteed cash equivalent may be accepted within the three-month 'guarantee period' without being subject to recalculation. Generally, provided any requirement to obtain advice is satisfied *(see above)*, the trustees are required to pay the transfer value within six months of the date of calculation where the cash equivalent is guaranteed and within six months of the original request where it is not (for example, where the benefits are money purchase). Trustees are also required to inform members of schemes providing non-money purchase benefits:

- that the Financial Conduct Authority, the Pensions Advisory Service and the Pensions Regulator provide information that may assist in their decision on whether to transfer
- of the existence of the Pension Protection Fund and that the scheme is eligible for it (eligible schemes only), *and*
- that it is recommended that they should take financial advice before making a decision.

Under the Financial Guidance and Claims Act 2018, where a member with flexible benefits applies to transfer they will need to be referred to appropriate pensions guidance. Before the member proceeds to transfer the managers must check that they have either received, or opted out of, such guidance. Implementation details will be confirmed in regulations.

Failure to follow the required processes could result in liabilities not being discharged properly. This is particularly relevant in relation to recent warnings about pension scams *(see below)*: although trustees must act on a valid transfer application within the appropriate timescales, they must take all reasonable steps to ensure that the receiving scheme is acting in good faith in order for the statutory discharge to apply.

If the transferring scheme has been informed that the alternative annual allowance provisions *(see Section 9)* apply to the member transferring, this information must be passed on to the receiving scheme within 31 days of the transfer (or within 31 days of the scheme administrator becoming aware that the member has flexibly accessed their pension rights).

Tax considerations

Since 6 April 2006, the majority of restrictions on pension transfers and the benefits that could be provided in respect of them under previous tax regimes have been removed. In general, under the Finance Act 2004 tax regime, transfers of 'uncrystallised' pension rights can be made between registered pension schemes (or to deferred annuity contracts or buy-out policies) without restriction, provided that scheme rules permit. Transfers can also be made to 'qualifying recognised overseas pension schemes' *(see below)*. The previous restrictions on partial transfers were removed by the Finance Act 2004.

Pensions already in payment can also be transferred without incurring unauthorised payment charges, provided that scheme rules allow and certain conditions are met *(see Section 9)*. Drawdown pension funds may be transferred to another such arrangement (which may not be used to hold any other funds).

Certain forms of transitional protection *(see Section 9)* may be lost on transfer, unless prescribed conditions are satisfied. In particular, enhanced protection or the various types of fixed protection will be lost unless the transfer is a 'permitted transfer' (requiring, *inter alia*, that the transfer is to a money purchase, but not cash balance, arrangement, or a bulk transfer that meets specified criteria).

Pension scams

Pension scams, or pensions liberation, refer to the transfer of a member's pension savings to an arrangement that is illegitimate and/or will allow them to access their funds before they are entitled to receive them.

The Regulator has encouraged trustees to ensure that members are aware of the risks. It notes that some arrangements may be illegal and even those that appear to operate within the law may result in the member facing unauthorised payment tax charges, in addition to high charges and high investment risks. The Regulator has produced material to assist trustees in communicating the issues to their members.

To counter pension scams, HMRC will confirm a scheme is registered only if the information it holds does not indicate a significant risk that the scheme is being used to facilitate a pension scam.

The Pension Scams Industry Group's voluntary Code of Good Practice is intended to set an industry standard for trustees, administrators and providers dealing with requests for transfers from members.

The Pensions Ombudsman has received well over a hundred complaints relating to pension scams. The complaints relate to both providers that have not allowed a transfer because liberation is suspected and providers that have allowed transfers with adverse consequences for the members.

Overseas transfers

A transfer to an overseas arrangement would only be a 'recognised transfer' for tax purposes if that arrangement falls within the definition of a qualifying recognised overseas pension scheme (QROPS). *(See Appendix 2, Glossary of Terms.)* It is the responsibility of the member and transferring scheme to check whether the receiving scheme is a QROPS. While HMRC maintains a list of recognised overseas pension schemes, it does not guarantee that a scheme is a QROPS. If such a transfer takes place, the scheme administrator of the registered pension scheme must ensure that certain information detailing the transfer is submitted to HMRC within 60 days of the transfer. Information may also be required by HMRC from the manager of the overseas scheme. Other transfers to overseas arrangements are likely to be treated as unauthorised payments for tax purposes *(see Section 9)*. For all transfers to overseas arrangements, the transferring member must acknowledge that unauthorised payment charges may apply if the transfer is not to a QROPS.

A new 'overseas transfer charge' was introduced from 9 March 2017. This 25% charge applies to recognised transfers to a QROPS unless the member has provided certain information to the administrator and at least one of a number of conditions are satisfied – for example, the QROPS is based in the same country as the individual or the QROPS is an occupational pension scheme sponsored by the individual's employer.

SECTION 14

MONEY PURCHASE RETIREMENT OPTIONS AND ADVICE

INTRODUCTION

The money purchase flexibilities introduced in April 2015 have changed the way in which money purchase benefits can be taken, providing individuals with greater choice about what to do with their funds on retirement. This choice has increased the focus on the information and advice available to individuals to ensure they can make good decisions on the use of their funds and that they understand the risks of the options available, in particular to ensure that they do not run out of retirement funds before they die. New products are likely to develop to help those who are less willing or able to make their own choices, and the regulatory system will also change over time to ensure members are appropriately protected.

Prior to 6 April 2015, most individuals used their funds to buy an annuity. Some members opted to draw down funds, but the amount individuals could draw down was capped unless they could demonstrate a minimum level of guaranteed income from other sources.

The regime that came into force on 6 April 2015 allows members of money purchase arrangements, once they have reached normal minimum pension age (usually 55), to flexibly access their savings how and when they want, subject to their pension scheme rules. The money purchase flexibilities apply to cash balance arrangements and money purchase additional voluntary contributions (AVCs) within defined benefit schemes as well as pure money purchase funds.

This section outlines the different options available, covers the importance of making informed choices and explains some recent developments. The pensions taxation rules for registered pension schemes are summarised in *Section 9*.

OPTIONS AT RETIREMENT

Whether or not a particular scheme offers any of the flexibilities will depend on the scheme rules.

Trustees are not required to offer any or all of the flexibilities. If they wish to adopt any of the flexible options but the scheme rules do not allow them to do so, the legislation provides for them to amend the rules by resolution (with employer consent) to achieve this, or alternatively to rely on a statutory override which allows trustees to make the various flexible payments even where not permitted by the scheme rules.

Flexible retirement options

Subject to scheme rules, the following options are generally available on retirement for members of money purchase arrangements:

- **Leave some retirement savings where they are** – benefits can be taken at any time from normal minimum pension age, but can otherwise be left invested until the member wishes to use the funds.
- **Take the whole pension pot in one go, or as a number of lump sums** – all or part of the member's benefits can be taken as a lump sum known as an uncrystallised funds pension lump sum (UFPLS). The member can take a series of UFPLS – up to 25% of each lump sum will be tax free, with the remainder being taxed as income. An UFPLS can only be taken from uncrystallised funds, i.e. those that have not been designated for flexi-access drawdown, used to pay a scheme pension, or converted into an annuity.
- **Take a flexible retirement income** – members can put funds into a drawdown arrangement, known as a flexi-access drawdown fund, from which they can draw down any amount over whatever period they choose. When funds are placed in drawdown, the member can take a separate, tax-free, pension commencement lump sum from the remainder of the fund of up to one-third of the funds being allocated to drawdown (equivalent to taking 25% of the funds as tax-free cash and the remainder as drawdown). Other withdrawals would be taxed as income.
- **Purchase an annuity** – the member can buy a lifetime annuity from an insurance company (or scheme pension if offered by the occupational pension scheme). This option typically involves taking a tax-free cash sum of 25% of the fund and purchasing an annuity with the balance of the fund based on the annuity rates the provider is offering. Short-term annuities are also available.
- **Choose a combination of these options** – a combination of some or all of the options could be taken over time.

Transferring to access the flexibilities

If their scheme does not offer all of the flexibilities, members may wish to transfer to a different arrangement to access these options. From 6 April 2015, members have a statutory right to transfer *flexible benefits* (broadly money purchase or cash balance benefits) to a different arrangement at any point before they come into payment, provided that they have stopped contributing and have not yet started taking benefits. They are also allowed to transfer separate categories of benefit – for example they can transfer money purchase funds (such as AVCs) in isolation from defined benefits in the same scheme.

Members of defined benefit arrangements providing *safeguarded benefits* (broadly benefits that are neither money purchase nor cash balance) may elect to transfer some or all of their accrued benefits to a money purchase scheme in order to take advantage of the flexibilities. Members may be required to take independent financial advice before transferring such benefits.

Evidence indicates that schemes have seen an increase in requests from members for transfer values, following the introduction of the flexibilities.

In response, in 2018 the Financial Conduct Authority (FCA) introduced new rules and guidance intended to improve advice for those transferring safeguarded benefits. The changes include a requirement for all pension transfer advice to be provided as a personal recommendation, alongside a tailored appropriate pension transfer analysis of the individual's options and a comparison to show the value of the benefits that are being given up.

The rules regarding transfers and the advice requirement are covered further in *Section 13*.

Communicating retirement options

Trustees need to consider carefully how best to communicate retirement options to members in a way that encourages them to consider their choices and alerts them to the decisions they will need to make.

The disclosure regulations include detailed requirements for scheme members with flexible benefits who are at, or approaching, retirement, which are outlined in *Section 15*. The information to be provided varies depending upon what has triggered it, but in all cases includes signposting to the Pension Wise guidance service *(see below)*. The Pensions Regulator has issued an *Essential guide to communicating with members about pensions flexibilities* which trustees may find helpful.

In a bid to help members better understand their retirement options the Association of British Insurers (ABI) has produced a guide, *Making Retirement Choices Clear*, which aims to simplify language on retirement options. The intention is for language to be simple, clear and consistent and avoid technical terms and jargon where possible, in order to help individuals make confident, appropriate and informed decisions. Schemes that wish to help members better understand their options may find the guide useful when reviewing their scheme literature.

In July 2018, the FCA began consulting on a package of proposed remedies to address the concerns identified in its retirement outcomes review. The review looked at how the retirement income market has changed since the introduction of the money purchase flexibilities, with a focus on those who do not take regulated advice. Among other things, the FCA proposes that:

- wake-up packs are sent to members from age 50, including a single-page summary (sometimes called a pensions passport) and risk warnings; these packs should be sent every five years until the member's pot has been fully taken
- providers should develop ready-made drawdown investment solutions (which it calls investment pathways) to help confused customers; also, the key features illustration they give to money purchase savers should include a one-year charge figure in pounds and pence.

The initial changes are due to be introduced from January 2019.

Retirement risk warnings and guidance

As well as signposting members to Pension Wise, schemes must give written risk warnings to members who indicate that they want to access their pension savings.

Providers of contract-based schemes *(see also Section 27)* such as group personal pensions must give tailored risk warnings, which involve asking the member questions (such as on health and marital status) that relate to the way they want to access their funds. This is intended to identify if a risk factor is present, in which case relevant risk warnings must be given. They must also highlight to members that using Pension Wise, or taking regulated advice, is a key part of protecting themselves and their family.

There are similar requirements for trust-based schemes, although they are less onerous *(see also Section 15)*. Trustees need to give generic (rather than targeted) risk warnings to members who may be intending to take their benefits flexibly. These only have to cover the options the member is able to access under the scheme, rather than all the options available under the flexibilities. Each risk warning should set out characteristic attributes and features that have the potential to adversely affect retirement income, and factors that have the potential to affect the appropriateness of options (such as health status and lifestyle choices, and whether a member has dependants, is in debt or in receipt of means-tested benefits).

The Financial Guidance and Claims Act 2018 will extend these requirements. Where a member with flexible benefits applies to transfer or start receiving their benefits, the trustees or personal pension provider will have to refer them to appropriate pensions guidance and explain the nature of such guidance. Before proceeding with the application, the trustees or provider will have to check that the member has either received, or opted out of, the guidance. The details of the new requirements will be set out in regulations, for which timescales are not yet known.

Schemes are also required to provide tailored risk warnings for members who have safeguarded-flexible benefits (meaning benefits that are safeguarded for the purpose of the independent advice requirement and are also flexible benefits – such as guaranteed annuity rates that exist in certain money purchase arrangements) and are considering options that might result in the loss of these guarantees. Among other things, the risk warning must explain that the individual has a potentially valuable guarantee, which would be lost if they proceed with the transaction.

PENSIONS GUIDANCE AND ADVICE

It is important that members understand the impact of the choices available and consider all of the options when making any decisions. In order to identify the most appropriate retirement income product for their circumstances, both information and advice are needed – not just at the point of retirement, but also leading up to and beyond it.

The complexity of retirement options available has led to an increase in focus on empowering members with knowledge about their options to help them make the necessary decisions.

Reports indicate that there is a lot of confusion around pension savings and that take-up of the free Pension Wise guidance service *(see below)* is low.

Also, while Pension Wise provides access to guidance, it is not tailored to the individual's needs and is not a recommendation of the kind delivered through regulated financial advice. However, regulated financial advice is costly. Changes in the UK's financial advice market have highlighted concerns that there are situations in which consumers are unable to get advice and guidance on a need they have at a price they are willing to pay. A number of changes have been introduced in an attempt to rectify this.

Employers have a role to play in helping with at-retirement decision-making and should have a strategy that supports employees with pensions decision-making by telling them about their options and helping them to understand these to make good choices. However, it is important that both employers and members understand the difference between guidance and regulated advice. The FCA and the Pensions Regulator have jointly published a guide for employers and trustees on what support they can provide on financial matters without being subject to regulation.

The right to financial guidance (Pension Wise)

The money purchase flexibilities have introduced new risks as the ability to take funds however and whenever members want means they can potentially take their money with the risk of running out of funds later in life. The complexity of the options available prompted the government to introduce from April 2015 a new right to impartial financial guidance at the point of retirement for anyone with money purchase funds.

The government-sponsored Pension Wise service offers guidance intended to help people aged 50 or over make informed decisions about their pension savings. It is a free and impartial service that aims to help individuals with money purchase benefits access information on all of the options available to them.

Each member is entitled to one appointment by telephone (by the Pensions Advisory Service), or face to face (by Citizens Advice). There is also information online. Sessions are normally 45 to 60 minutes, at the end of which the member will get a printed summary of the options and tips on what to do next. Pension Wise guidance specialists will not recommend any products or tell the member what to do.

Trustees and providers are required to signpost members to Pension Wise, and also have to issue retirement risk warnings *(see above)* to members taking flexible benefits.

Single financial guidance body

The Financial Guidance and Claims Act 2018 sets the framework for a new single financial guidance body (SFGB) that will be created by merging the Money Advice Service, the Pensions Advisory Service *(see Section 8)* and Pension Wise. The merger is expected to occur in January 2019 and the new public body will be responsible for the coordination of the provision of debt advice, money guidance and pensions guidance. Regulations are needed to set out the detailed provisions.

Paying for advice

In order to encourage members to take tailored advice, the Government introduced the following from 6 April 2017:

- A Pension Advice Allowance that allows members to withdraw up to £500 tax free from their money purchase pension to put towards the cost of 'retirement financial advice' (i.e. advice in respect of the person's financial position, including their pension arrangements and the use of their pension funds), that is fully regulated financial advice. There are no age restrictions; the allowance can be taken on up to three separate occasions during a member's lifetime, but only once in any tax year.
- A tax exemption for 'relevant pensions advice'. This exempts from income tax and National Insurance contributions the first £500 worth of employer-arranged advice provided to a current, former or prospective employee in a tax year.

Creating a pensions dashboard

In Budget 2016 the Government tasked the pensions industry with ensuring that by 2019 it had designed, funded and launched a pensions dashboard service, a free-to-consumer online resource that will allow people to find their retirement savings and view them all (including their state pension) in one place.

The ABI coordinated the initial stage of the project and in 2017 it demonstrated a prototype of the dashboard, in conjunction with a number of pension providers. The Government has indicated that eventually every provider will run a dashboard to share data with its members. However, the Work and Pensions Committee has recommended that there should be a single pensions dashboard, publicly hosted by the new SFGB *(see above)*, rather than multiple dashboards hosted by pension providers. The Government is considering this further and will set out its conclusions in its feasibility report, to be published in due course.

There is hope that the dashboard might be able to satisfy the disclosure requirements of the forthcoming Pensions Directive (including deferred member statements).

SECTION 15

DISCLOSURE OF INFORMATION

Pensions legislation requires the trustees of occupational pension schemes to disclose actuarial and accounting information, as well as individual benefit details for each member. These rules override any provisions in schemes' trust documents if the two are in conflict.

Details to be disclosed differ depending on the type of benefits provided. Information must normally be accompanied by the postal and electronic addresses for further enquiries.

Particular requirements apply in relation to flexible benefits (broadly, money purchase or cash balance benefits) and safeguarded benefits (broadly, defined benefits).

The following pages set out the main disclosure requirements for occupational schemes. The disclosure requirements relating to personal pensions and stakeholder schemes are generally the same as those for money purchase occupational pensions. Also, as such schemes are provided by a regulated insurance company, they must comply with additional disclosure requirements imposed by the Financial Conduct Authority.

In divorce cases, information must also be disclosed to pension credit members and further disclosure requirements also arise at the time when pension sharing arrangements are being made. These are too extensive to describe in detail here, but an outline is included in *Section 17*.

Disclosure rules relating to automatic enrolment are summarised in *Section 5*.

There are separate requirements for members and administrators to exchange information for pension taxation purposes; these do not fall under the disclosure regulations but key requirements are covered within the summary below.

SUMMARY OF DISCLOSURE REQUIREMENTS FOR OCCUPATIONAL PENSION SCHEMES

Information	To be Disclosed to	In What Circumstances	Time Limits/Other Details
Basic scheme information *(see later in this section for details).*	**Members**,* **prospective members,** their **spouses** and **civil partners**; **beneficiaries**; and recognised independent **trade unions**.	**New members** must be given basic scheme information **automatically** (and in advance where practicable).	New members (other than those being automatically enrolled – *see Section 5*) must receive this information within two months of joining the scheme.

(continues...)

Note: * Throughout this summary 'members' includes pension credit members, as well as pensioners and deferred pensioners.

Information	To be Disclosed to	In What Circumstances	Time Limits/Other Details
Basic scheme information *(continued)*			Trustees of automatic enrolment schemes must normally provide this within one month of receiving jobholder information.
		On request, no more than **once a year**.	Within two months of the request being made.
			Any **material change** in basic scheme information must be notified to all members and beneficiaries, before or as soon as possible after the alteration and in any case within three months.
Statement of Prospective Transfer Credits	**Members** and **prospective members**.	**On request**, no more than **once a year**.	Within two months of the request.
Benefit Statements – non-money purchase benefits *(see later for details)*.	**Active, deferred** and **pension credit members**.	**On request**, no more than **once a year**.	Within two months of the request. Information varies depending on the type of member.
Benefit Statements – money purchase benefits *(see later for details)*.	**Active** and **most deferred members**.	**Automatically, once a year.**	A benefit statement and Statutory Money Purchase Illustration (SMPI) must be provided within 12 months of each scheme year's end.
Early leaver benefits	**Members** who leave a scheme before normal pension age.	**Automatically** to early leavers.	Leavers with rights to preserved benefits must be told their rights and options within two months of the trustees being notified that the member has left service.
			Leavers with between three months and two years of qualifying service but without rights to preserved benefits must be informed of their options for a cash transfer sum or contribution refund as soon as possible (normally within three months).
	Active and **prospective members**.	**On request**, no more than **once a year**.	Within two months of the request.

INFORMATION	TO BE DISCLOSED TO	IN WHAT CIRCUMSTANCES	TIME LIMITS/OTHER DETAILS
Statement of entitlement to cash equivalent – non-money purchase benefits	**Deferred** and **pension credit members** with non-money purchase benefits.	**On request**, no more than **once a year**.	To be calculated within three months of the request and passed to the member within ten working days of calculation.
Estimate of cash equivalent transfer value	**Active members** still accruing a category of benefits; and **deferred members** with money purchase benefits.	**On request,** no more than **once a year**.	Within three months of the request the member should be told whether a cash equivalent or transfer value is available, or would be if the member was no longer accruing benefits, along with estimates of the amount and details of the rights to which it relates. Separate statements are required for money purchase and non-money purchase benefits.
Advice requirement – conversion or transfer of safeguarded benefits	**Members** or **survivors** with safeguarded benefits in the scheme exceeding £30,000 in value.	The individual makes a **written request** for a valuation of their safeguarded benefits, or information on how to carry out a transfer or apply for a statement of entitlement, or **applies** for a statement of entitlement.	Within one month, trustees must explain that they are required to check that appropriate independent advice has been received by the member or survivor; and that unless the member or survivor confirms otherwise, the trustees will assume that the purpose of any transfer is to provide flexible benefits. *See Section 13 for further details on transfers.*
	Members or **survivors** with safeguarded benefits in the scheme worth £30,000 or less.		Within one month, trustees must explain that the requirement for independent advice does not apply.
Risk warnings – conversion or transfer of safeguarded-flexible benefits	**Members** or **survivors** with safeguarded-flexible benefits in the scheme.	The individual makes a **written request** for a valuation of their safeguarded-flexible benefits, or for information on how to carry out a transfer or apply for a statement of entitlement, or **applies** for a statement of entitlement, **but not** if this has already been given in the last 12 months.	Within one month and no later than two weeks before the relevant transaction, trustees must provide a personalised risk warning. It must include two illustrations comparing the potential income if the member exercised the guarantee with the income that would be available on the open market; and information on the guarantee that would be lost.

Information	To be Disclosed to	In What Circumstances	Time Limits/Other Details
Lifestyling – money purchase benefits	**Members.**	**Automatically** where the scheme offers lifestyling, unless it has been provided within the last year as part of the basic scheme information.	Between 5 and 15 years before a member's retirement date, a statement must be provided explaining lifestyling, its advantages and disadvantages and when it will be adopted if not already.
Flexible benefits	**Members**, with a right to flexible benefits and the opportunity to transfer them, who are over or within four months of normal minimum pension age (usually 55) or are retiring on grounds of ill health.	Member **requests** information about taking flexible benefits, or **informs** trustees they are considering or have made a decision about what to do with such benefits, **but not** if this has already been given in the last 12 months.	Within two months of the request or contact, the member must be given options under the rules along with information about transferring flexible benefits (including the various options and implications) and how to access Pension Wise.
		Where there is **contact (other than a request)** between trustees and member about flexible benefits. There are **exceptions** (e.g. member has accessed Pension Wise or taken independent advice in last 12 months).	Within 20 days of initial contact, limited information on flexible benefits should be provided, and the member should be informed about Pension Wise.
Accessing flexible benefits	**Members** approaching retirement.	**Automatically.**	A retirement pack must be sent at least four months before the member's retirement date. If the retirement date is agreed during that four-month period, the information must be provided within 20 days of the agreement and in any event before retirement. The pack should include details of the member's benefits and options available; an explanation of the opportunity to transfer and that there may be tax and other implications from doing so. The member must also be told how to access Pension Wise. If relevant, the member should also be told of rights to benefits other than flexible benefits.

(continues...)

Information	To be Disclosed to	In What Circumstances	Time Limits/Other Details
Before flexible benefits are paid	**Members** making a final decision about taking their retirement benefits.	**Automatically** when the member is given the means to access flexible benefits, **unless** already provided in relation to the same type of benefit in the last 12 months.	Generic risk warnings about the retirement options available under the scheme must be given, along with a statement noting the importance of reading the warnings and of accessing pensions guidance or independent advice.
The Pensions Regulator's *Essential guide to communicating with members about pension flexibilities* provides further information and good practice suggestions on retirement communications.			
Benefits on death	**Beneficiaries** over age 18. **Personal representatives** of **members** or **beneficiaries** who have died.	**Automatically.** **On request.**	Beneficiaries must be notified of rights and options within two months of trustees being notified of death. Personal representatives must be notified within two months of request. Where there are rights or options relating to flexible benefits, information on Pension Wise should be provided.
Pension savings statement	**Members.**	**Automatically** to those: • whose pension input exceeds the annual allowance for the pension input period (defined benefit or money purchase as appropriate), *or* • who the trustees have reason to believe have flexibly accessed their pension savings and whose money purchase input amounts exceed the money purchase annual allowance *(see Section 9)*.	Within 6 months of the end of the tax year, a standard pension savings statement or a money purchase savings statement (as appropriate) will be provided. Figures must be given for the relevant tax year and for the previous three years.
		On request, if the individual will not get a statement automatically.	Within three months of the request, or by 6 October if later.
After accessing benefits flexibly	**Members.**	On **first 'accessing benefits flexibly'** *(see Section 9)*.	Within 31 days of payment, information must be given about the money purchase annual allowance and the duty to notify other schemes.

Information	To be Disclosed to	In What Circumstances	Time Limits/Other Details
Benefits on retirement	**Members** and **beneficiaries.**	**Automatically**, when benefits become payable. Where there are rights or options relating to **flexible benefits**, information on Pension Wise should be provided.	Details of benefits payable and of any rights and options, including selection of annuity and designation for drawdown, must be given before benefits become payable or within one month after (two months in the case case of early retirement).
Information about Benefit Crystallisation Events (BCEs)	**Members** who have taken some or all of their benefits (or their **personal representatives** if the BCE arises on death).	**Automatically**, following a BCE unless an annual pensioner statement will be supplied *(see below)*.	Within three months of the BCE, confirming the percentage of lifetime allowance expended and details of any lifetime allowance charge.
Annual pensioner statements	**Pensioners.**	**Automatically** to those retiring with a scheme pension or taking drawdown income since 6 April 2006 (unless drawdown funds are extinguished).	Once each tax year up to age 75. A statement of the cumulative total percentage of lifetime allowance crystallised in respect of the scheme (or benefit transferred into the scheme).
Change of benefits in payment	**Pensioners** (including **beneficiaries**).	**Automatically,** unless already informed about the anticipated increase.	Before, or within one month of, the change, the new amount of pension benefit and any changes to rights and options on death.
Summary Funding Statement *(see later for details)*	**Members** and **beneficiaries**.	**Automatically**, except where a member is entitled to only money purchase benefits.	Annually, to include information on the funding and solvency positions of the scheme. Must be issued within a **reasonable period** (generally three months) after the deadline for completion of actuarial valuation or actuarial report.
Trust Deed and Rules or other documents constituting the scheme, including names and addresses of participating employers.	**Members**, **prospective members**, their **spouses** and **civil partners**; **beneficiaries**; and recognised independent **trade unions.**	**For inspection on request**, free of charge at a reasonably accessible place or on a website. A copy **to keep on request**, unless the documents are publicly available; any charge must be limited to the cost of producing and sending it.	Within two months of the request being made, but no more than once a year. Any documentation not relevant to the rights of the particular person does not need to be disclosed.

Information	To be Disclosed to	In What Circumstances	Time Limits/Other Details
Trustees' Annual Report *(see later for details)* including: • audited accounts • latest certification of schedule of contributions • investment report • if relevant, money purchase governance statement, including details on costs and charges that must also be published on a publicly accessible website *(see later)*.	**Members**, **prospective members**, their **spouses** and **civil partners**; **beneficiaries**; and recognised independent **trade unions**.	Reports covering the previous five years must be available: • **for inspection**, free of charge, at a reasonably accessible place or on a website • a copy of the most recent report **on request**, free of charge, unless the documents are publicly available; can be provided electronically • copies of earlier reports **on request, to keep**, unless the documents are publicly available; any charge must be limited to the cost of producing and giving it.	The report must be available within seven months of the end of the scheme year. It should be provided within two months of the request, unless it has been given before.
Actuarial Valuation Report, Schedule of Contributions, Payment Schedule, Recovery Plan,** **Statements of Funding** and **Investment Principles**,** and outline **Winding-Up Procedure** (if applicable)	**Members, prospective members,** their **spouses** and **civil partners**; **beneficiaries**; and recognised independent **trade unions**.	**For inspection,** free of charge at a reasonably accessible place or on a website. A copy **to keep, on request**, unless the documents are publicly available; any charge must be limited to the cost of producing and giving it.	Within two months of the request being made.

Note: ** *See Section 18.*

BASIC SCHEME INFORMATION

Basic scheme information must include:

- eligibility and conditions for membership
- the period of notice which a member must give to leave pensionable service
- whether re-entry to pensionable service is permitted and, if so, upon what conditions
- how employers' and members' normal contributions are calculated
- any arrangements made for members to pay Additional Voluntary Contributions (AVCs)

- HMRC registration status
- the benefits payable, and how they are calculated, including the definition of pensionable earnings and the accrual rate
- for money purchase and cash balance benefits, a statement explaining that the value of pensions will depend on several factors
- if the scheme has provision for a lifestyle strategy, a statement explaining lifestyling and its advantages and disadvantages, and either that it has been adopted or an indication of when it will be
- the conditions on which benefits, including survivors' benefits, are payable and how and when any pension increases are applied
- whether the trustees accept transfers in to the scheme
- a summary of what can be done with accrued rights for early leavers, including transfers out, whether a charge will be made and a statement that further information is available on request
- where the member has flexible benefits, a statement explaining in what circumstances those rights can be transferred
- where the member has safeguarded benefits, a statement explaining that independent advice may be required before those benefits can be converted into flexible benefits or transferred in order to access flexible benefits
- a statement that the scheme annual report is available on request, except for public service pension schemes
- the procedure for internal resolution of disputes and the address and job title of the contact, *and*
- a statement explaining the functions and addresses (postal and electronic) of the Pensions Ombudsman, The Pensions Advisory Service and the Pensions Regulator.

BENEFIT STATEMENTS

Active and deferred members with non-money purchase benefits

On request, an active member must be given information including:

- the amount of the member's and survivors' accrued benefits, based on current salary, and assuming pensionable service ceases at a date specified by the trustees, or at normal pension age, or at a date agreed between the member and trustees; *and*
- the amount of the benefits payable if the member were to die in service at a date specified by the trustees, with details of how they are calculated.

The trustees need not comply with a request made within a year of providing the information, so if they provide benefit statements automatically once a year there is no need to respond to one-off requests.

On subsequent request, a deferred member must be given a statement of the date pensionable service ceased and the amount of his/her own benefits, and any survivors' benefits, payable from normal pension age or on death.

For both active and deferred members the information must include:

- the date on which pensionable service commenced
- a summary of the method for calculating the member's own benefits and any survivors' benefits
- the amount of the member's pensionable earnings (at the date pensionable service ceased for a deferred member and at a specified date for an active member), *and*
- details of how any deduction from benefits (e.g. an offset for State pension or any pension debit) is calculated.

On request, a member with *cash balance benefits* must be given an illustration showing the amount of pension that is likely to be secured at retirement. The member is also entitled to an illustration of their money purchase benefits.

Pension credit members with non-money purchase benefits

On request, the member must be given a statement of the amount of his/her own benefits, and any survivors' benefits, payable from normal benefit age or on death. The information must include:

- a summary of the method for calculating the member's own benefits and any survivors' benefits, *and*
- details of how any deduction from benefits is calculated.

All members with money purchase benefits

Statements must be given automatically within 12 months of the end of each scheme year. They are optional if the member has just joined and no contributions have yet been credited, or the member is in the auto-enrolment opt-out period. The money purchase benefit statement must show:

- contributions credited to the member (before deductions) during the immediately preceding scheme year
- value of any accrued rights at a specified date, *and*
- cash equivalents of these rights at the specified dates, if they differ from the values.

Statutory money purchase illustrations (SMPIs) of projected benefits are required in addition to the above information, unless the member is within two years of retirement, or the fund value is less than £5,000 and certain other conditions are met.

The SMPI must show the amount of pension the member is likely to receive at retirement in respect of his/her money purchase benefits. It must be prepared in accordance with the methodology and assumptions set out in the latest version of the Technical Memorandum (AS TM1).

The statement must explain that it is an illustration in today's terms and not guaranteed and that general assumptions have been used. The illustration and retirement dates should be provided, along with details of where to obtain further information. It should also include certain information and statements about the calculations and assumptions used e.g. in relation to investments, future contributions, lump sums taken, pension increases and dependants' pensions.

Additional requirements apply where the scheme is required to produce a money purchase governance statement *(see later)*:

- **From 6 April 2018**, certain information from the chair's statement *(see below)* must be made publicly available on a website. Where this applies, the annual benefit statement must also include: a statement that the information is available on the website, the website address, details of the place on the website where the information may be read, an explanation of how the recipient may read the information on the website, and a statement explaining the circumstances in which the information will be provided, on request, in hard copy form.
- **From 6 April 2019**, the benefit statement must include details of how the member may obtain, on request, certain information about pooled funds.

SUMMARY FUNDING STATEMENTS

Summary funding statements (SFS) must be given annually to most members and beneficiaries with defined benefits. As well as the information required by legislation, the Pensions Regulator's code of practice on funding defined benefits suggests items to be included. Taking into account these suggestions, the statement should include:

- a summary of the extent to which the assets of the scheme are adequate to cover its technical provisions
- the actuary's estimate of scheme solvency contained in the last valuation
- an explanation of any change in the funding position since the previous SFS
- a summary of any recovery plan in force
- whether the Pensions Regulator has exercised its powers in relation to the scheme and, if so, details of the circumstances, *and*
- whether any payment of surplus has been made to the sponsoring employer and, if so, the amount.

TRUSTEES' ANNUAL REPORT

The report must include:

- audited accounts, including auditor's statement
- latest actuarial certificate certifying the adequacy of the schedule of contributions
- names of trustees (or directors of the trust company), and the rules for changing trustees; names of the professional advisers, custodians and banks acting for the trustees, indicating any changes during the year

- a copy of the statement which any auditor or actuary of the scheme has made on resignation or removal as auditor or actuary during the year
- numbers of active, deferred and pensioner members and beneficiaries at a date during the year
- except for money purchase schemes, percentage increases made during the year to pensions and deferred pensions, in excess of those required by law – the extent to which increases were discretionary is to be stated
- except for money purchase schemes which are wholly insured, if transfer values paid during the year were not calculated in accordance with the law, an explanation as to why they have differed; if any were less than the full value of the member's preserved or pension credit benefits, an explanation as to why and when full values are likely to be available; and a statement as to whether discretionary benefits are included in the calculation and, if so, how they are assessed
- name of investment manager, and the extent to which the trustees have delegated their responsibility to him
- whether the trustees have produced a statement of investment principles and, if so, that a copy is available on request, and information on investments made other than in accordance with the statement
- except for wholly insured schemes, a statement of the trustees' policy on the custody of scheme assets
- investment report including review of performance, over the year and over a period of between three and five years; an assessment of the scheme's assets including any policies on rights attaching to investments; and details of social, environmental or ethical considerations
- details and percentage of any employer-related investment and steps taken or proposed to reduce excessive employer-related investment
- postal and electronic addresses for enquiries
- an explanation, where applicable, of why the auditor's statement about scheme contributions is negative or qualified and a statement as to how the situation has been, or is likely to be, resolved, *and*
- if relevant, money purchase governance statement *(see later)*.

The Pensions Research Accountants Group's Statement of Recommended Practice (SORP), last updated for accounting years commencing on or after 1 January 2015, gives guidance on best practice for financial accounting and reporting of pension schemes. The pensions SORP includes additional recommendations for information that should be included in the annual report.

Money purchase governance statement (the chair's statement)

Most occupational pension schemes that provide money purchase benefits must also prepare an annual governance statement. It must include:

- the latest statement on the investment principles for the default arrangement *(see Section 7)*, including a report on any review during the year and resulting actions, or the date of the last review if none was undertaken during the year
- a description of how the trustees have assessed the requirement to process core scheme financial transactions promptly and accurately
- a report on the level of charges and transaction costs in each default arrangement and the levels of charges and transaction costs applicable to each fund which members are able to select and in which assets relating to members are invested during the scheme year; the trustees' assessment of the extent to which these represent good value for members; and an illustration of the compounding effect of costs and charges; if trustees have been unable to obtain information about transaction costs, they must explain what steps are being taken to obtain that information in future
- a description of how the trustee knowledge and understanding requirements have been met during the year; and an assessment of how the combined knowledge and understanding of the trustees, together with the advice available to them, enables them to properly exercise their functions as trustees, *and*
- signature by the chair, or acting chair, of trustees, on behalf of the trustees.

Additional information must be included on the statement for relevant multi-employer schemes (including master trusts).

From 6 April 2018, certain information from the scheme's most recent chair's statement must be made publicly available free of charge on a website. Members must be made aware that this information is available, via their annual benefit statements.

AUTOMATIC DISCLOSURE IN SPECIAL CIRCUMSTANCES

Certain information about the scheme must be disclosed automatically, rather than on request, in the following circumstances.

(a) **If any contributions are not paid by the due date,** and the trustees believe that this will be of material significance to the Pensions Regulator, members must be informed within a reasonable period (generally within 30 days of having reported to the Regulator).

(b) **Details of any proposed transfer without the member's consent** *(see Section 25)*, must be provided at least one month before the proposed date of the transfer.

(c) **If a scheme is being wound up** *(see Section 23)*, all members and beneficiaries (except deferred pensioners and pension credit members who cannot be traced) must be notified at various stages.

(d) **Where a refund of surplus is proposed** *(see Section 18)* to be made to the employer from a scheme that *is not winding up*, all members of the scheme must be notified, at least three months before the date of payment.

(e) **Details of any independent trustee appointed on employer insolvency** *(see Section 23)* must be provided to all members and recognised independent trade unions within a reasonable period of the appointment being made.

(f) **In relation to the appointment of member-nominated trustees or directors** *(see Section 7)*, information about the nomination and selection processes should be communicated appropriately.

(g) **Consultation by employers** *(see Section 2)* with members and prospective members of occupational pension and personal pension schemes is required before they can make certain 'listed changes' to the scheme.

(h) **Modification of the accrued benefits provided by an occupational pension scheme** *(see Section 2)* requires notification to members within a reasonable period. The Pensions Regulator's code of practice 'Modification of subsisting rights' provides guidance on the trustees' duties and responsibilities under the various stages of the requirements.

(i) **Modification of future benefit accrual by the Pensions Regulator** must be notified to all active members, within one month of the change.

SCHEMES EXEMPT FROM DISCLOSURE

The following schemes are required only to disclose certain basic scheme information:

- schemes with fewer than two members
- schemes providing only death benefits, *and*
- schemes neither established in the UK nor with a trustee resident in the UK.

Certain public service pension schemes are not required to obtain audited accounts or an actuarial valuation, or to publish an annual report.

ELECTRONIC PROVISION OF INFORMATION

Subject to certain safeguards, schemes may provide information electronically if they are satisfied that recipients are able to access and store or print the information and that the communications meet the needs of people with disabilities.

Certain conditions must be met where trustees wish to meet requests for information, such as scheme documents, by using a website. For instance, a notification must be given to recipients each time information is disclosed in this way, with some exceptions for uncontactable members.

Trustees' obligations will not be met by means of email or website if the member requests otherwise in writing.

If a scheme wishes to convert from paper to electronic communication, the member must be given written notification and the opportunity to opt for continued paper communication.

MEMBER COMMUNICATIONS

The disclosure of accurate, adequate and timely information to members and beneficiaries is crucial. It is important that scheme material, such as the scheme booklet, is maintained as many complaints are made to the Pensions Ombudsman on the basis that information scheme documents contain is inaccurate, misleading or out of date.

As well as complying with legal requirements, trustees should consider the language that is used when communicating with members as this can influence how well they engage with the information. Various initiatives aim to ensure that pensions communications are clear and jargon free.

SECTION 16

EQUAL TREATMENT

Over several years, the UK government has incorporated into UK statute a number of provisions mostly designed to implement the various equal treatment requirements imposed by European law. Under EU law, there are a number of equal treatment principles that are of particular relevance to UK pensions. Because these principles have been incorporated into UK legislation, the UK's withdrawal from the EU will have no immediate impact on the requirements set out in this section. In the longer term, the terms of the UK's withdrawal will affect whether UK legislation can be amended in future without reference to EU law.

The Equality Act 2010 consolidated and harmonised previous legislation on equal treatment and strengthened the law to support progress on equality. Most aspects of the Act, as they relate to pensions, are the same as or very similar to provisions under previous legislation. The Act requires a single 'non-discrimination' rule in respect of various 'protected characteristics' to be deemed to be included in the rules of occupational pension schemes, together with separate equality rules in respect of sex and maternity. These generally prohibit indirect discrimination unless it can be justified as a proportionate means of achieving a legitimate aim. Direct discrimination based on age and disability can also be justified on these grounds, but indirect discrimination on the grounds of pregnancy or maternity cannot be so justified.

Further details of the principles of equal treatment, and how the Equality Act and associated regulations seek to implement them, are given below.

GENERAL PRINCIPLES OF EQUAL TREATMENT BY SEX

The deemed 'sex equality rule' under the Equality Act 2010 covers both admission of members and benefits. This arises from Article 157 of the Treaty on the Functioning of the European Union ('the Treaty of Rome'), which requires men and women performing work of equal value to receive equal pay. Case law at the Court of Justice of the European Union (CJEU) has shown that occupational pensions (though not social security schemes) fall within the definition of pay.

Equal benefits

The Equality Act 2010, together with other legislation, requires equality for benefits accrued in respect of service on or after 17 May 1990, except for claims initiated earlier. *(See 'Pension age and benefit accrual' below.)*

Equal access

Men and women must have equal rights to join their employer's pension scheme. The exclusion of part-timers may thus constitute 'indirect' sex discrimination if the exclusion affects a much greater number of one sex than the other, *unless* the employer shows that it may be explained by objectively justified factors unrelated to sex. There are time limits for bringing claims in relation to unequal access as well as to the extent to which membership can be backdated *(see below)*.

Role of trustees, employers and the courts

Trustees must observe the principle of equal treatment in performing their duties. Both trustees and employers are bound to use all the means available under national laws in order to eliminate discrimination. National courts must apply the principle of Article 157 in the context of domestic laws, taking due account of the respective liabilities of employers and trustees. Article 157 may be relied on in claims against trustees as well as against employers.

APPLICATION OF PRINCIPLES OF EQUAL TREATMENT BY SEX TO OCCUPATIONAL AND STATE PENSIONS

Member contributions

The equal treatment principle of Article 157 applies to the whole benefit paid by an occupational pension scheme, and no distinction need be made between the parts derived from the employer's and from the employee's contractual contributions. However, benefits derived from members' additional voluntary contributions are not pay and so do not fall within the scope of Article 157.

Pension age and benefit accrual

Normal pension ages for men and women must not be discriminatory for benefits accrued since 17 May 1990. In respect of service from 17 May 1990 up to the date benefits are equalised (the equalisation date), the provisions applying to the less-favoured sex must be levelled up to those of the more-favoured sex. For periods of service after the equalisation date, Article 157 does not preclude equal treatment being achieved by levelling benefits down, e.g. by raising the lower pension age. If members have a right to retire early, this right must not be discriminatory for benefits accrued since 17 May 1990. This can result in members having different pension ages for different periods of service.

Benefit accrual for service since 17 May 1990 must be equalised not only for scheme members but also for their dependants. For benefits not linked to length of service, e.g. lump sum benefits on death in service, equal benefits must be provided for men and women when the event triggering payment of the benefit occurs on or after 17 May 1990.

Where the funds held by the trustees are insufficient, any decision on how equalisation of benefits should be achieved must be resolved on the basis of national law. In 2009 the Court of Appeal ruled in the *Foster Wheeler* case *(see Section 30)* that any resolution should involve minimum interference with the scheme's provisions, and should not result in members receiving a windfall (for example, members with mixed pension ages should not be allowed to take all their benefits at the lowest age, without an actuarial reduction being applied to benefits accrued by reference to a higher pension age).

Bridging pensions and State pension offsets

Unequal bridging pensions (and State pension offsets) that allow for the difference between men's and women's State pension ages are permitted. The extra pension payable to a man may not exceed the total State retirement pension payable to a woman with the same earnings history in respect of his period of pensionable service under the scheme. Furthermore, it may be paid only between the corresponding female and male State pension ages.

The High Court ruled in the *Uppingham School v Shillcock* case *(see Section 30)* that, for the purposes of calculating contributions and benefits, the operation of a Lower Earnings Limit (LEL) deduction from pensionable pay without pro-rating for part-timers (who were mostly female) did not constitute indirect sex discrimination and was, in any case, a reasonable method of implementing the legitimate objective of integration with State benefits and so was objectively justified.

Transfers

Schemes may, if they wish, calculate transfers out using actuarial factors which vary according to sex. The benefits to which the factors are applied are required to be equalised for service since 17 May 1990. Where a transfer value has in fact been based on unequal benefits for a period of service after 16 May 1990, the transfer value might be lower than it would have been if it had been based on equalised benefits. In such circumstances the *receiving* scheme must increase the benefits provided to those which could have been bought by the higher transfer value that should have been paid.

Actuarial factors and insurance premiums

Under current UK legislation, actuarial factors that vary according to sex may be used for commutation, early and late retirement, and surrender of pension for a dependant (as well as transfers out, *as above*). Emerging pension benefits from money purchase arrangements may also be calculated using sex-dependent factors.

However, since 21 December 2012, the use of gender-based insurance premiums has been unlawful following the 2011 CJEU ruling in the *Test-Achats* case *(see Section 30)*. This affects Purchased Life Annuities and annuities purchased by individuals with individual personal pensions. It does not directly affect occupational pensions, nor group personal pensions 'arranged by employers', although annuities purchased by members of such schemes as part of the normal open market option process are affected.

Contracting-out problems

Formerly contracted-out schemes have particular difficulties in equalising the benefits they provide because GMPs accrued at different rates and are required to come into payment at different ages for men and women. This issue was partly addressed by regulations which give contracted-out schemes some scope to provide unequal pension increases that reflect sex-related differences in the ways in which the increase in members' State pensions are calculated. However, this exemption does not fully address the problems associated with differences under the anti-franking legislation (primarily concerning increases in deferment).

In October 2018, the High Court published a ruling on the equalisation of GMPs, with regard to three schemes of Lloyds Banking Group. The Court ruled that the trustees are under a duty to equalise for the effect of GMPs and that several methods can be used to achieve this. In addition, the employer can require that the minimum cost option be adopted. The ruling helps to address the long-running uncertainty surrounding the requirements and assists other trustees in addressing the issue. Given the complexity of the possible methods, the ruling is expected to have significant implications for schemes contracted out between 1990 and 1997.

Time limits for bringing claims and backdating membership

The ECJ (now CJEU) ruling in the indirect sex discrimination part-timer case of *Preston v Wolverhampton (see Section 30)* and subsequent UK legislation require that:

- claims for unlawful equal treatment must be brought to industrial tribunals within six months of leaving service, *and*
- individuals may claim backdated membership in respect of service back to 8 April 1976.

Maternity, adoption and paternity leave

The Equality Act 2010 (and previously the Employment Rights Act 1996) requires *all* benefits in kind, including pension accrual, to be maintained during *statutory* ordinary maternity leave (whether paid or unpaid). The Employment Act 2002 gave similar rights to adoptive parents with the introduction of statutory adoption leave, and also introduced new requirements for continued pension accrual during statutory paternity leave and statutory parental leave.

Legislation also requires all *paid* maternity, adoption and paternity absence to be treated as a period of normal service as far as an employer-related benefit scheme is concerned. When assessing benefits (or employer contributions to a money purchase occupational scheme) it should be assumed that the normal pay for the job was received. However, the member is required to pay contributions based only on the remuneration actually received. For paid (but non-statutory) 'family leave' (other than maternity, adoption or paternity leave), legislation only requires benefits to be based on actual (not on normal) remuneration.

Since 5 April 2015 the mother has been able to share 50 of her 52 weeks of maternity leave with the father (or other person), subject to conditions. Shared parental leave provides more flexibility than the previous provisions for additional statutory paternity leave. After the initial two weeks, which can only be taken by the mother, the remaining period can be shared and can be taken successively or concurrently, with pay and conditions applying as they would have for maternity leave.

State pension ages

Since November 2018, State pension age has been equalised for men and women, initially at 65 *(see Section 1)*.

EQUAL TREATMENT FOR PART-TIMERS

UK regulations implementing the EU part-time worker directive came into force on 1 July 2000. A part-timer cannot be treated less favourably than a 'comparable' full-timer, unless the less favourable treatment is justified on objective grounds. The regulations provide that, in determining whether or not treatment is unfavourable, a 'pro-rata' principle applies, 'unless it is inappropriate'. The extent to which it is legal to provide inferior (or no) benefits to part-timers (on grounds such as non-comparability with full-timers, 'objective justification' or inappropriateness of a pro rata principle) is only likely to become clear as case law is built up. For example, see *Ministry of Justice v O'Brien (see Section 30)*. Complaints by individuals under this legislation must generally be taken to an employment tribunal within three months of the last day on which they consider they were unfavourably treated.

EQUAL TREATMENT FOR FIXED-TERM WORKERS

UK regulations implementing the EU fixed-term worker directive came into force on 1 October 2002. Direct discrimination against fixed-term workers in relation to terms and conditions including pensions is prohibited when compared to permanent employees, unless it is justified on objective grounds. The regulations specifically provide that less favourable treatment in relation to some contractual terms is objectively justified where the fixed-term employee's overall employment package is no less favourable than that of a comparable permanent employee. Complaints by individuals under this legislation must generally be taken to an employment tribunal within three months of the last day on which they consider they were unfavourably treated.

Separate UK regulations implemented the EU agency workers directive with effect from 1 October 2011. These do not cover participation in occupational pension schemes but workers are eligible for the auto-enrolment provisions *(see Sections 3 and 4)*.

EQUAL TREATMENT AND SEXUAL ORIENTATION

The deemed non-discrimination rule under the Equality Act 2010 prevents trustees and employers from discriminating against, harassing or victimising members and prospective members on grounds of sexual orientation or gender reassignment. However, preventing or restricting access to a benefit by reference to marital status remains lawful (*but see below*), as do discriminatory benefits in respect of service before 1 December 2003.

The Civil Partnership Act took effect from 5 December 2005. It introduced a facility for same-sex partners to register civil partnerships and thereby receive increased legal recognition. It extended the divorce pension sharing and earmarking regulations and social security legislation in line with the principle that civil partners should be treated in the same way as opposite-sex married people. Under the Act, the same contracted-out benefits must be provided to civil partners as to spouses for all service after 5 April 1988. In addition, subsequent legislation requires all schemes to treat civil partners in the same way as spouses for service on or after 5 December 2005.

The Marriage (Same Sex Couples) Act 2013 came into force on 13 March 2014 in England and Wales (similar provisions came into force in Scotland on 16 December 2014), allowing same-sex couples to marry. The provisions require occupational pension schemes to provide benefits for most same-sex spouses only in the same way as for civil partners, rather than opposite-sex spouses.

However, the July 2017 Supreme Court ruling in the case of *Innospec v Walker (see Section 30)* means that civil partners and same-sex spouses are entitled to a spouse's pension in respect of all service, and not just service on or after 5 December 2005. At the time of writing, the legislation is expected to be reviewed in light of this ruling.

The Gender Recognition Act came into force on 4 April 2005. It is designed to give formal recognition to transsexuals who successfully register in their acquired gender.

EQUAL TREATMENT AND RACE, RELIGION OR BELIEF

The deemed non-discrimination rule under the Equality Act 2010 prevents trustees and employers from discriminating against, harassing or victimising members and prospective members on grounds of race, religion or belief. The anti-discrimination requirements cover admission to schemes as well as treatment once admitted. Particularly in the realm of indirect discrimination, potential issues could possibly arise for pension schemes, for example where all investment funds offered under a money purchase arrangement are unacceptable to members of a particular religion.

EQUAL TREATMENT AND DISABILITY

The deemed non-discrimination rule under the Equality Act 2010 prevents trustees and employers from discriminating against, harassing or victimising members and prospective members on grounds of disability. Trustees are also required to make 'reasonable adjustments'. Both direct and indirect discrimination can potentially be objectively justified as a 'proportionate means of achieving a legitimate aim'. Although the legislation does not in general affect benefits earned before October 2004, it does extend to communications with members in relation to such rights.

EQUAL TREATMENT AND AGE

Regulations under the Equality Act 2010 replaced identical age discrimination legislation, which mostly took effect from 1 October 2006, although the provisions relating to pensions took effect from 1 December 2006.

Both direct and indirect discrimination by employers and by trustees of pension schemes are prohibited, unless such a practice can be objectively justified as a 'proportionate means of achieving a legitimate aim'. There are a number of occupational pension scheme practices that are specifically exempted from being age-discriminatory. These include:

- the use of a minimum or maximum age for admission to a scheme
- the use of age-based actuarial factors in benefit calculations
- the use of a maximum period of service for benefit calculations
- limiting the payment of benefits to a minimum age
- the application of age restrictions which would be required to ensure the scheme is eligible for taxation concessions under the Finance Act 2004
- the provision of age-related employer contributions to money purchase schemes, where the aim is to provide benefits that do not vary by age of member (or to provide 'more nearly equal' benefits) in respect of each year of pensionable service, *and*
- the payment of equal contributions to money purchase schemes, irrespective of age, even though this will provide different levels of benefit to members of different ages.

Many previously common occupational pension scheme practices are, however, not exempt under the legislation. For example, benefit accrual may not generally cease at a fixed retirement age. In addition, there is a great deal of uncertainty concerning how much of the legislation will be interpreted, and clarification is expected to emerge only slowly as actual cases are considered by tribunals and courts.

The Equality Act 2010 retained a default retirement age of 65, but this was abolished with effect from 1 October 2011. Employers wishing to dismiss or retire an older employee will need to go through a fair procedure. A compulsory retirement age will be permitted only if it can be objectively justified as a proportionate means of achieving a legitimate aim. There is an exemption, however, which allows group risk insured benefits provided by employers to cease at age 65.

Complaints by individuals under this legislation must generally be taken to an employment tribunal within three months of the last day on which they consider they were unfavourably treated. A number of court cases, both in the UK and in Europe (such as *Seldon v Clarkson Wright and Jakes* and *Rosenbladt v Oellerking – see Section 30*), have considered whether an employer can objectively justify maintaining a compulsory retirement age. These provide guidance on the factors that can be considered in determining whether compulsory retirement can be objectively justified.

SECTION 17

PENSIONS AND DIVORCE

Courts are required to take benefits under pension schemes into account when considering financial provision on divorce. In many cases, this may be achieved by making a divorce settlement which distributes other marital assets in such a way as to keep pension rights intact. However, there are also two alternative approaches available for allowing one party to the divorce to benefit directly from the benefit entitlements under a pension scheme of the other party.

The first alternative, *earmarking*, was introduced in 1996 but is now rarely used. It orders a specified portion of a scheme member's benefits to be paid instead to his or her ex-spouse.

The second alternative, *pension sharing*, was introduced in 2000 and results in a 'clean break' between the divorcing parties. This is the option on which we focus in this Section.

A pension share may be triggered by a UK court order. However, where the divorce is governed by Scots law, a pension share might instead be triggered by a corresponding provision in a 'qualifying agreement' made between the divorcing parties. In the remainder of this Section, references to orders should be read to include provisions under qualifying agreements.

The provisions for pension sharing (and earmarking) also apply when civil partnerships are dissolved. In the remainder of this Section, 'divorce' should be read to include 'dissolution of civil partnership', 'ex-spouse' to include 'ex-civil partner' etc., as the context requires. The provisions apply equally to same-sex and opposite-sex marriages.

PENSION SHARING

Provision of information

Where schemes have been asked for a valuation of pension rights in connection with a divorce, they must supply this and other basic information within three months of the request; or within six weeks, where the member has notified them that proceedings for financial provision on divorce have commenced; or within such shorter period as may be specified in a court order. If no benefit valuation is to be included the basic information must be provided within one month. Further information must be provided within 21 days of being notified that a pension sharing order may be made, unless the prescribed information has already been supplied. Additional information requirements arise subsequently if it is decided that a pension sharing order will be made.

What rights may be shared?

All rights under occupational and personal pensions and retirement annuity policies (including pensions in payment and annuities or insurance policies purchased to give effect to any such rights) may be shared. However, the regulations exclude survivors' pensions payable as a result of a previous marriage. SERPS/S2P rights are also included, but the State Graduated Scheme and the Basic State Pension are not. The new State Pension *(see Section 1)* is not generally shareable; however, where under transitional arrangements an individual's Starting Amount is greater than the standard rate, the excess is shareable. Compensation payments under the PPF *(see Section 20)* may be shared on divorce and on dissolution of a civil partnership.

What triggers pension sharing?

Any decision on sharing is triggered by a court order between the parties. The order is stayed until any appeals process has been completed. The order is expressed in terms of a transfer from one party to the other of a percentage of rights accrued prior to the date the order takes effect. In Scotland, these rights are restricted to those that accrued during the marriage and the transfer can alternatively be expressed as a fixed amount.

Rights to be provided to ex-spouse

The person receiving a share of his or her ex-spouse's rights usually has to be offered a transfer value in respect of those rights. Rights under unfunded schemes, including state benefits, are excluded from this requirement.

Schemes that are obliged to offer an external transfer to another suitable pension arrangement may, but do not have to, offer the ex-spouse the alternative option of a pension credit benefit within the scheme calculated on the scheme's normal transfer-in basis. Ex-spouse members of pension schemes are, essentially, treated like deferred pensioners. If the ex-spouse is also an employee member of the scheme that provides the pension credit benefit, in most cases the scheme can insist that, on taking a subsequent cash equivalent, both sets of rights are transferred.

Basis of calculation for sharing

Calculations for pension sharing are based on the scheme's current established cash equivalent basis, extended to cover cases (like pensions in payment) where a transfer value would not normally arise. There is a facility for transfer values for ex-spouses (along with other transfer values) to be reduced if the scheme is underfunded. However, the legislation provides that such a reduction is to be applied only if the ex-spouse has been offered (but has declined) the alternative of a pension credit benefit within the scheme based on the unreduced transfer value.

Pension credit benefits

Pension credit benefits, if offered under the scheme, should be determined on the incoming transfer value basis, with appropriate adjustments where added-years pensions are normally awarded and the ex-spouse is not an active member of the scheme. Benefits are generally payable from normal benefit age but can be paid early where the member has attained normal minimum pension age or qualifies for an ill-health pension. Pension credit benefits can also be partially commuted for a pension commencement lump sum, or fully commuted in certain circumstances. Pension credit benefits provided on a money purchase basis can be used to take advantage of the flexibilities introduced in 2015 to the extent permitted under the scheme rules. Alternatively, pension credit benefits may be transferred to a different arrangement in order to access these flexibilities. The regulations require LPI indexation of any defined benefits derived from post-97 rights (other than those derived from AVCs). For this purpose, LPI is capped at 5% if the pension credit benefit was awarded before 6 April 2005, or 2.5% if awarded after 5 April 2005. Schemes are not prevented from indexing the whole of the pension credit benefit, in order to simplify administration.

Pension debits

In defined benefit schemes, the member's benefit becomes subject to a debit, designed to be of equal value to the amount transferred to the ex-spouse. For non-pensioners, this is, essentially, a negative deferred pension. Each part of the member's vested benefit entitlement immediately prior to the date the pension sharing order takes effect is reduced in the same proportion (including contracted-out benefits). Defined contribution scheme debits are the stipulated proportion of the fund value or, if applicable, of the benefit already in payment.

Timing of implementation

Schemes generally have four months, after the date the relevant court order takes effect or (if later) receipt of all relevant divorce documentation and personal information about the divorcing parties, to implement the pension share in accordance with the option chosen by the ex-spouse. If no valid instructions are given, the pension share can be implemented in accordance with the scheme's chosen default procedure. The Pensions Regulator may (on application) extend the implementation period, in circumstances broadly similar to those which apply for the late payment of normal cash equivalents.

Expense charges

Schemes are allowed to charge the divorcing parties for costs reasonably incurred in providing information for and implementing the pension share, and are usually able to insist on receiving these before they have to provide the information or implement the share. However, most charges are allowable only to the extent that they were disclosed in a Schedule of Charges at the outset, and no charge may be made for information that would be available for free under the Disclosure requirements *(see Section 15)*. The trustees can require that the charges are paid in cash, with deduction from the benefits being an alternative. Only costs specifically relating to an individual divorce case can be charged (so, for example, costs involved in setting up administrative procedures to deal with pension sharing may not be passed on).

Tax treatment

The benefits tested against an individual's lifetime allowance *(see Section 9)* are the actual benefits payable after taking account of a pension debit or credit. Therefore in most circumstances a pension credit received by someone will normally count against their lifetime allowance, whereas individuals whose benefits are reduced by pension debits will usually have scope within their lifetime allowance to rebuild the lost rights unless those benefits were already in payment.

If an entitlement to a pension credit relates to a pension put in payment after 5 April 2006, the ex-spouse can apply for an increased lifetime allowance within a prescribed timescale.

The tax treatment of pension credits and debits for individuals whose benefits are protected under transitional arrangements *(see Section 9)* will depend on the type of protection. *See below for restrictions on rebuilding rights, and the possible loss or reduction of protection, under different types of protection.*

Under *primary protection*, a divorcing member with protection will see his or her lifetime allowance reduced to take account of a post-5 April 2006 pension debit.

Under *enhanced protection*, for a divorcing member with protection, rights lost under a defined benefit or cash balance arrangement as a result of a post-5 April 2006 pension debit can – in general – be rebuilt, although this would not be possible under a money purchase arrangement. An ex-spouse would lose enhanced protection if a post-5 April 2006 pension credit paid to his or her defined benefit or cash balance arrangement caused the permitted limits to be breached. However, enhanced protection is not lost if the pension credit is paid to a money purchase arrangement that is not a cash balance arrangement, provided that this arrangement existed at 5 April 2006.

Under *fixed protection, fixed protection 2014* and *fixed protection 2016* there is limited scope in defined benefit and cash balance arrangements for a divorcing member to rebuild some of the lost rights without losing protection. An ex-spouse's protection will not be lost if a pension credit is paid to a money purchase arrangement that is not a cash balance arrangement, provided that the arrangement existed at 5 April 2012, 2014 or 2016 as appropriate. If it is paid into an existing defined benefit or cash balance arrangement, protection will be lost if the limit on the increase in benefits for the tax year is exceeded.

Under *individual protection 2014* and *individual protection 2016*, where a divorcing member with protection is subject to a pension debit after 5 April 2014 or 2016 respectively, the lifetime allowance will be reduced to take account of the debit.

SECTION 18

PENSION SCHEME FUNDING

Actuarial valuations are central to the process of funding defined benefit (DB) schemes. They are also used for other purposes, including accounting for pension costs *(see Section 26)*. In this section, we consider the concept of a valuation in principle, the requirements for a scheme funding valuation under the Pensions Act 2004 (reflecting the Pensions Regulator's Code of Practice and funding policy), the potential impact of the Government's 2018 White Paper on protecting DB pension schemes, alternative financing and the latest developments in monitoring scheme funding.

Trustees and sponsors may have more than one funding target. Some trustees have developed 'flight plans', which set out how they intend to achieve their ultimate objectives – perhaps de-risking the scheme or securing benefits with an insurance company – and the White Paper encourages trustees to set appropriate long-term objectives and take these into account in scheme funding.

ACTUARIAL VALUATIONS

Different types of valuation may be called for in different circumstances. The basic principles of two of the main types, 'ongoing' and 'solvency' valuations, are described briefly below.

Ongoing valuation

When a DB scheme is established, the actuary's calculations of the amount of contributions to be paid have to be based on assumptions about how the scheme will evolve. However, events will invariably unfold differently from the original assumptions, and it is necessary to examine the scheme periodically to value the assets and liabilities and to revise the contribution rate.

To value the liabilities, the actuary receives relevant individual details of the scheme's active, retired and deferred members. Data relating to changes in membership since the previous valuation may also be supplied to enable a reconciliation of the membership numbers to be carried out and to test actual experience against the assumptions of the last valuation.

Various assumptions need to be made; these are financial (e.g. the discount rate and rates of salary and pension increases) and demographic (e.g. rates of mortality, ill-health, commutation, early retirement and leaving service). The starting point for the financial assumptions is often either the yields on fixed-interest and index-linked securities or anticipated returns on other scheme assets at the valuation date. Valuations may be based on a 'yield curve', reflecting the variation in market yields by term, or a single flat-rate approximation.

Various different valuation methods are used according to the individual needs of the scheme and the employer, and to meet statutory requirements.

The differences only relate to the valuation of 'active members' – the most common method is the *Projected Unit Method*, which allows for expected salary increases to retirement, leaving service or death, as appropriate. An alternative is the *Current Unit Method* in which members are assumed to leave service at the end of a specified period.

The actuary also requires details of the assets held by the scheme. Assets are given at market value in the audited accounts, and this is the value that is used in actuarial valuations in conjunction with market-based yields for valuing liabilities. Some assets, such as insurance policies, may not have an appropriate value in the accounts, and the actuary will need to calculate a value that is consistent with the value applied to the corresponding liabilities (or possibly exclude such assets, and the corresponding liabilities).

Solvency valuation

The solvency, or discontinuance, valuation assesses whether the scheme's assets would be sufficient to cover the liabilities if the scheme were to be discontinued at the valuation date and no further contributions were received from the employer. The liability for active members is usually based on service to and salary at the valuation date. Future expenses should be allowed for.

This assessment can be made on various bases. However, the scheme funding legislation *discussed below* requires the actuary to disclose the extent to which the assets of the scheme would be sufficient, at the valuation date, to cover the liabilities assessed on an annuity buy-out basis. As an alternative to using the cost actually quoted by a suitable insurance company for buying out the benefits at the valuation date, the actuary may use an estimate of the buy-out cost based on the principles likely to be adopted by an insurance company. Liabilities must include a realistic allowance for expenses. Assets must be taken at market value although adjustments can be made for some assets, such as insurance policies *(see above)*.

SCHEME FUNDING UNDER THE PENSIONS ACT 2004

Under the 'statutory funding objective', a DB scheme is required to 'have sufficient and appropriate assets to cover its technical provisions', i.e. 'the amount required, on an actuarial calculation, to make provision for the scheme's liabilities'. Regulations require the technical provisions to be determined on a (normally 'ongoing') scheme-specific basis. There is no legal requirement for schemes to fund on a prescribed basis. Each actuarial valuation must, however, include an estimate by the actuary of the solvency of the scheme, *as described above*. The trustees have ultimate responsibility for the funding decisions, but are required to take advice from the scheme actuary and – normally – to obtain the employer's agreement. However, where the trustees have power under the scheme's rules to set contribution rates without the employer's agreement, that requirement is replaced by one for consultation (although agreement should be obtained if possible). If the rules provide for the actuary to determine the contributions, the trustees and employer must still agree the contributions payable, but in addition the actuary's certification of the schedule of contributions *(see below)* must state that the contributions are not lower than the actuary would have set had he or she had responsibility for preparing the schedule, the statement of funding principles and any recovery plan *(see below)*.

Actuarial valuations are required with effective dates no more than three years apart, with additional written 'actuarial reports', covering developments since the last valuation, in each intervening year (for schemes with 100 or more members). There is a general exception from the scheme funding requirement for schemes in wind-up, conditional upon the preparation of annual solvency estimates by the scheme actuary (on a buy-out basis) and a winding-up procedure *(see Section 23)*.

Cross-border schemes *(see Section 2)* are subject to more onerous requirements, including a specified deadline for meeting the statutory funding objective and full actuarial valuations every 12 months. At the time of writing, it is not clear how these schemes will be impacted by the UK's decision to leave the European Union.

The Regulator has competing objectives – to protect members' benefits; to reduce the risk of calls on the PPF; and 'to minimise any adverse impact on the sustainable growth of an employer' in relation to scheme funding *(see Section 8)*. The Regulator's Code of Practice and funding policy reflect these objectives.

Integrated risk management

The Regulator expects integrated risk management to be embedded within a scheme's governance framework and has published guidance on this approach. In the annual scheme return, it requests details of any 'Value at Risk' calculations schemes use to review and monitor risks. Trustees should seek to understand the risks across scheme funding, employer's covenant and investment.

The Code of Practice states that trustees should understand the strength of the employer's covenant and that this involves forming a view of the covenant now, and how it could grow and develop in the future. In 2015, the Regulator published guidance on 'assessing and monitoring the employer covenant'. The guidance sets out good practice on how to assess and monitor an employer's covenant – the employer's legal obligation and its financial ability to support the scheme now and in the future.

Particular considerations apply to multi-employer schemes and the Regulator has produced specific guidance on 'Multi-employer schemes and employer departures'. Trustees also need to identify the scheme's 'statutory employers' on their scheme returns. A statutory employer is responsible for some or all of: scheme funding, any debt on the employer *(see Section 25)* and triggering entry into the PPF *(see Section 20)*.

On investment, the Code sets out considerations for trustees in setting their investment strategy. They should engage with the employer as they develop this, even where this is not required by law. Trustees should understand the scheme's potential reliance on the employer over time based on a range of scenarios which capture investment risk. The Regulator published 'Investment guidance for defined benefit pension schemes' in 2017.

Statement of funding principles

The trustees must have a written statement of funding principles (SFP) setting out their policy for securing that the statutory funding objective is met and recording decisions as to the basis for calculating the technical provisions and the period within which any shortfall is to be remedied. The SFP must be reviewed at each valuation and, if amended, finalised (along with the valuation report and schedule of contributions) within 15 months of the effective date of the valuation.

Calculation of technical provisions

The trustees must choose an 'accrued benefits' funding method, such as the projected unit method *(see above)*, for calculating the technical provisions.

It is also the trustees' responsibility (having received advice from the scheme actuary) to choose the assumptions to be adopted for the calculation of the scheme's technical provisions. The trustees should also agree the assumptions with the employer (unless there is only a requirement for consultation – *see above*).

Legislation requires the assumptions to be chosen 'prudently', taking account, if applicable, of an appropriate margin for adverse deviation. The Regulator's Code of Practice states that assessment of the employer's covenant is required, as part of an integrated approach to risk management *(see above)*, to inform decisions on both the technical provisions and the recovery plan.

Recovery plan

If an actuarial valuation shows that the statutory funding objective is not met, the trustees must prepare a 'recovery plan' setting out the steps to be taken (and over what period) to make up the shortfall. The current Code of Practice states that trustees should aim for the shortfall to be eliminated 'over an appropriate period'. A copy of the recovery plan must be sent to the Regulator.

Schedule of contributions

The trustees must have in place a schedule of contributions setting out the rates and due dates of contributions payable to the scheme, which will normally have been agreed with the employer (unless there is only a requirement for consultation – *see above*). The schedule must be certified by the actuary, stating that the funding objective can be expected to continue to be met whilst the schedule is in force, or to be met by the end of the recovery period. In the latter case, a copy of the schedule must be sent to the Regulator. If contributions are not paid or are paid late, the trustees (and actuary or auditor, if they become aware of this) must inform the Regulator (and must alert members) if they believe that the failure is likely to be 'of material significance'.

Regulator's approach

The Regulator publishes annual statements on scheme funding. It believes that if trustees and employers follow the guidance in these statements, they will be more likely to reach funding agreements that will avoid the need for regulatory involvement. Where an approach is not in line with the statement, the Regulator will consider the case in more depth. The Regulator also pro-actively engages with some schemes from an early stage of their valuation process.

The Regulator's funding policy document sets out how it assesses risk and defines acceptable outcomes on an annual basis, how it identifies schemes to investigate, how it intervenes and how it measures its impact. It places schemes into one of four segments based on employer covenant: strong, tending to strong, tending to weak and weak. It then applies a Funding Risk Indicator, which, along with a suite of other risk indicators, is taken into account in deciding whether intervention is necessary. The majority of schemes receive an acknowledgement confirming that the Regulator has no further questions.

The Regulator also has powers to intervene in cases where agreement cannot be reached between the trustees and employer or where the actuary is unable to provide the necessary certification. In addition, the Regulator has powers to intervene if it views the technical provisions as insufficiently prudent, even if the trustees and employer are in agreement. Possible courses of action include imposing a funding basis, modifying future accrual and freezing or winding up the scheme. The Regulator has published a number of reports under section 89 of the Pensions Act 2004, setting out its consideration of the use of its powers in particular cases, in respect of scheme funding and other regulatory issues.

In its 2018 annual funding statement, the Regulator stated that 'We are now clearer about what we expect from trustees, are quicker to act and are tougher on those who fail to act in the interests of members'. The statement indicates that it will fine trustees who are late submitting a valuation – unless they have acted responsibly and taken all reasonable steps to finalise it, and there remains a genuine reason why the valuation cannot be finalised.

Recently, the Regulator used its long-standing power under section 231 of the Pensions Act 2004 to impose a schedule of contributions for the first time.

White Paper on protecting defined benefit pension schemes

In March 2018, the Government published a White Paper on protecting defined benefit pension schemes, including proposals relating to scheme funding. It proposes to strengthen the Regulator's ability to enforce funding standards through a revised and 'enforceable' Code of Practice, which will focus on:

- how prudence is demonstrated when assessing scheme liabilities
- appropriate factors when considering recovery plans, *and*
- ensuring a long-term view is considered when setting the statutory funding objective.

A revised Code is expected to be consulted on in 2019.

Disclosure to members

Schemes are required to send members a 'summary funding statement', following each actuarial valuation or actuarial report, including information about the funding and solvency positions of the scheme and an explanation of any changes since the previous statement *(see Section 15)*.

Refunds of surplus

A power to repay surplus from the scheme to an employer can only be exercised by the trustees (subject to the agreement of the employer, if the power was originally conferred on the employer) and only if it is in the members' interests and they have been notified.

Furthermore, a payment of surplus from the scheme to the employer will only be permitted to the extent that the scheme's assets exceed the full buy-out cost of the accrued liabilities, as indicated by a valuation carried out under the Pensions Act 2004 funding regime or a special valuation carried out for this purpose.

ALTERNATIVE FINANCING

A significant number of schemes have put in place funding mechanisms that go beyond just paying cash into the pension scheme. Some of these arrangements are treated as assets of the scheme, and those that are not aim to increase the strength of the employer's covenant and the overall security of the pension scheme. These mechanisms help create pensions stability by bridging the gap between the views of the employer and the trustees in relation to issues such as funding strategy, investment strategy and change in employer covenant, for example during corporate activity *(see Section 25)*.

There are a number of types of alternative financing that have been used to date, including:

- transferring company assets (e.g. property or brand names) to the scheme, an escrow account or a special purpose vehicle (also known as asset-backed contributions) which the scheme owns fully or partially; the trustees might initially just have a right to an income stream from the assets, with final ownership to be determined at a later stage, possibly depending on the funding position of the scheme and other circumstances at that time
- contingent assets, such as group company guarantees, security over assets, surety bonds and bank letters of credit, which pay out to the scheme if a specified event occurs, such as employer insolvency or increased employer borrowing; certain forms of contingent asset can reduce a scheme's PPF levy *(see Section 20), and*
- market instruments such as credit default swaps, which pay out if a company defaults on its corporate bond payments.

Trustees need to take specialist advice on the suitability of a proposed alternative financing arrangement, including on any legal issues such as employer-related investment. Ongoing advice is needed to ensure that it continues to be available if needed and is properly enforceable.

The Regulator's guidance on assessing and monitoring the employer covenant and its guidance on asset-backed contributions set out considerations for trustees in relation to such arrangements.

MONITORING FUNDING

Although legislation only requires trustees to monitor their scheme's funding position once a year, in practice they typically monitor it more frequently. A common approach is for trustees to look at funding quarterly or monthly, but increasingly they also expect up-to-date funding positions to be readily available whenever they need them. Similarly, sponsors increasingly expect accounting figures to be available whenever they require them.

Online tools now make this achievable, by maintaining up-to-date estimates of the scheme's funding position – on funding, accounting and solvency bases – so that trustees and sponsors have access to that information whenever they need it.

Such tools also facilitate more dynamic investment strategies. Many schemes now have 'flight plans', which include agreed actions to take when scheme funding reaches certain levels – and ensure a scheme is well placed to address the White Paper's proposals on long-term planning. Automated daily updates, linked to emails alerting trustees or advisers when pre-determined triggers are reached, allow agreed actions to be taken at the right time, and ensure opportunities are not missed.

SECTION 19

LONGEVITY

Ongoing high life expectancy and low interest rates mean that the cost of providing pensions continues to be high. Trustees of defined benefit schemes need to understand the risks arising from changes in life expectancy and how they can manage them. For example, trustees can purchase bulk annuities or enter into longevity swaps to reduce longevity risk. The risks arising from changes in life expectancy impact upon scheme members with money purchase benefits, including where individuals make use of the money purchase flexibilities introduced in 2015 *(see Sections 9 and 14)*.

LONGEVITY RISK

Different types of mortality-related risk can be identified. One such risk, commonly referred to as 'mortality risk', is the risk of dying sooner than expected. 'Longevity risk' refers to the risk of living longer than expected. This is typically more of an issue for pension schemes, given continued increases in life expectancy and uncertainty over how these will persist. We will concentrate on 'longevity risk' in the rest of this section.

Longevity risk has different elements. Past data may tell us fairly accurately the historic mortality rates for the general population. But for any given pension scheme there is uncertainty over:

- how mortality rates for its members differ from those for the general population (because of factors like location, social class, diet and smoking)
- how mortality rates will change in the future – will past improvements continue? *and*
- whether there might be a 'jump' in mortality rates in the future (e.g. caused by an epidemic or, in the other direction, a medical breakthrough).

Longevity risk can fall on different parties depending on what type of pension scheme we are considering.

The risk under a traditional final salary scheme falls on the sponsoring employer (although members' future benefit accrual could be reduced if increases in life expectancy cause the scheme to become too expensive).

The risk under a pure money purchase scheme falls on the scheme members (since they do not know how much pension their money will buy until the point that they purchase an annuity, or how long they will live and be able to draw on their fund if they do not buy an annuity), and also on the insurance company if an annuity is purchased (since the annuity rates it sets may turn out to be wrong).

ASSUMPTIONS

To place a value on the liabilities of a defined benefit pension scheme, the trustees need to make assumptions about how long its members will live. An insurance company selling annuities needs to do the same thing in order to set its annuity rates.

Mortality rates

Life expectancies are usually calculated based on mortality rates. 'Mortality rate' in this context means the assumed probability that an individual of a given age will die in the next year. The lower the mortality rates are, the longer the life expectancy is. The assumptions needed are in two parts: the rates assumed to apply for the next 12 months (the 'base tables') and how these rates are expected to change in future years (the 'future improvement'). Different mortality rates are calculated for men and women.

Base tables

There are two approaches to determining base mortality rates using data for individual scheme members. The first is to measure the scheme's actual mortality experience. This approach is limited to larger schemes because the experience needs to be of sufficient size to be statistically credible. The second approach is to use a postcode mortality model. Such models are created using a very large set of mortality experience data derived from a number of schemes. These models relate postcodes to mortality rates by assuming similar mortality either for individuals of similar socio-economic type (typically assessed using a third-party postcode marketing database) or for individuals living in the same area (by using postcodes to determine geographic locations). These approaches may be combined in practice (whereby a pension scheme's mortality experience is combined with a postcode model, allowing for the relative statistical credibility of each).

In most cases, published standard tables are used as a starting point, which are then adjusted for the results of any analyses. These are usually tables prepared by the Continuous Mortality Investigation (CMI), a limited company wholly owned by the Institute and Faculty of Actuaries, based on data collated from life insurance companies or from self-administered pension schemes. At the time of writing, the current pension scheme CMI tables are the 'S2' series, (based on self-administered pension scheme experience from 2004 to 2011), published in 2014. The 'S3' series (based on self-administered pension scheme experience from 2009 to 2016) are due to be published in late 2018. The current insured annuitant CMI tables are the '08' series tables, published in 2015 (based on life office experience from 2007 to 2010).

If more detailed analysis is not available, the trustees and actuary may adjust the mortality rates from the standard tables based on broad principles to make them more appropriate for their own scheme's members (to reflect, for example, their locations and occupations).

Future improvements

It is normal to make an explicit allowance for expected future improvements in longevity. These are of course unknown. The CMI publishes a projections model to allow for ongoing improvements in longevity, which is usually updated annually. At the time of writing, the current version of the model is 'CMI_2017', which reflects population data for England and Wales up to 31 December 2017. The next version of the model, 'CMI_2018', is due to be released in March 2019.

Another possibility is to adopt a stochastic approach. This involves assigning an assumed probability distribution for future mortality rates and then carrying out a large number of simulations to assess the range of outcomes. (A similar approach is often used to illustrate the effect on schemes' funding levels of different rates of future investment return.)

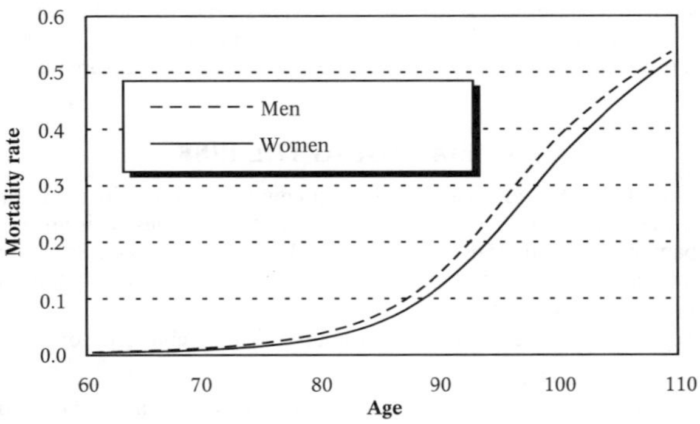

Mortality rate (probability that an individual of a given age will die in the next year)

Source: From the S2 series (pensioners, amounts), adjusted to 1 January 2019, allowing for CMI_2017 Core Projections with a long-term rate of improvement of 1.5% p.a.

LOOKING AHEAD

Predicting future improvements in longevity is extremely difficult, not least because of the huge uncertainties surrounding the impact that future events may have. Medical advances, especially the availability of life-extending medical treatments, increases in obesity, changes in social behaviours and general prosperity will all have an impact.

In the past, it was common to hear the view that life expectancy would level off in the future (because it was difficult to foresee how future improvements would arise). However, estimates based on this view have consistently underestimated future life expectancy and, as a result, it is now common to assume that the rate of mortality improvement will continue at similar levels into the future indefinitely, albeit with variation along the way. The current debate around mortality improvement focuses on whether recent rates of improvement for the population of England and Wales (which have been lower than over the period from 2000 to 2011) will revert to a higher level or whether the lower rates of improvement observed since 2012 are the new norm. Other areas of debate include how mortality improvement varies by socio-economic type and the extent to which each new year of mortality data should be reflected when projecting future improvements (bearing in mind that population deaths are volatile from year to year).

This uncertainty makes it difficult for trustees and actuaries to decide what allowance to make for future improvements in longevity. However, the Pensions Regulator's guidance on mortality assumptions for scheme-specific funding *(see Section 18)* states that, in its view, these should be chosen prudently. For base tables, the Regulator views prudence as taking a margin below best estimate rates; for future mortality improvements, the Regulator views prudence as not assuming any rates lower than are reasonable based on up-to-date evidence.

MANAGING THE RISK

There are a number of ways trustees and employers can reduce the longevity risk a defined benefit scheme faces. Purchasing annuities with an insurance company removes the longevity risk entirely *(see Section 24)*. Some financial institutions offer longevity swaps, which can reduce longevity risk in pension schemes *(see Section 21)*.

For future service, the benefit structure could be changed, to:

- money purchase
- cash balance, where a lump sum based on service and salary is used to purchase pension based on conversion terms that can change over time, *or*
- defined benefit, but where the normal retirement date is increased or a longevity adjustment factor is used to calculate pensions – for example, a factor based on a ratio of annuity values based on appropriate assumptions at the date of retirement and at a specified date in the past.

SECTION 20

THE PENSION PROTECTION FUND AND LEVIES

The Pension Protection Fund (PPF) was formally established under the Pensions Act 2004 and commenced on 6 April 2005, with the aim, in the words of the government, of 'guaranteeing members a specified minimum level of pension when the sponsoring employer becomes insolvent'.

The PPF covers eligible schemes where an insolvency event occurs to the employer on or after 6 April 2005. Schemes already in wind-up on that date are not covered by the PPF. The PPF is not underwritten by the government, but is funded by levies on eligible schemes. A separate Financial Assistance Scheme (FAS), which is funded by the government and managed by the PPF, provides assistance to members of schemes that went into wind-up on or after 1 January 1997 and were not eligible for the PPF. The Fraud Compensation Fund is also the responsibility of the PPF and covers claims from schemes that have lost assets as a result of an offence such as theft or fraud, where the employer is insolvent.

The CJEU ruling in *Hampshire v PPF* is likely to result in changes to the level of compensation paid by the PPF *(see below)* as it requires that every member receives compensation of at least 50% of the value of their accrued rights in a pension scheme in the event of the insolvency of the scheme's employer. At the time of writing, the PPF is considering what action it can take prior to legislative change and/or the conclusion of UK court proceedings.

ADMISSION

The PPF will 'assume responsibility' for 'eligible schemes' if their assets immediately before the insolvency event are insufficient to cover the 'protected liabilities' *(see below)*. 'Eligible schemes' excludes, in particular, pure money purchase schemes. 'Assuming responsibility' entails the PPF taking over the assets of the scheme and paying members the benefits provided under the 'pension compensation provisions' *(see below)*. The trustees are discharged from their obligations to pay benefits and administer the scheme.

The assessment period

During the 'assessment period', the PPF will determine whether or not the scheme is eligible. This period begins with the employer's insolvency (or, in certain circumstances, with either the trustees' application for the PPF to assume responsibility or a notification from the Pensions Regulator to the same effect). The legislation contains a lot of detail on the process for notifying insolvency events and confirming whether or not a 'scheme rescue' is possible (if, for example, the employer can continue as a going concern). Schemes must have a 'statutory employer' *(see Section 7)* in order to access the PPF; if a company supporting a pension scheme never employed any of those who have pension entitlements in the scheme, its insolvency would not trigger an assessment period.

The funding position of the scheme has to be determined, which may require an actuarial 'entry valuation' *(see below)* on a prescribed basis to be carried out. This assesses whether or not the scheme has sufficient assets to cover the 'protected liabilities' (i.e. the cost of securing the benefits provided for under the pension compensation provisions, together with any non-benefit-related liabilities and the estimated costs of wind-up). Once the PPF has determined the funding position of the scheme, normally either it will proceed to assume responsibility and issue a formal 'transfer notice' to the trustees, or (if there are sufficient assets to meet the protected liabilities) the trustees must proceed with winding up. In the latter case, the trustees can make an application to the PPF for reconsideration. Where winding up takes place, this may be subject to directions made by the PPF and/or the Regulator.

During an assessment period, various restrictions apply. Further benefits may not accrue and further contributions may not be made. Normally, transfers out are not permitted and a wind-up cannot be started. Benefit payments must be restricted to those payable under the pension compensation provisions. The PPF can also give directions to the trustees regarding, for example, scheme investment.

The assessment period ends when the 'transfer notice' is served, or when the PPF ceases to be involved with the scheme, or if the entry valuation indicates that the scheme has sufficient assets to cover its protected liabilities, normally *(but see below)* leaving it to be wound up outside the PPF. Reasons for the PPF ceasing to be involved include a scheme rescue and a refusal to assume responsibility for the scheme because it has been set up to exploit the PPF.

Closed schemes

Schemes that are too well funded to be taken on by the PPF but are too big to be able to find an insurer to buy out the liabilities must apply to the PPF to continue as 'closed schemes'. These closed schemes would then be subject to the same restrictions on contributions and accrual of benefits, and to directions from the PPF, that apply during an assessment period. Closed schemes are required to undertake regular valuations and, if at some point the assets have fallen below the value of the PPF liabilities, the PPF will then assume responsibility.

COMPENSATION

The admissible rules

The starting point for determining the benefits payable to members under the pension compensation provisions is the scheme's 'admissible rules'. Essentially, this means the rules as at the assessment date (i.e. the start of the assessment period), but disregarding rule changes within the previous three years that would increase the level of PPF compensation. Discretionary pension increases within the same period are also excluded to the extent that they exceed the increase in prices since the pension was last increased.

Discretionary early retirement pensions that came into payment under a rule that is to be disregarded may have to cease, and the PPF can review – and, if necessary, adjust – ill-health pensions granted in the last three years.

Members' and dependants' benefits

Members over NPA at the assessment date and ill-health pensioners are entitled to 100% of the level of benefits under their scheme's admissible rules. Payments made by the scheme during the assessment period are offset against the PPF compensation. Members under NPA, including those already receiving pension, are entitled to 90% of the level of accrued benefits under the admissible rules (subject to the compensation cap).

A future widow or widower is entitled to 50% of the compensation payable to the member (unless the admissible rules had no provision for a survivor's pension). A 'relevant partner' (of either sex, living with the member as 'man and wife') has the same entitlement. Benefits for children are payable until age 18 (or 25 in some circumstances); their amount depends on the number of children and on whether or not there is a widow, widower or relevant partner.

Compensation can be shared or earmarked, on divorce or dissolution of a civil partnership, in a similar way to occupational pension scheme benefits *(see Section 17)*. The resulting pension credits are retained in the PPF and cannot be transferred elsewhere.

The compensation cap

For members whose compensation is subject to the 90% restriction, the initial rate of compensation is capped at the date benefits come into payment. For 2018/19, a maximum pension of £35,106 p.a. at age 65 applies. The level of this cap increases in line with earnings each year. The PPF has set adjustment factors to derive amounts applicable where benefits come into payment at ages above and below 65. The cap is increased by 3% for every full year of service above 20 years, up to a maximum of double the standard cap.

Revaluation and indexation

Benefits not in payment and accrued before 6 April 2009 are revalued between the assessment date and NPA (or earlier retirement) in line with CPI (RPI for periods up to 31 March 2011) up to a maximum of 5% p.a. The 5% p.a. limit is reduced to 2.5% p.a. in respect of benefits accrued from 6 April 2009.

Where the scheme provides no revaluation to any member in any circumstances, legislation provides that PPF compensation benefits are not revalued.

For deferred pensioners, revaluation between date of leaving and assessment date is based on the scheme rules.

Benefits in payment are increased annually in line with inflation up to a maximum of 2.5%. Increases apply only to benefits attributable to service from 6 April 1997. RPI was originally used as the measure of inflation but this was changed to CPI from 1 January 2012.

Options

Lump sum commutation, of up to 25% of benefits, is permitted using factors specified by the PPF. Early payment of benefits from age 55 (or from the later of age 50 and the 'protected pension age', if any, that would have applied under the member's scheme) is permitted subject to actuarial reduction using factors specified by the PPF. Late payment of benefits is permitted under certain conditions, subject to actuarial increase using factors specified by the PPF. Trivial commutation and terminal ill-health lump sums are also available in certain circumstances.

Money purchase benefits

Money purchase benefits are excluded from the compensation provisions, so the PPF may direct the trustees to discharge these liabilities before entry. The money purchase flexibilities introduced in 2015 do not apply to the PPF or the compensation it pays.

Adjustments by the PPF

Where the scheme rules are such that the appropriate compensation benefits cannot be determined in accordance with the legislation, the PPF can decide the level of compensation that will apply to members.

The PPF received legal advice that it is required to equalise benefits to take account of differences in the way GMPs are calculated for men and women and has confirmed the approach to be adopted. Schemes transferring to the PPF since 1 June 2013 are required to adjust benefits during the assessment process in accordance with the PPF's guidance. For other schemes the PPF has made the necessary adjustments.

The PPF has the ability (after consultation) to adjust the rates of revaluation and increases in payment if necessary. If both of these have been reduced to zero they can recommend that the Secretary of State reduce the 90% and/or 100% levels of compensation. Such reductions would only apply in 'extreme circumstances'.

VALUATIONS

Two types of actuarial valuation are required by the PPF, each for a specific purpose – for levy calculations and to determine whether a scheme should enter the PPF.

Levy valuation

An eligible scheme must provide a 'section 179 valuation' to the PPF in order for it to determine the Pension Protection Levy payable by the scheme. These valuations must be carried out by the scheme actuary at intervals of no more than three years, and completed (and submitted via the Regulator's online 'Exchange' system) within fifteen months of the effective date.

For the purposes of the valuation, assets are generally taken at the value shown in the scheme's audited accounts.

Liabilities are valued, using assumptions set out in guidance issued by the PPF, to reflect the estimated cost of buying out the benefits with an insurance company. The benefits valued are broadly those provided under the scheme's rules, but allowing for members under NPA receiving 90% (not 100%) of benefits, the compensation cap, and the PPF levels of revaluation, indexation and spouse's pension.

Entry valuation

In most cases, a 'section 143 valuation' is required by the PPF to determine whether or not it should assume responsibility for a scheme that has entered an assessment period. The PPF will obtain this from the trustees, who will usually ask the scheme actuary to carry it out. It has to be obtained as soon as reasonably practicable after the insolvency event. Assets are generally taken at the value shown in the audited accounts. Liabilities are valued using assumptions set out in guidance issued by the PPF (which are similar to those for levy valuations but differ for some of the demographic assumptions to reflect the circumstances of the scheme), but the actual PPF compensation benefits are taken into account, rather than the broad approximations used in the section 179 valuation.

LEVIES

Schemes that are eligible for future entry to the PPF are required to pay two PPF-related levies, the Pension Protection Levy and the PPF Administration Levy. These are charged in respect of each levy year, which begins on 1 April.

Pension Protection Levy

The Pension Protection Levy consists of two parts: the risk-based levy (which must represent at least 80% of the total collected from all schemes) and the scheme-based levy. There are limits each year on the total estimated levy and the amount by which it can increase. These limits can only be changed by the Secretary of State following consultation and with the approval of the Treasury. Legislation allows the PPF to charge interest (at 5% above base rate) on any Pension Protection Levy that has not been paid within 28 days of the invoice date, although the PPF does have discretion to waive interest in certain circumstances.

The levy formula (including the risk-based levy scaling factor, risk-based levy cap and scheme-based levy multiplier – *see below*) is normally fixed for three years at a time, except in certain 'extreme' circumstances.

The current 'triennium' covers levy years 2018/19 to 2020/21. For 2018/19, the total levy estimate is £550m.

At the time of writing, the PPF has announced that for 2019/20 the proposed total levy estimate is £500m.

Risk-based levy

The risk-based levy formula is based on:

(a) The *assumed probability of insolvency of the employer* (or a weighted average probability for multi-employer schemes). The PPF uses published credit ratings, where available, and PPF-specific measures calculated by Experian for most other employers, which are largely based on financial information, as the measures of insolvency risk. Insolvency scores are averaged over a 12-month period prior to the start of each levy year (a 6-month period applied for 2018/19 only), and employers are assigned to one of ten bands.

(b) *Underfunding risk*. This is calculated as a specified percentage of the scheme's estimated PPF liabilities, averaged over the previous five years (i.e. up to the last day of the previous levy year) and also adjusted to reflect the risk posed by a scheme's investment strategy in adverse market conditions (so schemes with a riskier strategy pay a higher levy). The PPF calculates the investment risk for most schemes, but schemes with liabilities of £1.5 billion or more must carry out their own more detailed test (and smaller schemes can choose to) which takes account of a wider range of asset classes, including derivatives. Any such test must be submitted via Exchange in the same way as the valuation.

The amount is scaled to ensure that the total levy collected matches the levy estimate, and capped to protect the weakest schemes; for 2018/19, the risk-based levy scaling factor is 0.48 and the risk-based levy cap is 0.5% of a scheme's estimated PPF liabilities. At the time of writing, the PPF has announced that, subject to consultation, for 2019/20 the scaling factor will be 0.48 and the cap will be 0.5% of a scheme's estimated PPF liabilities, unchanged from 2018/19.

There are several actions that may be taken to manage a scheme's risk-based levy, including:

- *monitor an employer's insolvency measure* – there is limited scope to improve scores (other than submission of certain voluntary information), but it is important to ensure that Experian's records are correct
- *carry out the more detailed investment risk test* – schemes with liabilities of less than £1.5 billion have the option of doing this rather than relying on the PPF's default calculations
- *submit an out-of-cycle s179 valuation* to reflect action taken to improve the scheme's funding position
- *submit details of deficit reduction contributions* made since the relevant valuation date, over and above the cost of accruing scheme benefits, and as certified by an actuary (or for small schemes in certain circumstances, the trustees or employer) in accordance with guidance published by the PPF – this reduces the underfunding risk

- *put in place contingent assets* (if in a standard form and legally binding) that produce cash for the scheme when an insolvency event occurs in relation to the employer – these can be in the form of a guarantee from another group company, a charge over assets of the employer, a letter of credit or a surety bond, and they reduce the underfunding risk or the assumed insolvency probability, depending on the type of contingent asset. The PPF continues to take a strict view on the appropriateness of group company guarantees as contingent assets. Trustees are expected to fully consider guarantor strength, taking independent advice if necessary, and must submit a report, prepared by a professional adviser, to the PPF if the levy saving from the guarantee is £100,000 or higher. Trustees have to certify a 'realisable recovery' amount for use in the levy calculation, based on their assessment of the amount they could recover in an insolvency event, *and*
- *certify details of asset-backed contribution arrangements* in order for the PPF to assign any value to them. Trustees are required to obtain an insolvency valuation of the underlying assets and certify this annually.

Scheme-based levy

For 2018/19, the scheme-based levy is calculated as 0.0021% of a scheme's estimated PPF liabilities. At the time of writing, the PPF has announced that, subject to consultation, for 2019/20 the scheme-based levy multiplier will remain at 0.0021% of a scheme's estimated PPF liabilities.

PPF Administration Levy

This is charged to meet the costs of running the PPF (other than the cost of paying compensation). It is based on the number of members on the last day of the scheme year which ended before the beginning of the previous levy year, and (for 2017/18 onwards) ranges from £4.88 per member (for schemes with 12 to 99 members) to £1.45 per member (for schemes with 10,000 or more members but subject to a minimum of £20,700). It is invoiced with the General Levy *(see Section 8)*, and not with the Pension Protection Levy.

FINANCIAL ASSISTANCE SCHEME

The Financial Assistance Scheme (FAS) provides government-funded support for members of underfunded pension schemes which began to be wound up between 1 January 1997 and 22 December 2008 and in limited other circumstances, where the scheme was not eligible to enter the PPF but met other eligibility criteria. In response to the requirement for there to be a 'statutory employer' *(see Section 7)* if a scheme is to enter the PPF, regulations enabled pension schemes to qualify for the FAS if they began winding up between 23 December 2008 and 27 March 2014 and the connection with the last statutory employer was severed before 10 June 2011. From 1 September 2016, the FAS ceased to accept notifications from schemes, or assess schemes for FAS eligibility.

The FAS provides a top-up to a member's benefits so that the total benefits received by the member are broadly the same as those provided by the PPF. Members who would receive higher benefits from the scheme's assets under the statutory priority order maintain that higher level of benefit.

When the FAS was set up, it did not cover all schemes described above, and was restricted to pensioners and members near retirement. The level of FAS benefits has also been increased over time, as the original benefits were much lower than those provided by the PPF.

The FAS initially provided top-up payments, after the scheme had been wound up and members' benefits had been bought out with an insurance company. (Schemes dealt with in this way are now referred to as 'FAS1' schemes.) However, with effect from 26 September 2007, schemes eligible for FAS support were prohibited from purchasing annuities where they had not already done so. From April 2010, the government has taken on the assets of these 'FAS2' schemes and made combined payments of scheme and FAS benefits to members. The PPF now manages the FAS and is aiming to have transferred all FAS1 schemes to the government by 2018, and all FAS2 schemes by 2019. FAS compensation is subject to an equalisation process in respect of GMPs, similar to that for the PPF *(see above)*.

FRAUD COMPENSATION FUND

An occupational pension scheme that has lost assets as a result of an offence (such as theft or fraud) committed after 6 April 1997 may be eligible for compensation if the employer is insolvent. The amount of any compensation payment is determined by the PPF, and is limited to the amount of any loss that cannot reasonably be recovered. Applications for compensation may be made by the trustees, administrators or scheme members.

The Fund is financed by a Fraud Compensation Levy, potentially payable by all schemes eligible for this compensation (a wider group than for the PPF). For the amount of the Fraud Compensation Levy *see Section 8.*

SECTION 21

LIABILITY MANAGEMENT EXERCISES

In recent years, employers have looked at a number of ways of managing defined benefit (DB) liabilities. A common theme is the reduction of risk and, in some cases, possible improvement in the financial position of the scheme for funding or accounting purposes. Some of the approaches which have been considered are outlined below.

There has been a large increase in transfer values paid out of DB schemes since the money purchase flexibilities were introduced in 2015 *(see Section 9 and Section 14)*, particularly for members close to retirement. This has fuelled an increase in flexible retirement offers (FROs) being made to DB members over 55.

MEMBER OPTIONS

There are a number of options that can be offered to members to change the structure of their benefits within a DB scheme or to remove liability for these benefits altogether.

Flexible retirement offer (FRO)

It is becoming increasingly common to manage risk through a FRO where members who are of an age where they can take their benefits (age 55 for most schemes) have the option to transfer all or part of their benefits out of the scheme at the point of retirement *(see Section 13)*. These offers can allow members to benefit from the money purchase flexibilities *(see Section 14)*, or to receive other benefits that better suit their circumstances.

A FRO can be offered as a standard option to members when they request details of their retirement options, or carried out as a bulk exercise across a group of members and actively communicated to those members.

The transferred liabilities – and associated risks – are removed from the scheme and, depending on the terms of the transfer, the scheme's funding position can also be improved.

Pension increase exchange (PIE) exercises

Under a PIE exercise:

- an offer could be made to existing pensioners to exchange future increases on part of their pension for a higher immediate, but non-increasing, pension, *and/or*
- an option could be given to members to exchange the increases on part of their pension when it comes into payment for a higher, level pension at retirement.

In either case, some elements of pension, such as benefit relating to post-5 April 1997 service, will need to continue to be increased to meet statutory requirements.

These exercises are typically proposed by sponsoring employers, as a way of reducing exposure to inflation and longevity risk. Depending on the terms of the conversion, the employer might also benefit from an improvement in the scheme's funding position and/or their accounting results. Some members may find the immediate increase to their pension more attractive than protection against the impact of inflation.

There can be significant legal issues depending on the terms of the conversion *(see comments under 'Scheme modifications' in Section 2)*. Scheme amendment powers would need detailed consideration and there are also potential tax issues to consider as an increase in annual pension may trigger an annual allowance and/or lifetime allowance charge *(see Section 9)*.

Enhanced transfer value (ETV) exercises

Under ETV exercises, members are encouraged to transfer their defined benefits elsewhere, through the offer of an enhancement to the standard transfer value. The enhancement is usually only available for a limited period.

These exercises are typically proposed by sponsoring employers as a way of reducing exposure to investment and longevity risk. The employer might also benefit from an improvement in the scheme's funding position and/or their accounting results. This is because the value placed on benefits for funding or accounting purposes can significantly exceed the statutory minimum transfer value *(see Section 13)*, which is broadly equal to the expected cost of providing the benefit within the scheme. This means there is usually scope to pay a higher transfer value, whilst still remaining below the prudent reserves targeted for scheme funding *(see Section 18)*. This enhanced transfer value may be attractive to some members.

It is a statutory requirement for transferring schemes to check that individuals whose total DB transfer value from the scheme would be broadly over £30,000 have taken independent financial advice before transferring *(see Section 13)*. Where the transfer is part of an employer-led transfer exercise, the employer would need to pay for such advice.

Code of Good Practice and Regulator guidance

An industry Code of Good Practice on Incentive Exercises (which includes bulk PIE and ETV exercises) sets a benchmark for such exercises. The Code was reviewed in 2018 when it was concluded that it remained fit for purpose. The Code is voluntary and has no legal standing. There is however an expectation that employers, trustees and their advisers will follow the spirit and principles of the Code and not look for creative ways to work around it. The Pensions Act 2014 enables legislation to be passed that would prohibit transfer incentive exercises if the voluntary approach proves ineffective.

The key objectives of the Code are to help ensure that all incentive exercises enable members to make informed decisions and better choices, whilst permitting exercises and options to be offered in a responsible manner. The Code sets out seven principles that should be followed:

(1) Cash incentives that are contingent on the member's decision to accept the offer should not be offered.
(2) Advice should be provided to members unless certain conditions are met.
(3) Communications with members should be fair, clear, unbiased and straightforward.
(4) Records should be retained so that an audit trail can be maintained and examined in future.
(5) Members should have sufficient time to decide, with no undue pressure applied.
(6) Incentive exercises should only be offered to those over age 80 on an 'opt-in' basis. Special care should be taken when advising 'vulnerable clients'.
(7) All parties should be aware of their roles and responsibilities, and should act in good faith.

A booklet of examples was published alongside the updated Code.

The Pensions Regulator's statement on incentive exercises complements the Code. This highlights the role of trustees, and says that trustees should start from the presumption that such exercises are not in most members' interests. It sets out five principles that should be adhered to:

- the offer should be clear, fair and not misleading
- the offer should be open and transparent
- conflicts of interest should be identified and managed appropriately
- trustees should be involved from the start of the process, *and*
- independent financial advice should be made available and promoted to members.

Questions on incentive exercises are now included in the scheme return *(see Section 8)* including the number of offers made and accepted in relation to ETV and PIE exercises.

OTHER WAYS OF AMENDING LIABILITIES

There are a number of other ways in which the level or nature of liabilities can potentially be controlled or amended. Examples include:

- ceasing future accrual *(see Section 22)*
- capping future increases in pensionable salary
- commutation of small pensions *(see Section 9), and*
- encouraging early retirements (as it is cheaper to buy out benefits in payment than benefits for members who have not yet retired).

INVESTMENT SOLUTIONS TO MANAGE LIABILITIES

Various forms of liability management have been developed over recent years that focus on the investment of assets to manage liability risks. Two options, liability-driven investment and longevity swaps, are described below.

These two options can be combined to form a 'synthetic' or 'DIY' buy-in – significantly reducing risk by replicating the effect of a bulk annuity policy *(see Section 24)*. This may be at a lower cost and provide more flexibility than paying a one-off insurance premium.

Liability-driven investment

Liability-driven investment is an investment strategy based on the asset cashflows needed to meet the projected future benefit payments from a scheme.

This can be done by constructing a theoretical portfolio of gilts and index-linked gilts where the annual coupon and redemption proceeds closely match the amount and timing of the projected future nominal and inflation-linked payments from the scheme.

Pension schemes can buy the gilts needed outright. Alternatively, schemes can use interest rate and inflation swaps, or gilt repurchase agreements (gilt repos). These allow schemes to protect the projected future benefit payments from changes in inflation expectations and gilt yields without tying up as much of their assets in the strategy as would be needed if they bought the gilts outright.

Many pension schemes of all sizes are now making use of such assets in their investment strategies, either directly or via pooled funds. However, the use of the Consumer Prices Index (CPI) for increasing some pension liabilities has added complexity in this area as there is currently no developed market in CPI-linked assets.

Longevity swaps

Removing interest rate and inflation risks leaves increasing longevity as the main risk remaining for a typical DB pension scheme. 'Longevity swaps' can be used to reduce this risk. These allow the scheme to pay cashflows over a fixed period of time based on the expected longevity of a group of individuals, and receive cashflows over a period of time related to the actual longevity of that group.

This removes the risk to the scheme from members living longer than expected. At one time, swaps were only available for large deals – typically large schemes covering pensioner liabilities of over £500 million. However, as the market has become more established, smaller deals have been transacted – bespoke longevity swaps now range from £50 million (scheme not disclosed, October 2016) to £16 billion (BT Pension Scheme, July 2014). The market continues to innovate with streamlined contracts becoming available and the removal of collateral requirements for small to medium-sized longevity swaps.

INSURANCE APPROACHES

In addition to the relatively recent innovations outlined above for managing a scheme's liabilities, insurance policies are often used to help protect the scheme from adverse death-in-service experience. Examples include:

- insuring the lump sum payable on death
- insuring the dependant's pension either directly or (as the insurance of dependants' pensions is expensive and a number of insurers have withdrawn from this market) insuring a lump sum amount calculated by reference to the cost of providing a dependant's pension, *and*
- some form of partial insurance, for example insuring benefits in excess of a predetermined limit (such as £1 million), or benefits in relation to a specific group of employees (such as an executive group), or some form of catastrophe cover.

Due to the competitive insurance market, advantageous terms can often be secured which, in the long run, can be broadly equivalent to the actual underlying death claims experience for larger schemes. This can be an extremely cost-effective way to reduce risk to a pension scheme.

SECTION 22

CEASING ACCRUAL IN DEFINED BENEFIT SCHEMES

This section sets out the issues that employers and trustees need to consider before stopping any further benefits building up in a defined benefit (DB) arrangement. It includes some consideration of the benefits that may be provided in the future for affected members – further detail on the benefit design aspects is in *Section 2*.

Most final salary arrangements in the private sector have been closed to new members, with new employees instead being offered membership of a money purchase (MP) arrangement or a DB arrangement with lower costs and/or risks to the employer (e.g. Career Average Revalued Earnings (CARE) or cash balance: *see Section 2*). Current employees had generally continued to build up final salary benefits with these new benefit arrangements typically applying to new joiners only.

In recent years it has become common for employers to go further and stop final salary benefits (and other defined benefits) for all their employees. This is referred to as 'ceasing accrual'. A scheme with no further benefits accruing is known as a 'frozen scheme'.

Ceasing accrual is not a simple exercise. There are a number of actions that have to be carried out by law, and others that employers may want to go through in order to maintain good employee relations. The process will require a significant amount of planning and involve a number of functions within the employer as well as other parties. Careful due diligence and good project management are important in order to identify potential issues and to set a realistic timeframe.

CONSIDERATIONS FOR EMPLOYERS

Business case

The main reason for ceasing accrual is often to reduce the significant cost of pension benefits. However, employers may need to be able to justify the need for these cost savings to affected employees and other parties such as trade unions and the pension scheme trustees. These parties will often want to ensure that the employer has considered a range of possible options and be satisfied that ceasing accrual is a reasonable solution in the circumstances. Many employers propose moving members to a MP scheme to achieve these cost savings. But it may be possible to arrive at a similar result by retaining a DB structure, and making a combination of changes to the benefits that are offered (e.g. moving from final salary to CARE, reducing the accrual rate or other benefit design changes, or increasing member contributions).

Immediate financial savings may not be the only consideration. Employers may want to reduce the risk that the costs turn out to be higher than expected over the longer term. This would involve passing some or all of the risks inherent in a pension arrangement (for example, inflation, longevity and investment) on to members.

Members may be prepared to accept the cessation of DB accrual and its replacement with a more flexible MP arrangement.

Whereas in the past employers might have closed a scheme to new entrants only, feeling that stopping future accrual entirely was a step too far, several years of natural turnover will in many cases have resulted in a 'two-tier' workforce – those in the DB scheme being rewarded more generously than those (typically younger) members of the MP scheme. The employee group as a whole might now see stopping future accrual and rationalising benefits as a fair and reasonable approach.

In proposing changes, employers should always bear in mind that they have a legal obligation to act in good faith in dealings with employees. The Appeal Court ruling in the case of *IBM v Dalgleish (see Section 30)* highlighted the importance of proper consultation and confirmed that member expectations are just one of the factors that need to be taken into account (although the earlier High Court ruling had suggested that reasonable member expectations were of overriding significance).

Design of future benefits

Employers will need to consider what pension benefits they will offer to members to replace their defined benefits. If an employer has already set up a new arrangement for employees who joined after a certain date, then it may want to move all employees to this arrangement. However, the employer will want to ensure that this arrangement continues to be appropriate.

In many cases, employees are moved into a MP arrangement. However, this can be seen as moving from one extreme to the other (with all the risks passing from the employer to the member). Some employers may consider that sharing risks to some extent is a more desirable outcome *(see Section 2)*. Although legislation to facilitate risk sharing was put on hold, the Government is considering whether existing legislation can be amended to enable the introduction of collective defined contribution schemes.

The accounting impact of both ceasing accrual in the DB arrangement (particularly final salary), and the new benefit structure, will need to be considered *(see Section 26)*. The savings in cash terms are unlikely to be the same as the savings in accounting terms, and in some cases there could actually be an adverse effect on the employer's profit and loss account.

There are a number of other issues in changing benefit structures, particularly if moving from DB to MP:

- employers should ensure that the proposed new arrangement will meet the minimum requirements for auto-enrolment *(see Section 4)*
- employers should consider whether the new arrangement should be under the same trust as the DB arrangement: this approach can involve complex issues including implications for funding cross-subsidies and winding up

- benefits payable on death or ill health cannot be funded in a MP arrangement in the same way that they can in a DB arrangement: advice on appropriate insurance arrangements will be needed and the costs should be considered
- DB arrangements have in the past had more flexibility to provide extra benefits in cases of redundancy and other workforce management exercises, although this has been constrained more recently by funding pressures; MP arrangements are less flexible for this purpose, and employers will need to consider how to provide such benefits, particularly if these are contractual entitlements
- the investment options, particularly the default investment option, will need to be carefully designed, monitored and communicated
- there are additional considerations for higher earners:
  - the tax implications for those who are affected by the annual and lifetime allowances *(see Section 9)*: there may be a requirement for additional remuneration or benefits provided through a separate arrangement (bearing in mind the disguised remuneration requirements – *see Section 11), and*
  - setting up a new arrangement may in itself cause members to lose some protections and provision of life cover may impact on exemptions from the annual allowance, which may also create additional administration for the scheme.

Design of accrued benefits

There may also be various ways in which active members' final salary benefits in respect of past service can be calculated. For example, depending on scheme rules, the employer may have the following options for increasing pension between date of implementation and retirement:

- statutory minimum increases in line with leaving service benefits
- increases in line with price inflation, *or*
- maintaining full salary linking.

This is also an area in which legal advice is particularly important – *see below*.

If the scheme had been contracted out of the Additional State Pension *(see Reference Section 5)*, there are further considerations. For schemes that remained contracted out until 6 April 2016 (when contracting out was abolished), subsequent cessation of pensionable service will now trigger the anti-franking requirements from the time of cessation. For schemes that ceased contracted-out benefit accrual before 6 April 2016, a 'Protection Rule' needed to be added to the scheme rules to ensure that any contracted-out benefits retained within the scheme were protected (at normal pension age and on death) from being franked against benefits accrued during periods of subsequent non-contracted-out pensionable service; this was in addition to the anti-franking requirements that applied from cessation of contracted-out service.

Legal issues

There are a number of areas where employers will need to take legal advice.

Members' employment contracts will need to be reviewed. This is to check how membership of the pension scheme is described. For example, some contracts give the right to membership of a DB pension scheme. Some contracts may also contain individual pension promises. It may therefore be necessary to consult on contractual changes.

The scheme's trust deed and rules should be consulted and may need amendment. They should be checked to ensure that the scheme does not restrict the types of amendment that can be made, and to confirm which employers will remain liable for future contributions, either under the scheme rules or as 'statutory employers' *(see Section 7)*. If trustee consent is required for any amendment, the trustees may see this as an opportunity for negotiation *(see below)*.

One specific issue may arise if the employer wishes to break the link to final salary for accrued benefits (for example by capping increases to pensionable salary). Case law has suggested that the wording of some trust deeds and rules may require members' benefits to be calculated by reference to their salary when they leave or retire from the employer. If the final salary link cannot be broken in a scheme, this may reduce the cost savings the employer would otherwise make.

The case of *MNRPF v Stena Line (see Section 30)* has identified another legal issue by suggesting that even where salary linkage is retained when accrual ceases, the affected members would no longer be regarded as active members. The subsequent case of *G4S v G4S Trustees Limited* confirmed this point. This interpretation may have implications for employer debts *(see Section 25)* and entitlement to transfer values.

In some cases, amending the scheme rules or members leaving the scheme as a result of ceasing accrual may trigger a wind-up *(see Section 23)* or a debt on the employer *(see Section 25)*. This could have significant financial implications, and the employer will usually want to ensure that the changes are carried out in such a way as to avoid this.

Consultation and communication with employees

Ceasing accrual is a 'listed change' under the Pensions Act 2004 consultation requirements *(see Section 2)*. Most employers will therefore have to carry out a 60-day consultation with affected members or their representatives and consider any representations made during the consultation before they can implement any changes. This process could take significantly longer than 60 days, particularly if member representative groups need to be set up. It is important that this communication is clear and that the consultation is open.

Many employers will want to do more than the legal minimum, and put in place a detailed communication strategy to ensure members understand the reasons for change, the effect on their defined benefits built up to date, and the likely benefits they will receive from the new arrangement. For many members, the headline is likely to be a significant reduction in their projected benefits at retirement. However the detailed implications will affect individual members in different ways.

In the case of a new MP arrangement, employers may wish to encourage former DB members to take more responsibility than they have in the past for ensuring their benefits will meet their needs at retirement. This is likely to involve taking decisions relating to the level of contributions paid and their investment options. Employers may want to provide a range of information to employees about this, reflecting the level of financial literacy of the workforce.

Other protections for employees

There are additional considerations if the scheme has any ex-public sector workers, or if the employer might consider bidding for public sector outsourcing contracts in the future. Employers may be required to offer a certain level of DB pensions to ex-public sector workers. It is not always easy to identify ex-public sector workers, particularly if they have joined the scheme as a result of subsequent transactions between private sector companies.

Some rights (for example redundancy or early retirement enhancements) may need to be protected by the new employer. This applies particularly for ex-public sector workers but employers who have taken on private sector employees may also find that they need to protect such benefits and may seek indemnities from the seller.

CONSIDERATIONS FOR TRUSTEES

Trustees' duty

The conventionally accepted view is that trustees' primary duty is to safeguard accrued rights and administer the scheme in accordance with the rules, and that it is the employer's role to decide the basis of pension benefits it wishes to provide to its employees for future service.

However, as well as protecting members' existing benefits, trustees will want to satisfy themselves that the employer's business case for any proposal to cease accrual is properly reasoned, the proposals are workable in practice, and that they do not breach any legal obligations. Trustees should also bear in mind that they need to consider the interests of all members of the scheme, not just the active members who will be directly affected by the ceasing of future accrual.

As noted above, if trustee consent is required in order to amend the scheme to allow the ceasing of future accrual, the trustees may use this as an opportunity for negotiation with the employer over funding, security of benefits, and even benefits themselves. The trustees may need to take legal advice, particularly where their trust deed and rules provides them with a power to veto changes to future benefits.

Scheme funding implications

The issue of ceasing accrual may be raised during the valuation process *(see Section 18)*. The scheme funding regulations allow trustees (with employer agreement) to modify or cease future accrual if it appears to them that it is not otherwise possible to obtain the employer's agreement to the various required elements of the funding process. Alternatively, the issue may be raised by the employer during funding negotiations.

The trustees will need to consider whether a proposal to cease accrual, and the background to such a proposal, reflects a weakening in the employer's covenant – its ability and willingness to continue to fund the scheme *(see Section 18)*. This could have implications for the level of technical provisions the trustees consider necessary to safeguard accrued rights.

Even if the proposal is not made as part of the valuation process, the trustees will need to consider the effect of ceasing accrual on the funding position of the scheme *(see Section 18)*. This will include considering whether the current funding plan remains appropriate. The trustees should also confirm which employers will remain liable for future contributions, either under the scheme rules or as 'statutory employers' *(see Section 7)*.

Trustees and employers are likely to pay closer attention to the risks remaining in the scheme, and look for ways to manage these *(see Section 21)*. This may include buying out portions of the liabilities over time *(see Section 24)*. Ceasing accrual will also require ongoing review of cashflow requirements, and the disinvestment of assets, as the proportion of the scheme's liabilities that relates to pension in payment rises.

Any changes to the adopted funding principles are likely to require a review of actuarial factors, such as commutation and early retirement terms, as well as transfer value assumptions. The employer's consent may be required to change some factors.

Benefit changes

As part of any negotiation with the employer, trustees may decide it is appropriate to suggest alternative future benefits. As the employer's proposals are likely to be aimed at cutting costs, the scope for alternative approaches may be limited. Trade unions and representations from members may also suggest approaches which partially offset the ending of accrual.

Governance, administration and communication

If the new pension arrangement is being set up under the same trust, trustees will also need to deal with the different governance issues in relation to any MP section *(see Section 7)*. They will need to understand their responsibilities and any features of the new benefits with which they are not familiar, and will need to consider how the administration of two separate benefit structures for the same members will work, and ensure that administration systems can cope with both the new benefits and the past service benefits (including consideration of any residual contracting-out requirements).

Under the disclosure requirements *(see Section 15)* trustees will need to inform the members of the change, and general communications will need to reflect the new benefits. More generally, trustees may want to be involved in the employer's communication process, to ensure that the employer is explaining the issues clearly and properly. Once any changes have been implemented, trustees may want to review how they communicate with members more widely, taking care not to set any inappropriate expectations for future benefit provision.

SECTION 23

SCHEME CLOSURE AND WIND-UP

The winding up of occupational pension schemes can raise complex legal and practical issues. The process can take several years, although legislation exists that is intended to speed it up. The trustees of a scheme that is being wound up need to understand their continuing responsibilities under the relevant provisions of the trust deed and rules. It is important for the trustees to take legal and actuarial advice both before wind-up commences and throughout the wind-up period.

Commencement of wind-up

The events that can trigger wind-up are normally set out in the scheme trust deed and rules. These can include the employer ceasing to contribute (or not being prepared to contribute at a rate the trustees consider adequate for funding the scheme), or becoming insolvent. The scheme rules may allow the alternative of postponing wind-up, and instead continuing to operate on a 'frozen scheme' basis with no further accrual of benefits. Where the scheme's rules require wind-up, the trustees have an overriding power under the Pensions Act 1995 to choose instead to follow this 'frozen scheme' route. This overriding power does not apply in certain circumstances, including where a Pension Protection Fund (PPF) assessment period *(see Section 20)* has been completed but the scheme is found to be too well funded to be taken on by the PPF and is required to be wound up.

It is important for the date on which wind-up is treated as having commenced to be clearly identified and recorded. This can vary depending on the circumstances, but for most purposes can be taken as the earliest date when there are no members in pensionable service and either (i) the scheme rules provide that wind-up should commence or (ii) the power to wind up is exercised by the trustees (or by any other person or body, such as the Pensions Regulator or a court, having the authority to do so).

Winding-up procedure

The trustees of an underfunded occupational scheme that enters wind-up during a recovery period *(see Section 18)* must as soon as practicable prepare a 'winding-up procedure'. This procedure includes details of the action that will be taken to establish the liabilities and the method that will be used to discharge them, an indication of any accrued rights or benefits that are likely to be affected by a reduction in actuarial value, and an estimate of the amount of time that will be taken to complete these steps. The procedure must be submitted to the Pensions Regulator.

Schemes in wind-up are generally exempt from the scheme funding requirements *(see Section 18)*.

Appointment of an independent trustee and role of the Pensions Regulator

If the employer has become insolvent, the insolvency practitioner (or, if applicable, official receiver) must notify the Pensions Regulator. The Regulator then has the power to appoint an independent trustee although it does not have to do this (e.g. if one has already been appointed).

Subject to various safeguards relating to members' rights, the Regulator may modify a scheme with a view to ensuring that it is properly wound up following an application from the trustees (which must include specified information and documents). The Regulator may also order a scheme to be wound up, or give legally binding directions to trustees, administrators and others if it considers that these are necessary to speed up the process. The Regulator, the PPF and the Department for Work and Pensions (on behalf of the Financial Assistance Scheme) have published a joint statement saying that the important parts of a wind-up should generally be completed within a two-year period. The Regulator also maintains guidance that sets out examples of good practice in order to help schemes through the winding-up process.

Debt on the employer

Under Section 75 of the Pensions Act 1995, where a scheme has insufficient assets to cover the scheme liabilities, the employer may have a legal obligation to make up the shortfall. This does not apply to schemes providing only money purchase benefits.

For wind-ups starting on or after 15 February 2005, the value of liabilities for the calculation of the debt must be based on an estimate of the actual cost of buying out benefits and meeting the expenses of wind-up.

If the wind-up was triggered by an 'insolvency event' of the sponsoring employer, any 'debt on the employer' must be treated by the trustees as having arisen immediately before this occurred. Otherwise, the debt can be treated by the trustees as having arisen at *any* time after the commencement of wind-up and before the employer goes into liquidation.

The Regulator has highlighted the importance of trustees being able to identify a scheme's statutory employer(s) who would be liable for any such debt *(see Section 7)*.

Discharging scheme liabilities

In order to wind up a scheme, its assets must be applied to discharge its liabilities. This can be done by transfer to another occupational scheme (including master trusts and Superfunds – *see Sections 6 and 24 respectively*) or to personal pensions, by purchasing insurance company annuities *(see Section 24)*, by assigning existing annuity contracts to members or, in certain circumstances, by the payment of lump sums *(see Section 9)*.

Priority order

Because of the possibility that the assets will be insufficient to fully discharge all liabilities in this way, scheme rules normally contain a 'priority order' setting out the order in which the different liability classes (e.g. pensions already in payment, accrued pensions of active members) are to be dealt with. However, the Pensions Act 1995 introduced a statutory priority order with effect from 6 April 1997, modified by subsequent legislation, which generally overrides 'scheme-specific' priority orders. For the purpose of assigning them to appropriate priority classes, scheme liabilities are normally treated as having 'crystallised' according to their status at the date when wind-up commenced.

For wind-ups commencing on or after 6 April 2005, the statutory priority order is as follows:

(1) benefits under certain contracts of insurance

(2) benefits corresponding to those that would be provided if the scheme entered the PPF *(see Section 20)*

(3) benefits from AVCs, to the extent that these are not included in the categories above

(4) all other liabilities.

Any money purchase assets and liabilities are generally excluded from the above calculations. Such benefits would normally be expected to have priority over non-money purchase benefits, but this is dependent on the scheme rules.

The liabilities set out in the statutory priority order must be valued by the scheme actuary using a specified basis. For wind-ups commencing on or after 15 February 2005, the basis used is the actual cost of securing the benefits, for example by means of an annuity buy-out.

Deficiency

Where the full buy-out debt basis *(see above)* does not apply, or such a debt cannot be collected, the assets of the scheme may be insufficient to discharge all of the scheme's liabilities. In this event, the benefits provided for the lowest priority class(es) will have to be cut back accordingly. Legislation allows schemes in wind-up to reduce pensions already in payment, due to underfunding, without giving rise to unauthorised payments charges *(see Section 9)*.

The PPF *(see Section 20)* was established with effect from 6 April 2005. It provides some protection for eligible schemes with employers that become insolvent on or after that date. The Financial Assistance Scheme *(see Section 20)* was established to provide some support for workers who have lost pensions through underfunding in certain schemes that went into wind-up after 1996 and are not covered by the PPF, but since September 2016 it has ceased to accept new schemes.

Surplus

If a surplus of assets remains after all of the scheme liabilities have been discharged, this must also be dealt with in accordance with the scheme rules and relevant legislative requirements. As well as providing for the augmentation of benefits, either at the sole discretion of the trustees, or in consultation with (or with the consent of) the employer, there may be provision for payment of a refund to the employer. Before this can be done, a number of requirements under the Pensions Act 1995 (as amended by the 2004 Act) must be satisfied. These requirements include sending written notices to members inviting them to make representations in respect of the proposal.

Disclosure and reporting requirements

A notice must be given to members within one month of the commencement of wind-up, followed by annual progress reports. For defined benefit schemes, members must also be provided with details of the trustees' proposals for discharging liabilities before they are implemented. In all cases, once the assets have been applied to provide benefits, members must be given full details within three months.

Annual progress reports must also be given to the Pensions Regulator. The first such report must be filed within three months of the second anniversary of the commencement of wind-up.

Scheme operation during wind-up

The process of winding up can take several years. During this period, no new members will be admitted and no further benefits will accrue. The trustees may pay provisional benefits to members on retirement, with final benefits to be confirmed when winding up is complete. Legislation specifically provides for benefits paid during the winding-up period to be reduced in line with what the priority order will ultimately require *(see above)*. Trustees should also review the terms for member options and the scheme's investment strategy to ensure they remain appropriate, particularly if the employer has become insolvent. It is possible to apply to the Pensions Regulator for permission to delay paying cash equivalent transfer values.

Operating as a frozen scheme

Schemes also sometimes operate as 'frozen schemes' (with no further accrual of benefits) *without* having started a winding-up process. For example, this may happen where a scheme's sponsoring employer has decided to cease accrual *(see Section 22)* but can still fund the scheme. Alternatively, if the sponsoring employer has become insolvent but the scheme is too well funded to be taken on by the PPF *(see Section 20)*, it may be unable to wind up and purchase insurance company annuities, perhaps because it is too large.

SECTION 24

BULK ANNUITIES

Under a bulk annuity contract, a pension scheme pays a premium to an insurer and the insurer commits to providing the income needed to meet future benefit payments to a number of the scheme's members. The income stream is payable as long as they or their dependants live. An annuity thus provides protection against the interest rate, inflation, longevity and other risks connected to these liabilities. Ultimately, if all liabilities are bought-out with annuities, the scheme can cease operation (*in Section 23, scheme closure and wind-up are described.*)

It is our understanding that bulk annuities are protected under the Financial Services Compensation Scheme, to the full policy value - *see Section 27.*

The pricing of annuities tends to be considered relative to the yields on gilts or swaps, given that an annuity represents a bond-like asset whose price increases when other bonds are more expensive. Relative to these measures, annuity pricing is sensitive to the additional yield spread that the annuity provider can earn from investing in other long-term assets with predictable income, and to the reserving requirements for annuity products (which have changed markedly over the years) and their dependency on the insurance company's own investment strategy. It also depends on the provider's capacity and appetite for new business, and which transactions can deliver an acceptable profit margin.

Market capacity is an important consideration. As more defined benefit (DB) schemes cease accrual *(see Section 22)*, liability transfer becomes a long-term objective for many, often forming part of a 'flight-plan' strategy *(see Section 18)*. The annual capacity of the bulk annuity market depends on capital, asset sourcing, longevity reinsurance capacity, and suitably experienced manpower. Recently, available assets and manpower have been the key constraints at busy periods in the market. The volume of bulk annuity business written has recently tended to be £10–20 billion a year, which compares with overall unsecured liabilities in private sector DB schemes that have been estimated at around £2,000 billion. The capacity made available by insurance companies is also dependent on rival opportunities, including annuity back-book purchases from other insurers and new individual annuities.

As the UK bulk annuity market is partly dependent on the capacity of the global reinsurance market, which is also used to support other annuity markets (notably the US), this makes the availability of ultimate risk takers a key long-term factor in the sustainability of competitively priced annuities.

UK bulk annuity capacity was tested in 2018, following a number of large transactions taking place around the same time after a period of positive investment experience and improved annuity pricing. Capacity may be tested more often as more schemes mature and address funding deficits.

The growth of the bulk annuity market also reflects an increased focus on the risks associated with DB schemes and the potential impact on the sponsor's financial statements *(see Section 26)*.

For most schemes annuities are only currently affordable for retired members, partly because the scheme trustees set a less conservative funding reserve for other members to reflect the anticipated asset returns available from investing partially in growth assets. Hence many schemes planning to secure their liabilities would in practice enter into more than one bulk annuity transaction, securing some of the existing pensioners first and later securing more members after they have retired.

Schemes that are the most ready to transact may be positioned to take advantage of favourable price movements as and when they occur. Increasingly schemes carry out preparatory work, such as feasibility studies and data cleansing, with this in mind.

BUY-IN

Under a 'buy-in', the bulk annuity is held as an asset of the trustees. The income from the annuity is typically paid to the trustees' administrators, with the trustees remaining responsible for paying the benefits of the members covered by the annuity. The membership of the scheme is therefore not usually directly affected by a buy-in – the individuals covered remain scheme members.

The buy-in is intended to match a specific part of the scheme's liabilities closely, but not necessarily exactly. For example, where there are issues with data quality or where discretionary pension increases may be given, the buy-in policy may not exactly match the scheme's liabilities at all times, but the contract can include scope to amend the benefits covered.

This also provides trustees with the option of deliberately not precisely matching the annuity terms to the underlying benefit entitlements until buy-out, where there are aspects of the benefit structure that are comparatively expensive to insure, such as more complicated inflation-linked pension increases.

The sponsor remains responsible for funding all of the scheme, but in practice is only likely to be called upon for any further funding in respect of the benefits covered by the annuities to the extent that the insurance is corrected later for data changes.

If the scheme enters financial difficulty and cannot afford full benefits for members, the buy-in can usually be reallocated to partly pay income for members other than those originally covered.

A buy-in can also be converted into a buy-out contract (*discussed below*), for example when the scheme is being wound up.

Buy-in with additional security

Bulk annuity products are subject to the solvency and monitoring regime applicable to insurance companies. Some larger buy-ins have included a bespoke layer of additional security, such as a charge on assets, or the depositing in a ring-fenced account of backing assets. These become accessible to the pension scheme in the event of certain trigger events occurring before buy-out, such as a lasting deterioration in the solvency of the insurer below a threshold level. For contracts written from 1 January 2016 (commencement date of the Solvency II regulatory regime for insurance companies), there are constraints on the quantum of assets that can be used in this manner without materially increasing the annuity price.

BUY-OUT

Under a buy-out, individual annuity policies are provided in respect of each member covered. Each individual policy is a contract between the member and the insurer. This allows the link between the member and the trustees to be broken. The members' benefits are then paid and administered directly by the annuity provider. For the scheme sponsor, this should remove legal exposure to the potential cost of funding these members' benefits, including exposure to the risk of legislative change creating new pension costs in respect of these members.

Most commonly, buy-out is associated with the wind-up of a pension scheme with all members' benefits being secured under individual annuity contracts including the conversion of any older, existing 'buy-in' policies into individual annuity contracts.

To complete the wind-up of the scheme, any residual uncertainties over benefit entitlements, arising for example from incomplete data or any inadequacies in past equalisation measures *(see Section 16)*, need to be resolved.

To address the price impact of changes in the data, a final balancing premium is normally payable to or from the annuity provider post transaction to reflect the change in the value of the liabilities covered.

Some larger buy-out transactions have included a different feature – with the annuity provider giving additional cover in respect of residual data and benefit specification risks. This is normally paid for by an additional upfront premium, but avoids the need for a later balancing premium adjustment once the data is fully cleansed. Also, the additional cover secured normally lasts beyond scheme wind-up, giving members the potential ability to claim against the insurer if they later believe that the benefits secured were incorrect despite the cleansing work conducted.

Partial buy-out

A partial buy-out allows for the discharge of some of the liabilities of a pension scheme. As with a full buy-out, this results in the provision of annuity policies from an insurance company in the names of scheme members. They become policyholders of the insurer, ceasing to be members of the scheme.

A partial buy-out is usually difficult to achieve for a few reasons. Firstly, the rules of the scheme may not include provision for partial buy-out and it may be concluded that the rules do not give an adequate discharge of liabilities where the whole scheme is not winding up. In some instances partial buyout can require member consent for at least some of the members being secured under the annuity. There are potential solutions to this but they involve careful planning and may require the establishment of a new pension arrangement.

Secondly, the trustees need to consider the security of all members' benefits. Buying out the liabilities of current pensioners (for example) will generally increase the security of those benefits. Trustees will need to ensure that this is not to the material detriment of non-pensioners, particularly where the scheme is underfunded and no extra funding is provided at the time of the partial buy-out transaction.

For these reasons, partial buy-out has rarely occurred to date, with a buy-in *(see above)* conducted instead.

OTHER RELATED PRODUCTS

Medically underwritten bulk annuities

Medically underwritten bulk annuities are priced using information provided by members regarding their health and lifestyle as well as the information to which a pension scheme normally has access. This can sometimes lower the pricing of longevity risk by reducing uncertainty over measurement of the risk.

Synthetic buy-in

'Synthetic' or 'DIY' buy-ins can be constructed by the trustees by using a combination of investments including a longevity swap to provide a predictable level of income that, as far as practical, matches required benefit cash-flows in a manner similar to an annuity contract. This may be an attractive option for larger schemes (e.g. above £1 billion in size), with this approach retaining investment freedom otherwise lost on annuity purchase. For smaller schemes, the substantial effort involved in constructing (and then maintaining) a portfolio of assets to closely match liabilities, and the possible inefficiencies in running a pension scheme indefinitely as it matures and shrinks, can make annuities more attractive. As all closed schemes will ultimately shrink over time, this suggests that annuity purchase will ultimately be a common objective for most schemes. *Section 21 provides further detail on investment solutions to manage liabilities.*

Commercial consolidators

In 2018 the Government's White Paper on protecting DB pension schemes indicated that it would consult by the end of 2018 on a legislative framework and authorisation regime within which new forms of consolidation vehicles could operate. The consultation is expected to focus on 'commercial consolidators', which enable the sponsor to discharge their liabilities, subject to a minimum level of funding on entry. These arrangements are expected to operate as occupational pension schemes, and so be subject to the potentially less onerous scheme funding regime, rather than the solvency regime applicable to insurance companies. There were previous attempts to launch consolidator schemes when the bulk annuity market expanded in 2007, but without success. The greater maturity of typical DB schemes now, plus current Government efforts to derive an acceptable legislative framework and authorisation regime for consolidation vehicles to operate in, may make them more successful than before. These consolidation vehicles may then seek to hold liabilities indefinitely, profiting from earning investment returns that exceed those needed to meet liabilities, or may seek to ultimately secure annuities in respect of each scheme taken on.

SALES, PURCHASES & CORPORATE ACTIVITY

The pension aspects of corporate sales and acquisitions require careful consideration, particularly where UK defined benefit schemes are involved. All parties will need to take expert legal and actuarial advice.

PRICING PENSIONS IN THE DEAL

Pension costs will have a significant impact on the pricing of most deals.

Where personnel represents a material business cost and the deal is priced on the basis of future income, the purchaser should consider future pension costs, which might be different from the equivalent costs for the vendor.

If the purchaser is taking on accrued defined benefit pension liabilities, for example by acquiring an entire pension scheme or accepting a 'bulk transfer' *(see below)*, actuarial advice will be required on the net cost to the purchaser. This could be material and will need to be considered as part of the pricing.

The purchaser should also consider the impact of the ongoing defined benefit pension risk and develop options to limit that risk as far as possible in the post-integration plan. The level of pension risk relative to the business may also affect the purchase price adjustment for pensions.

The cost of any debt on the employer may also have to be allowed for *(see below)* although it is not uncommon to seek an indemnity for any such debt.

ACQUISITION OF WHOLE SCHEME

If the company being acquired has its own pension scheme and this will be acquired as part of the deal, then the scheme liabilities and funding will need to be examined carefully. The current financial position on the accounting basis may not be suitable for pricing purposes in isolation.

The ongoing costs of benefits, and any possible changes in the trustees' funding or investment strategies as a result of the sale or of the subsequent restructuring, should be considered. These may have a substantial impact on the future profitability, and even perhaps viability, of the business. If the business being acquired is publicly listed, the trustees may have set out their opinion on the effects of the proposed deal on the scheme in a document attached to the target company's board response.

BULK TRANSFER ARRANGEMENTS

If the transferring employees are members of the vendor's group scheme (and the scheme will be retained by the vendor), the employees may simply become deferred pensioners in the vendor's scheme but it is often desirable, in the interest of good employee relations, for a 'bulk transfer' to be arranged. The risks associated with such a transfer need to be compared against its benefits.

Bulk transfers are now relatively rare (with the exception of public sector outsourcing) as few purchasers make defined benefit provision for future service except where contractually required.

Under a bulk transfer, employees exchange their accrued benefits in the vendor's scheme for benefits in the purchaser's scheme and a transfer payment is made. In some circumstances there may exist a legal or contractual obligation to arrange a bulk transfer. The bulk transfer terms are a matter of commercial negotiation between the purchaser and the vendor. These will normally be set out in the 'pensions clause' of (or 'schedule' to) the legal agreement governing the transaction. This agreement may be accompanied by a side letter between the actuaries advising both parties, setting out the actuarial assumptions in detail. The amount transferred between schemes may not be equal to the value placed on the liabilities for pricing purposes and so there might also need to be a pricing adjustment.

As well as specifying the assumptions for calculating the amount of the bulk transfer payment, the pensions clause will usually also specify the terms for the benefits in the new scheme, the treatment of any excess or shortfall in the trustee transfer payment *(see 'Trustee considerations', below)*, the communications, and the transfer process.

After contracting out was abolished in April 2016, regulations prohibited the transfer of contracted-out liability (broadly Guaranteed Minimum Pensions and post-1997 rights) to a pension scheme that had never previously been contracted out, unless the consent of members was obtained. This was changed from 6 April 2018; regulations now allow contracted-out liability to be transferred without member consent to any other salary-related scheme, subject to the two schemes relating to connected employers and to other conditions being met.

Trustee considerations

The commercially agreed bulk transfer terms will not normally be binding on the trustees of the vendor's scheme. The trustees will need to consider, having regard to their trust deed and rules and the interests of *all* scheme members and beneficiaries, whether it is appropriate to pay a bulk transfer and, if so, the assumptions on which it should be calculated. If they decide that the payment should be calculated on assumptions different from the commercial bulk transfer terms, then the shortfall or excess payment clause (if any) in the sale agreement may be triggered between the vendor and purchaser.

Similarly, the trustees of the purchaser's scheme are not obliged to accept the proposed bulk transfer payment or provide the commercially agreed level of benefits, and may seek additional funding from the purchaser.

Member consent or actuarial certificate

For a bulk transfer to be paid from the vendor's scheme, *either* the transfer must be restricted to only those members who give their consent, *or* the trustees may decide that a transfer without consent is appropriate. For a without-consent transfer of defined benefits, the trustees will need to obtain a certificate from their scheme actuary confirming that the past service benefits of each transferring member will still be 'broadly no less favourable'. For money purchase without-consent transfers, the trustees may, in some circumstances, be required to consult with an appropriate adviser.

Where individual consents are sought, the trustees will need to ensure that members are provided with the information necessary to understand all of the options open to them and make an informed choice. Similarly, where a 'without-consent' transfer is anticipated, the members must be provided with appropriate information on the proposed transfer.

EMPLOYER COVENANT

The sale, or any subsequent transfer of assets, could have a material impact on the employer covenant provided to the scheme.

Whether or not a bulk transfer of pension assets and liabilities takes place, both the purchaser's and the vendor's schemes' trustees will need to consider the impact on their employer's covenant and the subsequent impact on their scheme. They may request additional funding in mitigation and/or review the investment and funding strategies if they believe the impact is detrimental.

A lack of information directly from the employer may lead to a more conservative assessment of the covenant – with potential adverse consequences for the ongoing funding requirements. Employers can therefore act to mitigate trustee concerns by actively engaging with them and providing as much information as possible to alleviate their concerns.

The impact on security can be complex and so the trustees may seek specialist covenant, legal and actuarial advice.

POTENTIAL 'DEBT ON EMPLOYER'

If the sale results in a participating employer ceasing to have any active members in the scheme, then a section 75 debt on the employer could be triggered. This might arise at the time of the sale, at the end of a participation period, or on any subsequent restructuring. The debt can be significant and is calculated using a similar approach to that which applies on a wind-up *(see Section 23)*.

The debt arises in respect of the benefits accrued whilst in service with the employer and covers both current and ex-employees. The debt also includes a proportion relating to any 'orphan' members (i.e. current or deferred pensioners with no currently participating employer). Depending on the previous corporate activity of the group, these orphan members can represent a high percentage of the total membership and therefore can substantially increase the debt for which a participating employer is liable.

The debt is payable by the participating employer involved and so can effectively fall to either the purchaser or the vendor depending on the terms of the deal. If the purchaser acquires one or more whole companies, then the debt would fall to the purchaser but the purchaser is likely to seek either a price reduction or an indemnity from the vendor. If business assets are being sold and a shell company is being retained by the vendor, and this shell ceases to have eligible active employees, then a debt effectively falls to the vendor.

There are a number of ways in which the level of a debt might be reduced, including:

- a Flexible Apportionment Arrangement – the company agrees with the trustees to apportion its whole pension liability to one or more other participating employers without triggering a Section 75 debt
- a Scheme Apportionment Arrangement – the company and trustees agree that some or all of the debt is reapportioned to other participating employers
- a Regulated Apportionment Arrangement – a restructuring mechanism that allows a financially troubled employer in extreme circumstances to detach itself from its pension liabilities, having obtained Pensions Regulator and PPF approval
- a Withdrawal Arrangement – the trustees agree that the ceasing employer pays a lower amount, at least equal to its share of any deficit relative to technical provisions *(see Section 18)*, and that a contingent guarantor will stand behind the remaining debt
- an Approved Withdrawal Arrangement – this is similar to a Withdrawal Arrangement but the Regulator's approval is required, and it applies when the proposed immediate payment is less than the employer's share of the technical provisions deficit
- a Deferred Debt Arrangement – on ceasing to employ active members, an employer can defer payment of the debt, if it retains its responsibilities to the scheme and the trustees consent, *or*
- transferring the accrued liabilities to the purchaser's scheme – this can reduce the debt, potentially down to nil, although the impact depends heavily on the terms of the transfer and the position of the vendor's scheme.

THE PENSIONS REGULATOR, MORAL HAZARD AND CLEARANCE

The Pensions Regulator can impact on a transaction through the 'moral hazard' provisions. These are designed to prevent employers avoiding their obligations and give the Regulator sweeping powers, including the power to issue Contribution Notices, Financial Support Directions and Restoration Orders *(see also Section 8)*. For example, a Contribution Notice can be issued if the effect of an act, regardless of the employer's intent, is materially detrimental to the security of members' benefits. Contribution Notices may be issued in relation to a variety of events, including (but not limited to) sale or acquisition of a business, group restructuring and capital restructuring. A statutory defence prevents the Regulator acting in this way where the employer reasonably concluded that there was no material detriment and certain other conditions are met. The application of the Regulator's powers is not limited to the current employer of the scheme.

A company or individual can avoid the risk of the Regulator later taking action by applying for clearance. Once given, clearance is binding on the Regulator unless the actual circumstances were materially different from those disclosed at the time.

The Regulator has issued guidance on clearance and this includes:

- a pension scheme in deficit should be treated like any other material creditor
- the Regulator wishes to know about all events having a materially detrimental effect on a pension scheme's ability to meet liabilities, *and*
- trustees and employers should work together in relation to potentially detrimental events, communicating and sharing appropriate information.

The 'notifiable events' framework requires the trustees of an underfunded scheme to notify the Regulator if a bulk or individual transfer payment exceeding £1.5 million (or, if lower, 5% of scheme assets) is made.

The Government's March 2018 White Paper on protecting defined benefit schemes proposed strengthening the notifiable events framework and the clearance regime, so that pensions are given appropriate regard in corporate transactions. Further changes to improve the effectiveness and efficiency of the Regulator's existing powers will also be considered.

TUPE

The TUPE requirements, and separate provisions for occupational pension scheme benefits, protect the terms and conditions relating to future benefits for employees who are compulsorily transferred as part of a deal. (Accrued pension rights are protected under preservation legislation.)

Transferring employees currently entitled to occupational scheme benefits must be entitled to pension benefits from the new employer. Where the new employer offers money purchase benefits, it must, at least, either match the employee's contributions, up to a maximum of 6% of basic pay, or match the old employer's contributions. The latter option appears to be restricted to employees who were members of the previous occupational pension scheme (whereas the former option applies to all those who were eligible to join the previous scheme).

If the new employer offers a defined benefit scheme, it must provide benefits that are at least as valuable as the sum of 6% of pensionable pay for each year of employment and the contributions paid by the member (although required member contributions can be no higher than 6%).

Transferring employees with rights to pension schemes established under contract (such as a group personal pension) may have their current pension rights preserved by TUPE, depending on the terms of their contracts.

In some circumstances, early retirement and redundancy terms and benefits in respect of accrued service may be preserved by the TUPE requirements. Actuarial and legal advice should be taken on the issue and, in general, purchasers should seek appropriate indemnities against hidden liability.

SECTION 26

PENSION COSTS IN COMPANY ACCOUNTS

Companies must show the cost of employee pension benefits in their accounts in accordance with relevant accounting standards. In the UK, International Accounting Standard IAS 19 is mandatory for listed companies' consolidated group accounts. Individual company accounts and the consolidated group accounts of unlisted companies may use either IAS 19 or section 28 of the UK standard, FRS 102, which is essentially a simplified version of IAS 19. There is a further option for qualifying entities to comply with FRS 101, which basically allows companies to use the same results as IAS 19. For the remainder of this section, references to IAS 19 also cover the requirements of FRS 101 for pensions. This section describes the requirements of these standards.

Additional disclosure requirements also apply to benefits, including pensions, paid to company directors. *These are also summarised below.*

ACCOUNTING FOR PENSION COSTS UNDER IAS 19

Requirement to use international standards

Companies governed by the law of an EU Member State, whose securities are admitted to trading on a regulated market in any EU Member State, are generally required to prepare their consolidated accounts in compliance with International Accounting Standards. For the UK, this covers companies listed on AIM (Alternative Investment Market) as well as those with a full London Stock Exchange (LSE) listing.

Coverage

IAS 19 covers four categories of employee benefits, with separate requirements for each:

- short-term employee benefits, such as salaries and social security contributions
- post-employment benefits, such as pensions and post-employment medical care
- other long-term employee benefits, including long-service leave (which are now largely treated in the same way as post-employment benefits, although gains/losses are recognised through profit and loss), *and*
- termination benefits.

Application to multi-employer schemes

Under IAS 19, only plans that are operated by companies which are *not under common control* are 'multi-employer' plans. If participants in a DB multi-employer plan are unable to identify separately the assets and liabilities, they can account for the plan on a cash contribution basis.

Where a DB plan is operated by a group of companies which are *under common control*, the principal sponsoring employer is required to account for the plan on a DB basis and other participating employers are allowed to use a cash contribution basis, unless there is a contractual agreement on the sharing of future pension costs, in which case each company should recognise its share of the DB cost.

A: DEFINED CONTRIBUTION SCHEMES

A DC scheme is defined as one 'into which an employer pays regular contributions fixed as an amount or as a percentage of pay' without a 'legal or constructive obligation to pay further contributions if the scheme does not have sufficient assets to pay all employee benefits relating to employee service in the current and prior periods'. A scheme may be taken to be a DC scheme for the purposes of this definition, even where salary-related death-in-service benefits are provided.

The only disclosure required by IAS 19 for DC schemes is the pension expense recognised, which is equal to the amount of contributions due in respect of the accounting period.

B: DEFINED BENEFIT SCHEMES

Overview

A DB scheme is defined as a 'pension or other retirement benefit scheme other than a defined contribution scheme'. Financial statements should reflect pension assets and liabilities, measured at fair value. Retirement benefit-related operating costs, financing costs and any other changes in value of assets and scheme liabilities should be recognised in the period in which the benefit is earned or in which they arise, with no smoothing or spreading.

Benefits to value

Benefits promised under the formal terms of the scheme must be valued. Benefits should be attributed to periods of service according to the scheme's benefit formula, except that uniform accrual should be assumed where the benefit formula is rear-end loaded.

Discretionary benefits are to be included only where the employer has a constructive obligation to provide them.

The *Lloyds* case is expected to result in guidance on how to equalise benefits to reflect unequal GMP, which will require changes to a plan's benefit formula *(see Section 16)*. The trustees may make further changes to benefits if they decide that the most efficient method for achieving equalisation is to convert the relevant pensions to a new unisex pension.

Actuarial assumptions and methodology

IAS 19 requires assets and liabilities to be valued regularly enough that the amounts recognised in the accounts are not materially different from the amounts that would be determined from an up-to-date valuation. The involvement of a qualified actuary is encouraged but not required.

Assets must be measured at fair value. Auditors may require fair value to be taken as bid value rather than mid-market. Liabilities are measured using the projected unit method.

IAS 19 is silent on the treatment of risk benefits. We understand that most auditors expect the 'attribution method' to be used. For benefits that are not service-related, this method allocates benefits in proportion to the ratio of completed years of service to either the vesting period or, if the benefit is unvested, total projected years of service.

The actuarial assumptions are the responsibility of the directors and must be unbiased and mutually compatible, being best estimates of the variables determining the ultimate cost of the benefits. The discount rate to be used should be determined by reference to market yields at the valuation date on high-quality corporate bonds of consistent term and currency.

In February 2018, the IASB amended IAS 19 to clarify the accounting treatment when a plan amendment, curtailment or settlement occurs during a period. On such an event, the net defined benefit liability (asset) is re-measured using the current fair value of plan assets and current actuarial assumptions and the effect of the event assessed at this date. The current service cost and net interest for the period after the re-measurement are determined using the assumptions used for the re-measurement, and the net interest is based on the re-measured net defined benefit liability (asset). The changes are to apply to accounting periods beginning on or after 1 January 2019 (with early adoption allowed).

Balance sheet

Any surplus at the balance sheet date of assets over scheme liabilities calculated as above should be recognised in the balance sheet, subject to any restriction from IFRIC 14 *(see below)*.

IFRIC 14, published by the Interpretation Committee of the IASB, addresses the impact of minimum funding requirements, the limit on an asset for a DB scheme and the interaction of these. IFRIC 14 explains that a refund or a reduction in future contributions may be considered available even if it cannot be realised at the balance sheet date. The company must have a right to any refund, without recourse to the trustees. The available reduction in future contributions must be restricted to allow for any contributions payable under any 'minimum funding requirement' that may apply. The balance sheet asset or liability must also be adjusted to reflect any irrecoverable surplus (on the accounting basis) that will be created in future by the payment of minimum contributions in respect of a past service deficit on the minimum funding basis.

Pension cost

The different components making up the pension cost are shown in the table *on the next page*, along with definitions, details of where they should be recognised in the performance statements, and brief comments.

IAS 19: SUMMARY OF CALCULATION OF PENSION COST

	Component	Where recognised	Description and notes
	Current service cost	Staff cost section of operating cost in the P&L[1]	The increase in the scheme liabilities expected to arise from employees' service in the accounting period, calculated using financial assumptions based on conditions at the beginning of the period. Includes the cost, for the accounting period, of death-in-service and other risk benefits, as well as an allowance for administration expenses (except investment expenses). Expected employees' contributions are offset from the gross cost.
+	Net interest income (expense)	Financing section of the P&L	The interest cost on the net balance sheet position, calculated at the discount rate. This combines: • the increase over the period in the present value of the scheme liabilities because they are closer to settlement, *and* • the expected return on the scheme's assets, calculated using the discount rate. Appropriate allowance should be made for expected cashflows into and out of the fund during the year. May be restricted if there is an irrecoverable surplus.[2]
+	Past service cost	Staff cost section of operating cost in the P&L, unless it attaches to an exceptional item immediately after operating profit in the P&L	A past service cost (PSC) is any increase in the scheme liabilities related to employees' service in prior periods, arising in the current period as a result of a plan amendment or curtailment.
+	Loss (gain) on settlement	Staff cost section of operating cost in the P&L, unless it attaches to an exceptional item immediately after operating profit in the P&L	Settlement occurs where the responsibility for, and risk attaching to, a pension obligation is irrevocably transferred to another party, e.g. by buying matching annuities or by paying a bulk transfer value. Losses or gains arising as a result of settlement instigated by the employer and falling outside the scope of the actuarial assumptions are included in this component of pension cost.
+	Actuarial loss (gain)	OCI[3]	Changes in actuarial surpluses or deficits that arise because events have not coincided with the actuarial assumptions made for the last valuation or because the actuarial assumptions have changed. Investment gains recognised are offset by investment expenses. An adjustment may be required where there is an irrecoverable surplus.[2]

Notes: [1] Profit and loss account. [2] Where the surplus recognised in the balance sheet has to be restricted (as described under the heading '**Balance sheet**'), IAS 19 sets out details of the adjustments required to the performance statements. [3] Other Comprehensive Income.

It is expected that equalising benefits to reflect unequal GMP *(see Section 16)* will be accounted for as a prior service cost resulting in a one-off impact in the P&L under IFRS. There could be a further cost if equalisation is achieved by converting relevant pensions to new unisex pensions in the plan. At this stage, it appears that companies will generally be required to recognise an allowance for equalisation from the date of the judgment of 26 October 2018.

Administration expenses (except investment expenses) are recognised as operating costs in the profit and loss account in the year in which they occur. Investment expenses are offset from actual investment returns and therefore from investment gains recognised in Other Comprehensive Income (OCI).

Disclosure

The disclosures required in respect of defined benefit schemes are as follows:

- a general description of the characteristics of the scheme, including the nature of the benefits provided, the regulatory framework and its impact and responsibilities for governance (including trustee powers)
- a description of the risks associated with the scheme
- a description of any amendments, curtailments and settlements
- a reconciliation of the scheme assets and liabilities to the net asset or liability recognised in the balance sheet, showing separate reconciliations for the scheme assets, the present value of the defined benefit obligation and the effect of any asset ceiling, where each reconciliation shows at least:
  - current service cost
  - interest income or expense
  - re-measurements of the net defined benefit liability or asset, showing separately:
    - the return on scheme assets
    - actuarial gains and losses arising from changes in demographic assumptions
    - actuarial gains and losses arising from changes in financial assumptions
    - changes in the effect of any asset ceiling
  - past service cost and gains or losses from settlements
  - the effect of any changes in foreign exchange rates
  - contributions to the scheme, split between employer and employee
  - payments from the scheme, with the amounts paid in respect of any settlement shown separately
  - the effect of any business mergers, acquisitions or disposals
- a disaggregation of the scheme assets according to nature and risks, and split between those that have a quoted price and those that do not
- the fair value of the employer-related investments, including property occupied by the employer

- the significant actuarial assumptions used to determine the defined benefit obligation
- a sensitivity analysis for each of the significant actuarial assumptions
- a description of any asset–liability matching strategies to manage risk
- an indication of the effect of the scheme on the employer's cashflows, including a description of the funding arrangements and policy, the expected contributions to the scheme over the following year and information on the maturity profile of the scheme
- additional disclosures for multi-employer schemes, such as information on funding arrangements, liability for the obligations of other participating employers, allocation of surplus or deficit, *and*
- additional disclosures for schemes where risk is shared between participating employers.

Future developments

The IASB has a project looking at amendments to IFRIC 14 to address how an entity assesses the availability of a refund when determining the defined benefit asset to disclose. It believes it is feasible to develop a principles-based approach to how an entity assesses the availability of a refund and when an entity can assume gradual settlement of the plan liabilities over time versus when it has to assume full settlement of the plan liabilities at an earlier date. Following its meeting in June 2018, the IASB plans to perform further work on the possible effects of amendments to IFRIC 14 before proceeding to draft amendments. Changes to the amendments would need to be re-exposed so would be unlikely to come into effect until at least 2020.

ACCOUNTING FOR PENSION COSTS UNDER FRS 102

FRS 102 (Section 28) is derived from the IASB's IFRS for SME (Small and Medium-sized Entities), but adapted to reflect UK legislation. The requirements of FRS 102 are simplified compared to IAS 19. In particular, the surplus/deficit does not need to be adjusted for the impact of committed future deficit contributions and the disclosure requirements are reduced to the following:

- a general description of the type of plan, including the funding policy
- the date of the most recent actuarial valuation and a description of the adjustments made to measure the defined benefit obligation at the reporting date if different from the valuation date
- a reconciliation of the opening and closing balances for the defined benefit obligation and the fair value of assets. Each reconciliation shall show the following if applicable:
  - the change in defined benefit liability arising from employee service rendered during the reporting period
  - interest income or expense

  - re-measurement of the net defined benefit liability, showing separately:
    - the return on plan assets less the amount included in interest income or expense
    - actuarial gains and losses
    - any change in the amount of surplus that is not recoverable (excluding amounts included in net interest on the defined benefit liability)
  - plan introductions, changes, curtailments and settlements
- the total cost relating to defined benefit plans for the period, disclosing separately the amounts:
  - recognised in profit or loss as an expense
  - included in the cost of an asset
- for each major asset class (including, but not limited to, equity instruments, debt instruments, property and all other assets) the percentage or amount that each major class constitutes of the fair value of the total plan assets at the reporting date
- the amounts included in the fair value of plan assets for:
  - the entity's own financial instruments
  - property occupied by, or other assets used by, the entity
- the return on plan assets
- the principal actuarial assumptions used, including:
  - discount rates
  - salary increase rates
  - medical cost trend rates
  - any other material actuarial assumption used
- additional disclosures for multi-employer schemes, such as information on funding arrangements, liability for the obligations of other participating employers, allocation of surplus or deficit, *and*
- additional disclosures for schemes where risk is shared between participating employers.

In November 2017, the FRC published the results of its thematic review of corporate pension disclosures. The key messages from the FRC were that it expects companies to:

- identify and explain their bases of pension valuation and the differences between the IAS 19 valuation and the cash funding valuation
- clearly quantify future funding requirements and describe the funding mechanisms adopted
- give clear information about the maturity profile of their obligations
- clearly explain their investment strategy and associated risks, including details of any asset–liability matching strategy
- disclose any significant judgements made when assessing trustee rights

- present meaningful classes of plan assets
- disclose information about their valuation methodology for unquoted assets (e.g. for LDI assets: clearly describing the nature of the components of their LDI portfolio, quantifying and clearly explaining how the fair value of the components has been estimated, explaining why they hold those respective components)
- consider whether aspects of their pension schemes constitute a principal risk or uncertainty and, where appropriate, supplement their pension disclosures with additional information in the strategic report.

RELATED PARTY DISCLOSURES (IAS 24)

Companies complying with IAS 19 also have to provide disclosure figures under IAS 24 – *Related Party Disclosures*. This standard requires information to be disclosed for key management personnel (in aggregate) for each of the following categories:

- short-term employee benefits
- post-employment benefits
- other long-term benefits
- termination benefits, *and*
- share-based payment.

IAS 24 defines key management personnel as persons having authority and responsibility for planning, directing and controlling the activities of the entity, directly or indirectly. This includes (but is not limited to) directors.

For each category, only a single figure is required. For some benefits this one figure is easy to access (for example, actual contributions paid to a DC plan). In our experience, a salary-weighted proportion of the total service cost is typically used for DB plans, although other approaches may also be acceptable.

DISCLOSURE OF DIRECTORS' PENSIONS

Companies Act disclosure requirements have applied to quoted companies for years ending on or after 30 September 2013 in relation to directors' pensions, and the additional disclosure requirements previously imposed by the FCA's Listing Rules ceased to apply from this date.

The legislative requirements apply in addition to the requirements of IAS 24 – *Related Party Disclosures* where applicable. A summary of the current legislative disclosure requirements relating to directors' pensions is *given below*.

Unquoted company disclosures

Unquoted companies are required to make the following disclosures in the notes to their accounts:

- the aggregate value of company contributions paid or treated as paid to a pension scheme to provide money purchase benefits in respect of directors' service
- the number of directors accruing retirement benefits under money purchase schemes and the number accruing benefits under DB schemes
- except where, broadly, aggregate directors' pay and other specified emoluments fall below a specified threshold, the following must be disclosed in respect of the highest-paid director: company contributions in respect of money purchase benefits, and accrued DB pension and lump sum (both excluding benefits from AVCs) at the year-end, *and*
- the aggregate amount by which directors' retirement benefits in payment exceeded the amount they were entitled to at 31 March 1997, or the date the benefits became payable, if later. This does not apply if the benefits were sufficiently funded without recourse to additional contributions and benefits were paid to all pensioner members of the scheme on the same basis.

Quoted company disclosures

The directors' remuneration report must show a single total remuneration figure for all types of reward received by each director over the year, including pension benefits. Defined benefit pensions are valued using similar methodology to that for calculating the annual allowance, but with a factor of 20 rather than 16 for valuing pension accrual.

In addition to the single figure, companies also need to provide details of any defined benefit or cash balance pension rights at the end of the year plus the director's normal retirement date and a description of any additional benefit that will be receivable on early retirement (split between different types of benefit).

Other disclosures are also required, including the link between company performance and pay for the reporting period and scenarios for what directors will be paid for performance at minimum, maximum or on-target levels.

SECTION 27

FINANCIAL SERVICES LEGISLATION AND PENSION SCHEMES

The Financial Conduct Authority (FCA) is responsible for the conduct supervision of all regulated financial firms. Some responsibilities in relation to deposit-taking institutions, insurers and investment firms rest with the Prudential Regulation Authority (PRA) – the FCA is also responsible for the prudential supervision of those institutions not supervised by the PRA.

The Financial Services and Markets Act 2000 (FSMA) is the principal legislation for the regulation of the financial services market. It specifies that 'regulated activities' may only be carried out as a business in the UK by persons who are either authorised or exempt. Regulated activities include dealing or arranging deals in investments, managing investments, advising on investments, safeguarding and administering investments, and establishing collective investment schemes and certain pension schemes. Authorisation is granted by the FCA or the PRA. Firms set up in other EEA states may obtain authorisation through a system of 'passporting'. It is not yet clear what impact the UK's exit from the EU will have on this aspect. The Pensions Regulator *(see Section 8)* also has a regulatory role in respect of workplace contract-based pension arrangements.

Professional firms may be licensed by 'Designated Professional Bodies', such as the Institute and Faculty of Actuaries, to carry out a limited range of 'exempt' regulated activities that are incidental to their main business without FCA authorisation. Firms that are managed or controlled by suitably qualified professionals and fall within the FCA's definition of 'Authorised Professional Firms' may also be able to avail themselves of corresponding exemptions when carrying out similar, non-mainstream, regulated activities.

Implications for pension schemes

Pension scheme trustees and administrators are clearly concerned with investments in various ways. They may be:

- responsible for the management of the scheme's assets (whether in insurance policies or directly invested)
- involved in giving advice or information to scheme members and prospective members, *and/or*
- involved in arranging investments for individual members, such as money purchase fund choices, additional voluntary contributions, purchase of annuities, assigning annuities to individual members, and insurance company buy-outs.

Each of the above can be a 'regulated activity' requiring authorisation by the FCA, for which stringent requirements must be met, unless covered by an exemption. Establishing whether authorisation is required for a particular action can be complicated, particularly when considering relationships between trustees and individual members. The FCA has formal 'perimeter guidance' setting out the circumstances in which authorisation is or is not required.

The definition of 'advice' was amended with effect from 3 January 2018 so that regulated firms give financial advice only when a personal recommendation is made.

Definition of investments

Under the FSMA, the definition of investments includes cash deposits (and also mortgages and general insurance contracts), shares, debentures, government and public securities, options and futures, units in unit trust schemes and long-term insurance contracts. However, the provisions relating to managing, dealing in and advising on investments do not apply to cash deposits.

Generally, a scheme member's interests under the trusts of an occupational pension scheme are not classed as investments. However, rights under a stakeholder scheme are specifically included (even if it is an occupational scheme), as are rights under a personal pension scheme (including a Self-Invested Personal Pension). Rights under any occupational scheme providing safeguarded benefits (i.e. any benefits other than money purchase or cash balance benefits) are also included, but only in relation to advice on conversion or transfer *(see below)*.

Management of investments

The legislation specifically provides that those engaged 'by way of business' in managing investments must be authorised or exempt. This would also apply to trustees managing the assets of occupational pension schemes, even if (as is the case with many trustees) they would not normally be regarded as doing so as a business. However, the legislation exempts them from authorisation if all day-to-day decisions about the management of investments are taken on their behalf by a person who is themself authorised or exempt. Trustees are also permitted to make 'day-to-day' decisions on pooled investment products and insurance contracts, provided that they have first obtained and considered advice from an appropriate authorised or exempt person.

The Pensions Act 1995 also imposes a requirement on pension schemes for trustees to appoint a competent and experienced fund manager who has the necessary authorisation or exemption. It identifies certain matters on which trustees are required to obtain investment advice and also sets out a requirement for most schemes to prepare a written statement of investment principles (SIP) to govern the investment of the scheme's assets. In 2018 the DWP confirmed changes to trustees' investment duties, applying from October 2019. Trustees will be required to set out in their SIP how they take account of financially material considerations, including climate change, and to set out their policies on stewardship. Money purchase schemes will need to disclose on a website the new information, along with an implementation report.

The Myners principles, guidance from the Investment Governance Group and the FRC Stewardship Code set out best practice for pension scheme (and wider institutional) investment activity. Investment guidance for trustees has also been published by the Law Commission and by the Pensions Regulator. *See Section 7 for further details.*

Governance standards and charging restrictions

Minimum governance standards apply to workplace money purchase arrangements. Contract-based schemes must have Independent Governance Committees (IGCs) to assess and report on compliance with the standards, and FCA rules require providers to set up and maintain these IGCs.

Charging restrictions are imposed on qualifying workplace personal pension schemes, similar to those that apply to occupational pension schemes *(see Section 7)*. These are covered in the FCA's rules, which cap charges within default arrangements equivalent to 0.75% per year of funds under management, and prevent firms from paying or receiving consultancy charges. Further restrictions include a ban on 'active member discounts' in qualifying schemes and restrictions on member-borne commissions.

A cap on early exit charges has applied from 31 March 2017 for personal pension schemes, and from 1 October 2017 for occupational pension schemes. In each case the cap is 1% of the member's benefits for existing schemes, and 0% for contracts set up after the relevant cap came into effect.

Advice and guidance

The money purchase flexibilities *(see Section 9)* have created a need to protect members from making poor decisions when accessing pensions. Occupational pension schemes must, where a member's safeguarded benefits in the scheme are valued at over £30,000, check that the member has taken independent financial advice before transferring any safeguarded benefits (or converting them within the scheme), to obtain flexible benefits (i.e. broadly money purchase or cash balance benefits). FCA rules require that all such advice on pension transfers is provided or checked by a Pension Transfer Specialist. The rules were updated in 2018, adding a requirement that such advice must be provided as a personal recommendation, and replacing the previous transfer value analysis requirement with a requirement to undertake appropriate analysis of the client's options.

From 6 April 2017, the Pension Advice Allowance enables members with money purchase benefits to withdraw up to £500 in a year, no more than three times, to pay for retirement financial advice. From the same date, the level of employer-funded 'relevant pensions advice' that members can receive without it being taxed as a benefit in kind was increased. Members with flexible benefits are entitled to free and impartial guidance on their choices through the 'Pension Wise' service. Schemes must also provide retirement risk warnings to members intending to take their benefits flexibly. Once in force, provisions under the Financial Guidance and Claims Act 2018 will require members with flexible benefits to be referred to 'appropriate pensions guidance' before they transfer or start receiving the benefits. From 1 October 2018, the Act also establishes a single financial guidance body responsible for coordinating the provision of debt advice, money guidance and pension guidance (including 'Pension Wise'). *See Section 14 for further details.*

Communication with members

In September 2017, the FCA and the Pensions Regulator issued a new guide explaining what advice employers and trustees can provide on pensions and other financial matters without being subject to formal regulation.

To reflect the requirements of the EU Distance Marketing Directive, UK legislation prevents an employee from being supplied with financial services without a 'prior request'. This means that any information given to employees offering membership of a stakeholder or group personal pension arrangement will need to include a reply slip, unless consent is obtained and recorded by some other means.

However, employers are not prevented from auto-enrolling employees into group personal pension and stakeholder schemes, as an alternative to master trusts such as NEST or their own occupational trust-based scheme *(see Sections 3 to 5).*

The FSMA also places restrictions on financial promotion, prohibiting the communication of any 'invitation or inducement to engage in investment activity', unless it is issued or approved by an authorised person. There are certain exemptions set out in secondary legislation, covering some (but not all) communications involving trustees, beneficiaries and trust settlors (generally, employers in a pension scheme context), but these are generally relevant only to occupational schemes. However, employers offering stakeholder or group personal pension arrangements and third-party administrators acting on their behalf can avoid the restrictions, provided certain conditions are met. These include requirements that the employer must contribute and must not receive any direct financial benefit.

The Government has consulted on regulations to enforce the ban on cold-calling in relation to pensions, introduced under the Financial Guidance and Claims Act. These are expected to be laid in Autumn 2018.

Other activities of the Financial Conduct Authority

The FCA's strategic objective is to ensure that the financial markets function well. As part of this, it regulates the marketing and promotion of all personal pension and stakeholder pension schemes, the authorisation of such schemes' managers, and the activities of pension scheme investment managers. *For further details of its objectives and activities see Section 8.*

Role of the Pensions Regulator

See Section 7 for details of the Regulator's role in scheme governance and Section 8 for more information on the Regulator itself.

The regulation of workplace contract-based pension schemes (such as group personal pension arrangements) is shared between the Pensions Regulator and the FCA. A Memorandum of Understanding explains their respective roles.

The Pensions Regulator is responsible for maximising employers' compliance with their automatic enrolment duties. The Regulator's role also includes dealing with late payment of contributions and other breaches of legislation, promoting good administration, and providing information and education.

The Regulator has published strategy documents for regulating workplace money purchase schemes, including compliance and enforcement policy documents. These emphasise the Regulator's commitment to work with the FCA and relevant government departments with the aim of ensuring that the regulation of occupational and other workplace pensions is joined up, quality standards are consistent and the regulatory framework offers similar levels of member protection. The documents also highlight areas of formal interaction with the FCA, including the sharing of information, sharing and aligning of risks, and joint working on supervision and enforcement. In 2018 the FCA and the Regulator consulted on how they should tackle the key risks facing the sector.

The Financial Services Compensation Scheme (FSCS)

The FSCS is a safety net for customers of financial services firms, dealing with all financial-services-related claims.

The FSCS was set up to pay compensation where an authorised firm (or a firm that has taken over its responsibilities) is unable, or unlikely to be able, to pay claims against it. This is generally when a firm is insolvent or has gone out of business. It covers deposit-related claims, insurance- and investment-related claims and claims related to mortgage advice and arranging. Stakeholder and group personal pension arrangements are covered. From 29 April 2016, all occupational pension schemes providing money purchase benefits are covered, regardless of the size of the company; trustees of schemes providing defined benefits (including small self-administered schemes) can claim only if the employer is small. Claims are limited to £50,000 per member for money purchase benefits, but to £50,000 in total for the trustees of a scheme providing defined benefits. The FCA has consulted on increasing this limit to £85,000 with effect from 1 April 2019.

For long-term insurance (such as pensions), the FSCS protects 100% of the claim, with no upper limit.

SECTION 28

RECENT DEVELOPMENTS

1 Oct 2017	Regulations introduced a cap on early exit charges in occupational money purchase schemes. For such schemes used for automatic enrolment, the ban on member-borne commission is extended to all arrangements.
1 Oct 2017	Changes to the calculation of insolvency risk apply in the calculation of PPF levies for 2018/19 onwards.
18 Dec 2017	The DWP published a report, 'Maintaining the Momentum', recommending changes to the automatic enrolment framework.
22 Jan 2018	HM Treasury published the Government's response to the consultation on indexing and equalising GMPs in public service pension schemes.
1 Feb 2018	With the end of staging, the automatic enrolment duties apply to all employers.
19 Mar 2018	The DWP published a White Paper on 'Protecting defined benefit pension schemes', setting out plans for a stronger Pensions Regulator, clarification of scheme funding principles and promotion of scheme consolidation.
1 Apr 2018	The Pensions Ombudsman took over responsibility for all pension complaints, including those previously dealt with by The Pensions Advisory Service.
6 Apr 2018	New requirements apply to schemes providing money purchase benefits to disclose more details of costs and charges.
6 Apr 2018	Amending regulations enable contracted-out rights to be transferred without member consent to a scheme that has never been contracted-out.
6 Apr 2018	Amending regulations take effect, to simplify the bulk transfer of money purchase benefits without member consent.
6 Apr 2018	Employers can defer paying a section 75 debt on ceasing to employ any active members, through a new deferred debt arrangement.
6 Apr 2018	The standard lifetime allowance increased from £1.0 million to £1.03 million.
6 Apr 2018	Minimum contributions to money purchase schemes used for automatic enrolment increased, following the end of the first transitional period.
6 Apr 2018	New income tax rates and bands for Scottish taxpayers took effect.
16 Apr 2018	The Pensions Regulator published guidance for trustees on cyber security principles for pension schemes.

10 May 2018	The Financial Guidance and Claims Act received Royal Assent. It includes provisions to establish the single financial guidance body.
25 May 2018	The General Data Protection Regulation took effect, introducing a uniform data protection regime across the EU.
4 Jun 2018	HMRC launched the first phase of its Manage and Register Pension Schemes, a new digital platform for pension scheme registration and administration.
26 Jun 2018	The DWP consulted on several proposed measures to strengthen the Pensions Regulator's powers for defined benefit schemes. This was the first of the consultations arising from its White Paper of March 2018.
29 Jun 2018	The Transfers and Re-registration Industry Group published a framework that aims to make transferring money purchase rights between schemes more efficient.
16 Jul 2018	The FRC published a new Corporate Governance Code, applying from 1 January 2019.
20 Jul 2018	HM Treasury issued a consultation on regulations to ban cold calling in relation to pensions.
6 Sep 2018	The Court of Justice of the European Union published a ruling in the case of *Hampshire v PPF*, which could result in changes to PPF compensation levels.
11 Sep 2018	The DWP published the Government's response to its consultation on changes to the investment regulations, which will come into force from 1 October 2019. The changes include a requirement for trustees to set out in their statement of investment principles how they take account of risks such as climate change.
18 Sep 2018	The Pensions Regulator announced a new approach to regulating workplace pension schemes. It will monitor schemes more closely, including higher- and lower-intensity interventions depending on the risks identified, and introduce one-to-one supervision for 60 of the largest schemes.
1 Oct 2018	A new authorisation and supervision regime applies to master trusts. It is administered by the Pensions Regulator, with a Code of Practice providing guidance.
26 Oct 2018	The High Court ruled that trustees have a duty 'to equalise benefits for men and women so as to alter the result which is at present produced in relation to GMPs' and suggested several methods that can be used to achieve this.
6 Nov 2018	State Pension Age was equalised at 65 for men and women.

SECTION 29

SIGNIFICANT PENSION DATES

AUTOMATIC ENROLMENT

01.07.12	Earliest date to which large employers could bring forward their staging date for automatic enrolment.
01.10.12	(i) Employer automatic enrolment obligations start, staged over a period of some five years dependent on employer payroll size. (ii) Minimum contribution of 2% (including minimum 1% employer) of qualifying earnings for money purchase arrangements.
01.04.17	Removal of NEST annual contribution limit and some transfer restrictions.
30.09.17	End of the transitional period that allowed DB and hybrid schemes to defer automatic enrolment.
06.04.18	Minimum contribution of 5% (including minimum 2% employer) of qualifying earnings for money purchase schemes.
06.04.19	Minimum contribution of 8% (including minimum 3% employer) of qualifying earnings for money purchase schemes.

DISCLOSURE AND ACCOUNTING

01.11.86	Pension scheme disclosure requirements introduced.
06.04.97	New disclosure requirements introduced by Pensions Act 1995.
22.06.01	FRS 17 accounting procedures gradually introduced.
31.12.02	New directors' remuneration reporting standards introduced.
06.04.03	Statutory money purchase illustrations (SMPIs) to be provided to pension scheme members with money purchase benefits.
01.01.05	Consolidated group accounts of companies listed and regulated in EU member states generally required to comply with International Accounting Standards (IAS). Full implementation of FRS 17 required by UK companies not adopting IAS.
30.12.05	Trustees to provide defined benefit members with an annual summary funding statement.
06.04.07	FRS 17 disclosure requirements brought into line with those of IAS 19.
01.12.10	Pension schemes permitted to meet disclosure requirements by providing some information electronically.
01.01.13	Revised IAS 19 for reporting years beginning on or after this date.

30.09.13	New directors' remuneration reporting standards for reporting years ending on or after this date. 'Greenbury' Listing Rules requirements removed.
06.04.14	Revised disclosure regulations in force, including a requirement in money purchase arrangements for 'lifestyling' information where relevant.
01.07.14	Implementation of the US–UK agreement on US Foreign Account Tax Compliance Act (FATCA).
01.01.15	FRS 102 replaced FRS 17. Early adoption allowed for years ending on or after 31.12.12. Revised SORP for pension scheme accounts.
06.04.15	New disclosure requirements introduced in relation to 'flexible benefits' in money purchase and cash balance arrangements.
06.04.16	Generic risk warnings required when benefits in occupational schemes can be accessed flexibly.
06.04.18	(i) Tailored risk warnings required when a member considers accessing safeguarded-flexible benefits. (ii) New disclosures of costs, charges and investment information for money purchase schemes are required.
06.04.19	Information about pooled funds must be provided on request.

DIVORCE

01.07.96	Courts in England and Wales required to take pension rights into account when making financial provision orders on petitions for divorce.
19.08.96	Courts in Scotland required to take pension rights into account when making financial provision orders on actions for divorce.
01.12.00	Pension sharing provisions in force.
05.12.05	Revised forms and procedures introduced for pension sharing and earmarking.
06.04.09	Abolition of legislative restrictions on pension credit benefits arising from contracted-out rights (safeguarded rights).
06.04.11	PPF compensation can be shared on divorce or dissolution of a civil partnership.

EQUAL TREATMENT

08.04.76	*Defrenne* judgment in ECJ established (after later clarification) the right of men and women to equal access to pension schemes.
07.11.87	Sex Discrimination Act 1986 came into force: compulsory retirement ages must be the same for men and women.

17.05.90	*Barber* judgment (as clarified by later cases): occupational pensions are pay, and benefits in respect of service from 17.05.90 must be equal.
23.06.94	Maternity and family leave provisions of Social Security Act 1989 brought into effect. Benefits during periods of paid maternity absence must continue to accrue based on notional full salary.
16.10.94	All employment rights (other than pay) to be maintained during statutory ordinary maternity leave.
02.12.96	Parts of Disability Discrimination Act 1995 dealing with employment and the supply of services effective.
01.07.00	Discrimination against part-timers illegal under the terms of Employment Relations Act 1999 unless objectively justified.
01.10.02	Discrimination against fixed-term workers became illegal unless objectively justified.
01.12.03	Legislation against discrimination by sexual orientation in force.
02.12.03	Legislation against discrimination by religion or belief in force.
01.10.04	Revised disability discrimination legislation in force.
05.12.05	Under the Civil Partnership Act 2004, civil partners must be given the same benefits, for future service, as those who are married.
01.12.06	Legislation against discrimination by age in force.
01.04.07	Statutory maternity and adoption pay periods increased from 26 to 39 weeks.
08.07.09	The *Foster Wheeler* judgment established that consent to retirement from age 60 could not be withheld from members with service in the *Barber* window (with a normal retirement age of 60).
08.04.10	Equality Act 2010 received Royal Assent, harmonising, and in some respects extending, existing discrimination laws.
01.10.11	Default retirement age of 65 abolished.
21.12.12	Insurance premiums based on gender not permitted from this date, as a result of the *Test-Achats* judgment by CJEU.
13.03.14	Marriage (Same Sex Couples) Act 2013 in force. Marriage includes same-sex couples and conversion of civil partnerships.
16.12.14	Marriage and Civil Partnership (Scotland) Act in force, bringing same-sex marriage provisions to Scotland.
05.04.15	Shared parental leave introduced.

PROTECTING MEMBERS

06.04.88	Compulsory membership of occupational schemes prohibited.

17.08.90	No surplus refund to employer unless LPI given.
12.11.90	Requirement to appoint independent trustee on employer insolvency.
02.04.91	Pensions Ombudsman in operation.
09.03.92	Self-investment restrictions effective.
29.06.92	Debt on employer on winding up of pension scheme.
06.10.96	'Member-nominated trustees' legislation commenced (and became fully effective from 06.04.97).
06.04.97	(i) Minimum Funding Requirement (MFR) and Statement of Investment Principles introduced. (ii) LPI increases became compulsory for future benefit accrual. (iii) Appointments of scheme actuary and auditor required. (iv) Internal Dispute Resolution Procedures required. (v) Pensions Compensation Board powers commenced. (vi) Opra could remove or suspend trustees and impose civil penalties.
29.05.00	Protection of pension rights on bankruptcy under approved pension schemes introduced.
06.04.01	Requirement for monitoring contributions to personal pensions.
19.03.02	Interim MFR changes: lengthened deficit correction periods; partial abolition of annual recertification; changes to wind-up asset allocation priority calculations and debt-on-employer calculations where employer solvent.
11.06.03	Employer debt increased to full buyout level for solvent employer scheme wind-ups.
06.04.05	First provisions of Pensions Act 2004 came into force, including Pension Protection Fund, new Pensions Regulator and: (i) introduction of pension protection on transfer of employment to which TUPE regulations apply, *and* (ii) changes to LPI cap from 5% p.a. to 2.5% p.a. for future service. Money purchase benefits exempt from LPI.
01.09.05	Financial Assistance Scheme came into operation.
02.09.05	Debt on employer when leaving multi-employer schemes increases to share of full buy-out deficiency, unless approved withdrawal arrangement put in place.
30.12.05	(i) Scheme-specific funding requirement contained in Pensions Act 2004, replacing the MFR. (ii) New requirements for schemes operating as 'cross-border' within the EEA.

06.04.06	Remaining Pensions Act 2004 provisions in force, including: (i) new regulations on scheme modifications (section 67) (ii) new requirements for member-nominated trustees, including removal of the facility to opt out, *and* (iii) requirements placed on trustees to have specific knowledge and understanding of pension issues.
06.04.08	Revised debt-on-employer provisions give more flexibility in multi-employer schemes.
06.04.10	Corporate restructuring permitted without triggering an employer debt provided certain conditions are satisfied.
06.04.12	Further amendments to debt-on-employer provisions provide more flexibility in multi-employer schemes.
01.07.12	Time limits for employers to pay over member contributions to schemes changed.
01.04.13	The Financial Services Authority is replaced by two bodies, the Prudential Regulation Authority and the Financial Conduct Authority.
21.11.13	Regulator's code of practice on the governance and administration of trust-based money purchase schemes came into force.
24.07.14	Definition of money purchase benefits changed by Pensions Act 2011.
29.07.14	Regulator's revised code of practice on funding defined benefits in force.
06.04.15	Trustees of money purchase schemes must appoint a chair within three months, responsible for signing off an annual statement explaining how new governance standards and charge controls are being met.
06.04.16	Revised deadline for trustees to amend their rules using a 'section 251 resolution' in order to keep the option of a refund of surplus.
28.07.16	Regulator's revised code of practice on trust-based schemes providing money purchase benefits came into force.
01.09.16	Financial Assistance Scheme closed to new schemes.
06.04.17	PPF compensation cap increased for members with over 20 years' service.
01.10.17	Cap (of 1%) on exit charges for existing members, and ban for new members, for occupational schemes.
01.04.18	All dispute resolution functions transferred to Pensions Ombudsman.
06.04.18	(i) Simplified process for pure DC to DC transfers. (ii) Deferred debt option introduced for multi-employer schemes.

25.05.18	EU General Data Protection Regulation (GDPR) and new Data Protection Act apply.
01.10.18	(i) Master trust authorisation and supervision regime in force. (ii) Single financial guidance body introduced: it will replace the Money Advice Service, Pensions Advisory Service and Pension Wise.
13.01.19	Deadline for revised EU pensions directive to be incorporated into EU states' national legislation.
01.10.19	Option to use actuarial certification process for pure DC to DC transfers removed.

STATE SCHEMES AND CONTRACTING OUT

06.04.75	Benefits under Graduated Scheme cease to accrue.
06.04.78	Start of SERPS. DB schemes can contract out.
01.01.85	Anti-franking introduced for leavers on or after this date.
01.11.86	Contracting-out quality test removed.
06.04.87	Contracting out via personal pension could be backdated to this date.
06.04.88	(i) SERPS benefits reduced for retirement after 2000. (ii) GMP accrual rates reduced. (iii) GMPs accrued after this date must receive increases of up to 3% p.a. from scheme. (iv) Fixed rate GMP revaluation for future leavers 7.5%. (v) Widowers' GMPs introduced. (vi) Money purchase contracting out (COMPS) introduced. (vii) 2% incentive payments introduced.
06.04.93	(i) Fixed rate GMP revaluation for future leavers 7%. (ii) 2% incentive payments ceased; 1% incentive payments introduced for personal pension contributors aged 30 or over.
06.04.97	(i) 1% incentive payments paid to personal pension contributors aged 30 or over ceased. (ii) Age-related rebates introduced for contracted-out money purchase (COMP) schemes and appropriate personal pensions (APPs). (iii) Link with SERPS broken. (iv) GMP accruals cease and Reference Scheme Test introduced for contracted-out salary-related (COSR) schemes . (v) Limited Revaluation and State Scheme premium options (other than contributions equivalent premiums – CEPs) removed. (vi) Fixed rate GMP revaluation for future leavers reduced to 6.25%. (vii) Contracted-out mixed benefit (COMB) schemes permitted.

06.04.02	(i) State Second Pension (S2P) replaces SERPS. (ii) New table of rebates to 2007, with different levels of rebates applying to different tranches of earnings for personal pensions. (iii) Fixed rate GMP revaluation for future leavers reduced to 4.5%. (iv) Automatic periodic certification of COSR assets ends.
06.10.03	State Pension Credit replaces Minimum Income Guarantee.
06.04.07	(i) New table of rebates to 2012. (ii) Fixed rate GMP revaluation for future leavers reduced to 4%.
06.04.09	Trustees, with employer consent, able to convert GMPs into 'normal' scheme pensions.
06.04.10	State Pension Age for women starts to increase from 60 to 65, over a transitional period now due to last until December 2018.
06.04.10	Pensions Act 2007 introduces extensive changes to State pensions, including: (i) 30 contributory years for full Basic State Pension (BSP), *and* (ii) S2P reformed to make it a flat-rate top-up to BSP.
06.04.11	(i) BSP to increase each year in line with the highest of earnings increases, price increases and 2.5% ('triple lock'). (ii) First GMP increase order based on CPI rather than RPI.
06.04.12	(i) Abolition of contracting out on a money purchase basis and removal of all protected rights restrictions. (ii) New rebates for COSR schemes effective to 2017. (iii) Transfers of COSR rights to non-COSR schemes permitted. (iv) Fixed rate GMP revaluation for future leavers 4.75%.
06.04.16	(i) New State pension for those reaching State Pension Age on or after this date. (ii) Salary-related contracting out abolished. (iii) Bulk transfers of contracted-out rights only permitted to formerly contracted-out schemes (rules extended from 6 April 2018 – *see below*). (iv) Statutory power to amend previously contracted-out schemes effective from this date.
06.04.17	Fixed rate GMP revaluation for future leavers 3.5%.
06.04.18	Bulk transfers of contracted-out rights permitted to schemes that have never been contracted-out.
06.12.18	State Pension Age for men and women to start increasing from 65 to 66 over a transitional period to October 2020.
05.04.21	Statutory power to amend previously contracted-out schemes will end.
06.04.26	State Pension Age for men and women to start increasing from 66 to 67 over a transitional period to April 2028.

TAXATION

17.03.87	Revised limits for new members on or after this date.
06.04.87	Controls on surplus.
01.07.88	Personal pensions available.
14.03.89 & 01.06.89	1989 Revenue limits regime introduced for members joining newly established schemes on or after 14.03.89 and existing schemes on or after 01.06.89.
27.07.89	Concurrent membership of approved and unapproved schemes permissible.
30.06.95	Annuity purchase deferral and income withdrawal permitted for personal pensions.
01.01.97	Reinstatement to pension schemes permitted on special terms for those mis-sold personal pensions.
02.07.97	Tax credits on UK dividend income can no longer be claimed by pension schemes.
30.06.99	Annuity purchase deferral and income drawdown introduced for money purchase occupational schemes and buy-out contracts.
06.04.01	Changes to personal pension tax regime: (i) contributions of up to £3,600 p.a. permitted irrespective of earnings (ii) 'carry forward' facility removed (iii) 'carry back' facility radically reduced (iv) contributions for risk benefits, for new entrants, limited to 10% of total contribution paid for year, *and* (v) concurrent membership of occupational and personal pension schemes permitted for those earning under £30,000 p.a.
11.05.01	Rate of tax on refund of surplus reduced from 40% to 35%.
06.04.06	(i) New tax regime replaces former contribution and benefit limits; lifetime allowance introduced, with transitional protections. (ii) Requirement for occupational pension schemes to offer an AVC facility removed.
22.04.09	Special annual allowance charge introduced for 2009/10 and 2010/11.
01.12.09	Additional authorised payments permitted, including *de minimis* commutation payments of up to £2,000.
06.04.10	Increase in the normal minimum pension age from 50 to 55.
06.04.11	(i) Annual allowance reduced to £50,000. (ii) Requirement to annuitise before age 75 removed; flexible drawdown introduced.

06.04.11 *(continued)*	(iii) Lump sum death benefits paid from age 75 authorised but, along with certain other lump sum death benefits, taxed at 55%.
06.04.12	Lifetime allowance reduced to £1.5 million. Fixed Protection effective.
27.03.14	Transitional flexibility ahead of 06.04.15 changes, and increased limits for the commutation of small benefits and capped drawdown.
06.04.14	Lifetime allowance reduced to £1.25 million and the annual allowance reduced to £40,000. Fixed Protection 2014 and Individual Protection effective.
06.04.15	(i) Money purchase flexibility – full access to money purchase (and cash balance) accounts as lump sums or as unrestricted drawdown. (ii) Money purchase annual allowance of £10,000 applies from first tax year in which an individual accesses pension rights flexibly. (iii) Reduction in tax on certain money purchase funds on death. (iv) Introduction of the 'guidance guarantee', and Pension Wise to provide it.
08.07.15	All Pension Input Periods close and a new PIP runs from 09.07.15 to 05.04.16. Subsequent PIPs to be aligned with tax year.
06.04.16	(i) Scotland Act 2012 empowers the Scottish Parliament to set income tax at a different rate in Scotland. (ii) Lifetime allowance reduced to £1.0 million. Fixed Protection 2016 and Individual Protection 2016 effective. (iii) Tapered reduction in annual allowance for those earning above £150,000 p.a. (iv) Marginal tax rate applies for certain death benefits which were previously charged at 45%.
09.03.17	Overseas transfer charge on certain transfers.
06.04.17	(i) Pension advice exemption from income tax for first £500 of relevant pensions advice provided by employer. (ii) Money purchase annual allowance reduced to £4,000. (iii) Lifetime ISA introduced. (iv) Scottish income tax thresholds start to diverge from rest of UK.
06.04.18	(i) Lifetime allowance increased to £1.03 million (and set to increase in line with CPI, annually from this date). (ii) Scottish income tax rates/bands start to diverge from rest of UK.

TRANSFERS, PRESERVATION AND REVALUATION

06.04.75	Leavers on or after this date aged at least 26 and with 5 years' qualifying service entitled to preserved benefits.

01.01.86	(i) Statutory right to cash equivalent for leavers on or after this date. Non-GMP deferred pensions of such leavers accrued from 01.01.85 to be revalued, broadly at lower of 5% p.a. or price inflation. (ii) Age 26 requirement for preservation removed.
06.04.88	Minimum period of qualifying service for entitlement to preserved benefits amended to two years, for leavers on or after this date.
01.01.91	Leavers on or after this date receive revaluations on whole non-GMP deferred pension.
19.03.97	Occupational pension scheme members permitted to transfer personal pension benefits into a FSAVC.
06.04.97	(i) Rights to cash equivalent extended to pre-01.01.86 leavers. (ii) Three-month guarantee on cash equivalent quotations for salary-related benefits introduced. (iii) Cash equivalents subject to a minimum of the MFR value.
01.12.00	Investment-linked annuity allowed as an alternative to LPI increase for non-protected rights under a money purchase scheme.
04.08.03	Trustees permitted to cut back individual transfer values where scheme is underfunded.
06.04.06	Leavers with between 3 and 24 months' pensionable service entitled to a cash transfer sum as an option.
01.10.08	Transfer values to be set by trustees (on at least a 'best estimate' basis after taking actuarial advice).
06.04.09	Minimum revaluation of non-GMP deferred pensions accrued from this date reduced to the lower of 2.5% p.a. or price inflation.
01.01.11	First statutory revaluation order based on CPI rather than RPI effective.
06.04.15	Independent financial advice must be obtained for transfers or conversion of safeguarded benefits valued at more than £30,000 into flexible benefits.
01.10.15	New joiners to money purchase schemes acquire a right to preserved benefits after 30 days (and short service refunds cannot then be paid).
06.04.17	Revised QROPS and QOPS definitions.

EFRBS/UNAPPROVED BENEFITS

27.07.89	Membership of unapproved schemes to provide benefits on top of those from approved schemes permitted.

01.12.93	Taxation of lump sum benefits from certain offshore Funded Unapproved Retirement Benefit Schemes (FURBS).
06.04.98	National Insurance contributions payable on contributions to money purchase FURBS.
06.04.99	National Insurance contributions payable on contributions to final salary FURBS.
06.04.06	Special tax treatment of unapproved pension arrangements removed (subject to transitional provisions). Unapproved schemes become Employer-Financed Retirement Benefit Schemes (EFRBS).
06.04.11	Finance Act 2011 provisions apply, amending the taxation of funded and certain unfunded secured EFRBS.
04.11.13	Introduction of the 'employment income hallmark' under the Disclosure of Tax Avoidance Schemes (DOTAS) regulations; certain EFRBS set up on or after this date may need to be disclosed.

SECTION 30

UK PENSIONS CASE LAW

This section lists a number of legal cases that are of significance in the development and understanding of pensions. We have included summaries of cases heard in courts of law and tribunals, and significant determinations by the Pensions Ombudsman and the Pensions Regulator.

The list is not intended to be exhaustive and the comments given are merely an indication of the case content. No reliance should be placed on these summary comments. Legal advice should always be sought for guidance as to the applicability of case law. The year quoted below for each case usually refers to the date of a published law report. This may be a later year than the judgment or determination.

TRUSTEESHIP

Re Whiteley (Court of Appeal) [1886]

The duty of a trustee is to take such care as an ordinary prudent man would take if he were minded to make investment for the benefit of other people for whom he felt bound to provide.

Learoyd v Whiteley (House of Lords) [1887]

A trustee must use ordinary care and caution and is entitled to rely upon skilled persons.

Re Skeats' Settlement (High Court) [1889]

The power of appointment of trustees is fiduciary. The person in whom the power is vested cannot appoint themselves as a trustee.

Re Hastings-Bass (Court of Appeal) [1975]

Concerns the ability of trustees to have their past mistakes corrected by the courts. Subsequent cases (such as *Pitt v Holt* [2011] and see in particular *Futter v HMRC* [2013]) have limited the application of the 'rule in *Hastings-Bass*', which broadly states that where trustees have acted without taking relevant considerations into account, resulting in an unintended effect, the court may intervene to correct the error.

Cowan v Scargill (High Court) [1984]

The duty of trustees to act in the best interests of the present and future beneficiaries of the trust is paramount. Normally this means the best *financial* interests.

Martin v City of Edinburgh District Council (Court of Session, Scotland) [1989]

Whilst trustees cannot be expected to set aside completely all personal preferences and conscientiously held principles, they must exercise fair and impartial judgement on the merits of the issues before them. The investment duty of a trustee is not merely to rubber-stamp the professional advice of financial advisers.

Wilson v Law Debenture (High Court) [1995]

Courts will not compel trustees to disclose the reasons for the exercise of a discretion (but see *Allen v TKM Group Pension Scheme* [2002]).

Elliott v Pensions Ombudsman (High Court) [1998]

Trustees can exercise discretion to favour certain categories of members over other categories.

Harding and Others (Trustees of Joy Manufacturing Holdings Ltd Pension and Life Assurance Scheme), petitioners (Court of Session, Inner House, Scotland) [1999]

Trustees in Scotland may not surrender the exercise of their discretion to the Court.

Edge v Pensions Ombudsman (Court of Appeal) [2000]

The main purpose of a pension scheme is not served by putting an employer out of business, nor by setting contributions or benefits at levels that deter employees from joining. Trustees are not obliged to put forward proposals on use of surplus that they do not think are fair to the employers.

When exercising discretions, trustees must give proper consideration to all relevant matters, and may reach a decision that appears to favour one interest over others. However, any explanation given may be evaluated critically, and appropriate inferences drawn from a failure to give an explanation when called for.

Allen v TKM Group Pension Scheme (Pensions Ombudsman) [2002]

Trustees may find themselves judged to have acted with maladministration even where they have not acted unlawfully. It is good administrative practice for trustees to provide reasons for their decisions to those with a legitimate interest in the matter, and they should generally make the minutes of their meetings available to scheme members.

The Ombudsman's ruling appears to contradict an established trust law principle that trustees are not obliged to reveal the reasons for their decisions when exercising discretions (see *Wilson v Law Debenture* [1995]). An Ombudsman's ruling is, however, not a binding precedent on schemes generally and it may be that a Court would take a different view from the Ombudsman.

Lawrence Graham Trust Corporation v Trustees of Greenup and Thompson Limited Pension Scheme (Pensions Ombudsman) [2008]

On liquidation of the employer, a loan from the trustees, made in breach of section 40 of the Pensions Act 1995 and the terms of the trust, had not been repaid. The Ombudsman determined that the trustees were guilty of breach of trust and personally liable for the outstanding amount.

Gregson v HAE Trustees (High Court) [2008]

Beneficiaries cannot bring indirect 'dog-leg' claims against directors of a corporate trustee, as this would circumvent the principle that no direct duty is owed by the directors to the beneficiaries. However, this appears to conflict with a 1997 ruling allowing an indirect claim in a case where the trustee company was the trustee of only one trust and had no other business interest.

Independent Trustee Services Limited v Hope (High Court) [2009]
Trustees cannot take account of the PPF in making certain decisions. Although this 'Ilford' case related specifically to the purchase of annuities to secure certain benefits, similar principles can be expected to apply in other situations.

Futter v HMRC (Supreme Court) [2013]
The rule in *Hastings-Bass* [1975] may only be applied where the error made by the trustees and their failure to carry out the correct decision-making process amounted to a breach of their fiduciary duty (such breach would not normally be the case where they have relied in good faith on incorrect professional advice). However, in the case of *Futter,* the court was able to use the legal rule of Mistake to correct the error.

EMPLOYERS

Re Courage Group's Pension Schemes, Ryan v Imperial Brewing (High Court) [1987]
The ability to substitute a principal employer is dependent on the purpose for which the intended substitution would be made. A rule-amending power could not be used to change the principal employer to a holding company that had no connection with the previous principal employer and whose purpose was to retain control of a surplus contributed by companies that the holding company had bought.

Imperial Group Pension Trust v Imperial Tobacco (High Court) [1991]
Pension benefits are part of the consideration received by employees for their services. The employer owes his employees a duty of good faith in relation to a pension scheme, and should not act so as to destroy or seriously damage their relationship of confidence and trust. But see *Dalgleish v IBM* [2017].

Hillsdown v Pensions Ombudsman (High Court) [1997]
Under the scheme, the trustees had sole power to deal with a surplus. The employer threatened to bring in employees of new employers to run down the surplus, and persuaded the trustees to agree to an amendment enabling a transfer to another scheme from which a refund to the employer could be made. The Court ruled that the amendment and transfer were for an improper purpose and ordered the refunded surplus to be returned to the scheme. It further ruled that the employer's implied obligation of trust and confidence prevented it from using a power to suspend contributions, whilst at the same time using a power to adhere further employers.

Air Jamaica v Charlton (Privy Council) [1999]
Bearing in mind the employer's obligation to exercise powers in good faith, it was difficult to see how the scheme could be amended in any significant respect once it had discontinued and wind-up was anticipated.

University of Nottingham v Eyett (High Court) [1999]

Where all the relevant information is available to the employee to make his own informed choice, the employer's implied obligation of good faith does not require it to draw the member's attention to the fact that he might have done better financially by changing the timing of his choice. See *Imperial Group Pension Trust v Imperial Tobacco* [1991].

Prudential Staff Pensions v Prudential Assurance (High Court) [2011]

In 2006, after granting discretionary pension increases broadly in line with the Retail Prices Index (RPI) for a number of years, the employer revised its policy by capping annual increases at 2.5%. The Court ruled that, in doing so, the employer had not breached its duty of good faith.

Cherry v Police & Crime Commissioners of South Wales (Pensions Ombudsman) [2014]

An employer owes a duty of care to its employees to inform them of the tax implications of re-employment. Here the protected pension age of 50 was lost on re-employment. Providing such generic information would not amount to giving regulated advice.

Dalgleish v IBM (Court of Appeal) [2017]

The High Court had previously ruled that the employer breached its contractual duty of trust and confidence as well as its duty of good faith to members because of the way it restructured its pension arrangements, and taking into account IBM's previous conduct and communications that had given rise to members' reasonable expectations about the scheme's future. However the Court of Appeal overturned this decision, ruling that, while the company's conduct had given rise to member expectations, these were just one of many considerations that the company should take into account, and that the High Court had been wrong to treat them as being of paramount significance. See also *Imperial Group Pension Trust v Imperial Tobacco* [1991].

Pimlico Plumbers v Smith (Supreme Court) [2018]

Restrictions placed on Mr Smith, a plumber, were inconsistent with him being a self-employed contractor so he was a worker and he should have benefited from employment rights. These would have included automatic enrolment into a workplace pension scheme assuming other eligibility conditions were satisfied. The decision was upheld by the Supreme Court, on appeal.

BENEFITS AND CONTRIBUTIONS

Packwood v APS (Pensions Ombudsman) [1995]

Where trustees failed to consider the use of a power of amendment to increase benefits, this was held to be a breach of trust and maladministration. However, the employer did not breach his implied obligation of good faith by preferring his own interests, having first considered the interests of pensioners.

Barclays Bank v Holmes (High Court) [2000]

Where a defined contribution section has been added to a defined benefit scheme, the surplus in the defined benefit section may (provided that this is not contrary to the trust deed) be used to meet the defined contributions.

Merchant Navy Ratings Pension Fund Trustees v Chambers (High Court) [2001]

An amendment that allows a pensioner's benefits to be transferred without consent is not automatically prohibited. It is for the actuary to consider whether to give a 'section 67' certificate.

Royal Masonic Hospital v Pensions Ombudsman (High Court) [2001]

Unfunded pension schemes are not subject to the preservation requirements.

Hagen v ICI Chemicals and Polymers Ltd (High Court) [2001]

The Court ruled that the employer had misrepresented the position to employees, when informing them that they would receive broadly similar benefits on transfer to a new scheme following a business transfer.

Beckmann v Dynamco Whicheloe Macfarlane Ltd (European Court of Justice) [2002]

Scheme benefits payable on redundancy, before normal pension age, do not fall under the exemption for occupational pension scheme rights under the TUPE legislation. The 2003 ruling in *Martin and Others v South Bank University* built on this decision, extending it to some other early retirement situations.

The 2012 High Court ruling in *Procter & Gamble v SCA* provided further clarification and confirmed that the principles applied to private sector schemes. It has been reported that the parties settled out of court, so some uncertainties about TUPE legislation remain.

Aon Trust Corporation Ltd v KPMG (Court of Appeal) [2005]

The exercise of an express power in the scheme rules (to reduce benefits when the scheme was in deficit) was a power to modify the scheme, coming within the ambit of section 67 of the Pensions Act 1995. Consequently, the power could not be exercised (without member consent) if it would adversely affect accrued rights or entitlements.

Pinsent Curtis v Capital Cranfield Trustees Ltd (Court of Appeal) [2005]

Under a scheme rule which empowered the trustees to determine 'appropriate' contributions, the trustees could seek a lump sum contribution equal to the buy-out deficit during the period for which notice had been given by the employer that he would terminate the scheme.

PNPF Trust Co Ltd v Taylor & Others (High Court) [2010]

The rules of the Pilots' National Pension Fund, an industry-wide scheme, gave the trustees the power to set contributions subject to certain conditions. The scheme funding legislation could be used to set contributions in excess of those allowable under the rules, although this would require the employer's agreement.

IMG v German (Court of Appeal) [2010]

Section 91 of the Pensions Act 1995 does not prevent the bona fide compromise of disputed or doubtful entitlements or rights under an occupational pension scheme.

Houldsworth v Bridge Trustees (Court of Appeal) [2010], (Supreme Court) [2011] (the *Imperial Home Décor* case)

Pensions deriving from money purchase assets but paid directly by the scheme, defined contribution funds with notional investment returns, and money purchase benefits subject to a GMP underpin all remain money purchase benefits for the purposes of the statutory winding-up provisions (and, by implication, other areas of legislation where the same definition is used). The judgment meant that a scheme considered to be a money purchase scheme could have a deficit (or surplus) on winding up, but not be covered by the PPF, and it therefore raised doubts about the UK's compliance with EU legislation protecting pension schemes. As a result the legislative definition of money purchase benefits, for various purposes, was amended by the Pensions Act 2011.

QinetiQ Trustees v QinetiQ Holdings (High Court) [2012]

The rules of the QinetiQ scheme related indexation and revaluation to the RPI 'or any other suitable cost-of-living index selected by the Trustees'. The Court ruled that the particular scheme rules gave the trustees the power to switch to using the Consumer Prices Index (CPI) to calculate future pension increases and revaluation in respect of all service. See also *Arcadia Group v Arcadia Group Pension Trust* [2014].

Arcadia Group v Arcadia Group Pension Trust (High Court) [2014]

The High Court held that the rules of two schemes provide the power to switch from RPI to CPI increases for revaluation and pension increases. The rules link these increases to RPI, defined as 'the Government's Index of Retail Prices or any similar index satisfactory for the purposes of the Inland Revenue'. But see *Buckinghamshire v Barnardo's* [2016].

Horton v Henry (Court of Appeal) [2016]

The Court ruled that an Income Payments Order could not be made against the pension of a bankrupt member, because he could not be compelled to exercise his options at retirement and elect to put his pension into payment. An entitlement to payment was established only where there is a pension in payment under which definite amounts have become contractually payable. This contradicted the ruling in *Raithatha v Williamson,* which was rejected by the Court of Appeal, removing any remaining uncertainty from this area. See also *Hinton v Wotherspoon* [2016].

Buckinghamshire v Barnardo's (Court of Appeal) [2016]

The Court upheld the ruling that the precise wording in the scheme's rules ('General index of Retail Prices published by the Department of Employment or any replacement adopted by the Trustees without prejudicing approval') prevented a switch from RPI to another index while RPI continues to be an officially published index. The *QinetiQ* and *Arcadia* rulings were also confirmed, i.e. that under the particular wording of those schemes' rules, moving to a less generous index was not a detrimental modification for section 67 of Pensions Act 1995.

Hinton v Wotherspoon (High Court) [2016]

The Court ruled that an Income Payments Order could be made against the pension of a bankrupt member who had already put funds into drawdown and had taken income payments. However, if he had put funds into drawdown but not yet taken payment, an IPO could not be made against those funds as an 'entitlement' to payment had not been created (see *Horton v Henry* [2016]).

Hughes v Royal London (High Court) [2016]

The Court overturned a previous Ombudsman decision; it ruled that a statutory right to transfer to an occupational pension scheme required the member to have earnings; but these did not necessarily need to come from an employer participating in that scheme.

Bradbury v BBC (Court of Appeal) [2017]

In 2011, Mr Bradbury was offered a pay rise, on condition of acceptance of a split in salary between pensionable and non-pensionable salary. The High Court ruled that the employer's conduct was not contrary to the scheme rules and there would have been no alienation of an entitlement or right under section 91 of the Pensions Act 1995. In a later ruling, it also ruled that the employer did not breach its implied duties arising from Mr Bradbury's employment contract. The Court of Appeal upheld both rulings. See also *Dalgleish v IBM* [2017].

British Telecom plc v BT Pension Schemes Trustees Ltd (High Court) [2018]

The Court ruled that the BT Pension Scheme could not change its indexation approach from RPI to CPI. The specific scheme rule under consideration would have allowed such a change if RPI had 'become inappropriate'. The Court decided that this was not the case, noting that some of the flaws in RPI were present and known to be present when the rule was written. The employer is appealing the ruling.

WINDING UP AND COMPANY INSOLVENCY

Robins and others v Secretary of State for Work and Pensions (European Court of Justice) [2007] (the *Allied Steel Workers (ASW)* case)

The ECJ ruled that the UK government had not adequately protected the rights of workers in occupational schemes in the event of insolvency (in particular, an insolvency occurring in April 2003), under the 1980 European Insolvency Directive. This case was cited in *Hampshire v PPF* [2018].

NBPF Pension Trustees Ltd v Warnock-Smith (High Court) [2008]

Trustees may use scheme assets on wind-up to purchase insurance to protect themselves against 'run-off' liabilities and claims from overlooked beneficiaries.

MCP v Aon (High Court) [2009]
Trustees are not discharged from liabilities in a scheme wind-up despite giving notice under section 27 of the Trustee Act 1925 to which beneficiaries failed to respond, as the trustees should have been aware of their interests.

Bonas UK (Upper Tribunal) [2011]
The purpose of a Contribution Notice should be to compensate the scheme for the detriment suffered, rather than to actively penalise the company.

Nortel and Lehman Brothers v The Pensions Regulator (Supreme Court) [2013]
A Financial Support Direction can be issued after the insolvency of the employer. However, the debt arising would rank as a 'provable debt' (not an expense of liquidating the company) and so the trustees trying to enforce the debt would be unsecured, non-preferential creditors. This overturns the rulings from inferior courts giving FSDs a 'super-priority'.

Olympic Airlines Pension Scheme v Olympic Airlines (Supreme Court) [2015]
In some circumstances, the UK courts have jurisdiction to wind up a company in England (which might then result in its scheme being eligible to enter the PPF) as a secondary proceeding under European insolvency legislation, even if the company is already in liquidation abroad. In particular, the company must have an 'establishment' in the UK, which entails it carrying out 'economic activity with human means and goods', when secondary proceedings commence. Subsequently the legislation was amended, allowing PPF entry even where a sponsoring employer cannot have an 'insolvency event'.

MNRPF v Stena Line (High Court) [2015]
This ruling confirmed that providing an enhanced revaluation rate, which was not conditional on continued employment by a participating employer, did not prevent pensionable service from having ended.

Carrington Wire (Pensions Regulator's Determinations Panel) [2015]
When a Contribution Notice is issued, because the 'main purpose' is to avoid a section 75 debt, the 'main purpose' test extends to acts that prevent recovery under a guarantee including acts before the debt arose.

Hampshire v PPF (Court of Justice of the European Union) [2018]
Mr Hampshire challenged the level of compensation provided by the PPF after his previous employer became insolvent. The Court of Appeal referred several questions to the CJEU.

The Court ruled that the EU Insolvency Directive should be interpreted to the effect that the PPF is required to provide compensation of at least 50% of the value of every individual's accrued rights in a pension scheme in the event of the insolvency of the scheme's employer. At the time of writing, the PPF is considering what action it can take prior to legislative change and/or the conclusion of UK court proceedings.

SURPLUS AND DEFICITS

British Coal Corporation v British Coal Staff Superannuation Scheme Trustees (High Court) [1995]

An employer's liability to pay future standard contributions may be set against any scheme surplus.

National Grid Co plc v Laws (Court of Appeal) [1999]

Members have no rights in a surplus, only a reasonable expectation that, when contemplating any use of that surplus, fair regard will be paid to their interests.

Wrightson Ltd v Fletcher Challenge Nominees Ltd (Privy Council) [2001]

In a balance of cost scheme, any surplus on a final dissolution is generally to be considered as resulting from past overfunding by the employer.

Sarjeant v Rigid Group (High Court) [2013]

During winding-up the trustees were able to maximise the debt due from the employer by buying out some benefits before fixing the date for calculating the section 75 debt. This reduced the scheme's assets by the full amount of the buy-out cost, which was greater than the value would have been on a section 75 basis.

EQUAL TREATMENT

Defrenne v Sabena (No. 2) (European Court of Justice) [1976]

The principle of equal pay, under Article 119 (now Article 141) of the Treaty of Rome, may be relied upon by the national courts. However, this cannot be applied to claims for periods prior to 8 April 1976. (This case has been taken to indicate that *access* to pension schemes should be equal for men and women from 8 April 1976.)

Bilka-Kaufhaus GmbH v Weber von Hartz (European Court of Justice) [1986]

Where the exclusion of part-timers affected a far greater number of women than men, the equal pay requirements of the Treaty of Rome were infringed unless the employer could show that the exclusion was objectively justified.

Barber v GRE (European Court of Justice) [1990]

Benefits under a pension scheme are deferred pay and therefore subject to equal treatment between men and women.

Roberts v Birds Eye Walls (European Court of Justice) [1993]

The principle of equal treatment presupposes that men and women are in identical situations. Therefore, where a 'bridging pension' is paid only to a male member to offset the fact that a woman's State pension starts earlier, this is not direct sex discrimination. [*Note:* a later case in the ECJ, *Bestuur van het Algemeen Burgerlijk Pensioenfonds v Beune*, seemingly contradicts this, although arguments have been advanced, reconciling the results.]

Ten Oever v Stichting Bedrijfspensioenfonds voor het Glazenwassers (European Court of Justice) [1993]

A survivor's pension falls within the scope of the equal pay requirements.

Coloroll Pension Trustees v Russell (European Court of Justice) [1994]

Equal pension benefits for men and women need only be provided for service from 17 May 1990, except where a claim had been initiated earlier. Unequal benefits must be levelled up for any service after 17 May 1990, but schemes can, in principle, change benefit structures to level down for any service after the date of change. Benefits from voluntary contributions paid by employees are not pay and so not subject to the same equal treatment requirements.

Preston v Wolverhampton (European Court of Justice) [2000]

Part-timers whose exclusion from membership of an occupational pension scheme amounts to indirect sex discrimination can claim retrospective membership as far back as 8 April 1976. The House of Lords later confirmed that the time limit for making such claims is six months from the date of leaving service.

Uppingham School v Shillcock (High Court) [2002]

Offsets from pensionable salary without pro-rating for part-timers are not discriminatory where applied equally to all members. The approach adopted was in any case objectively justifiable as a reasonable method of implementing the legitimate objective of integration with the State scheme.

Allonby v Accrington & Rossendale College (European Court of Justice) [2004]

The female claimant did not have to identify a male comparator with the same employer, where the indirect sex discrimination arose from a wider 'single source'. (Here this was the entry rules to a particular pension scheme.)

Bloxham v Freshfields (Employment Tribunal) [2007]

The tribunal held that the treatment suffered by Mr Bloxham when Freshfields introduced new pension arrangements was potentially discriminatory on grounds of age, but that Freshfields' actions were objectively justified as no less discriminatory means were available to them.

Foster Wheeler v Hanley (Court of Appeal) [2009]

To give effect to rights to equal treatment, the modification of a scheme should be the minimum substantive change and should not give rise to windfall benefits. In the context of the scheme rules, here minimal interference was to prohibit consent to retirement from age 60 from being withheld from members with service in the *Barber* window (with a normal retirement age of 60). The scheme was also modified so that an early retirement reduction could be applied for any part of the benefit due from age 65.

Rosenbladt v Oellerking (Court of Justice of the European Union) [2010]

A collective agreement providing for the automatic retirement of employees at age 65 constituted age discrimination, but was justified as a proportionate means of achieving legitimate aims. The Supreme Court judgment in *Seldon v Clarkson Wright and Jakes* [2012] provides further help in defining the criteria that need to be met to establish the legitimate aim leg of the justification for discrimination.

Belgian Annuities (Court of Justice of the European Union) [2011] (the *Test-Achats* case)

The Court found that the use of insurance premiums based on gender is incompatible with the principle of equal treatment for men and women, and decided that the use of gender-based premiums would be unlawful from 21 December 2012.

Seldon v Clarkson Wright and Jakes (Employment Appeal Tribunal) [2014]

The EAT confirmed earlier decisions that a mandatory retirement age of 65 for partners (the default retirement age at the time) amounted to a proportionate means of achieving the firm's legitimate aims of staffing retention and workforce planning. The subsequent removal of the default retirement age leaves in doubt what would now be considered proportionate. See also *Rosenbladt v Oellerking* [2010].

Kristensen v Experien (Court of Justice of the European Union) [2014]

In this Danish case the CJEU ruled that the use of age-related defined contributions can be objectively justified.

Lock v British Gas (Court of Appeal) [2016]

Contractual 'results-based' commission must be included in the calculation of holiday pay (which may affect pensionable salary).

Safeway v Newton (Court of Appeal) [2017]

The High Court ruled that purported retrospective changes to equalise scheme benefits were invalid. The Court of Appeal upheld the ruling that the amendment had to be made by deed but referred the matter of retrospective change to the CJEU.

Walker v Innospec (Supreme Court) [2017]

A surviving same-sex spouse's or civil partner's entitlement to spouse's pension is determined when it falls to be paid, and not over the member's accrual period. It therefore cannot be restricted to service from 5 December 2005, and the Equality Act 2010 exemption permitting this is a form of discrimination which is incompatible with EU law.

O'Brien v Ministry of Justice (Supreme Court) [2017]

The Supreme Court had determined that there was no objective justification for refusing to give a part-time judge paid on a daily fee basis a pension calculated on a basis pro rata to that of a full-time circuit judge. The Employment Appeal Tribunal subsequently determined that a pro rata pension need only be given in respect of service after 7 April 2000 (when the EU directive should have come into force in the UK). On appeal, the Supreme Court has referred the matter of accrual up to 7 April 2000 to the CJEU.

Re Denise Brewster Judicial Review (Northern Ireland) (Supreme Court) [2017]

The Court ruled that the Local Government Pension Scheme Northern Ireland had to pay Ms Brewster, an unmarried woman, a survivor's pension. The scheme required cohabitees to 'opt in' by completing a nomination form, and refused to pay a pension on the grounds that a form had not been completed. The Court found this requirement to be unlawful. The ruling is of most relevance to public sector schemes in Northern Ireland.

Lloyds Banking Group Pensions Trustees Limited v Lloyds Bank plc and others (High Court) [2018]

Equalisation for the effect of unequal GMPs is required; the trustees have a duty 'to equalise benefits for men and women so as to alter the result which is at present produced in relation to GMPs'. Several methods can be used to achieve this; the employer can require that the minimum cost option be adopted.

ADVISERS AND PROFESSIONALS

Re George Newnes Group Pension Fund (High Court) [1969]

An actuary is an expert. If an actuary acts honestly and does not make an objective mistake, the decision is not open to challenge.

Bartlett v Barclays Trust Co Ltd (No. 1) (High Court) [1980]

A higher duty of care is expected from professional trustees.

Auty v National Coal Board (Court of Appeal) [1985]

Actuarial evidence (relating to loss of value dependent on future economic trends) can be rejected by courts on the grounds that it is based on hearsay and speculative in nature.

Re Imperial Foods Ltd Pension Scheme (High Court) [1986]

An actuarial certificate (relating to a bulk transfer payment) could not be successfully challenged in the absence of a cardinal error of principle or a mathematical error.

Re the Minworth Limited Pension Scheme, Anderson v William M Mercer (Pensions Ombudsman) [1999]

A professional trustee who had failed to give proper thought to risks associated with investment mismatching during a wind-up was 'recklessly indifferent' to the fact that they were in breach of their duties, and was therefore not entitled to be exonerated by a clause exempting trustees from liability other than arising from wilful default or fraud. In addition, the Ombudsman ruled that an actuary was inherently 'concerned with the administration' of the scheme, and so a complaint against the actuary came within his jurisdiction. But see *Armitage v Nurse* [1997].

Wirral BC v Evans (Court of Appeal) [2000]

Administrators have no general duty to advise present or potential future members of the scheme.

Gleave v PPF (High Court) [2008]

Insolvency practitioners cannot dispute section 75 debt claims as calculated by the scheme actuary. The companies went into administration in 2001. The insolvency practitioners had argued that the actuary had overestimated the claim, exercisable by the PPF, by using later mortality tables.

Pollock v Reed (Halcrow Pension Scheme) (High Court) [2015]

The Court ruled that, on a proposed bulk transfer without consent, the actuary could not take into account the security of the benefits when certifying that the benefits in the receiving arrangement were broadly no less favourable than those in the transferring scheme.

TAXATION

Hillsdown v Commissioners of Inland Revenue (High Court) [1999]

The employer had been obliged to repay a refund of surplus on which tax had been paid. The Inland Revenue had originally refused to reimburse this tax. The Court ruled that a repayment of surplus in which no beneficial interest passed was not a payment for the purposes of section 601 ICTA 1988.

JP Morgan Fleming Claverhouse Investment Trust plc and the Association of Investment Trust Companies v Commissioners of HM Revenue & Customs (European Court of Justice) [2007] (the *Wheels* case)

The ECJ suggested that Investment Trust Companies (ITC) should be exempt from paying VAT in respect of investment management charges. The NAPF and the Wheels Common Investment Fund launched a joint challenge against HMRC in the ECJ (now CJEU) on the grounds that the exemption should also apply to pension schemes. The CJEU ruled that UK workplace defined benefit pension funds are not 'special investment funds' and are therefore not exempt (but in relation to defined contribution schemes, see *ATP* [2014]).

Re PPG Holding BV (Court of Justice of the European Union) [2013]

In a Dutch case involving a defined benefit scheme, the CJEU ruled that both the day-to-day management costs and the investment management fees paid by a sponsor (as opposed to those paid by the scheme as in the 2007 *Wheels* case) should be exempt from VAT as long as the investment services provided to the scheme have a direct and immediate link with the employer's taxable activities.

BT Pension Scheme v HMRC (Court of Appeal) [2014]

A CJEU ruling on the different tax treatment of foreign and domestic dividends resulted in claims for tax credits. The trustees argued that exempt approved pension schemes did not need to make a claim for the tax credits because of their exemption from tax on investment income.

However, the court disagreed and further ruled that failure to claim tax credits in previous annual returns meant that BT was now time-barred from obtaining relief.

ATP Pension Service v Skatteministeriet (Court of Justice of the European Union) [2014]

The CJEU ruled that usually a money purchase scheme where assets are pooled should be exempt from VAT on investment management services and that specific administration services could fall within the finance VAT exemptions for payment and transfers. Whether a particular scheme falls within the exemption is up to the national courts to decide.

In money purchase schemes, the members bear the risk of the investments that are being managed and therefore should be subject to the same VAT treatment as investors in other 'special investment funds' which are exempt from VAT on the management of investments (but see the *Wheels* case [2007] for the consideration of defined benefit schemes).

ERRORS AND DISPUTES

Armitage v Nurse (Court of Appeal) [1997]

Trustees can be indemnified under an exoneration clause, even where they have been grossly negligent, provided that they were not reckless. But see *Re the Minworth Limited Pension Scheme, Anderson v William M Mercer* [1999].

Hogg Robinson v Pensions Ombudsman (High Court) [1998]

The trustees were not guilty of maladministration by refusing to extend a guarantee period where the member had had problems because of an incorrect quotation. (But subsequently the Ombudsman determined that the failure to produce an accurate quotation in good time was maladministration.)

Derby v Scottish Equitable (Court of Appeal) [2001]

A member who had received a substantial overpayment from a personal pension was obliged to give up the overpayment after the insurer had realised its mistake, except to the limited extent to which he had spent the money irreversibly and could claim a 'change of position'.

Steria v Hutchison (Court of Appeal) [2006]

The appeal judges ruled that a caveat in the booklet that it did not override the trust deed and rules was adequate to prevent an override if it was clear and 'not tucked away in tiny print in a footnote'. A letter to the member that did not contain a caveat could be overriding, but was irrelevant to the case.

Tyler v Robert Fleming Benefit Consultants and Minet Benefit Consultancy (Pensions Ombudsman) [2008]

The Ombudsman held that Minet (the former administrators) were responsible for the disappearance of data in respect of Mr Tyler. He directed Minet to put Mr Tyler in the position he would have been in had he been included in the subsequent bulk buy-out by purchasing a deferred annuity for him.

Colorcon v Huckell (High Court) [2009]

The Court granted an order for rectification of the scheme rules. Evidence showed that the rules relating to the revaluation of deferred pensions had been amended incorrectly and contrary to the common intention of the employer and trustees.

IBM UK Pensions Trust v IBM UK Holdings (High Court) [2012]

Evidence showed that a rule requiring employer consent for retirement at 60 from active service had been unintentionally introduced in 1983. The trustee successfully argued for the removal of the requirement for consent. The Court granted an order for rectification of the scheme rules.

BCA Pension Trustees (High Court) [2015]

The Court gave an order stating how to correctly interpret the rules to include additional wording, omitted due to a drafting error, because the rules would not work without them. This ruling will protect the trustees against any claim of wrongly administering the scheme, but it is not rectification and members may still contest the interpretation if they wish to do so.

Burgess and others v BIC UK (High Court) [2018]

This judgment considered whether a rule amendment for increases to pensions in payment was valid, and, if not, whether and how overpayments could be recovered. The court held that the increases had been properly paid. Nevertheless, the judge went on to consider the extent to which the trustees could have recovered past overpayments. He commented that the trustees would have had a duty to exercise their equitable right of recoupment (i.e. recovery by adjustment of future pension payments), and took the view that this would not be subject to the six-year limitation period that applies when seeking to recover overpayments by way of a one-off repayment. If the member disputes the amount, the set-off cannot be exercised without the order of a competent court to enforce the payment. As they did not form part of the decision, these comments are not binding, but they give an indication of how the Court might approach this issue in the future.

GENERAL AND MISCELLANEOUS

Mettoy Pension Trustees v Evans (High Court) [1991]

Interpretation of pension scheme documents should be practical and purposive, rather than detailed and literal.

Nuthall v Merrill Lynch (UK) Final Salary Plan trustees (Pensions Ombudsman) [1999]

Trustees can be guilty of maladministration for unnecessary delays in transferring money to individual members' accounts, even if the payments have been made within the maximum timescales permitted by the Pensions Act 1995 (see also *Jones v Tyco Holding (UK) Ltd CARE Pension Scheme* [2011]). In *Bonner v NHS Pension Scheme* [2004], the Ombudsman essentially extended the 1999 determination to other types of pension scheme transaction – ruling that the scheme's inability to deal quickly with a transfer payment was maladministration.

Hoover Ltd v Hetherington (High Court) [2002]

The word 'retires' signifies final withdrawal from some office, without prejudicing the individual's entitlement to work for another office or business. The Court also held that retirement from service by reason of incapacity included retirement in circumstances where the member was in fact capable of full-time work, albeit not of the kind normally undertaken by him or her.

Durant v Financial Services Authority (Court of Appeal) [2003]

Personal data is information that affects an individual's privacy. Two questions can assist in determining the nature of the information: is the information 'biographical', and who is the focus of the information? The fact that an individual's name appears in a document does not mean it will necessarily be personal data about that individual.

The Data Protection Act applies to manual data held in a 'relevant filing system'. A filing system will only be such if it is of sufficient sophistication to provide 'ready accessibility' broadly equivalent to a computerised filing system.

Jones v Tyco Holding (UK) Ltd CARE Pension Scheme (Pensions Ombudsman) [2011]

Administrators should take no more than five working days to raise and issue a cheque for a transfer value once they have all the necessary documentation; and to take longer than that is maladministration, even if the payment is made within the statutory timescale. See also *Nuthall v Merrill Lynch (UK) Final Salary Plan trustees* [1999].

SECTION 31

INTERNATIONAL

Introduction

These summaries highlight key design and financing features in some markets with high levels of employer-sponsored retirement provision. They are an extract from Aon Hewitt's Global Retirement Country Overviews. Readers interested in seeing more details, more countries, or exploring improving their governance of retirement plans globally should email *global.retirement.mailbox@aon.com*.

Countries covered:

- Americas:
  - Canada
  - United States of America
- Europe:
  - Belgium
  - Germany
  - Ireland
  - The Netherlands
  - Switzerland
- Asia Pacific:
  - India
  - Japan.

Abbreviations used in this section

CBA	Collective bargaining agreement
CPI	Consumer prices index
GAAP	Generally accepted accounting principles
IFRS	International Financial Reporting Standard
SSCC	Social security contribution ceiling

BELGIUM

	DB	*DC*
Social security	• Social security pension benefits for salaried workers have a low salary replacement ratio: 40% for a median earner. This should be compared with civil servant workers that have a replacement ratio of 75% in the case of a full career. • Legal retirement age: age 67 as from 1 February 2030; age 66 between 1 February 2025 and 31 January 2030 and age 65 before 1 February 2025. Legal retirement before normal retirement age is possible but under strict conditions: as from 2019 this is possible as from age 63 with 42 years of activity.	• No statutory defined contribution (DC) component. • Mandatory industrywide DC plans exist mainly for blue collar workers.
Programme design	• About 15% of employers provide ongoing defined benefit (DB) plans; a further 50% have closed DB plans (either with or without allowing for future accruals). • Benefits are typically defined as lump sums at retirement and provide about 2.5 times salary below social security ceiling and 6 times salary above social security ceiling. • Employee contributions common.	• 85% of employers provide DC plans. • A median contribution is 2% for low earners; up to and above 6% for high earners. Some plans vary by age/service. • Plans pay lump sums at retirement. • Default plan is insured in the main fund of the insurance company *(see further below on funding)*. Some larger plans are collectively insured or in pension funds. • About 50% of plans have employee contributions, e.g. 2% to 4% of salary.
	• Employees can only take up their retirement benefit at the moment they legally retire. Pension plans are required to align the retirement age in the pension plan with the legal retirement age for new entrants as from 2019. • Employees have the option to convert the lump sum payment into annuity payments with legally defined (expensive) conversion factors but this is rarely applied. This, amongst other things, is due to the disadvantageous fiscal treatment for the recipient. Employers may face additional contribution requirements due to the cost of the annuity. • Where employee contributions are required, employers must receive employee consent when changing the plan. New plans are sometimes set up without employee contributions for this reason.	

(continues...)

BELGIUM *(continued)*

<table>
<tr><th></th><th>DB</th><th>DC</th></tr>
<tr><td>Programne design (continued)</td><td colspan="2">• Discrimination between blue collar and white collar workers must be fully phased out by 2025, meaning that there cannot be different pension plans based on these categories in the same company as from 2025. Different plan rules based on function classes are possible.
• Pre-retirement death benefits are typically part of the pension plan. The common benefit is 2 times annual salary. Post-retirement death benefits are uncommon as most plans are set up as lump sum plans.</td></tr>
<tr><td>Financial management</td><td colspan="2">• There is a 4.4% premium tax and 8.86% social security contribution on employer contributions. There is also a 4.4% premium tax on employee contributions but this tax is usually paid by the employer.</td></tr>
<tr><td></td><td>• Minimum funding requirement based on prescribed discount rate (6%), mortality table (MR/FR) and funding method. Any shortfall with respect to the minimum funding requirement must be settled immediately. The minimum funding requirements are rather lenient.
• For insured plans, financing depends on plan regulations but usually based on level annual premiums (individual accounts).
• For pension funds, LTP (long-term provision) must cover accumulated benefit obligation (ABO) with expected return as discount rate, and adjusted mortality tables. Any shortfall in LTP must be addressed in a recovery plan with a maximum horizon of 3 years.
• Funding is typically reviewed on an annual basis.
• Insured plans (85% prevalence) are usually in the main fund of the insurance company. Returns in the main fund are low (base return without profit sharing <1%; with profit sharing 2–3%). Employers cannot influence the asset management of the main fund. Main fund is typically invested in government and corporate bonds (90%).</td><td>• Plans are funded via individual accounts; however, employers are legally required to guarantee a minimum return on the defined contributions.
• Historically the minimum return was 3.25% for employer contributions and 3.75% for employee contributions. Since 2016, the minimum rate has been 1.75%.
• Actual guaranteed returns from the insurance companies are currently below the minimum returns that the employer has to guarantee (the insurer can unilaterally change the guaranteed return they provide). The guaranteed returns provided by insurance companies are expected to remain below the minimum return the employer has to guarantee for the next few years.
• Most DC plans are insured in the main fund of the insurance company. Returns in the main fund are low (base return without profit sharing <1%; with profit sharing 2–3%). Employers cannot influence the asset management of the main fund. Main fund is typically invested in government and corporate bonds (90%).</td></tr>
</table>

(continues...)

BELGIUM *(continued)*

	DB	*DC*
Financial management (continued)	• More flexible asset management with the insurance company is possible but typically requires scale (>€10m of assets). These plans are typically invested in equities (40–60%) and bonds (60–40%). • Pension funds (15% prevalence) have higher returns (4–5%) but rarely have active asset management due to size of the fund (<€50m). Pension funds are typically invested in equities (40–60%) and bonds (60–40%). • An emerging trend is multi-employer funds as a way for smaller funds to access more diverse and more efficient investment .	• There is a trend to move away from the main fund to more flexible asset management with the insurance company (via a selection of predefined investment funds) or via a pension fund. • Employees generally do not have asset allocation choice; there are some market discussions about providing lifecycle or products giving employees investment choice but this remains rare. Investment choices are typically in predefined investment funds (5–7) because of the requirement to guarantee returns. • In all funding cases the minimum returns by the employer apply. Under IAS19/US GAAP a provision is required for DC plans because of this minimum return.

CANADA

	DB	*DC*
Social security	• Social security (Canadian Pension Plan (CPP)) provides about 40% of pay for average earner: flat benefit of approx. C$590/month (OAS) plus 25% of the 5-year average indexed pay (YMPE). Separate but similar plan in Quebec. • There is an OAS clawback of C$0.15 per C$1 income over C$75,910 (2018). • CPP enhancement will increase the variable part of the CPP benefit from 25% of average indexed pay in 2018 to 33.33% in 2025, and covered earnings will increase by 14% above current levels. The pay replacement level will increase to about 50%. Enhancement is for future service only, full benefit will be earned over 40 years and the enhancement is being phased in from 2019 to 2025. • Ceiling set at national average wages (C$55,900 in 2018), total max. benefit C$20,650 (2018), increasing by about C$7,000 after phase-in. • Higher CPP contributions for the new additional CPP benefit will be phased in from 2019 to 2025. • Unreduced retirement age 65 (no planned increase). • No mandatory DC benefits.	

CANADA *(continued)*

	DB	DC
Programme design	• Fewer than 20% of large private employers provide DB plans open to new hires; in addition 33% still provide on a frozen or closed basis. • Salaried plans, generally final pay-based, provide a typical accrual of 2% per year integrated with social security, paid as lifetime annuity with lump sum equivalent option on termination, but not usually on retirement. Hourly benefits more likely flat-rate. • Normal retirement age 65, common to subsidise early retirement. Average actual age 63. • About 50% provide top-up plans for benefits above tax limits. About 50% of plans adjust for inflation to some degree. About 60% require employee contributions. • Pre-retirement death benefit commuted value; post-retirement upon election with actuarial reduction. • DB pensions continue to be poorly understood by employees (but unions now much better informed). • Recent social security enhancement triggering review of company-sponsored pensions.	• About 90% of large private employers offer DC plans (approx. 10% as DB supplement, remainder in lieu of). • 50% provide match savings plan; 25% provide direct contributions without match requirement, remainder provide combination of both. • Median total potential contribution 5–6%. • Auto-enrolment, escalation possible for some plan designs but not prevalent. • Employee portals are common, providing plan and investment information, modellers and ability to change investments. • Increasing emphasis on promoting retirement income adequacy to employees. • Benefit is paid out via structured payments; annuity possible but rare; small benefits paid as lump sum. • Target benefit plans are a new option between DB and DC, with plans having a target DB benefit and cost certainty. Plan sponsors are able to reduce benefits in case of a funding deficit.

Note: Plan prevalence information in the above material based on the salaried benefit programmes representing 364 large employers from Aon Hewitt's 2016 Benefit SpecSelect™ Online tool. Prevalence may differ for hourly plans, public employers or small employers.

Financial management	• Funding is mandatory, determined by province; reforms under way. Combination of long-term going-concern (expected asset return-based discount rate, projected benefits, 15-year deficit funding) and solvency (plan termination basis, government bond rates, 5-year funding).	• DC plans typically offered by an insurance company bundling investment, administration and communication into a single offering. Increasing interest in customised fund options (more employer control in optimising fund options), but still generally in an insured platform.

(continues...)

CANADA *(continued)*

	DB	*DC*
Financial management (continued)	• Provinces have granted solvency relief due to high solvency valuation contributions. Quebec has eliminated; Ontario will mostly eliminate. • Tax deferral for qualified plans; limit of C$2,944 (2018) annual accrual. • Typical asset mix has 50% growth assets and 40% fixed income/other, 10% real estate. • Liability-driven investing (LDI) and de-risking using flight plans are starting to be used. • Longevity swaps starting to make inroads. • Settlement market is primarily through insurance companies offering group annuities (e.g. buy-in and/or buy-out); lump sum settlements only possible for vested termination; mandatory to offer if more than 10 years from retirement.	• Target date or lifestyle investment options, which vary asset mix by age, are most common (75% of total assets); mandatory default in some provinces, but employees have wide range of investment options, typically 8–10 choices. • Tax deferral up to C$26,500 in 2018 for DC-only employees; maximum inclusive of DB accruals based on prescribed, simplified conversion to present value. After-tax option (returns tax-free) possible but generally found only among individual savers. • Benefits generally paid out via structured settlements (maximum and minimum annual withdrawal) within plan or transfer to another provider; fewer than 5% elect annuity. • Focus on minimising investment and administration costs as means of increasing account balances. • Pooled Retirement Pension Plans (PRPP) a new option where fiduciary responsibility with a third-party administrator. • Industry/policymaker interest in increasing risk-pooling opportunities post-retirement, but no product/vehicle yet.

GERMANY

	DB	*DC*
Social security	• Social security benefits provide about 48% of pay for average full-career earner; maximum covered earnings €78,000 (2018). • Retirement age now 65 years and 7 months – increasing to 67 in 2031.	• The *Riester-Rente* programme provides greater of tax deduction or savings grant for employees who save 4% of salary up to social security ceiling; may be directed to employer-sponsored or private savings.

GERMANY *(continued)*

	DB	*DC*
Programme design	• More than 90% of medium and large employers provide defined benefit (DB) plans; of these, about 90% are open to new hires. • Most plans that are open for new hires (80%) have a contribution-based formula (cash balance/notional account); the remainder (and the typical closed plan) have a traditional final pay formula. Employers may not reduce accruals without consent, so typical to have multiple grandfathered plans. • Common formulas are 1–4% below/4–12% above covered earnings ceiling for contribution-oriented plans. An interest rate guarantee of minimally 0% is required, but most companies (83%) provide higher guarantees. Some plans may require employee matching contributions. • Benefits focused on earnings above SSCC, with no requirements for even provision for lower earners. • In general, traditional plans are required to offer CPI-based pension adjustment or, alternatively, a guaranteed 1% per year increase; 70% of plans elect the latter option. • Trend is towards providing lump sum payments at retirement, but most plans (83%) offer option of annuity payments. Typically, survivor's annuities paid pre- and post-retirement. • Normal retirement age generally 65 with reduced early retirement; avg. actual retirement age 63, slowly increasing.	• Starting 01/01/2018, defined contribution (DC) plans are introduced as a legal option for 'tariff' (unionised) employees up to a maximum contribution of 8% of SSCC. These plans are 'Defined Ambition' – that is, target benefit with adjustment as needed. • DC plans may only be offered by companies if based on a union's collective bargaining agreement (CBA) (terms of agreement may offer other employees option to participate) and financed via direct insurance, *Pensionskasse* or *Pensionsfonds*. • Details of the new plans (investment types, plan management, etc.) are still unknown, to be determined via CBA. • Other than that, employers are not permitted to provide true DC plans, except when an external provider (direct insurance, *Pensionsfonds* or *Pensionskasse*) guarantees the minimum return; those insured plans may qualify as DC plans under IFRS/US GAAP. • Employers must offer salary sacrifice plans (voluntary purchase of pension accruals) upon request; these may simply take the form of the opportunity to pay into a direct insurance contract.
Financial management	• No funding required. • Contributions towards direct insurance, *Pensionsfonds* or *Pensionskasse* plans are tax free up to a maximum amount of 8% of the SSCC from 2018 (until 2017: 4% + €1,800 ≈ 6.4% of SSCC). Amounts in excess are immediately taxed. Book-reserved plans receive a tax deduction on the increase in liability calculated with a prescribed methodology.	

(continues...)

GERMANY *(continued)*

	DB	DC

Financial management (continued)

- Benefits are fully taxable for employees, tax deductible for employers when paid; partial tax relief for lump sum payments.
- Four recognised funding vehicles plus direct pension promises (% of total plans):
  - ***Pensionskasse* (6%)** = captive insurance company; typically used by large local companies or as industry plans
  - **direct insurance (11%)** = deferred annuity contract with a life insurance company
  - ***Pensionsfonds* (2%)** = external vehicle to finance pensions; typically, tariffs are on a best estimate basis with requirement of further contribution if funding level decreases below 100%
  - **support fund (13%)** = external vehicle that often reinsures benefits with a life insurance company: has the advantage of allowing for (mostly) unlimited contributions if reinsured; if not reinsured, contributions are discretionary but quite limited due to tax regulations
  - **direct promise – 68%** of plans are financed (from German legal perspective) only through book reserves.
- All four external funding vehicles may qualify for DC accounting as insured plans under IFRS/US GAAP if vehicle takes over minimum return guarantee.
- Contractual trust agreement (CTA): very popular among multinationals to fund direct promises; it confers no legal status in local law but meets IFRS/US GAAP criteria for funded plan. No funding requirements, full flexibility in investment strategy. 33% of direct promise plans funded via CTA.
- Pension Protection Fund (PSV):
  - mandatory insolvency protection scheme for all direct pension promises, support funds and *Pensionsfonds*
  - contribution base is the actuarial liability of the benefits calculated with 6% discount rate (tax liability); for *Pensionsfonds* the contribution base is only 20% of this liability
  - contribution rate is determined on an annual basis based on the claims to the PSV in the relevant year; 10-year average rate is approx. 0.3%. For 2018 a rate of 0.25% is expected (after a 0.2% rate in 2017).
- When changing pension plans, the benefit level for future service may not be reduced without material reasons; the accrued benefit level for past service may only be reduced in case of serious economic hardship (close to insolvency).
- Lump-sum settlement exercises for retirees are popular – a (closing) window of opportunity for settlement gains as pay-out is commonly calculated considering local GAAP discount rates; only for retirees with annuities started before 2005.

INDIA

	DB	*DC*
Social security	• Payment of a gratuity benefit is mandatory for companies with more than 10 employees. • Minimum benefit is a lump sum at retirement/resignation/death equal to 15 days' basic salary for each year of service with a cap of INR 2 million since late 2017 and a vesting criterion of 5 years. • No mandated retirement age in private sector but typically 58 to 60. • It is mandatory to accumulate earned leaves when not being able to take leave in a year. This becomes long-term/retirement benefits with corresponding defined benefit (DB) liabilities.	• All employers with with 20 and more employees must contribute 12% of applicable basic pay to the Provident Fund (PF) with equal mandatory contribution of 12% by the employee. • Although PF is applicable to employees earning less than the applicable wage of INR 15,000 per month, it is typical market practice for employers to make it mandatory for all employees and pay contributions on full basic pay. The accumulated PF account balance is payable at retirement. • PF has two sub-plans (Employees' Pension Scheme and Employees' Deposit Linked insurance), which provide pension and insurance benefits respectively. • Employees' Pension Scheme provides 50% of pay as pension on retirement (if a full 35-year career) up to a maximum of INR 7,500 per month.
Programme design	• DB pension schemes are no longer common. They can only be found among public sector employers (prior to 2004) and a few legacy large Indian business houses. • Tax exemption on gratuity is available only up to a limit of INR 2 million beyond which the payout is taxable. • Gratuity is accounted for as a retirement benefit but does not lead to adequate pay replacement at retirement hence not perceived highly by employees. • Approximately 50% of employers offer gratuity without a cap to enhance the offering.	• Superannuation and National Pension Scheme (NPS, launched in 2012) are two other voluntary defined contribution (DC) schemes available. • Superannuation are older pension arrangements. About 20%–30% of employers offer Superannuation plans, voluntary DC plans where typically the employer contributes 15% of basic salary (often carved out from the employee's salary). Although quite popular in the last decade, these plans are losing popularity in favour of NPS plans. • It is possible to transfer the Superannuation fund to NPS.

(continues...)

INDIA *(continued)*

	DB	*DC*
Programme design (continued)		• Under NPS, employers contributes 10% of base salary, again usually carved out of the employee salary. NPS has seen a significant growth since its inception in 2012. Funds are portable, and individual accounts are available. • PF contributions and payouts are tax exempt. • Superannuation contributions are tax exempt to INR 150,000 per year, payable 33% tax-free lump sum, 67% taxable annuity at retirement. • NPS contributions are tax exempt up to 10% of basic salary; at retirement 60% is taken as a lump sum, of which 20% is taxed; the balance (40%) is taken as a taxable annuity.
Financial management	• There are no funding requirements for gratuity benefits, but most medium and large employers (80% plus) choose to fund as the contributions are tax deductible. The average funding ratio is about 75%. • 70% plus of employers choose to invest the assets in a traditional cash accumulation scheme through Life Insurance Corporation of India (LIC), the State provider; the remaining employers self-manage the investments or use unit-linked funds (from an insurer). • In cases of in-house fund management, the investments have to be made in line with the investment pattern mandated by the government (mostly government and state bonds). • Leave schemes are mostly unfunded but balance sheet liabilities are provisioned.	• PF may be managed by the government (95% plus) or by the employer as a private trust (Exempted Provident Fund Trust). Exempted Provident Funds (EPFs) are required to match the investment return declared by the government-managed fund. • Companies providing EPF Trusts have in-house fund management with support from investment advisors. • Superannuation plans have a trust governing the scheme similar to the gratuity. The trust serves as an intermediary with the insurance company (80% LIC, 20% private providers) which provides actual investment management. • Self-managed EPF and Superannuation plan investment allocations are stipulated by law: at least 45% government bonds, at least 35% state bonds/bank deposits, no more than 15% equities.

(continues...)

INDIA *(continued)*

	DB	*DC*
Financial management (continued)		• NPS is a fully regulated pension plan managed by the regulator (PFRDA) at all stages. Pension fund managers (currently 8) are appointed by PFRDA; each employee may choose own fund manager, or default to employer choice. • Each fund manager offers a default investment choice, but employees may make their own fund elections as well. Options include equities, corporate bonds, and government bonds, with a limit of 50% equities (a rule passed in FY18 increases limit for equities to 75%).

IRELAND

	DB	*DC*
Social security	• The State Pension (Contributory) is paid to people who have sufficient Irish social insurance contributions paid by the time they reach State Pension Age. It is not means-tested. You can have other income and still get a State Pension (Contributory). This pension (currently approx. €12,652) is taxable but you are unlikely to pay tax if it is your only income. • State Pension Age is dependent on birth date – currently between 66 and 68, reaching 68 in January 2028.	• No statutory defined contribution (DC) provision. • Government has confirmed its intention to introduce a universal pension plan for all workers. Auto-enrolment is the most likely structure. • If no occupational pension arrangement is offered then the company must provide access to a personal pension arrangement for employees but is not required to contribute.
Programme design	• Private sector plans continue to be closed to new employees, with only about 10% remaining open. • Increasingly, private sector plans are now completely frozen, with approximately 30% now frozen.*	• DC is the predominant form of pension provision in the private sector for new employees and future service. • Membership is typically voluntary. Automatic enrolment exists but not prevalent.

(continues...)

* Pensions Authority DB review 2017.

IRELAND *(continued)*

	DB	*DC*
Programme design (continued)	• Trend has been away from DB to DC due to rising costs, driven by lower expected future asset returns, increasing longevity expectations and an onerous statutory funding standard for schemes as they mature. • Public sector plans typically continue to be fully open. • Historically typical benefit is final pay-based accrual of 1/60th of pay per year with little or no integration with State pensions. However, where DB schemes have remained open, commonly benefits are less generous. • Typical normal retirement age of 65. • Common for employees to choose to commute ~25% of pension into tax-free cash at retirement. • DB plans provide (by law) for limited pre-retirement indexation (plus death benefits). • Incapacity pension often provided through plan as enhanced and early pension. • Fixed employee contributions are common, e.g. 5% of pay less the State pension offset.	• Eligibility is generally from joining service or after 6 months. • Approximately 40% of schemes provide a matching contribution structure and 34% provide a fixed rate.* • Average total contribution rate in a fixed structure is 12.4% (7.7% employer rate and 4.7% member rate).* • In a matching structure the median maximum contribution rates are 8% (employer) and 6% (member).* • Employee portals are common; providing plan and investment information, modellers and ability to make investment switches. • Increasing focus on raising awareness of retirement income adequacy and target retirement income and encouraging additional voluntary contributions. • Annuity purchase had traditionally been the dominant form of retirement benefit but increasingly members with small funds are taking a large proportion as cash and as funds get bigger members are investing post-retirement for income drawdown.
Financial management	• Schemes are required to have a plan to get to full funding within a reasonable period when in deficit on the statutory funding standard (maximum of 6 years). • Pace of funding negotiated with trustees, and will depend on investment strategy and sponsor covenant strength.	• Plans are fully funded via contributions to individual accounts and provide no investment guarantees.

(continues...)

* Aon Hewitt Ireland DC Survey 2016.

IRELAND *(continued)*

	DB	*DC*
Financial management (continued)	• EET system where contributions and investment return are exempt from tax while pensions are taxed in retirement. Contributions are subject to age-related earnings limits as well as total earnings limit of €115,000. • Lifetime allowance €2m, above which additional tax applied. • Typical asset mix 60% growth assets and 40% fixed income. • Interest rate hedging is becoming more common albeit starting from a low base – typically sub-30% hedged as a broad average, but wide variation. Leverage used only in very large or sophisticated schemes but more interest of late from smaller schemes. • Settlement market consists of annuities offered by insurance companies, typically price for existing pensions similar to government bond investment with discounts for large transactions. • Pricing higher for pensions not in payment, so transferring risk to members common through transfer values (potentially with enhancements). • Liability-driven investing (LDI) and de-risking using dynamic funding level triggers are becoming more common. • Opportunities to improve portfolio diversification through alternative assets becoming more attainable.	• Tax treatment same as for DB. • DC plans typically offered through insured/bundled or self-administered/unbundled trust-based arrangements. • No restrictions on investment options but typically a range of equity, bond and diversified funds. • Target date and lifestyle options can vary significantly in asset mix by age; customised approaches becoming more common. • Innovation in bespoke individual lifestyle strategies becoming more commonplace. • Growing interest in master trust approaches to address increasing governance burden.

JAPAN

	DB	*DC*
Social security	• State pension payable from 63 (61 for females), rising to 65 by 2025 (2030 for females).	• No statutory defined contribution (DC) plan.

(continues...)

JAPAN *(continued)*

	DB	DC
Social security (continued)	• Flat-rate (¥780,000 p.a. with 40 years of coverage) plus earnings-related (based on career-average capped salary) pension benefits. Replacement ratio is broadly 60% for an average earner, but the ratio is projected to decrease to 50% or below in 20 to 25 years.	
Programme design	• Roughly 91% of companies offer retirement arrangements. • Of these, 32% are defined benefit (DB) only, 51% DB and DC. • Risk-sharing pension plan (DB with benefit decreases/ increases for deficits/surpluses) is new option, first implementation in late 2017. • Following implementation of DC plans in mid-2000s, employers electing to offer DC typically terminated DB and converted existing DB accruals to opening DC balances; remaining DB plans are open for new entrants and accrual. • Historical typical benefit form multiple of monthly pay as lump sum, but cash balance/notional account plans have become the norm. • Average account accrual is 6%–9%; if both DB and DC offered, DB is supplemental for accruals above tax limits. • RAP-type *(see next page)* typically allows lump sum only; other plans provide option of annuities, but usually only annuity certain. • Directors often (especially at domestic firms) have separate benefits, unfunded, more generous benefit levels.	• Of employers with retirement plans, 17% are DC only, 51% DB and DC. • Low contribution cap (¥660,000/year, or ¥330,000 if funded DB is also provided) makes DC only uncompetitive, pairing with unfunded DB (book-reserved RAP) preferred. • DC plans must be open to all employees. • Maximum vesting period is 3 years. • Pre-retirement withdrawal of funds possible only in very limited circumstances (death, serious disability). • Taking out loans against account balance is not common. • Assets are transferable to new employer's DC or personal DC account if none provided. • Employers with DC plans are often preferred by new hires (to avoid setting up a personal DC account). • Employee contributions possible at 22% of employers, but may not exceed employer contribution and cap applies to total. • Normal form of payment can be lump sum, annuity or a mix of both. Annuities are usually fixed term.

(continues...)

JAPAN *(continued)*

	DB	*DC*
Programme design (continued)	• Vesting is 0–1 years for involuntary and 3 years for voluntary termination, but may take up to 15–30 years to qualify for full benefit schedule in the case of voluntary termination. • Employee contribution is possible but unusual (less than 5%). • Retirement age is generally 60 years (both in plan provisions and actual practice). • While companies are obliged to provide continuous employment till 65 if the employee wishes so, most terminate at 60 and rehire on fixed-term contract afterwards; benefits are paid out or deferred.	
Financial management	• Multiple plan structures: book-reserved (RAP) and funded (CPP/CPF, EPF). Employee's Pension Fund (EPF) is a fund which contracts out of part of the social security pension; however legislation that promotes dissolving these funds is in force (2014). • Smaller companies usually operate RAP only. • Separate directors' benefits offered as RAP. • RAP plans can be pre-financed by individual insurance contracts but this practice is uncommon. • Strict and complex funding regulations, annual check-up to determine level of funding and sufficiency of contributions, detailed funding valuation required at least every 5 years. • No legal requirement on term to reach fully funded status; shortfall is usually amortised over 3 to 20 years (range is possible). • Employer contributions are tax deductible. In unfunded plans, the employer receives tax deduction when the benefit is paid. • Employees enjoy tax advantages for cash lump sums.	• Plans are financed in DC funds governed by the DC Law and managed by DC service providers. • The employer must offer a minimum of 3 investment options, with at least 1 option offering a guarantee of principal. • Avg. number of funds is 16 including equities, bonds, and balanced funds, but employees prefer conservative investments – 60% of assets are in cash/bank accounts. • Recent legislation changes made it easier to remove investment products and set the maximum number a company can offer at the same time to 35. • Accounts may not be invested in real estate or financial/commodity futures. • Target-date funds are not widespread. • Employer contributions are tax deductible (with limits). • Employees enjoy advantageous tax treatment on lump sum payment.

(continues...)

JAPAN *(continued)*

	DB	*DC*
Financial management (continued)	• Due to lump sum/annuity certain-focused environment, longevity pressure is smaller than in other countries despite aging population. • Typical asset allocation: 30% equities, 40% bonds, remainder insurance, cash, other. • Buy-out is **not** legally possible in Japan. • 'De-risking' done via more conservative assumptions, less risky portfolio, higher contributions. Hedging usually targets interest rate.	

NETHERLANDS

	DB	*DC*
Social security	• Flat benefit payable from age 66 and 3 months. Approximately €14,200 in 2018, nearly 40% of average earnings. • Age increase to 67 by 2021 and a longevity link thereafter.	• No statutory defined contribution (DC) component.
Programme design	• Over 90% of employees are covered by occupational plans; of these 75% are defined benefit (DB), and of these, most are industry-wide plans, and the remainder single-employer plans, declining in prevalence. • Typical benefit is an indexed career-average accrual of 1.875% per year, integrated with social security, paid as lifetime annuity; executive benefits generally similar. • Fiscal retirement age increases to 68 from January 2018. • Benefits (when not insured) are commonly indexed for inflation pre- and post-retirement, if funding permits.	• About 25% of employers provide either 'true' DC plans, or 'collective DC' (CDC) plans. Current trend is towards 'true' DC plans. • Contribution levels for DC plans are based on a target benefit at retirement. By law, contributions are age-graded and standardised for a given level of target benefit. Contributions are integrated with social security. • CDC plans explicitly express the benefit as a DB benefit accrual at retirement, though with potential for benefit cuts or lack of indexation.

(continues...)

NETHERLANDS *(continued)*

	DB	*DC*
Programme design (continued)	• Employee contributions common. Could be 5% of pensionable pay for single-employer, or up to 12% for industry-wide plans. • Ongoing industry/public policy debate about future of DB plans; move to individual plan member accounts with risk pooling at retirement under consideration.	• Employee contribution rates common; typically flat e.g. 5% pensionable earnings; additional voluntary savings possible. • Employee portals are required, providing plan and investment information, modellers and ability to make investment switches.
Financial management	• Multi-employer plans are functionally DC plans from employer's perspective – fixed contribution, risk borne by employees via potential benefit reductions or lack of indexation. • Single-employer plans may be funded via insurance (fixed deferred annuities) or pension fund; if the latter, require prefunding with specified interest rate; funded ratio of 104% or higher must be maintained or pension cuts are required; a ratio of 130% is required for full indexation. • EET tax treatment, provided accrual and compensation limits met; otherwise entire plan fully taxable. • Pension fund is a separate legal entity with employer obligations contractually agreed; contract may include cap to limit employer contributions. • Pension fund board determines asset mix; no control for employers. • Single-employer plans encouraged to use insurance, industry-wide plan, APF (General Pension Fund) or cross-border arrangement. • Cross-border plans outside the Netherlands (typically in Belgium) offer potential of lower funding costs and improved, centralised governance.	• Plans are fully funded via contributions to individual accounts; they provide no investment guarantees. • CDC plans are treated as DB under US GAAP, unless a multi-employer plan or insured. • EET tax treatment, provided accrual and compensation limits met; otherwise entire plan fully taxable. • DC plans typically offered by an insurance company, premium pension institution (PPI) or a pension fund bundling investment, administration and ommunication into a single offering. • Employees may select funds other than default funds; lifestyle/target date funds common. • Prior to 2016, fixed annuities were required at retirement; now variable annuities are permitted, offering lifetime income that varies based on market returns under very strict conditions. Pension funds (including cross-border funds outside the Netherlands) may also offer annuities in case the employee holds benefits within these funds. • Emerging interest in financial wellness.

SWITZERLAND

	DB	DC
Social security	• Social security benefits provide about 30% of pay for typical earner (CHF 84,600); benefit is progressive and drops considerably for higher earners (CHF 250,000) to about 10% of pay. • Retirement age 65/64 for men/women respectively.	• No pure defined contribution (DC) component in accordance with BVG/LPP law.
Programme design	• All employers are required to provide occupational pensions under BVG/LPP law. Most employers supplement the legally stipulated minimum benefits. Traditional percentage of pay times service accrual formulas have been replaced by cash balance formulas locally labelled 'Swiss DC'. Around 88%/12% of plans are Swiss DC/DB (defined benefit) respectively.* • Statutory accruals range from 7%–18% of pay between CHF 24,675 and CHF 84,600, by age. Employer pays between 50%–70% (minimum 50%) of the total premium. Mandatory minimum interest rate of 1.00% (2018) on mandatory part of the benefit. • Employers typically provide additional contributions of 1%–6% by age category, with employees typically making additional contributions of 0.5%–3% by age category. Maximum pensionable salary CHF 846,000. • Account balance is converted at retirement age into a pension; partial or total lump sums possible. Minimum annuity conversion rate (currently 6.8%) mandated for mandatory benefits.	• No true DC option. • New legislation (Art. 1e) permits pension fund to more easily offer investment choice for contributions (either employer or employee) on salary over CHF 126,900.

(continues...)

* Prevalence data from companies surveyed in the Aon Hewitt Swiss Pension Fund Data Collection 2016.

SWITZERLAND *(continued)*

	DB	*DC*
Programme design (continued)	• Most pension funds offer survivors', death or disability benefits greater than the mandatory pensions. Death – mandatory spouse's pension. Often the benefits are defined as a percentage of the insured salary. • Employers may not reduce future accruals without approval from the board of the foundation.	
Financial management	• 'Swiss DC' plans are funded as if DC plans. Funding involves a degree of discretion, and some variation by canton, as cantonal supervisors vary in interpretation/ implementation of federal regulation. When plan is deemed underfunded, a recovery plan of between 5 and 7 years is required. Typical recovery measures are increased contributions and potentially benefit reductions. • Contributions/earnings/pay-outs are exempt/exempt/ taxed respectively under the BVG/LPP law.	• Same tax treatment for Article 1e benefits as 'Swiss DC'.
	• Pensions are funded via the legal entity of a 'foundation'. • A company may have its own autonomous pension foundation or participate in a collective foundation. • A foundation can be fully insured, partially insured with shared risk or uninsured. • The Guarantee Fund guarantees benefits at insolvent occupational benefit institutions, up to pensionable salary of CHF 126,900, funded by a contribution of 0.1% of BVG salaries and 0.005% of a combination of BVG capital and 10 times pensions in payment. • The mandatory minimum required under BVG/LPP law is tracked via a shadow account.	• Same regulatory environment for Article 1e plans as 'Swiss DC' – separate legal entity required.

(continues...)

SWITZERLAND *(continued)*

	DB	*DC*
Financial management (continued)	• Typical asset allocation of 30% stocks, 40% bonds, 20% real estate and 10% other. Maximum legal limit of 30% allocation to foreign currency investments. Foreign currency fixed income investments are predominantly hedged in Swiss Francs. Foundation board determines allocation. • Asset–liability modelling is generally used (e.g. triennially), either with simplified models or more complex (50/50).	

UNITED STATES

	DB	*DC*
Social security	• Social security provides about 40% of pay for typical earner; benefit is progressive and accruals end at ceiling of US$128,400 in 2018. Max. benefit US$33,456 in 2018. • Unreduced retirement age now 66, increasing to 67 in 2027.	• Some states (e.g. California, Illinois) have passed laws to implement defined contribution (DC) retirement savings plans with auto-enrolment (opt-out possible) for workers without employer-sponsored retirement plans. Oregon plan now operational, others in process. Court challenges continue.
Programme design	• Fewer than 20% of large employers offer defined benefit (DB) open to new hires; about 40% provide on frozen or closed basis. • Pace of DB closures/freezes has slowed, as most employers still offering do so for its value to employees. • Typical benefit of open plans is cash balance (notional account) paid as lump sum with annuity available; for closed/frozen plans, final pay-based, e.g. 1.67% of pay with social security offset, paid as lifetime annuity; may have lump sum equivalent option; no indexation. • Survivor's annuities paid pre-retirement; only if elected with actuarial reduction.	• Nearly all large employers provide a matched savings plan; about half provide additional benefits not dependent on employee contributions. • Average contribution across all plan types about 6% of pay. Contribution may vary across business units. • Balance is drawn down after retirement, or transferred to another tax-qualified plan at retirement or termination. • Maximum employee deferral US$18,500; total employer plus employee contribution max. US$55,000 (2018). Only recognise pay up to US$275,000 (2018). • Survivor's benefits equal to account balance.

(continues...)

UNITED STATES *(continued)*

	DB	*DC*
Programme design (continued)	• Normal retirement age generally 65 with actuarially reduced early retirement; average actual retirement age 63. • Benefits typically the same for all participants across business units/divisions, but may differ for union and hourly vs. salaried. Executives typically receive supplemental plan for benefits above tax limits (US$275,000 pensionable pay limit for 2018). • Employee contributions rare due to administrative complexity *(see tax treatment below)*, poor perception.	• About 33% of plans offer auto-enrolment and auto-escalation; a further 33% offer auto-enrolment only. • Design strategies emphasise maximising employee voluntary contributions relative to a given employer spend; increasing emphasis on financial wellness to increase employee contributions. • Employee portals are now standard; providing plan and investment information, modellers, and ability to make investment changes.
Financial management	• Prefunding required for all but executive plans; calculation methodology, mortality, interest rate prescribed by law, with minimum and maximum annual contributions. Deficits amortised over 7 years. • Accruals untaxed, pensions taxed as income. Employee contributions are after-tax; benefits proportionately tax free. • Average asset mix: 44% fixed income, 39% equities, 14% other (generally growth assets), 3% real estate. • Liability-driven investments now commonplace; growing prevalence of flight paths, especially for frozen plans. • About 67% of plans have offered/will offer a temporary lump sum option, many others offer ongoing lump sums; annuity purchases less frequent but interest increasing. • Guarantee Fund (PBGC) US$74 per participant plus 3.8% of unfunded vested benefits in 2018 (increases thereafter). Tripled in past 10 years. Strategic mergers or splits can reduce.	• Generally, contributions and account growth tax free; taxed as income after retirement. • 67% of employers offer after-tax 'Roth' option (earnings grow tax free, income not taxed at retirement); 12% of employees elect when offered.[2] • Employers offer a variety of funds for employees to select among with varying risk levels; target date funds most popular choice. • Employers offer an average of 18 funds, when target date fund classes counted as a single fund. Target date funds growing in popularity – 33% of total balances but 54% of new contributions.[2] • Plans provide no investment guarantees. • Focus on minimising investment and administration costs as means of increasing account balances.

Notes: [1] Unless otherwise cited, plan prevalence information in the above material is based on the salaried benefit programs representing 1,100 large employers from Aon Hewitt's 2018 Benefit SpecSelect™ Online tool. Prevalence may differ for hourly plans, public employers or small employers.

[2] Source: Vanguard 'How America Saves 2018 – Vanguard 2017 defined contribution plan data'.

ECONOMIC & DEMOGRAPHIC DATA

CONSUMER PRICES INDEX (CPI)

Index based on 2015 = 100

	Jan.	Feb.	Mar.	Apr.	May	Jun.	Jul.	Aug.	Sep.	Oct.	Nov.	Dec.
2014	99.0	99.5	99.7	100.1	100.0	100.2	99.9	100.2	100.3	100.4	100.1	100.1
2015	99.3	99.5	99.7	99.9	100.1	100.2	100.0	100.3	100.2	100.3	100.3	100.3
2016	99.5	99.8	100.2	100.2	100.4	100.6	100.6	100.9	101.1	101.2	101.4	101.9
2017	101.4	102.1	102.5	102.9	103.3	103.3	103.2	103.8	104.1	104.2	104.6	104.9
2018	104.4	104.9	105.0	105.4	105.8	105.8	105.8	106.5	106.6	106.7		

Source: *World Economics*, compiled from government information.

CPI INFLATION

Percentage increase in the Consumer Prices Index over previous 12 months

	Jan. %	Feb. %	Mar. %	Apr. %	May %	Jun. %	Jul. %	Aug. %	Sep. %	Oct. %	Nov. %	Dec. %
2014	1.9	1.7	1.6	1.8	1.5	1.9	1.6	1.5	1.2	1.3	1.0	0.5
2015	0.3	0.0	0.0	–0.1	0.1	0.0	0.1	0.0	–0.1	–0.1	0.1	0.2
2016	0.3	0.3	0.5	0.3	0.3	0.5	0.6	0.6	1.0	0.9	1.2	1.6
2017	1.8	2.3	2.3	2.7	2.9	2.6	2.6	2.9	3.0	3.0	3.1	3.0
2018	3.0	2.7	2.5	2.4	2.4	2.4	2.5	2.7	2.4	2.4		

Source: *World Economics*, compiled from government information.

RETAIL PRICES INDEX (RPI)

Index based on January 1987 = 100

	Jan.	Feb.	Mar.	Apr.	May	Jun.	Jul.	Aug.	Sep.	Oct.	Nov.	Dec.
2014	252.6	254.2	254.8	255.7	255.9	256.3	256.0	257.0	257.6	257.7	257.1	257.5
2015	255.4	256.7	257.1	258.0	258.5	258.9	258.6	259.8	259.6	259.5	259.8	260.6
2016	258.8	260.0	261.1	261.4	262.1	263.1	263.4	264.4	264.9	264.8	265.5	267.1
2017	265.5	268.4	269.3	270.6	271.7	272.3	272.9	274.7	275.1	275.3	275.8	278.1
2018	276.0	278.1	278.3	279.7	280.7	281.5	281.7	284.2	284.1	284.5		

Source: *World Economics*, compiled from government information.

RPI INFLATION

Percentage increase in the Retail Prices Index over previous 12 months

	Jan. %	Feb. %	Mar. %	Apr. %	May %	Jun. %	Jul. %	Aug. %	Sep. %	Oct. %	Nov. %	Dec. %
2014	2.8	2.7	2.5	2.5	2.4	2.6	2.5	2.4	2.3	2.3	2.0	1.6
2015	1.1	1.0	0.9	0.9	1.0	1.0	1.0	1.1	0.8	0.7	1.1	1.2
2016	1.3	1.3	1.6	1.3	1.4	1.6	1.9	1.8	2.0	2.0	2.2	2.5
2017	2.6	3.2	3.1	3.5	3.7	3.5	3.6	3.9	3.9	4.0	3.9	4.1
2018	4.0	3.6	3.3	3.4	3.3	3.4	3.2	3.5	3.3	3.3		

Source: *World Economics*, compiled from government information.

TRENDS IN AVERAGE EARNINGS PER PERSON PER WEEK AND THE HOUSEHOLDS' SAVINGS RATIO

	at Current Prices		at Constant 2017 Prices[1]		Households' Savings Ratio[3] (%)
	Average Earnings[2] (£pw)	Annual Change (%)	Average Earnings[2] (£pw)	Annual Change (%)	
1977	70.62	9.0	416.91	–5.9	8.6 (7.6)
1978	79.69	12.8	434.58	4.2	10.4 (9.4)
1979	92.00	15.4	442.38	1.8	12.0 (10.9)
1980	111.15	20.8	453.09	2.4	13.5 (12.3)
1981	125.35	12.8	456.74	0.8	13.4 (12.0)
1982	137.15	9.4	460.16	0.8	12.5 (10.8)
1983	148.77	8.5	477.16	3.7	11.2 (9.0)
1984	157.67	6.0	481.80	1.0	12.7 (10.2)
1985	171.00	8.5	492.58	2.2	12.4 (9.7)
1986	184.80	8.1	514.72	4.5	11.5 (8.1)
1987	198.90	7.6	531.96	3.4	9.5 (5.2)
1988	218.70	10.0	557.56	4.8	7.9 (3.5)
1989	239.80	9.6	567.11	1.7	9.2 (5.3)
1990	263.20	9.8	568.59	0.3	11.1 (7.5)
1991	284.70	8.2	581.02	2.2	13.1 (9.6)
1992	304.80	7.1	599.66	3.2	14.5 (10.9)
1993	317.30	4.1	614.64	2.5	14.3 (9.9)
1994	326.10	2.8	616.42	0.3	12.5 (8.3)
1995	337.60	3.5	617.11	0.1	13.7 (9.2)
1996	351.50	4.1	627.35	1.7	12.7 (8.4)
1997	367.60	4.6	636.12	1.4	11.4 (8.0)
1998	392.50	6.8	656.69	3.2	9.7 (6.5)
1999	407.80	3.9	671.98	2.3	7.2 (4.7)
2000	425.10	4.2	680.33	1.2	9.1 (4.6)
2001	449.70	5.8	707.26	4.0	9.3 (5.9)
2002	472.10	5.0	730.26	3.3	9.0 (4.7)
2003	487.10	3.2	732.23	0.3	7.9 (4.3)
2004	498.20	2.3	727.25	–0.7	8.0 (3.8)
2005	516.40	3.7	733.02	0.8	7.5 (2.9)
2006	534.90	3.6	735.92	0.4	7.4 (3.4)
2007	550.30	2.9	725.95	–1.4	8.5 (2.1)
2008	575.60	4.6	730.34	0.6	7.6 (2.2)
2009	587.20	2.0	748.88	2.5	10.8 (7.0)
2010	598.60	1.9	729.65	–2.6	10.9 (7.3)
2011	602.90	0.7	698.44	–4.3	9.2 (6.7)
2012	607.80	0.8	682.31	–2.3	9.2 (6.8)
2013	620.20	2.0	675.65	–1.0	8.6
2014	620.80	0.1	660.68	–2.2	8.6
2015	627.00	1.0	660.80	0.0	9.4
2016	644.90	2.9	668.03	1.1	6.8
2017	662.50	2.7	662.50	–0.8	4.3

Notes:

1 **Constant 2017 Prices**: Deflated by the Retail Prices Index (2017 = 100).

2 **Earnings**: Wages and salaries of those in employment, excluding those whose pay is affected by absence. Data are derived from the earnings index of all adults in full-time employment.

3 **Households' Savings Ratio**: Savings as % Total Resources; the latter is the sum of Gross Household Disposable Income and the Adjustment for the net equity of the households in pension funds. The Adjustment has been recalculated and increased; figures in brackets are on the old basis.

Sources: *ASHE* and *UK Economic Accounts*, National Statistics © Crown Copyright 2018; *World Economics*.

POPULATION DATA, MID-2017

By Nation

Thousands

	Total	Males	Females
England	55,619	27,481	28,138
Wales	3,125	1,540	1,585
Scotland	5,425	2,640	2,785
Great Britain	**64,169**	**31,662**	**32,508**
Northern Ireland	1,871	920	951
United Kingdom	**66,040**	**32,582**	**33,458**

By Sex and Age, UK

	Total		**Males**		**Females**	
Age	*'000s*	*%*	*'000s*	*%*	*'000s*	*%*
0–4	3,961	6.0	2,031	3.1	1,930	2.9
5–9	4,113	6.2	2,105	3.2	2,008	3.0
10–14	3,733	5.7	1,913	2.9	1,820	2.8
15–19	3,704	5.6	1,902	2.9	1,803	2.7
20–24	4,207	6.4	2,158	3.3	2,049	3.1
25–29	4,542	6.9	2,294	3.5	2,248	3.4
30–34	4,422	6.7	2,203	3.3	2,219	3.4
35–39	4,282	6.5	2,126	3.2	2,156	3.3
40–44	4,059	6.1	2,014	3.0	2,046	3.1
45–49	4,575	6.9	2,255	3.4	2,320	3.5
50–54	4,668	7.1	2,298	3.5	2,370	3.6
55–59	4,184	6.3	2,064	3.1	2,120	3.2
60–64	3,599	5.4	1,763	2.7	1,835	2.8
65–69	3,474	5.3	1,682	2.5	1,791	2.7
70–74	3,111	4.7	1,488	2.3	1,623	2.5
75–79	2,177	3.3	1,002	1.5	1,175	1.8
80–84	1,635	2.5	711	1.1	924	1.4
85–89	1,013	1.5	393	0.6	620	0.9
90+	580	0.9	178	0.3	401	0.6
Total	**66,040**	**100.0**	**32,582**	**49.3**	**33,458**	**50.7**

Population Projections, UK

Thousands

			Projections		
	2017 (2016 base)	2022	2027	2032	2037
0–15	12,502	12,972	12,889	12,676	12,607
16–44	24,537	24,669	24,935	25,126	25,014
45–64	17,024	17,298	17,300	17,062	17,125
65–74	6,586	6,711	7,193	8,070	8,389
75+	5,402	6,312	7,217	7,946	8,900
Total	**66,051**	**67,961**	**69,533**	**70,881**	**72,035**

Sources: *Mid-2017 Population Estimates*, Office for National Statistics © Crown Copyright 2018; General Register Office for Scotland, Northern Ireland Statistics and Research Agency; Population projections by the Government Actuary's Department, 2016.

EXPECTATIONS OF LIFE

Age x	Males Expectation	Females Expectation	Age x	Males Expectation	Females Expectation
0	79.17	82.86			
1	78.51	82.15	51	30.37	33.33
2	77.53	81.17	52	29.48	32.41
3	76.54	80.18	53	28.59	31.49
4	75.55	79.19	54	27.70	30.58
5	74.56	78.20	55	26.82	29.67
6	73.57	77.20	56	25.95	28.77
7	72.57	76.21	57	25.09	27.87
8	71.58	75.21	58	24.23	26.98
9	70.58	74.22	59	23.39	26.09
10	69.59	73.22	60	22.55	25.22
11	68.60	72.23	61	21.73	24.35
12	67.60	71.23	62	20.92	23.48
13	66.61	70.24	63	20.11	22.63
14	65.62	69.24	64	19.32	21.78
15	64.62	68.25	65	18.54	20.94
16	63.63	67.26	66	17.76	20.10
17	62.65	66.27	67	16.99	19.27
18	61.67	65.28	68	16.23	18.45
19	60.69	64.30	69	15.49	17.64
20	59.72	63.31	70	14.75	16.84
21	58.75	62.32	71	14.03	16.06
22	57.78	61.34	72	13.33	15.28
23	56.80	60.35	73	12.65	14.52
24	55.84	59.36	74	11.97	13.78
25	54.87	58.38	75	11.33	13.05
26	53.90	57.39	76	10.70	12.34
27	52.93	56.41	77	10.08	11.64
28	51.96	55.42	78	9.48	10.96
29	51.00	54.44	79	8.89	10.29
30	50.03	53.46	80	8.32	9.65
31	49.07	52.48	81	7.78	9.03
32	48.11	51.50	82	7.26	8.43
33	47.15	50.52	83	6.77	7.85
34	46.19	49.55	84	6.30	7.31
35	45.24	48.57	85	5.86	6.79
36	44.28	47.60	86	5.45	6.30
37	43.33	46.63	87	5.06	5.84
38	42.38	45.67	88	4.69	5.41
39	41.44	44.70	89	4.36	5.01
40	40.49	43.74	90	4.04	4.64
41	39.55	42.78	91	3.76	4.30
42	38.62	41.82	92	3.48	3.98
43	37.69	40.86	93	3.23	3.68
44	36.76	39.91	94	3.01	3.41
45	35.84	38.96	95	2.82	3.17
46	34.91	38.02	96	2.64	2.96
47	34.00	37.07	97	2.49	2.76
48	33.09	36.13	98	2.31	2.55
49	32.18	35.20	99	2.19	2.38
50	31.27	34.26	100	2.07	2.23

Note: The table above shows the 'period' expectation of life at various ages, that is, the average number of additional years a person would live if he or she experienced the age-specific mortality rates of 2014–2016 for the rest of their life. No allowance is made for future improvements in mortality.

Source: *National Life Tables 2014–2016 for United Kingdom*, Office for National Statistics © Crown copyright 2017.

WORKING POPULATION – UNITED KINGDOM

	June 1998		June 2017		June 2018	
	'000s	%	'000s	%	'000s	%
Employees in employment:						
– Male	12,088	42.7	13,684	41.5	13,908	41.7
– Female	11,183	39.5	13,386	40.6	13,562	40.7
All employees	23,271	82.3	27,069	82.1	27,470	82.4
Self-employed persons	3,288	11.6	4,855	14.7	4,761	14.3
HM Forces	219	0.8	156	0.5	153	0.5
Government-supported trainees	162	0.6	71	0.2	45	0.1
Total employed labour force	26,939	95.2	32,152	97.6	32,429	97.3
Claimant unemployment	1,344	4.8	801	2.4	900	2.7
Total	28,283	100.0	32,953	100.0	33,329	100.0
Index (June 1998=100)	100.0		116.5		117.8	

Notes: [1] Seasonally adjusted.
[2] Totals might differ from sum of preceding figures owing to rounding.

Source: *Labour Market Statistics*, Office for National Statistics © Crown Copyright 2018.

INVESTMENT DATA

UK ANNUAL INFLATION

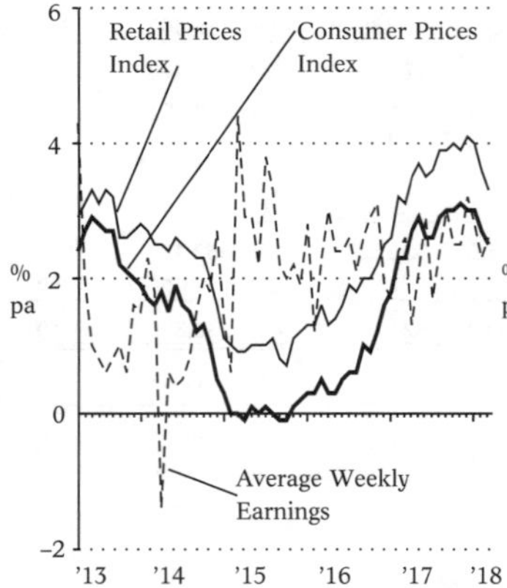

UK INVESTMENT YIELDS AND INFLATION

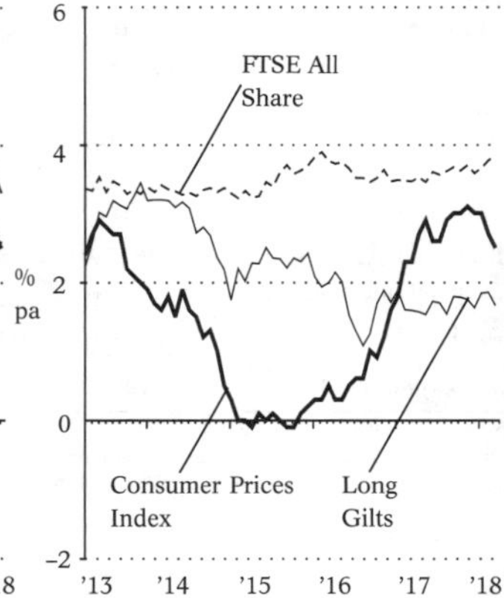

Notes:

1 Index for Long Gilts is based on all issues with a term of 15 years.

2 The 3-month bank rate shown is the LIBOR 3-month offer rate.

3 Annual return on cash deposits is calculated using the LIBOR Total Return Index for London Interbank 3-month deposits.

Sources:

CPI, RPI and AWE data derived from information published by the Office for National Statistics. AWE figures are based on the 2007 Standard Industrial Classification (SIC 2007) using the not-seasonally-adjusted index for the whole economy, including bonuses and arrears. All other figures collated by Aon.

UK INTEREST RATES AND INFLATION

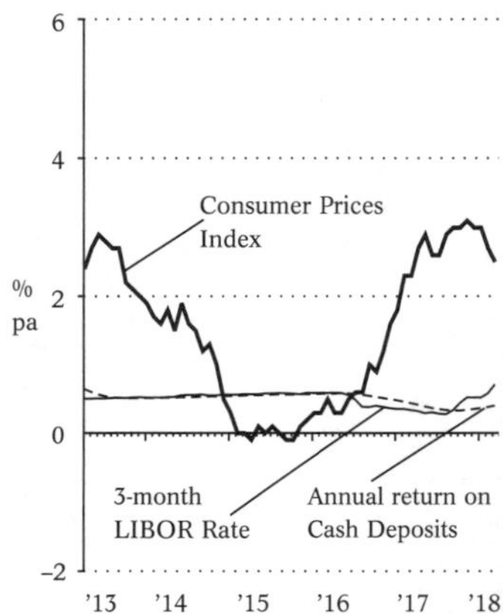

UK INVESTMENT HISTORY (1)

	Annual increase:[1]			Corresponding annual rate of return on investments:			
One year returns to end of:	*CPI* %	*RPI* %	*AWE*[2] %	*Cash Deposits*[3] %	*Long Gilts*[4] %	*Index-linked Gilts*[5] %	*UK Equities*[6] %
2008	3.1	0.9	2.5	5.7	13.6	3.7	–29.9
2009	2.9	2.4	0.7	1.2	–4.8	6.4	30.1
2010	3.7	4.8	1.2	0.7	8.8	8.9	14.5
2011	4.2	4.8	1.9	0.9	26.3	19.9	–3.5
2012	2.7	3.1	1.2	0.8	2.9	0.6	12.3
2013	2.0	2.7	1.6	0.5	–5.9	0.5	20.8
2014	0.5	1.6	2.7	0.5	26.1	19.0	1.2
2015	0.2	1.2	1.9	0.6	0.1	–1.0	1.0
2016	1.6	2.5	1.9	0.5	18.5	24.3	16.8
2017	3.0	4.1	3.2	0.4	3.3	2.3	13.1
Length of period:	*Average annual increases and rates of return for different periods to end of 2017:*						
10 years	2.4	2.8	1.9	1.2	8.3	8.1	6.3
9 years	2.3	3.0	1.8	0.7	7.7	8.6	11.4
8 years	2.2	3.1	2.0	0.6	9.4	8.9	9.2
7 years	2.0	2.9	2.1	0.6	9.5	8.9	8.5
6 years	1.6	2.5	2.1	0.6	6.9	7.2	10.6
5 years	1.5	2.4	2.3	0.5	7.8	8.6	10.3
4 years	1.3	2.4	2.4	0.5	11.5	10.7	7.8
3 years	1.6	2.6	2.3	0.5	7.0	8.0	10.1
2 years	2.3	3.3	2.5	0.4	10.6	12.8	14.9

Notes:
1 The increase shown is measured over the calendar year(s) from December to December.
2 Average Weekly Earnings, whole economy, not seasonally adjusted, including bonuses and arrears.
3 Annual return on cash deposits is calculated using the LIBOR Total Return Index for London Interbank 3-month deposits.
4 FTSE UK Gilts Over 15 Years total return.
5 FTSE Index Linked UK Gilts All Stocks total return.
6 FTSE All Share total return.

Source: Annual increases in indices and annual rates of return collated, and averages calculated, by Aon.

UK INVESTMENT HISTORY (2)

Historic yields and returns (% p.a.)

		UK assets: real rates of return		
5 years to end of:	Retail Prices Index	Equities	Government Bonds	Treasury Bills
1972	7.1	8.8	–2.4	–0.2
1977	16.2	–8.5	–3.7	–4.8
1982	11.6	6.6	2.0	1.4
1987	4.6	17.6	7.0	5.4
1992	6.1	8.0	4.9	6.0
1997	2.8	13.0	8.9	3.3
2002	2.2	–4.3	5.6	3.5
2007	3.4	11.2	0.9	1.3
2012	3.2	–0.9	5.9	–1.6
2017	2.4	7.5	2.3	–2.0
10 years to end of:				
1972	5.2	7.7	–1.8	0.8
1977	11.6	–0.2	–3.1	–2.5
1982	13.9	–1.2	–0.9	–1.8
1987	8.0	12.0	4.5	3.3
1992	5.4	12.7	6.0	5.7
1997	4.5	10.4	6.9	4.7
2002	2.5	3.9	7.2	3.4
2007	2.8	3.1	3.2	2.4
2012	3.3	5.0	3.4	–0.2
2017	2.8	3.2	4.0	–1.8

Sources: Barclays Equity Gilt Study 2018. Annual increases in Retail Prices Index collated, and averages calculated, by Aon.

CUMULATIVE INDEX RETURNS TO 31 MARCH 2018

Annualised returns (in sterling terms)	Last 12 months %	Last 3 years %	Last 5 years %	Last 10 years %
FTSE All Share	1.2	5.9	6.6	6.7
FTSE World North America	1.3	**12.3**	**14.4**	**12.9**
FTSE AW Developed Europe ex UK	4.1	8.6	10.3	6.5
FTSE Japan	7.5	11.4	11.6	8.3
FTSE AW Developed Asia Pacific ex Japan	1.9	9.8	6.5	8.9
FTSE AW Emerging Markets	**8.8**	10.4	6.9	7.0
FTSE All World Developed ex UK	2.4	11.3	12.7	10.7
FTSE AW All-World	2.9	10.9	11.6	10.0
FTSE UK Gilts All Stocks	0.5	3.4	4.2	5.6
BofA Merrill Lynch Non-Gilts All Stocks	1.3	3.6	5.1	6.6
FTSE Index Linked UK Gilts All Stocks	0.5	7.0	6.9	7.8

Note: The best performing sector over each period is highlighted in **bold** typeface.
Source: Increases in indices collated, and averages calculated, by Aon.

DB SCHEMES: WEIGHTED AVERAGE ASSET ALLOCATION

	2008	2009	2010	2011	2012	2013	2014	2015	2016	2017
	%	%	%	%	%	%	%	%	%	%
Equities	53.6	46.4	42.0	41.1	38.5	35.1	35.0	33.0	30.3	29.0
Bonds	32.9	37.1	40.4	40.1	43.2	44.8	44.1	47.7	51.3	55.7
Other investments	13.5	16.5	17.6	18.8	18.3	20.1	20.9	19.3	18.4	15.3
of which										
Insurance policies	1.1	1.4	1.4	1.6	0.2	0.1	0.1	0.1	0.1	0.1
Cash and deposits	3.0	3.9	3.9	4.1	5.1	6.7	6.1	3.5	3.0	–0.9
Property	5.6	5.2	4.6	4.4	4.9	4.7	4.6	4.9	4.8	5.3
Hedge funds	N/A	1.5	2.2	2.4	4.5	5.2	5.8	6.1	6.6	6.7
Other(note)	3.8	4.5	5.4	6.3	3.6	3.5	4.3	4.7	3.8	4.1

Note: Other alternative investments excluding hedge funds.

Source: The Pension Protection Fund, *The Purple Book, DB pensions universe risk profile*, 2017.

REFERENCE SECTION 3

PENSION STATISTICS

NOTES ON SOURCES USED

This section provides a snapshot of selected features of pension schemes in the UK. The charts and tables *on pages 249 to 253* are based on data from the following sources:

- **Annual Survey of Hours and Earnings (ASHE) 2017 (provisional)**: ASHE is based on a 1% sample of employee jobs taken from HMRC PAYE records.
- **The Association of Consulting Actuaries' (ACA) 2018 Pension trends survey**: this survey covers 349 employers of all sizes, sponsoring over 550 pension schemes.
- **The PLSA Annual Survey, 2017**: this survey is based on responses from fund members of the Pensions and Lifetime Savings Association, mainly in the private sector.
- **The Pensions Regulator's DC Trust 2017–18**: statistics on employer-sponsored schemes based on scheme return data 2017–18 and ASHE 2016.
- **Pension Funds Online** (*www.pensionfundsonline.co.uk*): an online database maintained by Wilmington plc that includes information on over 3,700 major UK pension funds (as at July 2018).
- **The Purple Book 2017, DB pensions universe risk profile**: a joint annual publication by the Pensions Regulator and the Pension Protection Fund (PPF) focusing mainly on private sector defined benefit schemes. Most of the analysis is based on a sample of 5,588 schemes, with much of the basic information coming from scheme returns provided to the Pensions Regulator. Data as at 31 March 2017.

Figures throughout may not total due to rounding.

PERCENTAGE OF EMPLOYEES WITH A WORKPLACE PENSION
By size of employer

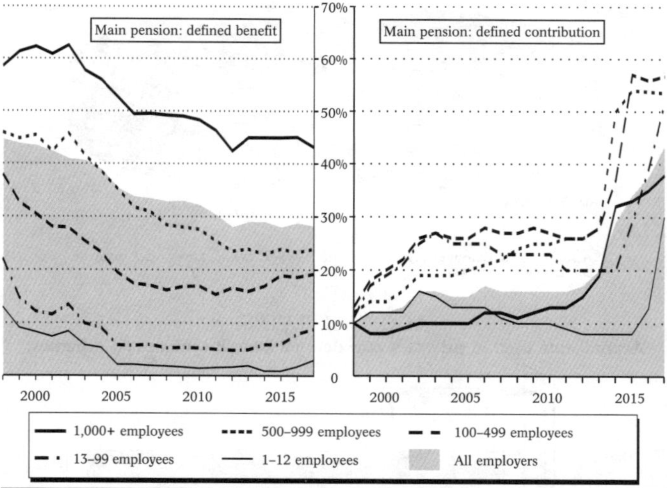

Note: Those whose pension type is unknown are treated as having no pension.
Source: Annual Survey of Hours and Earnings 2017, Office for National Statistics. (*See note on page 248 concerning this source.*)

PERCENTAGE OF PRIVATE SECTOR EMPLOYEES WITH A WORKPLACE PENSION
By main pension type

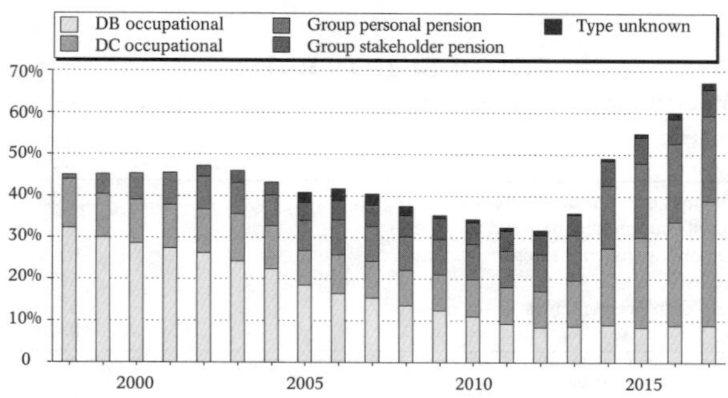

Source: Annual Survey of Hours and Earnings 2017, Office for National Statistics. (*See note on page 248 concerning this source.*)

TYPICAL CURRENT RETIREMENT AGES

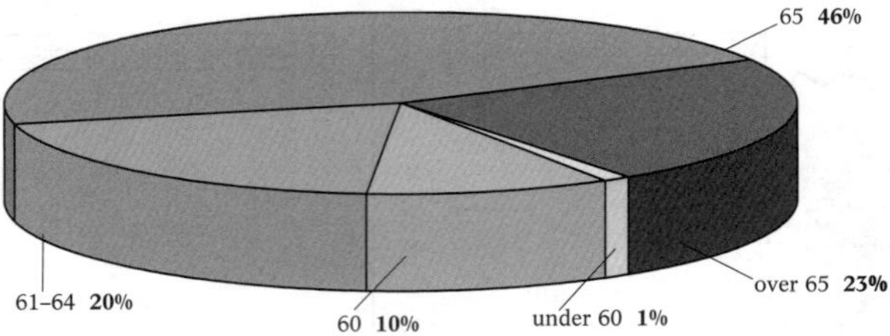

Source: Association of Consulting Actuaries' *2018 Pension trends survey*. (*See note on page 248 concerning this source.*)

ACCRUAL RATES

Accrual rate used in private sector defined benefit schemes (% schemes)

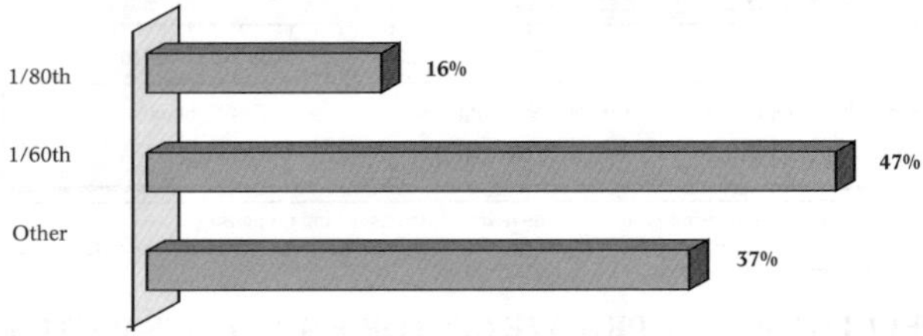

Note: Accrual rate is that for active members in an organisation's main defined benefit scheme. 'Other' rates typically were a mix of accrual rates ranging from 1/50th to 1/80th.

Source: Based on 73 responses to the PLSA *Annual Survey*, 2017. (*See note on page 248 concerning this source.*)

CONTRIBUTION RATES

Median contributions paid into pension schemes (% earnings)

% by benefit type	Member contributions	Employer contributions
Defined benefit occupational schemes	6	21–25
Defined contribution occupational schemes	4	6
Group personal pension arrangements	3	6
Master trusts	2	1–2
Other multi-employer schemes	2	3
Mixed DB/DC	6	16–20

Source: Association of Consulting Actuaries' *2018 Pension trends survey*. (*See note on page 248 concerning this source.*)

DC PENSION SCHEME MEMBERSHIP BY SCHEME STATUS

Private sector schemes ('000s)

	2012	2013	2014	2015	2016	2017
Open	1,707	1,965	4,074	6,332	9,249	12,012
Closed	393	472	430	432	424	441
Frozen	115	103	92	116	109	134
Winding up	50	74	73	51	37	36
Total	**2,265**	**2,614**	**4,669**	**6,931**	**9,819**	**12,622**

Source: The Pensions Regulator's *DC trust: a presentation of scheme return data 2017–18*. (Includes hybrid schemes with DC members.) (*See note on page 248 concerning this source.*)

PENSION SCHEME MEMBERSHIP BY BENEFIT TYPE

Employer-sponsored pension provision in the private sector

	DB	Hybrid: mixed benefit	Hybrid: dual-section	DC (trust)	DC (workplace contract)
Schemes	4,960	250	840	31,940	2,190
Open schemes	770	30	400	25,150	1,960
Total members ('000s)	6,697	1,104	4,900	11,364	N/A
Total active members ('000s)	898	84	1,075	6,778	5,188

Source: The Pensions Regulator's *DC trust: a presentation of scheme return data 2017–18*. (*See note on page 248 concerning this source.*)

PENSION SCHEME MEMBERSHIP BY AGE AND SEX, 2017

	Percentage of employees who are members, by age group						
Scheme members in Great Britain	16–21	22–29	30–39	40–49	50–59	60+	**All employees**
Males							
Defined benefit	5	15	22	28	31	20	23
Occupational DC	8	32	30	27	24	21	26
Personal pension	6	26	27	27	26	20	25
None*	81	27	21	19	19	39	27
Females							
Defined benefit	7	25	34	41	43	28	34
Occupational DC	7	26	22	20	19	14	20
Personal pension	3	20	19	16	15	11	16
None*	83	29	25	23	23	47	30

Note: The 'None' category includes a small number of individuals who did not know about their pension provision.

Source: Annual Survey of Hours and Earnings 2017, Office for National Statistics. (*See note on page 248 concerning this source.*)

THE LARGEST UK PENSION FUNDS

£ million	
60,546	Universities Superannuation Scheme
49,344	BT Pension Scheme
45,030	Royal Bank of Scotland Pension Fund
31,820	Barclays Bank UK Retirement Fund
31,187	Electricity Supply Pension Scheme
28,716	Pension Protection Fund
27,418	Railways Pension Scheme
26,002	BP plc Pension Fund
22,067	HSBC Bank plc DB Scheme
21,271	Greater Manchester Pension Fund
19,826	Lloyds Bank Pension Scheme No.1 DB Section
19,689	Strathclyde Pension Fund
16,841	National Grid UK Pension Scheme DB
16,383	Shell Contributory Pension Fund
16,062	New (British) Airways Pension Scheme (NAPS)
15,844	BBC Pension Scheme
14,755	HBOS Final Salary Pension Scheme
14,400	AVIVA Staff Pension Scheme
14,294	West Midlands Metropolitan Authorities Pension Fund
13,632	West Yorkshire Pension Fund
13,607	Rolls-Royce Pension Fund
13,196	Tesco plc Pension Scheme
13,013	BAE Systems plc BAE Systems Section
12,241	Mineworkers' Pension Scheme
11,955	Ford Motor Co Pension Funds
11,746	Santander Pension Scheme
11,306	Co-operative Group Pension (Average Career Earnings) Scheme
10,570	Marks & Spencer Group plc DB Scheme
10,388	ICI Pension Fund
9,920	J. Sainsbury plc Pension Scheme

£ million	
9,868	Transport for London Pension Fund
9,709	Royal Mail Pension Plan
9,356	British Coal Staff Superannuation Scheme
8,776	Unilever UK Pension Fund
8,594	Lloyds Bank Pension Scheme No.2 DB Section
8,557	TPT Retirement Solutions Defined Benefit Schemes
8,178	Merseyside Pension Fund
8,010	(British) Airways Pension Scheme (APS)
7,961	IBM Pension Plan – DB Section
7,951	Tyne & Wear Pension Fund
7,938	Centrica Combined Common Investment Fund Limited
7,650	South Yorkshire Pension Fund
7,288	Zurich Financial Services DB Section
7,209	Lancashire County Council Pension Fund
7,168	Alliance Boots DB Scheme
7,118	BMW Operations Pension Scheme
7,083	Northern Ireland Local Government Officers' Superannuation Scheme
7,061	Prudential plc DB Scheme
7,015	Diageo plc Pension Scheme
6,900	MMC UK Pension Fund
6,709	Vodafone Group Pension Scheme
6,635	British Energy Generation Group of the Electricity Supply Pensions Scheme DB Section
6,595	Lothian Pension Fund
6,571	RWE npower Group DB Scheme
6,337	Hampshire County Council Pension Fund
6,231	The Railways Pension Scheme Network Rail Section

Note: Certain figures relate to the total of several funds within a group; however in some cases the data available treat separate sections under the same trust as separate schemes. The list excludes some large funds that represent pooled assets of other pension funds.

Source: Based on information from *Pension Funds Online* (*www.pensionfundsonline.co.uk*), part of Wilmington plc, as at July 2018. Where the funds had not supplied up-to-date information, the latest figures available are shown. (*See note on page 248 concerning this source.*)

OVERALL FUNDING LEVELS

	Section 179 (£bn)	Full buy-out (£bn)
Total assets	1,541.1	1,541.1
Total liabilities	1,702.9	2,277.3
Total balance	–161.8	–736.2
Total balance (for schemes in deficit)	–246.7	–741.0
Total balance (for schemes in surplus)	84.9	45.4

Note: Shows estimated figures for a total of 5,588 schemes as at 31 March 2017.

Source: *The Purple Book, DB pensions universe risk profile*, the Pensions Regulator/PPF, 2017. *(See note on page 248 concerning this source.)*

SECTION 179 FUNDING LEVELS BY SCHEME SIZE

Scheme membership	Schemes in sample	Market value of assets (£bn)	Total s179 liabilities (£bn)	Weighted aggregate funding level (%)	Simple average funding level* (%)
2–99	1,994	16.1	16.2	99	95
100–999	2,458	133.2	152.3	88	85
1,000–4,999	759	255.4	293.7	87	84
5,000–9,999	180	195.4	214.9	91	89
10,000+	197	941.0	1,025.8	92	92
Total	**5,588**	**1,541.1**	**1,702.9**	**91**	**89**

Note: * Excludes 24 schemes with funding ratio over 200% (on a full buy-out measure) to avoid distortions. Data as at 31 March 2017.

Source: *The Purple Book, DB pensions universe risk profile*, the Pensions Regulator/PPF, 2017. *(See note on page 248 concerning this source.)*

SECTION 179 FUNDING LEVELS BY SCHEME MATURITY

Pensions in payment as % liabilities	Schemes in sample	Market value of assets (£bn)	Total s179 liabilities (£bn)	Aggregate funding level (%)	Simple average funding ratio* (%)
25% and less	1,754	240.4	326.2	74	78
25%–50%	2,705	938.1	1,031.3	91	87
50%–75%	943	332.8	322.0	103	107
75%–100%	186	29.8	23.5	127	126
Total	**5,588**	**1,541.1**	**1,702.9**	**91**	**89**

Note: * Excludes 24 schemes with funding ratio over 200% (on a full buy-out measure). Data as at 31 March 2017.

Source: *The Purple Book, DB pensions universe risk profile*, the Pensions Regulator/PPF, 2017. *(See note on page 248 concerning this source.)*

REFERENCE SECTION 4

SOCIAL SECURITY BENEFITS AND TAX RATES

INTRODUCTION

Social security benefits, and tax allowances and rates that may be relevant when considering private sector pension provision, are outlined in this section. Further information, including details of other state benefits, can be found at *www.gov.uk*. This section sets out rates for State pensions; *further detail on State pensions is set out in Section 1.*

SOCIAL SECURITY BENEFIT RATES AND ELIGIBILITY RULES

This table gives the rates for 2018/19 and 2019/20, and sets out the main eligibility rules. Receipt of some benefits affects entitlement to other benefits. **Eligibility conditions are not necessarily comprehensive and may also be subject to change.** Further information on benefits can be found at *www.gov.uk*. Information is correct as at 23 November 2018.

There is a limit on the amount of benefit that most people aged 16 to 64 can receive. From 7 November 2016, the cap is £384.62 per week for couples and lone parents, and £257.69 per week for single adults, living outside Greater London. For those living inside Greater London, the respective amounts are £442.31 per week and £296.35 per week. The cap does not apply where someone in the household is entitled to Working Tax Credit or to certain benefits. Where benefits are subject to the cap, a note to that effect is included in the table.

All rates are weekly unless otherwise specified

Benefit	Rates, 2018/19	2019/20	Eligibility
RETIREMENT BENEFITS			
The new State Pension (SPA on or after 6/4/2016)(note)	£164.35	£168.60	(i) Reached State Pension Age (SPA) *and* (ii) NIC record sufficient.
Basic State Pension (SPA before 6/4/2016)(note)	Based on own or late spouse's NICs: £125.95 Based on spouse's NICs: £75.50 Over 80 pension: £75.50 Over 80 addition: £0.25 *taxable*	£129.20 £77.45 £77.45 £0.25	(i) Reached SPA *and* (ii) NIC record sufficient. The Over 80 pension is non-contributory and subject to residence conditions. Payable to individuals who receive little/no other State pension.

Note: The Basic State Pension and Additional State Pension were replaced by the new State Pension for those reaching SPA on or after 6 April 2016 *(see Section 1)*.

All rates are weekly unless otherwise specified

Benefit	Rates, 2018/19	2019/20	Eligibility
RETIREMENT BENEFITS (continued)			
Additional State Pension (SPA before 6/4/2016)(note)	SERPS/State Second Pension (S2P) – *see Section 1.* *taxable*		(i) Reached SPA *and* (ii) paid Class 1 NICs and/or received credits.
Graduated Retirement Benefit (SPA before 6/4/2016)(note)	Per unit: 13.83p Employees may have been contracted-out and receive EPBs instead. *taxable*	14.16p	Based on NICs paid between April 1961 and April 1975.
State Pension Credit	Tops up weekly income to: single pensioner (minimum) £163.00 couple (minimum) £248.80 *tax free*	 £167.25 £255.25	Aged over women's SPA. Lower capital limit £10,000. *means tested*
WIDOW'S/WIDOWER'S BENEFITS			
Bereavement Allowance (replaced by **Bereavement Support Payment** for deaths from 6 April 2017)	Standard rate: £117.10 Lower rates where widow, widower or surviving civil partner was under age 55 when benefit became payable. *taxable; subject to the benefit cap*	£119.90	Husband's, wife's or civil partner's NIC record sufficient or their death was work-related *and*: (i) claimant is under SPA and was 45 or over when husband, wife or civil partner died *and* (ii) **Widowed Parent's Allowance** is not payable.
Widowed Parent's Allowance (replaced by **Bereavement Support Payment** for deaths from 6 April 2017)	Allowance: £117.10 *Plus* Additional State Pension. *taxable; subject to the benefit cap*	£119.90	Husband's, wife's or civil partner's NIC record sufficient or their death was work-related *and:* (i) claimant is entitled to Child Benefit for his/her child *and* (ii) is under SPA.
Bereavement Support Payment	First payment: £2,500, or £3,500 if has children under 20 in full-time education. *(continues)*	Amounts as for 2018/19	Husband, wife or civil partner died under SPA, *either* having paid NICs for at least 25 weeks *or* their death was work-related. *(continues)*

Note: The Basic State Pension and Additional State Pension were replaced by the new State Pension for those reaching SPA on or after 6 April 2016 *(see Section 1).*

All rates are weekly unless otherwise specified

Benefit	Rates, 2018/19	2019/20	Eligibility
WIDOW'S/WIDOWER'S BENEFITS (continued)			
Bereavement Support Payment (continued)	Monthly payments: £100, or £350 if has children under 20 in full-time education. *tax free*		Monthly payments continue for up to 18 instalments, depending on circumstances.
PARENTAL BENEFITS			
Maternity Allowance	For up to 39 weeks: Lesser of (a) 90% of average earnings *and* (b) £145.18. *tax free;* *subject to the benefit cap*	Lesser of (a) 90% of average earnings *and* (b) £148.68.	(i) Not eligible for **Statutory Maternity Pay** *and* (ii) employed/self-employed *and* (iii) must have been employed/ self-employed for at least 26 of the 66 weeks before baby is due, and average earnings at least £30.00 per week (the Maternity Allowance Threshold).
Statutory Maternity Pay	First 6 weeks: 90% of average earnings After 6 weeks, and up to week 39: Lesser of: (a) 90% of average earnings *and* (b) £145.18. *taxable;* *subject to NICs*	90% of average earnings Lesser of: (a) 90% of average earnings *and* (b) £148.68.	In the qualifying week (15th week before the baby is due): (i) employed with same employer for at least 26 weeks *and* (ii) average earnings above Lower Earnings Limit.
Statutory Paternity Pay	For up to 2 weeks: Lesser of: (a) 90% of average earnings *and* (b) £145.18. *taxable;* *subject to NICs*	Lesser of (a) 90% of average earnings *and* (b) £148.68.	As for **Statutory Maternity Pay.** Statutory Shared Parental Pay may be payable at the same rate, for up to 37 weeks if Statutory Maternity Leave and Pay are ended early.

(continues)

All rates are weekly unless otherwise specified

Benefit	Rates, 2018/19	2019/20	Eligibility
PARENTAL BENEFITS (continued)			
Statutory Adoption Pay	For up to 39 weeks: Amounts as for **Statutory Maternity Pay.** *taxable; subject to NICs*	Amounts as for **Statutory Maternity Pay.**	(i) Employed with same employer for at least 26 weeks before adoption agency informed that matched with child *and* (ii) earning above Lower Earnings Limit.
SICKNESS			
Statutory Sick Pay	Standard rate: £92.05 (up to 28 weeks) *taxable; subject to NICs*	£94.25	(i) Earnings at least equal to Lower Earnings Limit *and* (ii) has been sick for at least 4 consecutive days.

OTHER BENEFIT ENTITLEMENTS

There are other benefits for those who have an illness, health condition or disability that may have some relevance when considering private sector pension provision, including the following; *for details, see www.gov.uk*.

Disability Living Allowance
Personal Independence Payment
Attendance Allowance
Severe Disablement Allowance
Employment and Support Allowance (replaced Severe Disablement Allowance and Incapacity Benefit for new claims)
Carer's Allowance
Industrial Injuries Disablement Benefit
Reduced Earnings Allowance
Retirement Allowance
Constant Attendance Allowance
Exceptionally Severe Disablement Allowance

NATIONAL INSURANCE CONTRIBUTION RATES

Tax Year	Earnings per week (£)	National Insurance contribution rates: Employer (%)	Employee (%)	National Insurance earnings limits: LEL[1] per week (£)	LEL[1] per month (£)	UEL[1] per week (£)	UEL[1] per month (£)
2015/16							
	£155.01[2]–£156[2]	0.00	12.00	112	486	815	3,532
	£156.01[2]–UEL[3]	13.80	12.00				
	Above UEL	13.80	2.00				
2016/17							
	£155.01[2]–£156[2]	0.00	12.00	112	486	827	3,583
	£156.01[2]–UEL[3]	13.80	12.00				
	Above UEL	13.80	2.00				
2017/18							
	£157.01[2]–UEL[3]	13.80	12.00	113	490	866	3,750
	Above UEL	13.80	2.00				
2018/19							
	£162.01[2]–UEL[3]	13.80	12.00	116	503	892	3,863
	Above UEL	13.80	2.00				
2019/20							
	£166.01[2]–UEL[3]	13.80	12.00	118	___*	962	___*
	Above UEL	13.80	2.00				

Notes:

* As at 23 November 2018 the Government had not announced these limits for 2019/20. These figures can be found at *www.pensionspocketbook.com*.

1 **LEL**: Lower Earnings Limit; **UEL**: Upper Earnings Limit. These limits depend on the employee's earnings period. Weekly- and monthly-paid amounts are shown.

2 The Primary and Secondary Thresholds (above which, respectively, employee and employer contributions are payable) also depend on the employee's earnings period. The figures shown are for weekly-paid employees. The thresholds were aligned from 2017/18.

3 There is a zero rate band on earnings below the UEL for employer contributions from 2015/16 in respect of employees under the age of 21, and from 2016/17 in respect of apprentices under the age of 25.

STATE RETIREMENT PENSIONS

From	Basic State Pension: Single person £ per week	Basic State Pension: Married couple £ per week	New State Pension £ per week
11.04.2011	102.15	163.35	–
09.04.2012	107.45	171.85	–
08.04.2013	110.15	176.15	–
07.04.2014	113.10	180.90	–
06.04.2015	115.95	185.45	–
11.04.2016	119.30	190.80	155.65
10.04.2017	122.30	195.60	159.55
09.04.2018	125.95	201.45	164.35
08.04.2019	129.20	206.65	168.60

Note: For those reaching State Pension Age on or after 6 April 2016, the Basic State pension is not payable and was replaced by the new State Pension *(see page 254)*. For Basic State pensions in years from 1948, see *www.pensionspocketbook.com*.

TAX ON REGISTERED PENSION SCHEMES

(See Section 9 for further details)

Tax Charge	Tax Rate
Lifetime allowance charge	25% if benefits taken as pension/drawdown 55% if benefits taken as lump sum
Annual allowance charge	Taxed as top slice of income
Unauthorised payments charge	40%
Unauthorised payments surcharge	15%
Scheme sanction charge	40%, but may be reduced to as low as 15% where an unauthorised payments charge has been paid
Authorised surplus payments charge	35%
Short service refund lump sum charge	20% on first £20,000; 50% on balance
Charge on trivial commutation and winding-up lump sums	25% of uncrystallised rights tax free, balance taxed as the top slice of income
Charge on certain taxable lump sum death benefits[1]	Taxed as top slice of income
Charge on serious ill-health lump sums[2]	Taxed as top slice of income
Overseas transfer charge	25% of transferred value *(see Section 9)*

Notes: Each of these rates may change from time to time. The rates shown are those that apply in 2018/19.

1 This applies to pension protection, annuity protection, drawdown pension fund, flexi-access drawdown fund, defined benefits and uncrystallised funds lump sum death benefits, where death occurs at age 75 or over, and to lump sum death benefits where death occurs before age 75 and payment is made after the end of the statutory two-year period *(see Section 9)*. A special lump sum death benefit charge was payable, in relation to deaths at or after age 75, at the rate of 35% for deaths before 6 April 2011, 55% for deaths between 6 April 2011 and 5 April 2015, and 45% for deaths between 6 April 2015 and 5 April 2016. From 6 April 2016, this charge is payable (at 45%) where the lump sum death benefits are paid to a 'non-qualifying' person.

2 This applies to serious ill-health lump sums paid to members aged 75 or over. A serious ill-health lump sum charge was payable at the rate of 55% prior to 6 April 2015, and 45% between 6 April 2015 and 5 April 2016.

TAX ALLOWANCES AND RATES

Tax	2018/19	2019/20
Income Tax Allowances		
Personal allowance[1]	£11,850	£12,500
Married couple's allowance[2]		
– maximum amount	£8,695	£8,915
– minimum amount	£3,360	£3,450
Income limit[2]	£28,900	£29,600
Personal savings allowance[3]		
– basic rate taxpayers	£1,000	£1,000
– higher rate taxpayers	£500	£500
Dividend allowance[4]	£2,000	£2,000

TAX ALLOWANCES AND RATES *(continued)*

Tax		2018/19	2019/20
Income Tax Bands and Rates			
Starting rate for savings[5]	0%	£0–5,000	£0–5,000
Basic rate[6]	20%	£0–34,500	£0–37,500
Higher rate[6]	40%	£34,501–150,000	£37,501–150,000
Additional rate[6]	45%	over £150,000	over £150,000
Capital Gains Tax			
Exempt amount		£11,700	£12,000
Standard rate[7,8]		10%	10%
Higher rate[7,9,10]		20%	20%
Inheritance Tax			
Nil rate band[11]		£325,000	£325,000
Rate (above nil rate band)[12]		40%	40%
Corporation Tax		19%	19%
Value Added Tax (VAT)			
Registration level		£85,000	£85,000
Standard rate		20%	20%
Insurance Premium Tax (IPT)			
Standard rate		12% of gross premium	12% of gross premium
Higher rate[13]		20% of gross premium	20% of gross premium

Notes:

1 Allowance is reduced by £1 for every £2 above an income of £100,000. A transferable tax allowance – the marriage allowance – allows an individual to transfer unused personal allowance to his or her spouse or civil partner, limited to 10% of the personal allowance (i.e. £1,190 for 2018/19) provided that both parties pay tax only at the basic rate, the dividend ordinary rate or the starting rate for savings. Those claiming the married couple's allowance are not eligible for the marriage allowance.

2 Tax relief restricted to 10%. One spouse/civil partner must have been born before 6 April 1935. Amount depends on husband's income if married prior to 5 December 2005, and on person with the higher income if married on or after 5 December 2005 or in a civil partnership. For each £2 of income in excess of the income limit, the married couple's allowance reduces from the maximum amount by £1 (but is subject to the minimum amount). Those claiming the married couple's allowance are not eligible for the marriage allowance *(see note 1)*.

3 The first £1,000 of savings income is tax free for basic rate taxpayers, and the first £500 for higher rate taxpayers. This does not apply to additional rate taxpayers.

4 Individuals pay no tax on dividend income below the dividend allowance, regardless of non-dividend income.

5 Applies only if non-savings income above the personal allowance is below this limit. (Non-savings income is taxed first, then savings income, then dividends.)

6 The corresponding tax rates on dividends are 7.5%, 32.5% and 38.1%.

7 'Entrepreneurs' Relief' is available for gains made on certain disposals. A flat-rate 10% tax applies, subject to a lifetime limit of £10 million.

8 An 18% rate applies for taxable gains on residential property and 'carried interest'.

9 Where total income and gains exceed the higher-rate income tax threshold.

10 A 28% rate applies for taxable gains on residential property and 'carried interest'.

11 Unused nil rate band can be transferred to the surviving spouse or civil partner. An additional nil rate band applies for homes passed on to direct descendants. For 2018/19 and 2019/20 this is £125,000 and £150,000 per individual respectively (due to increase to £175,000 in 2020/21). The residence nil rate band is tapered away for estates over £2m.

12 A lower rate of 36% may apply if at least 10% of the estate is left to charity. A sliding scale of 'Taper Relief' applies on certain gifts (known as Potentially Exempt Transfers) made between three and seven years of death.

13 Applies to travel and breakdown insurance, and insurance sold with goods subject to VAT.

CONTRACTING OUT

The ability to contract out of the Additional State Pension was introduced alongside SERPS *(see Section 1)* in 1978 and lasted until 2016.

Between 1988 and 2012, it was possible to contract out on either a salary-related (COSR) basis or a money purchase (COMP) basis. However, contracting out on a money purchase basis was abolished from April 2012, and the introduction of the new State Pension involved the abolition of all contracting out from April 2016.

For former COSRs, legal requirements relating to contracted-out rights continue to apply. However, certain amendments were made for schemes that ceased to contract out in April 2016.

What did contracting out involve?

For periods when earners were contracted out, their State Pension entitlement *(see Section 1)* is adjusted. For those reaching State Pension Age before 6 April 2016, their Additional State Pension (SERPS between April 1978 and April 2002; State Second Pension (S2P) thereafter) is subject to a contracted-out deduction in respect of the periods of contracted-out service.

For those reaching State Pension Age on or after 6 April 2016 and therefore entitled instead to the new State Pension, their calculated 'starting amount' *(see 'Transitional arrangements' in Section 1)* is reduced, reflecting the deduction that would have applied to their SERPS/S2P entitlement for service up to 5 April 2016.

Under a COSR, the employee and employer paid reduced rates of National Insurance (NI) contributions until April 2016. For schemes contracted out on a COMP basis before April 2012, NI rebates worked differently for occupational schemes than for Appropriate Personal Pensions *(see below)*.

In order to protect contracted-out members' pensions, extra requirements and restrictions apply to former COSRs. The HMRC National Insurance Contributions and Employers Office has responsibility for contracting-out procedures and supervision, with some aspects being handled by the HMRC Pension Schemes Services office.

Contracted-out deductions from Additional State Pension

For those who reached State Pension Age before 6 April 2016, their Additional State Pension is subject to a contracted-out deduction.

Where an employee was contracted out prior to 6 April 1997, SERPS pension in payment for service up to that date is subject to a contracted-out deduction broadly equal to the guaranteed minimum pension (GMP) (or the 'notional' GMP in the case of a member of a contracted-out scheme other than a COSR). The calculation of annual increases in payment is applied to the gross SERPS pension, meaning that the state effectively tops up the increases in payment on the GMP provided by the scheme, where SERPS exceeds the GMP.

This does not apply to those reaching State Pension Age on or after 6 April 2016, whose 'starting amount' on that date is subject to a one-off, permanent deduction.

Between April 1997 and April 2002, the contracted-out deduction for members of all types of contracted-out scheme was equal to the full SERPS pension, and so they accrued no SERPS benefit.

Following the introduction of S2P in April 2002, members of contracted-out occupational schemes continued to have a contracted-out deduction based on the SERPS level of benefit with earnings limits changed as for S2P *(see Section 1)*. A top-up pension, payable by the state, accrued to such members, equal to the amount (if any) by which the member's S2P would have exceeded the SERPS level of benefit adjusted as for S2P. The same applied up to 5 April 2012 for members of COMPs. In contrast, the contracted-out deduction for members of APPs until April 2012 was equal to the full S2P and so they did not accrue a top-up pension from the state (except for members earning below the Low Earnings Threshold). These differences were reflected in the rebates available between 2002 and 2012.

SALARY-RELATED CONTRACTING OUT

Contracting out on a salary-related basis was abolished from 6 April 2016. Contracting-out certificates were automatically cancelled and all affected schemes automatically contracted back in.

Guaranteed Minimum Pensions (GMPs)

Before 6 April 1997, COSRs had to promise to pay at least a minimum pension (the GMP) to each participating employee; this reduced the employee's SERPS pension from the state and, in return, both the employer and the employee paid lower-rate NI contributions. Former COSRs still need to provide GMPs accrued before 6 April 1997.

These are subject to strict regulatory requirements, including revaluation for early leavers, as described in *Section 12*. Tables of revaluation rates are included *on pages 266 and 267*.

Legislation that allows schemes the option of converting GMPs to 'normal' scheme benefits of equal value came into effect on 6 April 2009. To use this option, trustees must have employer consent and have consulted affected members.

Because of the abolition of salary-related contracting out, HMRC developed a service for the reconciliation of membership and GMP data held by schemes. It intends reconciliation to be completed in early 2019 and to then issue final membership scans to schemes in March. A 'GMP Checker' allows schemes to calculate GMPs themselves.

Restrictions on GMPs remain, requiring them to be revalued and not to be 'franked' against excess pension. For these purposes, members in contracted-out service on 5 April 2016 are treated as remaining so until their pensionable service ends. However, the requirement for a 'Protection Rule' to be added to the rules of a scheme that has ceased to contract out *(see Section 22)* was removed for schemes ceasing to contract out on 6 April 2016.

The Reference Scheme Test (RST)

From 6 April 1997, no further GMPs accrued and, in order to contract out, schemes had to pass a 'Reference Scheme Test'.

A scheme's actuary was required to certify that the pensions provided by the scheme were 'broadly equivalent to' or 'better than' the pensions under a Reference Scheme that was specified in legislation. The main features of the Reference Scheme from 6 April 2009 were:

Pension age	65
Pension accrual rate	1/80
Pensionable salary	average qualifying earnings in the last three tax years
Qualifying earnings	90% of earnings between the Lower Earnings Limit (×52) and the Upper Accrual Point (×53)
Service	if limited to a maximum, this must not be less than 40 years
Spouse's or surviving civil partner's pension	50% of the member's pension (based on completed service for members who die before age 65)

Some schemes' own rules may still refer to the Reference Scheme, to define a minimum level of benefit.

Amending scheme rules following the end of contracting out

To reflect the removal of NI rebates from April 2016, employers were given an overriding power to amend the rules of formerly contracted-out schemes, which would apply in addition to any amendment powers under scheme rules. This power lasts for five years from April 2016, and may be used to increase employee contributions or to alter future accrual of benefit (or a combination of the two). An actuarial certificate must be provided to the employer and trustees, confirming that the amendments save no more than the increase in the employer's NI contributions. The employer chooses the calculation date and instructs an actuary to carry out the work. The employer may instruct the actuary to remove margins from the assumptions used to value benefits, so that the cash equivalent basis is used instead of the 'prudent' scheme funding basis.

Amendments are subject to the usual requirement for the employer to consult with members before making listed changes *(see Section 2)*. Employers may need legal advice, to ensure that communications with members are appropriate and that any contractual issues are dealt with.

Contracting back in

COSRs were automatically contracted back in from 6 April 2016 *(see above)*.

Before 6 April 2016 a COSR could decide to cease to contract out (and in some cases had to do so). In order to do so the trustees or managers notified

Pension Schemes Services and then received a notice from them setting out the date from which the contracting-out certificate was cancelled. From this date all affected members were contracted back in and the trustees or managers then had two years to either discharge the rights or determine to preserve them within the scheme, in which case the scheme needs to continue to comply with the relevant requirements. The following methods could be used to secure the liabilities:

- provision of benefits within the scheme that satisfy HMRC requirements
- transfer to another scheme *(see Section 13)* – member consent is required unless this is part of a bulk transfer exercise and prescribed conditions are met, *or*
- the purchase of an annuity or deferred annuity contract.

The scheme does not need to use the same method for all members.

Schemes that ceased to contract out after 6 April 2015 and have not yet reconciled their contracted-out liabilities with HMRC can apply for an extension of the time limits for paying transfer values, up to 6 April 2021.

Bulk transfers

A bulk transfer of contracted-out liabilities can be made to a former COSR. If individual members' consents are not obtained, an actuarial certificate is needed. From April 2018, such a 'without-consent' transfer can also be made to a scheme that is not a former COSR. *See Section 25.*

MONEY PURCHASE CONTRACTING OUT

Contracting out on a money purchase basis was abolished from 6 April 2012. Contracting-out certificates were automatically cancelled and all affected schemes automatically contracted back in. Protected Rights *(see below)* ceased to exist and are treated in exactly the same way as any other money purchase benefits, subject to any restrictions written into scheme rules.

COMPs

Before 2012, occupational schemes could contract out on a money purchase basis if contributions equal to the flat-rate contracted-out rebates were paid to the scheme by the employer. COMP NI rebates were age-related between April 1997 and April 2012. The age-related rebates were capped at 7.4% of Upper Band Earnings from April 2007.

The flat-rate part of the rebate (3% from April 2007) was paid by the employer to the trustees. Of this, 1.6% was attributed to, and could be recovered from, the employee. For members whose age-related rebate exceeded the flat-rate part, the balance was paid to the trustees in the following tax year by NICO. All rebates paid into the COMP, and any investment return on them, were known as Protected Rights and had to be used to provide benefits as set out in legislation, prior to 6 April 2012.

Arrangements for the payment and recovery of age-related rebates continued during a transitional period until April 2015. After then, any outstanding age-related payments are made directly to members.

Appropriate Personal Pension (APP)

Before 2012, employees could take out an APP contract in order to contract out. Employers and employees continued to pay full-rate NI contributions and, following the end of the tax year, NICO then rebated part of these NI contributions by making so-called ‘minimum contributions’ directly into the APP. A basic rate ‘tax rebate’ on that part of these minimum contributions deemed to be in respect of employee NI contributions was also paid into the scheme by NICO. These payments, and any investment return on them, were Protected Rights under an APP.

From April 1997, minimum contributions were age-related, again subject to a cap. From April 2010, earnings between the Lower Earnings Limit and the Upper Accrual Point were divided into two bands and different rebate rates applied to earnings falling within each band.

Contracted-out Mixed Benefit (COMB) scheme

Between 6 April 1997 and 5 April 2012, two sections of a single scheme were permitted to contract out concurrently on the two different bases.

STATE SCHEME PREMIUMS

Before 6 April 1997, contracted-out schemes were able to buy their members back into SERPS by payment of a State scheme premium in a number of circumstances, thereby extinguishing the scheme’s liability to provide the member with contracted-out benefits. Only the Contributions Equivalent Premium (CEP) now remains, which COSRs may pay in respect of members who have been contracted out and leave with less than two years’ qualifying service. This facility is extended until 6 April 2019 (and extended indefinitely in some limited circumstances).

FIXED RATE GMP REVALUATION FACTORS

	Terminations on or after:							
Number of years	6.4.1978 8.5%	6.4.1988 7.5%	6.4.1993 7.0%	6.4.1997 6.25%	6.4.2002 4.5%	6.4.2007 4.0%	6.4.2012 4.75%	6.4.2017 3.5%
1	1.085	1.075	1.070	1.0625	1.045	1.040	1.0475	1.035
2	1.177	1.156	1.145	1.1289	1.092	1.082	1.0973	1.071
3	1.277	1.242	1.225	1.1995	1.141	1.125	1.1494	1.109
4	1.386	1.335	1.311	1.2744	1.193	1.170	1.2040	1.148
5	1.504	1.436	1.403	1.3541	1.246	1.217	1.2612	1.188
6	1.631	1.543	1.501	1.4387	1.302	1.265	1.3211	1.229
7	1.770	1.659	1.606	1.5286	1.361	1.316	1.3838	1.272
8	1.921	1.783	1.718	1.6242	1.422	1.369	1.4495	1.317
9	2.084	1.917	1.838	1.7257	1.486	1.423	1.5184	1.363
10	2.261	2.061	1.967	1.8335	1.553	1.480	1.5905	1.411
11	2.453	2.216	2.105	1.9481	1.623	1.539	1.6661	1.460
12	2.662	2.382	2.252	2.0699	1.696	1.601	1.7452	1.511
13	2.888	2.560	2.410	2.1993	1.772	1.665	1.8281	1.564
14	3.133	2.752	2.579	2.3367	1.852	1.732	1.9149	1.619
15	3.400	2.959	2.759	2.4828	1.935	1.801	2.0059	1.675
16	3.689	3.181	2.952	2.6379	2.022	1.873	2.1012	1.734
17	4.002	3.419	3.159	2.8028	2.113	1.948	2.2010	1.795
18	4.342	3.676	3.380	2.9780	2.208	2.026	2.3055	1.857
19	4.712	3.951	3.617	3.1641	2.308	2.107	2.4151	1.923
20	5.112	4.248	3.870	3.3619	2.412	2.191	2.5298	1.990
21	5.547	4.566	4.141	3.5720	2.520	2.279	2.6499	2.059
22	6.018	4.909	4.430	3.7952	2.634	2.370	2.7758	2.132
23	6.530	5.277	4.741	4.0324	2.752	2.465	2.9077	2.206
24	7.085	5.673	5.072	4.2844	2.876	2.563	3.0458	2.283
25	7.687	6.098	5.427	4.5522	3.005	2.666	3.1904	2.363
26	8.340	6.556	5.807	4.8367	3.141	2.772	3.3420	2.446
27	9.049	7.047	6.214	5.1390	3.282	2.883	3.5007	2.532
28	9.818	7.576	6.649	5.4602	3.430	2.999	3.6670	2.620
29	10.653	8.144	7.114	5.8015	3.584	3.119	3.8412	2.712
30	11.558	8.755	7.612	6.1641	3.745	3.243	4.0237	2.807
31	12.541	9.412	8.145	6.5493	3.914	3.373	4.2148	2.905
32	13.607	10.117	8.715	6.9587	4.090	3.508	4.4150	3.007
33	14.763	10.876	9.325	7.3936	4.274	3.648	4.6247	3.112
34	16.018	11.692	9.978	7.8557	4.466	3.794	4.8444	3.221
35	17.380	12.569	10.677	8.3467	4.667	3.946	5.0745	3.334
36	18.857	13.512	11.424	8.8683	4.877	4.104	5.3155	3.450
37	20.460	14.525	12.224	9.4226	5.097	4.268	5.5680	3.571
38	22.199	15.614	13.079	10.0115	5.326	4.439	5.8325	3.696
39	24.086	16.785	13.995	10.6372	5.566	4.616	6.1095	3.825
40	26.133	18.044	14.974	11.3021	5.816	4.801	6.3997	3.959
41	28.354	19.398	16.023	12.0084	6.078	4.993	6.7037	4.098
42	30.764	20.852	17.144	12.7590	6.352	5.193	7.0221	4.241
43	33.379	22.416	18.344	13.5564	6.637	5.400	7.3557	4.390
44	36.217	24.098	19.628	14.4037	6.936	5.617	7.7051	4.543
45	39.295	25.905	21.002	15.3039	7.248	5.841	8.0711	4.702
46	42.635	27.848	22.473	16.2604	7.574	6.075	8.4545	4.867

Source: Aon.

SECTION 148 ORDERS: REVALUATION OF EARNINGS FACTORS (%)

Tax year of:	Termination								
Earnings	2018/19	2017/18	2016/17	2015/16	2014/15	2013/14	2012/13	2011/12	2010/11
1978/79	820.9	794.1	771.5	754.4	741.7	734.2	719.5	705.0	686.9
1979/80	712.8	689.2	669.2	654.1	642.9	636.3	623.3	610.5	594.5
1980/81	579.1	559.3	542.6	530.0	520.7	515.1	504.3	493.6	480.2
1981/82	468.7	452.2	438.2	427.6	419.8	415.2	406.1	397.1	385.9
1982/83	416.6	401.5	388.8	379.2	372.1	367.9	359.6	351.5	341.4
1983/84	379.6	365.7	353.9	345.0	338.4	334.5	326.8	319.2	309.8
1984/85	344.1	331.2	320.2	312.0	305.9	302.3	295.2	288.2	279.5
1985/86	316.6	304.5	294.2	286.5	280.8	277.4	270.7	264.2	256.0
1986/87	282.6	271.4	262.0	254.9	249.7	246.5	240.4	234.4	226.9
1987/88	256.2	245.8	237.1	230.4	225.6	222.7	217.0	211.3	204.3
1988/89	227.7	218.1	210.1	204.0	199.5	196.8	191.6	186.4	180.0
1989/90	195.7	187.1	179.9	174.4	170.3	167.9	163.2	158.5	152.7
1990/91	175.6	167.6	160.8	155.7	151.9	149.7	145.3	140.9	135.5
1991/92	150.3	143.0	136.9	132.2	128.8	126.8	122.8	118.8	113.9
1992/93	135.1	128.2	122.4	118.1	114.8	112.9	109.2	105.5	100.8
1993/94	123.9	117.3	111.8	107.7	104.6	102.8	99.2	95.7	91.3
1994/95	117.1	110.8	105.5	101.4	98.5	96.7	93.2	89.8	85.5
1995/96	108.0	101.9	96.8	93.0	90.1	88.4	85.1	81.8	77.7
1996/97	102.3	96.4	91.4	87.7	84.9	83.3	80.0	76.8	72.9
1997/98	92.7	87.1	82.3	78.8	76.1	74.5	71.5	68.4	64.6
1998/99	84.2	78.8	74.3	70.9	68.4	66.9	63.9	61.0	57.4
1999/00	76.8	71.6	67.3	64.0	61.6	60.1	57.3	54.5	51.1
2000/01	66.3	61.5	57.4	54.3	52.0	50.7	48.0	45.4	42.1
2001/02	59.9	55.3	51.3	48.4	46.2	44.9	42.3	39.8	36.6
2002/03	53.3	48.9	45.1	42.2	40.1	38.9	36.4	34.0	31.0
2003/04	48.0	43.7	40.0	37.3	35.3	34.1	31.7	29.4	26.5
2004/05	42.6	38.4	34.9	32.3	30.3	29.2	26.9	24.6	21.8
2005/06	37.0	33.0	29.6	27.1	25.2	24.1	21.9	19.7	17.0
2006/07	32.5	28.6	25.3	22.9	21.1	20.0	17.9	15.8	13.2
2007/08	27.2	23.5	20.4	18.0	16.3	15.3	13.2	11.2	8.7
2008/09	22.1	18.6	15.5	13.3	11.6	10.6	8.7	6.7	4.3
2009/10	18.4	15.0	12.1	9.9	8.3	7.3	5.4	3.5	1.2
2010/11	17.0	13.6	10.7	8.6	7.0	6.0	4.1	2.3	
2011/12	14.4	11.1	8.3	6.1	4.6	3.6	1.8		
2012/13	12.4	9.1	6.3	4.3	2.7	1.8			
2013/14	10.4	7.2	4.5	2.4	0.9				
2014/15	9.4	6.2	3.5	1.5					
2015/16	7.8	4.7	2.0						
2016/17	5.7	2.6							
2017/18	3.0								

Source: Aon, compiled from government information.

The full table can be found at *www.pensionspocketbook.com.*

APPENDIX 1

ABBREVIATIONS IN COMMON USE

AA	Annual Allowance
ABI	Association of British Insurers
ACA	Association of Consulting Actuaries
AE	Automatic Enrolment
APP	Appropriate Personal Pension
AVCs	Additional Voluntary Contributions
AWE	Average Weekly Earnings
BCE	Benefit Crystallisation Event
BEIS	Department for Business, Energy & Industrial Strategy
BSP	Basic State Pension
CA	Companies Act *or* Certified Amount
CARE	Career Average Revalued Earnings
CB	Cash Balance
CDC	Collective Defined Contribution
CEP	Contributions Equivalent Premium
CETV	Cash Equivalent Transfer Value
CGT	Capital Gains Tax
CJEU	Court of Justice of the European Union
CMI	Continuous Mortality Investigation
COMBS	Contracted-out Mixed Benefit Scheme
COMPS	Contracted-out Money Purchase Scheme
CoP	Code of Practice
COSRS	Contracted-out Salary-related Scheme
CPI	Consumer Prices Index
CPIH	Consumer Prices Index including owner occupiers' housing costs
DB	Defined Benefit
DC	Defined Contribution
DPA	Data Protection Act
DWP	Department for Work and Pensions
ECJ	European Court of Justice
EEA	European Economic Area
EFRBS	Employer-financed Retirement Benefit Scheme
EIOPA	European Insurance and Occupational Pensions Authority
EPB	Equivalent Pension Benefit

ERF	Early Retirement Factor
ESG	Environmental, Social and Governance
ETV	Enhanced Transfer Value
EU	European Union
FA	Finance Act
FAS	Financial Assistance Scheme *or* Financial Accounting Standard
FASB	Financial Accounting Standards Board
FATCA	Foreign Account Tax Compliance Act
FCA	Financial Conduct Authority
FCF	Fraud Compensation Fund
FP	Fixed Protection (*similarly* FP 2014, FP 2016)
FRC	Financial Reporting Council
FRS	Financial Reporting Standard
FSCS	Financial Services Compensation Scheme
FSD	Financial Support Direction
FSMA	Financial Services and Markets Act
GAD	Government Actuary's Department
GAR	Guaranteed Annuity Rate
GDPR	General Data Protection Regulation
GMP	Guaranteed Minimum Pension
GPP	Group Personal Pension
HMRC	Her Majesty's Revenue & Customs
HMT	Her Majesty's Treasury
IAS	International Accounting Standard
IASB	International Accounting Standards Board
ICO	Information Commissioner's Office
ICTA	Income & Corporation Taxes Act
IDRP	Internal Dispute Resolution Procedure
IFoA	Institute and Faculty of Actuaries
IFRS	International Financial Reporting Standard
IGC	Independent Governance Committee
IHT	Inheritance Tax
IORP	Institutions for Occupational Retirement Provision
IP 2014	Individual Protection 2014 (*similarly* IP 2016)
IRM	Integrated Risk Management
ISA	Individual Savings Account
ITEPA	Income Tax (Earnings and Pensions) Act

LDI	Liability-driven Investment
LEL	Lower Earnings Limit
LET	Low Earnings Threshold
LISA	Lifetime Individual Savings Account
LPI	Limited Price Indexation
LRF	Late Retirement Factor
LTA	Lifetime Allowance
MBD	Member-borne Deduction
MND	Member-nominated Director
MNT	Member-nominated Trustee
MPAA	Money Purchase Annual Allowance
NAMES	Non-associated Multi-employer Scheme
NEST	National Employment Savings Trust
NI	National Insurance
NICO	National Insurance Contributions Office
NISPI	National Insurance Services to Pensions Industry
NMPA	Normal Minimum Pension Age
NPA/NPD	Normal Pension Age/Normal Pension Date
NRA/NRD	Normal Retirement Age/Normal Retirement Date
OMO	Open Market Option
ONS	Office for National Statistics
OPS	Occupational Pension Scheme
PA	Pensions Act
PAYE	Pay As You Earn
PCLS	Pension Commencement Lump Sum
PIA	Pension Input Amount
PIE	Pension Increase Exchange
PIP	Pension Input Period
PLSA	Pensions and Lifetime Savings Association
PMI	Pensions Management Institute
PPF	Pension Protection Fund
PPP/PPS	Personal Pension Plan/Scheme
PRA	Prudential Regulation Authority
PRAG	Pensions Research Accountants Group
PSA	Pension Schemes Act
PSS	Pension Savings Statement
PTM	Pensions Tax Manual
QROPS	Qualifying Recognised Overseas Pension Scheme

RAA	Regulated Apportionment Arrangement
ROPS	Recognised Overseas Pension Scheme
RPI	Retail Prices Index
RST	Reference Scheme Test
S2P	State Second Pension
SERPS	State Earnings-related Pension Scheme
SFGB	Single Financial Guidance Body
SFO	Statutory Funding Objective
SFP	Statement of Funding Principles
SFS	Summary Funding Statement
SI	Statutory Instrument
SIP	Statement of Investment Principles
SIPP	Self-invested Personal Pension
SLA	Standard Lifetime Allowance
SMPI	Statutory Money Purchase Illustration
SoC	Schedule of Contributions
SORP	Statement of Recommended Practice
SPA	State Pension Age
SPP	Society of Pension Professionals
SRI	Socially Responsible Investment
SRIT	Scottish Rate of Income Tax
SSA	Social Security Act
SSAS	Small Self-administered Scheme
SSB	Short Service Benefit
SSPA	Social Security Pensions Act
TAS	Technical Actuarial Standard
TKU	Trustee Knowledge and Understanding
TPAS	The Pensions Advisory Service
TPO	The Pensions Ombudsman
TPR	The Pensions Regulator
TUPE	Transfer of Undertakings (Protection of Employment) Regulations
TV	Transfer Value
UAP	Upper Accrual Point
UEL	Upper Earnings Limit
UFPLS	Uncrystallised Funds Pension Lump Sum
WGMP	Widow's/Widower's Guaranteed Minimum Pension

Source: Aon.

APPENDIX 2

GLOSSARY OF TERMS

Bold Text:	Cross references that it is felt might improve the understanding of the term concerned.
Italicised Text:	Wording that, whilst not forming part of the basic definition, provides the reader with additional guidance.

DEFINITIONS

The definitions in this Glossary are current at the time of going to print (and include some terms associated with future legislation).

ACCRUAL RATE The rate at which rights build up for each year of **pensionable service** in a **DB scheme**.

ACCRUED BENEFITS The benefits for service up to a given point in time, whether **vested rights** or not. They may be calculated in relation to current earnings or projected earnings.

Allowance may also be made for **revaluation** *and/or* **pension increases** *required by the scheme rules or legislation.*

ACCRUED RIGHTS The benefits to which a member is entitled, as of right, under an **occupational pension scheme**. These include **accrued benefits**. Depending on the context, accrued rights for an **active member** can be based on benefits as if the member had left service or could include a right to have benefits linked to future salary changes.

The term is given various specific definitions in PSA 1993 for the purposes of **preservation** *and in the Disclosure Regulations. It is also given a specific meaning in PA 1995, e.g. in relation to scheme amendments.*

ACTIVE MEMBER A member of an **occupational pension scheme** who is at present accruing benefits under that scheme in respect of current service.

ACTUARIAL EQUIVALENCE A test of actuarial value that compares benefits, in particular, immediately before and after a modification. For the test to be satisfied, the total value of the member's subsisting rights immediately after the modification must be no less than the value of those rights immediately before the modification. This term is used in connection with **section 67** of PA 1995.

ACTUARIAL REDUCTION A reduction made to a member's **accrued benefits** in order to offset any additional cost arising from their payment in advance of the **normal pension date**.

ACTUARIAL REPORT A written report, prepared and signed by the **scheme actuary**, on the developments affecting the scheme's **technical provisions** since the last **actuarial valuation** was prepared.

ACTUARIAL VALUATION

(1) Commonly refers to an investigation by an actuary into the ability of a **DB scheme** to meet its liabilities. This is usually to assess the **funding level** and a recommended contribution rate based on comparing the value of the assets and the actuarial liability.

(2) Under PA 2004, specifically refers to a written report, prepared and signed by the **scheme actuary**, valuing the scheme's assets and calculating its **technical provisions**.

ADDED YEARS The provision of extra benefits by reference to an additional period of **pensionable service** in a **DB scheme**, arising from the receipt of a **transfer payment**, the paying of **AVCs** or by way of augmentation.

ADDITIONAL VOLUNTARY CONTRIBUTIONS (AVCs)

Contributions over and above a member's normal contributions if any, which the member elects to pay to an **occupational pension scheme** in order to secure additional benefits.

ADMINISTRATOR

(1) The **scheme administrator**.

(2) The person who is responsible for the day-to-day administration of the pension scheme.

ANNUAL ALLOWANCE The maximum amount of pension savings that can be built up in any one tax year before liability to an **annual allowance charge** arises. Some carry forward of unused allowance is permitted.

ANNUAL ALLOWANCE CHARGE The tax charge levied on an individual who is a member of one or more **registered pension schemes** in respect of the amount by which the total **pension input amount** for a tax year exceeds the **annual allowance** (taking account of any 'unused annual allowance' carried forward).

ANNUAL REPORT The means by which the **trustees** of an **occupational pension scheme** communicate financial and other

ANNUAL REPORT *(continued)*
information about the scheme to the members, the employer and other interested parties. The term is used to describe the specific information that is required to be made available by trustees in relation to each scheme year under the Disclosure Regulations. Subject to certain exemptions, this must include a copy of the audited accounts and other information specified, including an investment report. The detailed content of the audited accounts is described in the Pension Scheme **SORP**.

Trustees often publish a simplified annual report for members containing the above material suitably summarised.

ANNUITY A series of payments, which may be subject to increases, made at stated intervals until a particular event occurs. This event is most commonly the end of a specified period or the death of the person receiving the annuity.

An annuity may take one of a number of different forms including **compulsory purchase annuity**, *deferred annuity,* **purchased life annuity** *and* **short-term annuity**.

ANTI-FRANKING REQUIREMENTS The requirements that ban the process whereby statutory increases in **GMP** e.g. between termination of **pensionable service** and GMP coming into payment are offset against other scheme benefits, rather than being added to a member's total benefits.

The requirements are covered in Chapter III of Part IV PSA 1993.

ARRANGEMENT Under FA 2004, a contractual or **trust**-based arrangement made by or on behalf of a member of a pension scheme under that scheme. A member may have more than one arrangement under a scheme.

ASSESSMENT PERIOD The period of time when a scheme is being assessed to determine whether the **Pension Protection Fund** can assume responsibility for it.

ASSET AND LIABILITY MATCHING A process of selecting assets which are likely to generate proceeds broadly equal to the cashflow needed to meet the liabilities as they occur under different economic scenarios.

An example of this would be the matching of a level pension with fixed interest securities.

ASSET AND LIABILITY MODELLING A technique used to test the effect of different economic scenarios on the assets and liabilities of an **occupational pension scheme**, the inter-relationship between them, the **funding level** and the contribution rates.

ASSET-BACKED PENSION CONTRIBUTION (ABC) A non-cash business asset used by an employer to underpin regular cash contributions to a pension scheme.

ATTAINED AGE METHOD A funding method in which the actuarial liability makes allowance for projected earnings. The contribution rate is that necessary to cover the cost of all benefits that will accrue to existing members after the valuation date by reference to total earnings throughout their future working lifetimes projected to the dates on which benefits become payable.

AUTHORISED PAYMENT A payment made by a **registered pension scheme** to an employer or member that is permitted under the provisions of FA 2004.

AUTOMATIC ENROLMENT The process whereby employers must automatically enrol workers that meet specified eligibility conditions into an **automatic enrolment scheme**. Workers can subsequently opt out by giving notice within a prescribed period.

AUTOMATIC ENROLMENT SCHEME A **qualifying scheme** that does not contain provisions preventing the employer from making arrangements for **automatic enrolment** and does not require workers to provide information or express a choice.

BASIC PENSION The flat-rate (not earnings-related) State pension paid to all who have met the minimum NI contribution requirements. An individual may claim on the NI record of his/her spouse or civil partner.

It was replaced by the **new State Pension** *for those reaching* **State pensionable age** *after 5 April 2016.*

BENEFICIARY A person entitled to benefit under a pension scheme or who will become entitled on the happening of a specific event.

BENEFIT CRYSTALLISATION EVENT One of various events defined in FA 2004 that triggers a test of benefits 'crystallising' at that point against the individual's available **lifetime allowance**.

BRIDGING PENSION An additional pension paid from a scheme between retirement and **State pensionable age**, which is then usually replaced by the State pension payable from that age.

BULK TRANSFER The transfer of more than one member, from one **arrangement** to another.

BUY-IN The purchase by **trustees** of an **occupational pension scheme** of an insurance policy in the name of the trustees. This remains an asset of the trustees.

BUY-OUT The purchase by **trustees** of an **occupational pension scheme** of an insurance policy in the name of a member or other **beneficiary**, in lieu of entitlement to benefit from the scheme, following termination of the member's **pensionable service**.

CAPPED DRAWDOWN A form of drawdown. The maximum income is capped by reference to the level of an equivalent single life level **annuity** that could be provided from the **drawdown pension** fund.

From April 2015, it is not available other than for **arrangements** *under which funds had already been designated for capped drawdown.*

CAREER AVERAGE REVALUED EARNINGS (CARE) SCHEME A **DB scheme** in which the benefit for each year of membership is related to that year's **pensionable earnings**, revalued in line with an appropriate index during and after **pensionable service**.

CASH BALANCE BENEFIT

(1) A guaranteed cash sum built up on the basis of a formula directly related to the employee's **pensionable earnings** in each year of membership. The resulting 'cash balance' can be used either to purchase an **annuity** or to make other arrangements for retirement.

(2) Under FA 2004, a type of **money purchase benefit**, calculated by reference to an amount available for the provision of benefits, determined otherwise than wholly by reference to contributions paid.

CASH EQUIVALENT The amount that a member of a pension scheme may, under section 94 PSA 1993, require to be applied as a **transfer payment**.

CASH TRANSFER SUM The amount that a leaver with at least three months' **pensionable service** but without **preserved benefits** may require to be applied as a **transfer payment**, as an alternative to a refund of contributions.

CERTIFICATION In the context of **automatic enrolment**, formal confirmation by the employer or **scheme actuary** that a scheme meets the quality requirements necessary to be a **qualifying scheme**.

CHAIR'S STATEMENT An annual statement explaining how an **occupational pension scheme** providing **money purchase benefits** meets governance standards and charge controls.

CHARGE CAP The cap on **member-borne deductions** applying to default **arrangements** in most **occupational pension schemes** that provide **money purchase benefits** and are used as **qualifying schemes**.

CLOSED SCHEME A scheme that does not admit new members.

CODES OF PRACTICE The **Pensions Regulator** issues various codes of practice providing practical guidance on compliance with the requirements of relevant pensions legislation.

COLLECTIVE DEFINED CONTRIBUTION (CDC) SCHEME A scheme with no promised level of benefit, where the scheme's assets are pooled, allowing risk to be shared between members.

COMMUTATION The forgoing of a part or all of the pension payable from retirement for an immediate lump sum benefit.

COMPULSORY PURCHASE ANNUITY The term used to describe an **annuity** purchased on retirement for a member of a **registered pension scheme**.

CONTINGENT ASSETS Assets that produce cash for a scheme contingent on certain events, in particular when an insolvency event occurs to the employer. These include charges over employers' assets, group company guarantees and bank letters of credit.

CONTRACTED OUT/CONTRACTED IN A pension scheme was contracted out where it provided benefits (**protected rights**, **GMPs** or **section 9(2B) rights**) in place of **SERPS** or **S2P** and was given a contracting-out certificate by HMRC.

A pension scheme was commonly called contracted in where it was not contracted out.

Contracting out on a money purchase basis was abolished from 6 April 2012. Contracting out on a salary-related basis was abolished from 6 April 2016.

CONTRACTUAL ENROLMENT An alternative to **automatic enrolment**, whereby an employer fulfils its duties under PA 2008 by enrolling all workers into a suitable pension scheme when they start work with the employer.

CONTRIBUTION NOTICE A direction by the **Pensions Regulator** to a company or individual that is, or is connected to, an employer, to pay a contribution to that employer's scheme. The Regulator must be of the opinion that they have acted in order to prevent recovery of a **section 75 debt** or that a 'material detriment' test is met.

CROSS-BORDER SCHEME If a UK scheme has members working in another EEA state, who are not **seconded employees**, the scheme is operating as a cross-border scheme. Such schemes require regulatory approval to accept contributions in respect of cross-border operations and are subject to additional regulations, for example in relation to the **statutory funding objective**.

DEFAULT FUND In relation to **money purchase benefits**, the investments that are selected for members who do not make an active choice.

DEFERRED DEBT ARRANGEMENT An arrangement allowing an employer in a multi-employer scheme to defer payment of a **section 75 debt** on ceasing to employ **active members**.

DEFERRED MEMBER/DEFERRED PENSIONER A member entitled to **preserved benefits**.

DEFINED BENEFIT (DB) SCHEME A scheme where the scheme rules define the benefits independently of the contributions payable, and benefits are not directly related to the investments of the scheme. The scheme may be funded or unfunded.

DEFINED CONTRIBUTION (DC) SCHEME A scheme providing **money purchase benefits**.

DEPENDANT For HMRC purposes:

(1) a person who was married to, civil partner of or financially dependent on the member, or dependent on the member because of physical or mental impairment, at the date of the member's death, is a dependant of the member, *and*

(2) a child of the member is a dependant of the member if the child has not reached the age of 23, or has reached age 23 and, in the opinion of the **scheme administrator**, was at the date of the member's death dependent on the member because of physical or mental impairment.

DISCLOSURE

(1) A requirement introduced by PSA 1993 (formerly SSPA 1975) and strengthened by PA 1995 for pension schemes to disclose information about the scheme and benefits to interested parties.

(2) Rules introduced by regulatory bodies to disclose product and commission information to the purchasers of life assurance and insured pension products.

DISCONTINUANCE The cessation of the liability of the sponsoring employer to pay contributions to a pension scheme.

DISCRETIONARY INCREASE An increase to a pension in payment or to a **preserved benefit** arising on a discretionary basis, i.e. other than from a system of **escalation** or **indexation**. Such an increase may be of a regular or an ad hoc nature.

DRAWDOWN PENSION Pension paid in the form of **income withdrawal** and/or **short-term annuity**, without purchasing a **scheme pension** or **lifetime annuity**.

ELIGIBLE JOBHOLDER For the purposes of **automatic enrolment**, a **jobholder** who is at least age 22, has not reached **State pensionable age** and earns more than the 'earnings trigger'.

EMPLOYER COVENANT The extent of the employer's legal obligation and financial ability to support its pension scheme now and in the future.

EMPLOYER-FINANCED RETIREMENT BENEFIT SCHEME A scheme that is neither a **registered pension scheme** nor a section 615(3) scheme.

ENHANCED LIFETIME ALLOWANCE This is where the standard **lifetime allowance** has been increased as a result of **primary protection**, **pension credits** or transfers from **overseas pension schemes**, or where the member has not always had taxable UK earnings or been resident in the UK.

ENHANCED PROTECTION A form of protection from the **lifetime allowance charge** available for all members who registered for it under the FA 2004 tax regime, regardless of the amount of their benefits pre-6 April 2006.

ENTITLED WORKER For the purposes of **automatic enrolment**, a worker who ordinarily works in the UK, is aged at least 16 and under 75 and is in receipt of earnings of no more than the lower limit for **qualifying earnings**. Entitled workers are entitled to join a pension scheme but it need not be a **qualifying scheme** and the employer is not obliged to contribute.

ESCALATION A system whereby pensions in payment and/or **preserved benefits** are automatically increased at regular intervals and at a defined percentage rate.

EXPRESSION OF WISH A means by which a member can indicate a preference as to who should receive any lump sum death benefit. The choice is not binding on the **trustees**, and, as a result, inheritance tax is normally avoided.

FINAL PENSIONABLE EARNINGS/PAY/SALARY The **pensionable earnings** on which the benefits are calculated in a **DB scheme**. The earnings may be based on the average over a number of consecutive years prior to retirement, death or leaving **pensionable service**.

FINANCIAL ASSISTANCE SCHEME (FAS) A scheme introduced by the government to help workers who lost pension rights through

FINANCIAL ASSISTANCE SCHEME (FAS) *(continued)* company insolvency but whose schemes do not qualify for the **Pension Protection Fund**.

From 1 September 2016, the FAS no longer accepts schemes.

FINANCIAL SUPPORT DIRECTION A direction by the **Pensions Regulator**, requiring a company that is, or is connected to, an employer in relation to the scheme to put in place financial support arrangements where the effect of the corporate structure is that the employer is 'insufficiently resourced'.

FIXED PROTECTION A form of protection from the **lifetime allowance charge**. Different versions (fixed protection, fixed protection 2014 and fixed protection 2016) were introduced to coincide with reductions in the **lifetime allowance** from 6 April 2012.

FIXED RATE REVALUATION A method used by a former contracted-out salary-related scheme to revalue **GMP** e.g. between termination of **pensionable service** and age 65 (men), 60 (women) as one of the alternatives to applying **section 148 orders**.

The rate is reviewed periodically.

FLEXI-ACCESS DRAWDOWN A form of drawdown available from April 2015, from which individuals can take unlimited amounts as income. This replaces **flexible drawdown**.

FLEXIBLE BENEFITS **Money purchase benefits**, **cash balance benefits**, and other benefits calculated by reference to an amount available for their provision. Defined in section 74 PSA 2015 in relation to the money purchase flexibilities.

FLEXIBLE DRAWDOWN A form of drawdown available until April 2015 to individuals with a required minimum level of secure lifetime income and satisfying certain criteria. Individuals could take unlimited amounts as income and were not subject to **capped drawdown**. Replaced by **flexi-access drawdown**.

FLEXIBLE RETIREMENT OFFER An option allowing a member entitled to retire to take a **transfer payment**, which is used to access the money purchase flexibilities or purchase a higher level pension as an **annuity** from an insurance company.

FROZEN SCHEME A scheme with no further benefits accruing.

FUNDING LEVEL The relationship at a specified date between the value of the assets and the actuarial liability. Normally expressed as a percentage.

GENERAL DATA PROTECTION REGULATION The regulation that introduced a uniform data protection regime across the EU.

GMP CONVERSION The conversion of **GMPs** into 'normal' scheme benefits of equal actuarial value, permitted from 6 April 2009.

GMP EQUALISATION Equalising scheme benefits to take account of differences in the way that **GMPs** are calculated for men and women.

GUARANTEED ANNUITY RATE The right to apply the proceeds of an **arrangement** to buy an **annuity** at a rate guaranteed under that arrangement.

GUARANTEED MINIMUM PENSION (GMP) The minimum pension that an **occupational pension scheme** must provide as one of the conditions of contracting out for pre-6 April 1997 service (unless it was **contracted out** through the provision of **protected rights**).

HYBRID ARRANGEMENT Under FA 2004, an **arrangement** where only one type of benefit will ultimately be provided, but the type of benefit that will be provided is not known in advance because it will depend on certain circumstances at the point benefits are drawn.

HYBRID SCHEME An **occupational pension scheme** either:

(1) comprising **hybrid arrangements**, *or*
(2) providing more than one type of benefit, for example both defined benefit and **money purchase benefits**.

INCOME WITHDRAWAL An amount other than an **annuity** that a member is entitled to be paid from their **drawdown pension** fund or **flexi-access drawdown** fund.

INDEPENDENT GOVERNANCE COMMITTEE The committee that a workplace contract-based scheme must have, to oversee quality standards and protect members' interests.

INDEPENDENT TRUSTEE An independent trustee must be registered and an 'independent person in relation to the scheme'. This requirement will be satisfied if he or she has no interests in the assets of the employer or scheme and is not connected with the employer, insolvency practitioner or official receiver.

INDEXATION A system whereby pensions in payment and/or **preserved benefits** are automatically increased at regular intervals by reference to a specified index of prices or earnings.

INDIVIDUAL PROTECTION A form of protection from the **lifetime allowance charge**. Different versions (individual protection 2014 and individual protection 2016) were introduced to coincide with reductions in the **lifetime allowance** from 6 April 2014.

INTEGRATED RISK MANAGEMENT An approach to identifying and managing risk for **defined benefit schemes**, focusing on **employer covenant**, investment and funding.

INTERNAL DISPUTE RESOLUTION PROCEDURE (IDRP) **Occupational pension schemes** (subject to exceptions) are required to have a procedure to deal with disputes between **trustees** on the one hand and members and **beneficiaries** on the other hand.

JOBHOLDER For the purposes of **automatic enrolment,** a worker who ordinarily works in the UK, is aged at least 16 and under 75 and to whom **qualifying earnings** are payable.

LIFESTYLING An asset allocation strategy used mainly in relation to **money purchase benefits** whereby a member's investments are adjusted depending on the term until funds are drawn.

LIFETIME ALLOWANCE The lifetime allowance is an overall ceiling on the amount of tax-privileged savings that an individual can draw. The standard allowance is set in FA 2004; some individuals have a higher allowance.

LIFETIME ALLOWANCE CHARGE The tax charge levied on excess funds, following a **benefit crystallisation event**, for any individual crystallising more than their **lifetime allowance**.

LIFETIME ANNUITY Under FA 2004, an **annuity** contract purchased from an insurance company of the member's choosing that provides the member with an income for life.

LIFETIME ISA A type of individual savings account providing a means of saving for retirement or to purchase a first home, open to those under age 40 and attracting 'bonus' payments from the government up to age 50.

LIMITED PRICE INDEXATION (LPI) The requirement under PA 1995 to increase pensions in payment under an **occupational pension scheme** (excluding **AVCs** and **money purchase benefits**) by a minimum amount. The minimum is in line with price inflation or, if lower, 5% p.a. for benefits accrued between 6 April 1997 and 5 April 2005 and 2.5% p.a. for benefits accrued after 5 April 2005.

LOWER EARNINGS LIMIT (LEL) A threshold, the annual equivalent of which is the minimum that must be earned in a year in order for an individual to accrue State pension benefits.

MASTER TRUST An occupational **trust**-based scheme, promoted to provide benefits to employers that are not connected and where each employer group is not included in a separate section with its own **trustees**.

MEMBER-BORNE DEDUCTIONS All deductions (whether taken as a flat fee or a percentage) taken from money purchase funds under management, investment returns and contributions, but excluding transaction costs.

MONEY PURCHASE ANNUAL ALLOWANCE The reduced **annual allowance** applying to money purchase input where an individual with **money purchase benefits** has taken advantage of the money purchase flexibilities.

MONEY PURCHASE ARRANGEMENT Under FA 2004, an **arrangement** under which the member is entitled to benefits, the rate or amount of which is calculated by reference to an amount available for providing those benefits.

A cash balance arrangement is one type of money purchase arrangement.

MONEY PURCHASE BENEFITS Under PSA 1993, benefits the rate or amount of which is calculated solely by reference to assets that must necessarily suffice for provision. This includes pensions in payment that are secured by an **annuity** contract or insurance policy with an insurer and at all times before coming into payment met the above condition. This applies for the purposes of legislation including that in respect of scheme funding.

In some areas, money purchase benefits are referred to as defined contribution (DC) benefits.

NET PAY ARRANGEMENT The procedure whereby contributions to an **occupational pension scheme** are deducted from the member's pay before tax is calculated under PAYE, giving immediate tax relief at the highest applicable rate.

In some cases, **relief at source** *may be used instead, or relief claimed via self-assessment.*

NEW STATE PENSION The flat-rate State Pension that replaced the **Basic Pension** and **State Second Pension** for those reaching **State pensionable age** after 5 April 2016.

NOMINEE An individual, other than a **dependant** of the member, nominated by the member or **scheme administrator** to receive pension from a **money purchase arrangement** after the member's death.

NON-ASSOCIATED MULTI-EMPLOYER SCHEME (NAMES) A scheme, typically providing defined benefits, in which participating

NAMES *(continued)*
employers are not all connected (although they may be in the same industry).

NON-ELIGIBLE JOBHOLDER A **jobholder** who is not an **eligible jobholder**. A non-eligible jobholder is not eligible for **automatic enrolment** but can opt into an **automatic enrolment scheme**.

NORMAL MINIMUM PENSION AGE The earliest age, currently 55, at which a member is allowed to draw benefits from a **registered pension scheme**, other than in ill health. Transitional provisions allow members to protect existing rights at 5 April 2006 to receive their benefits from an earlier age.

NORMAL PENSION AGE (NPA)

(1) Commonly the age by reference to which the **normal pension date** is determined.

(2) The main statutory definition (relevant for **preservation** and **contracting-out** purposes) is the earliest age at which a member is entitled to receive benefits (other than **GMP**) on his/her retirement from employment to which the scheme relates, ignoring any special provisions as to early retirement on grounds of ill health or otherwise. This is commonly interpreted to mean the earliest age at which a member has the right to take benefits without reduction.

This may be different from definition (1) above or **normal retirement age**.

NORMAL PENSION DATE (NPD) The date at which a member of a pension scheme normally becomes entitled to receive his/her retirement benefits.

NORMAL RETIREMENT AGE (NRA)

(1) For employment purposes the age at which the employees holding a particular position normally retire from service.

This is often (but not always) the same as **normal pension age** *or definition (2) below.*

(2) The age of a member of an **occupational pension scheme** at the **normal retirement date** as specified in the scheme rules.

NORMAL RETIREMENT DATE (NRD) The date (usually the date of reaching a particular age) specified in the rules of an **occupational pension scheme** at which a member would normally retire.

NOTIFIABLE EVENTS Certain specified events to be automatically notified to the **Pensions Regulator** under section 69 of PA 2004.

OCCUPATIONAL PENSION SCHEME A scheme established by an employer or on behalf of a group of employers to provide pensions and/or other benefits for or in respect of one or more employees on leaving service or on death or on retirement.

The statutory definitions are in section 1 PSA 1993 and section 150 FA 2004.

OPEN MARKET OPTION The option to apply the proceeds of an insurance or investment contract to buy an **annuity** at a current market rate from the same or another insurance company.

OVERSEAS PENSION SCHEME A pension scheme established outside the UK for local residents of that country or employees of an international organisation, which is subject to local pension scheme and taxation regulations.

OVERSEAS TRANSFER CHARGE The tax charge applying on transfer to a **Qualifying Recognised Overseas Pension Scheme** unless certain conditions are met.

PARTICIPATING EMPLOYER An employer, some or all of whose employees have the right to become members of an **occupational pension scheme**.

Usually applied where more than one employer participates in a single scheme.

PAYMENT SCHEDULE A schedule, required under section 87 PA 1995 for money purchase **occupational pension schemes**, specifying contribution rates to be paid and the due dates for such payments.

PENSION ADVICE ALLOWANCE A type of **authorised payment** allowing individuals to withdraw up to £500 tax-free in a tax year (up to three times) from their **money purchase arrangement** or **hybrid arrangement** to put towards the cost of financial advice.

PENSION COMMENCEMENT LUMP SUM Under FA 2004, the term for the tax-free cash sum that may be paid to a member on taking pension benefits.

PENSION CREDIT The amount of benefit rights that an ex-spouse of a scheme member becomes entitled to following a **pension sharing order**.

PENSION DEBIT The amount of benefit rights given up by a scheme member when a **pension sharing order** is made in respect of them.

PENSION GUARANTEE An arrangement whereby, on the early death of a pensioner, the pension scheme pays a further sum or sums to meet a guaranteed total.

This total may be established by relation to, for instance, a multiple of the annual rate of pension or the accumulated contributions of the late member.

PENSION INCREASE An increase to a pension in payment.

Such an increase may arise as a result of **escalation** *or* **indexation** *or may be a* **discretionary increase**.

PENSION INCREASE EXCHANGE EXERCISE An offer to members to exchange future, non-statutory increases on their pensions for higher fixed pensions.

PENSION INPUT AMOUNT The amount of contributions paid or increase in value of a member's benefits in an **arrangement**, measured for **annual allowance** purposes.

PENSION INPUT PERIOD The period over which the **pension input amount** for an **arrangement** is measured.

PENSION PROTECTION FUND (PPF) A fund set up under PA 2004 to provide benefits to members of **DB schemes** that **wind up** due to the employer's insolvency with insufficient assets to pay benefits.

PENSION SALARY SACRIFICE An agreement between the employer and employee whereby the employee forgoes part of his/her future earnings in return for a corresponding contribution by the employer to a pension scheme.

PENSION SCAM The transfer (or release) of a member's pension savings to an arrangement that is illegitimate and/or inappropriate. Sometimes referred to as pensions liberation.

PENSION SCHEMES REGISTRY The register of **occupational pension schemes** and **personal pension schemes**, maintained by the **Pensions Regulator**.

The registry enables members to trace schemes with which they have lost touch.

PENSION SHARING ORDER An order making provision for the pension rights of a scheme member to be split on divorce.

PENSION WISE The government service introduced in 2015 to provide free and impartial guidance on financial choices for individuals with **flexible benefits**.

PENSIONABLE EARNINGS/PAY/SALARY The earnings on which contributions and/or benefits are calculated under the rules of an **occupational pension scheme**.

PENSIONABLE SERVICE The period of service that is taken into account in calculating benefits.

PSA 1993 gives the term a statutory definition for the purposes of the **preservation**, **revaluation** *and* **transfer payment** *requirements of the Act. PA 1995 gives a further statutory definition.*

PENSIONS DASHBOARD An online resource allowing individuals to find their retirement savings and view them all in one place.

PENSIONS OMBUDSMAN The Pensions Ombudsman deals with disputes about entitlement and complaints of maladministration from members of **occupational pension schemes** and **personal pension schemes**.

PENSIONS REGULATOR, THE (The Regulator, TPR) An independent body set up under PA 2004 to regulate **occupational pension schemes** from 6 April 2005.

PERSONAL LIFETIME ALLOWANCE The **lifetime allowance** applicable to individuals who have registered for **primary protection**. It is indexed in line with changes in the standard lifetime allowance but taking that allowance to be at least £1.8m for tax years following 5 April 2012.

See also **enhanced lifetime allowance**.

PERSONAL PENSION SCHEME A scheme provided by an insurance company (or another financial institution) to enable individuals to save for retirement.

The statutory definition is in section 1 PSA 1993.

POSTPONEMENT In the context of **automatic enrolment**, the use by an employer of a waiting period, of up to three months, to defer the obligation to automatically enrol a worker.

PRESERVATION The granting by a scheme of **preserved benefits** to a member leaving **pensionable service** before **normal pension age** under an **occupational pension scheme**, in particular in accordance with minimum requirements specified by PSA 1993.

PRESERVED BENEFITS Benefits arising on an individual ceasing to be an **active member** of an **occupational pension scheme**, payable at a later date.

PRIMARY PROTECTION A mechanism by which individuals could register pre-6 April 2006 rights of more than £1.5m and obtain an increased **personal lifetime allowance**.

PRINCIPAL EMPLOYER Commonly used in scheme documentation for the particular **participating employer** in which is vested special powers or duties in relation to such matters as the appointment of the **trustees**, amendments and **winding up**. Usually this will be the employer that established the scheme or its successor in business.

PRIORITY RULE The provisions contained within the scheme documentation setting out the order of precedence of liabilities to be followed if the scheme is wound up.

Section 73 PA 1995 introduced an overriding statutory order of priorities.

PROFESSIONAL TRUSTEE A **trustee** of an **occupational pension scheme** who is considered as professional by the **Pensions Regulator** because they act as a trustee in the course of the business of being a trustee. Higher standards are expected from professional trustees.

PROJECTED UNIT METHOD A funding method in which the actuarial liability makes allowance for projected earnings. The contribution rate is that necessary to cover the cost of all benefits that will accrue in the control period following the valuation date by reference to earnings projected to the dates on which the benefits become payable.

Also known as the projected unit credit method.

PROSPECTIVE MEMBER An individual, not currently a member of the pension scheme of his/her employer, who is either entitled to join or will become eligible to join in the future by virtue of continuing in employment with the employer.

PROTECTED PERSONS Certain employees of some formerly nationalised industries, in respect of whom legislation limits the ability of the employers and pension scheme **trustees** to change scheme rules.

PROTECTED RIGHTS The benefits from a scheme **contracted out** on a money purchase basis deriving from at least the minimum contributions or minimum payments, provided in a specified form as a necessary condition of contracting out.

Protected rights were abolished from 6 April 2012, when contracting out of **S2P** *on a money purchase basis was abolished.*

PUBLIC SECTOR PENSION SCHEME An **occupational pension scheme** for employees of central or local government, a nationalised industry or other statutory body.

PURCHASED LIFE ANNUITY An **annuity** purchased privately by an individual.

QUALIFYING EARNINGS The band of gross earnings between limits set each year on which minimum contributions for the purposes of **automatic enrolment** are calculated.

QUALIFYING OVERSEAS PENSION SCHEME (QOPS) An **overseas pension scheme** where the scheme manager has undertaken to provide HMRC with certain information.

QUALIFYING RECOGNISED OVERSEAS PENSION SCHEME (QROPS) A **recognised overseas pension scheme** where the scheme manager has advised HMRC of its status and undertaken to meet detailed requirements for providing information.

A **recognised transfer** *can be made to a QROPS.*

QUALIFYING SCHEME For the purposes of **automatic enrolment**, any **occupational** or **personal pension scheme** that meets statutory minimum criteria for the **jobholder** in question.

QUALIFYING SERVICE The term defined in section 71(7) PSA 1993 denoting the service to be taken into account to entitle the member to **short service benefit**.

From 1 October 2015, the minimum period required was reduced from 2 years to 30 days for members entitled only to **money purchase benefits**.

RECOGNISED OVERSEAS PENSION SCHEME (ROPS) Under FA 2004, an **overseas pension scheme** that is established and recognised in a prescribed country and satisfies all prescribed requirements.

RECOGNISED TRANSFER Under FA 2004, a transfer representing a member's **accrued rights** under a **registered pension scheme** to another registered pension scheme (or, in certain circumstances, to an insurance company) or a **qualifying recognised overseas pension scheme**.

RECOVERY PLAN If an **actuarial valuation** shows that the **statutory funding objective** is not met, the **trustees** will have to prepare a 'recovery plan' setting out the steps to be taken (and over what period) to make up the shortfall.

REGISTERED PENSION SCHEME A pension scheme is a registered pension scheme at any time when, either through having applied for **registration** and having been registered by HMRC, or through acquiring registered status by virtue of being an approved scheme on 5 April 2006, it is registered under FA 2004.

REGISTRATION The process of applying to HMRC and being accepted as a **registered pension scheme**. From 6 April 2006, registration

REGISTRATION *(continued)*
replaced 'HMRC approval' as the process by which schemes obtain tax-advantaged status. 'De-registration' refers to the withdrawal by HMRC of a scheme's registered status.

REGULATED APPORTIONMENT ARRANGEMENT An arrangement where the **section 75 debt** due from an employer is changed, usually by reapportionment of all or part to other employers. It must be approved by the **Pensions Regulator** and requires the scheme to be in, or there to be a reasonable likelihood it will enter, a PPF **assessment period**.

RELIEF AT SOURCE The procedure whereby member contributions are paid net of basic rate tax and the **scheme administrator** claims the tax from HMRC. Any higher-rate tax is claimed under self-assessment.

For an **occupational pension scheme***, a* **net pay arrangement** *is more likely to be used.*

RETIREMENT ANNUITY An **annuity** contract between an insurance company or friendly society and a self-employed individual or a person not in pensionable employment, which was established before 1 July 1988.

REVALUATION The application, particularly to **preserved benefits**, of **indexation** or **escalation** or the awarding of **discretionary increases**. PSA 1993 imposes a minimum level of revaluation in the calculation of **GMP** and of preserved benefits other than GMP.

RISK WARNING A written communication that must be given in certain circumstances to members with **flexible benefits**, explaining the factors that may affect their retirement income. In some cases, risk warnings must be tailored to the members' personal circumstances.

SAFEGUARDED BENEFITS Benefits other than **cash balance** and **money purchase benefits**. Defined in section 48 PSA 2015, in relation to the requirement for independent advice to be obtained before conversion or transfer.

SAFEGUARDED-FLEXIBLE BENEFITS Benefits, other than **cash balance** and **money purchase benefits**, calculated by reference to an amount available for their provision. These are benefits that fall within the definitions of both **flexible benefits** and **safeguarded benefits**.

This includes benefits with a **guaranteed annuity rate**.

SCHEDULE OF CONTRIBUTIONS A schedule specifying the contribution rates and payment dates (normally) agreed between the employer and the **trustees** of a **DB scheme** and certified by the **scheme actuary** as being adequate to satisfy the **statutory funding objective**.

SCHEME ACTUARY The named actuary appointed by the **trustees** or managers of an **occupational pension scheme** under section 47 PA 1995.

SCHEME ADMINISTRATION MEMBER PAYMENT Under FA 2004, a payment made by a **registered pension scheme** to a member, or in respect of a member, for the purposes of administration or management of the scheme.

SCHEME ADMINISTRATOR The person or persons notified to HMRC as being responsible for the management of a pension scheme.

SCHEME AUDITOR The auditor appointed by the **trustees** or managers of an **occupational pension scheme** under section 47 PA 1995.

SCHEME PAYS Where a member's pension savings exceed the **annual allowance** for the tax year, the member can oblige (or in some cases ask) the scheme to pay all or part of the charge on their behalf and reduce their benefit entitlement accordingly.

SCHEME PENSION Under FA 2004, a pension entitlement provided to a member of a **registered pension scheme**, which is an absolute right to a lifetime pension payable by the scheme.

SCHEME RETURN Information submitted by schemes to the **Pensions Regulator**, which it uses to make sure the details it holds on the register of pension schemes are accurate, calculate levies due from pension schemes and regulate pension schemes. The information collected is also used by the **Pension Protection Fund**.

SECONDED EMPLOYEE For the purposes of the legislation on **cross-border schemes**, an employee who is sent, by a UK employer, to work overseas for a limited period in another EEA state, is still providing services on behalf of the UK employer and intends to return to resume work for that employer in the UK or to retire at the end of that period.

SECTION 9(2B) RIGHTS Rights to benefits (other than from **AVCs**) under an **occupational pension scheme** contracted out on a salary-related basis by virtue of section 9(2B) PSA 1993 and which are attributable to **contracted-out** employment between 6 April 1997 and 5 April 2016 (when contracting out ended).

SECTION 32 POLICY Used widely to describe an insurance policy used for **buy-out** purposes. This term came into use as a result of section 32 FA 1981.

SECTION 67 Section 67 PA 1995 requires that **trustees** obtain members' consents, or a certificate from an actuary, before making any modification to an **occupational pension scheme** that would or might affect members' entitlements or **accrued rights** in respect of service before the modification.

SECTION 75 DEBT A debt due to a pension scheme under PA 1995 from a sponsoring employer if that employer becomes insolvent or leaves a multi-employer scheme, or the scheme starts to **wind up**, when the scheme is underfunded.

SECTION 143 VALUATION A written valuation of the scheme's assets and liabilities for the purposes of enabling the **Pension Protection Fund** to determine whether it must assume responsibility for the scheme.

SECTION 148 ORDERS Orders issued each year in accordance with section 148 Social Security Administration Act 1992 specifying the rates of increase to be applied to the earnings factors on which **GMPs** are based.

This **revaluation** *is based on the increase in national average earnings. Formerly known as section 21 orders.*

SECTION 179 VALUATION A written valuation of a scheme's assets and liabilities, prepared and signed by the **scheme actuary**, for the purposes of enabling **Pension Protection Fund** levies to be calculated.

SELF-ADMINISTERED SCHEME An **occupational pension scheme** where the assets are invested, other than wholly by payment of insurance premiums, by the **trustees**, an in-house investment manager or an external investment manager.

SELF-INVESTED PERSONAL PENSION (SIPP) A **personal pension scheme** that allows the member to choose the investments.

SELF-INVESTMENT The investment of the assets of an **occupational pension scheme** in employer-related investments.

A 5% limit is imposed on employer-related investments by PA 1995 (with certain exemptions).

SERIOUS ILL HEALTH COMMUTATION Full commutation of benefits if a member's life expectancy is less than 12 months.

SHARED RISK SCHEME A scheme that gives a promise, before retirement, about some but not all aspects of the benefits.

SHORT SERVICE BENEFIT The benefit that must be provided for an early leaver with a legal right under the **preservation** legislation.

SHORT SERVICE REFUND LUMP SUM A refund of contributions available to employees who have stopped accruing benefits under the scheme but are not entitled to **short service benefit** under section 71 PSA 1993.

SHORT-TERM ANNUITY Under FA 2004, an **annuity** contract purchased from a member's **drawdown pension** fund held under a **money purchase arrangement** that provides that member with pension income for a term of no more than five years.

SINGLE FINANCIAL GUIDANCE BODY The new statutory body responsible for providing debt advice, money guidance and pensions guidance.

SMALL SELF-ADMINISTERED SCHEME (SSAS) A **trust**-based **occupational pension scheme**, usually established for the directors of a limited company and allowing members to direct the investments.

A different definition, arising from legislation, applied before 6 April 2006.

SOCIALLY RESPONSIBLE INVESTMENT (SRI) Investment strategies or restrictions that take account of the environmental, social and governance (ESG) impacts that a company's activities can have on individuals and the environment. Pension funds are required to disclose in their **Statement of Investment Principles** the extent to which they take these factors into account.

SOLVENCY The ability of a **defined benefit scheme** to cover its liabilities on **discontinuance**.

STAGING The process of introducing employer duties for **automatic enrolment** at monthly stages on allocated dates between 2012 and 2018. The staging date for an employer depended on its size (as measured by the number in its PAYE scheme on 1 April 2012).

STAKEHOLDER PENSION SCHEME A scheme that provides **money purchase benefits**, is registered with HMRC and satisfies the CAT standards necessary to be registered with the **Pensions Regulator** as a stakeholder scheme.

STATE EARNINGS-RELATED PENSION SCHEME (SERPS) The additional pension provisions of the State pension scheme.

This was replaced by the **State Second Pension (S2P)** *from 6 April 2002.*

STATE PENSIONABLE AGE (SPA) The age from which pensions are normally payable by the State pension scheme as defined in Schedule 4 PA 1995.

STATE PENSION CREDIT An income-related (means-tested) benefit that supplements a pensioner's State pension to ensure they have a minimum level of income.

STATE SECOND PENSION (S2P) The State pension scheme introduced with effect from 6 April 2002 to replace **SERPS** and to enhance the **Basic Pension**.

It is replaced by the **new State Pension** *for those reaching* **State pensionable age** *after 5 April 2016.*

STATEMENT OF FUNDING PRINCIPLES Statement by the **trustees** setting out their policy for securing that the **statutory funding objective** is met and recording the decisions as to the basis for calculating the scheme's **technical provisions** and the period within which any shortfall is to be remedied.

STATEMENT OF INVESTMENT PRINCIPLES (SIP) A written statement of principles governing decisions about investment for an **occupational pension scheme**, which **trustees** are required to prepare and maintain. Trustees must have regard to advice from a suitably qualified person and consult with the employer.

STATEMENT OF RECOMMENDED PRACTICE (SORP) Guidance on best accounting practice for the presentation of financial information prepared by the particular industry to which the SORP relates.

STATUTORY EMPLOYER In a **DB scheme**, the employer legally responsible for meeting the **statutory funding objective**, paying any **section 75 debt** and triggering entry to the **PPF**.

STATUTORY FUNDING OBJECTIVE The requirement that a **DB scheme** 'must have sufficient and appropriate assets to cover its **technical provisions**'.

STATUTORY MONEY PURCHASE ILLUSTRATION (SMPI) An annual statement, which must be issued to members with **money purchase benefits**, illustrating on a prescribed statutory basis the projected value of a member's benefits at retirement, in today's terms.

SUCCESSOR An individual nominated to receive pension deriving from unused **drawdown pension** funds under a **money purchase arrangement** on the death of a **dependant**, a **nominee**, or a previous successor.

SUMMARY FUNDING STATEMENT A summary of the scheme's funding position. It must be issued, normally annually, to all scheme members and **beneficiaries**. Certain schemes, such as those in **wind-up**, are exempt.

TAPERED ANNUAL ALLOWANCE The reduced **annual allowance** applying from 6 April 2016 to certain higher earners.

TECHNICAL PROVISIONS Under the scheme funding provisions of PA 2004, the amount required on an actuarial calculation to make provision for the scheme's liabilities.

TRANSFER CLUB A group of employers and **occupational pension schemes** that has agreed to a common basis of **transfer payments**.

TRANSFER INCENTIVE EXERCISE An offer of an enhanced transfer value, to encourage members to transfer out their defined benefits.

TRANSFER PAYMENT A payment made from a pension scheme to another pension scheme, or to purchase a **buy-out** policy, in lieu of benefits that have accrued to the member or members concerned, to enable the receiving **arrangement** to provide alternative benefits.

The transfer payment may be made in accordance with the scheme rules or in exercise of a member's statutory rights under PSA 1993. See also **cash equivalent**.

TRIPLE LOCK Annual increases to some State pensions at the higher of average earnings growth, price inflation and 2.5%.

TRIVIAL COMMUTATION Payment of a member's rights under a defined benefit **arrangement** as a lump sum, permitted subject to certain conditions under FA 2004 if the member's total pension rights are valued below a specified amount.

TRUST A legal concept whereby property is held by one or more persons (the **trustees**) for the benefit of others (the **beneficiaries**) for the purposes specified by the trust instrument. The trustees may also be beneficiaries.

TRUST DEED A legal document, executed in the form of a deed, which establishes, regulates or amends a **trust**.

TRUSTEE An individual or company appointed to carry out the purposes of a **trust** in accordance with the provisions of the **trust deed** (or other documents by which a trust is created and governed) and general principles of trust law.

TRUSTEE REPORT A report by the **trustees** describing various aspects of an **occupational pension scheme**. It may form part of the **annual report.**

UNCRYSTALLISED FUNDS PENSION LUMP SUM (**UFPLS**) A lump sum from a member's uncrystallised funds in a **money purchase arrangement**.

UPPER ACCRUAL POINT (UAP) The maximum amount of earnings on which **S2P** and contracted-out rebates were based, until 5 April 2016.

UPPER BAND EARNINGS Earnings between the **lower earnings limit** and the **upper accrual point**.

UPPER EARNINGS LIMIT (UEL) The upper limit to earnings on which full-rate NI contributions are payable by employees. NI contributions are payable by employees at a lower rate on earnings above this limit.

VESTED RIGHTS

(1) For **active members**, benefits to which they would unconditionally be entitled on leaving the scheme

(2) for **deferred pensioners**, their **preserved benefits**, *and*

(3) for pensioners, pensions to which they are entitled including where appropriate the related benefits for spouses or other **dependants**.

WHISTLE-BLOWING The statutory duty imposed on **trustees**, employers, **administrators** and advisers to advise the **Pensions Regulator** as soon as practicable in writing if they have reasonable cause to believe there is a material problem with an **occupational pension scheme**.

WINDING UP The process of terminating an **occupational pension scheme** (or less commonly a **personal pension scheme**), usually by applying the assets to the purchase of immediate **annuities** and deferred annuities for the **beneficiaries**, or by transferring the assets and liabilities to another pension scheme, in accordance with the scheme documentation or statute (section 74 PA 1995).

WITH-PROFITS POLICY An insurance policy under which a share of the surpluses disclosed by actuarial valuations of the insurance company's life and pensions business is payable in addition to the guaranteed benefits or in reduction of future premiums.

Many of the definitions used in this Glossary of Terms originate from the Eighth edition of *Pensions Terminology*, published by the Pensions Management Institute and the Pensions Research Accountants Group, whose kind permission to reproduce here is gratefully acknowledged.

APPENDIX 3

COMPOUND INTEREST TABLES

How to use the compound interest tables to generate additional factors:

Present value of a payment of one unit due in *n* years' time	$v^n = \dfrac{1}{(1+i)^n}$
Present value of an annuity of one unit per annum payable annually in arrears for *n* years	$a_{\overline{n}\rceil} = \dfrac{1-v^n}{i}$
Present value of an annuity of one unit per annum payable annually in advance for *n* years	$\ddot{a}_{\overline{n}\rceil} = \dfrac{1-v^n}{d}$
Present value of an annuity of one unit per annum payable continuously for *n* years	$\bar{a}_{\overline{n}\rceil} = \dfrac{1-v^n}{\delta}$
Present value of an annuity of one unit per annum payable in two half-yearly instalments in arrears for *n* years	$a^{(2)}_{\overline{n}\rceil} = \dfrac{i}{i^{(2)}} a_{\overline{n}\rceil}$
Present value of an annuity of one unit per annum payable in four quarterly instalments in arrears for *n* years	$a^{(4)}_{\overline{n}\rceil} = \dfrac{i}{i^{(4)}} a_{\overline{n}\rceil}$
Present value of an annuity of one unit per annum payable in twelve monthly instalments in arrears for *n* years	$a^{(12)}_{\overline{n}\rceil} = \dfrac{i}{i^{(12)}} a_{\overline{n}\rceil}$
Accumulated value after *n* years of an annuity of one unit payable annually in arrears	$s_{\overline{n}\rceil} = \dfrac{(1+i)^n - 1}{i}$

Accumulated value after n years of a single unit payment $[(1+i)^n]$

n	i=1%	i=2%	i=3%	i=4%	i=5%
1	1.010000	1.020000	1.030000	1.040000	1.050000
2	1.020100	1.040400	1.060900	1.081600	1.102500
3	1.030301	1.061208	1.092727	1.124864	1.157625
4	1.040604	1.082432	1.125509	1.169859	1.215506
5	1.051010	1.104081	1.159274	1.216653	1.276282
6	1.061520	1.126162	1.194052	1.265319	1.340096
7	1.072135	1.148686	1.229874	1.315932	1.407100
8	1.082857	1.171659	1.266770	1.368569	1.477455
9	1.093685	1.195093	1.304773	1.423312	1.551328
10	1.104622	1.218994	1.343916	1.480244	1.628895
11	1.115668	1.243374	1.384234	1.539454	1.710339
12	1.126825	1.268242	1.425761	1.601032	1.795856
13	1.138093	1.293607	1.468534	1.665074	1.885649
14	1.149474	1.319479	1.512590	1.731676	1.979932
15	1.160969	1.345868	1.557967	1.800944	2.078928
16	1.172579	1.372786	1.604706	1.872981	2.182875
17	1.184304	1.400241	1.652848	1.947900	2.292018
18	1.196147	1.428246	1.702433	2.025817	2.406619
19	1.208109	1.456811	1.753506	2.106849	2.526950
20	1.220190	1.485947	1.806111	2.191123	2.653298
21	1.232392	1.515666	1.860295	2.278768	2.785963
22	1.244716	1.545980	1.916103	2.369919	2.925261
23	1.257163	1.576899	1.973587	2.464716	3.071524
24	1.269735	1.608437	2.032794	2.563304	3.225100
25	1.282432	1.640606	2.093778	2.665836	3.386355
26	1.295256	1.673418	2.156591	2.772470	3.555673
27	1.308209	1.706886	2.221289	2.883369	3.733456
28	1.321291	1.741024	2.287928	2.998703	3.920129
29	1.334504	1.775845	2.356566	3.118651	4.116136
30	1.347849	1.811362	2.427262	3.243398	4.321942
31	1.361327	1.847589	2.500080	3.373133	4.538039
32	1.374941	1.884541	2.575083	3.508059	4.764941
33	1.388690	1.922231	2.652335	3.648381	5.003189
34	1.402577	1.960676	2.731905	3.794316	5.253348
35	1.416603	1.999890	2.813862	3.946089	5.516015
36	1.430769	2.039887	2.898278	4.103933	5.791816
37	1.445076	2.080685	2.985227	4.268090	6.081407
38	1.459527	2.122299	3.074783	4.438813	6.385477
39	1.474123	2.164745	3.167027	4.616366	6.704751
40	1.488864	2.208040	3.262038	4.801021	7.039989

	i=1%	i=2%	i=3%	i=4%	i=5%
d	0.009901	0.019608	0.029126	0.038462	0.047619
$i^{(2)}$	0.009975	0.019901	0.029778	0.039608	0.049390
$i^{(4)}$	0.009963	0.019852	0.029668	0.039414	0.049089
$i^{(12)}$	0.009954	0.019819	0.029595	0.039285	0.048889
δ	0.009950	0.019803	0.029559	0.039221	0.048790

Note: For GMP fixed rate revaluation factors *see page 266*.

Accumulated value after *n* years of a single unit payment $[(1+i)^n]$

n	*i*=6%	*i*=7%	*i*=8%	*i*=9%	*i*=10%
1	1.060000	1.070000	1.080000	1.090000	1.100000
2	1.123600	1.144900	1.166400	1.188100	1.210000
3	1.191016	1.225043	1.259712	1.295029	1.331000
4	1.262477	1.310796	1.360489	1.411582	1.464100
5	1.338226	1.402552	1.469328	1.538624	1.610510
6	1.418519	1.500730	1.586874	1.677100	1.771561
7	1.503630	1.605781	1.713824	1.828039	1.948717
8	1.593848	1.718186	1.850930	1.992563	2.143589
9	1.689479	1.838459	1.999005	2.171893	2.357948
10	1.790848	1.967151	2.158925	2.367364	2.593742
11	1.898299	2.104852	2.331639	2.580426	2.853117
12	2.012196	2.252192	2.518170	2.812665	3.138428
13	2.132928	2.409845	2.719624	3.065805	3.452271
14	2.260904	2.578534	2.937194	3.341727	3.797498
15	2.396558	2.759032	3.172169	3.642482	4.177248
16	2.540352	2.952164	3.425943	3.970306	4.594973
17	2.692773	3.158815	3.700018	4.327633	5.054470
18	2.854339	3.379932	3.996019	4.717120	5.559917
19	3.025600	3.616528	4.315701	5.141661	6.115909
20	3.207135	3.869684	4.660957	5.604411	6.727500
21	3.399564	4.140562	5.033834	6.108808	7.400250
22	3.603537	4.430402	5.436540	6.658600	8.140275
23	3.819750	4.740530	5.871464	7.257874	8.954302
24	4.048935	5.072367	6.341181	7.911083	9.849733
25	4.291871	5.427433	6.848475	8.623081	10.834706
26	4.549383	5.807353	7.396353	9.399158	11.918177
27	4.822346	6.213868	7.988061	10.245082	13.109994
28	5.111687	6.648838	8.627106	11.167140	14.420994
29	5.418388	7.114257	9.317275	12.172182	15.863093
30	5.743491	7.612255	10.062657	13.267678	17.449402
31	6.088101	8.145113	10.867669	14.461770	19.194342
32	6.453387	8.715271	11.737083	15.763329	21.113777
33	6.840590	9.325340	12.676050	17.182028	23.225154
34	7.251025	9.978114	13.690134	18.728411	25.547670
35	7.686087	10.676581	14.785344	20.413968	28.102437
36	8.147252	11.423942	15.968172	22.251225	30.912681
37	8.636087	12.223618	17.245626	24.253835	34.003949
38	9.154252	13.079271	18.625276	26.436680	37.404343
39	9.703507	13.994820	20.115298	28.815982	41.144778
40	10.285718	14.974458	21.724521	31.409420	45.259256

	i=6%	*i*=7%	*i*=8%	*i*=9%	*i*=10%
d	0.056604	0.065421	0.074074	0.082569	0.090909
$i^{(2)}$	0.059126	0.068816	0.078461	0.088061	0.097618
$i^{(4)}$	0.058695	0.068234	0.077706	0.087113	0.096455
$i^{(12)}$	0.058411	0.067850	0.077208	0.086488	0.095690
δ	0.058269	0.067659	0.076961	0.086178	0.095310

Note: For GMP fixed rate revaluation factors *see page 266*.

APPENDIX 4

ANNUITY FACTORS

MALE LIFE ANNUITIES ON S2PMA (Year of Use=2019) TABLE

With future improvements in life expectancy based on the CMI_2017 Core Projections for males with a long-term rate of improvement of 1.5% p.a.

Exact age:	55	60	65	70	75
Interest					
0%	31.718	26.869	22.165	17.794	13.657
1%	26.787	23.208	19.571	16.045	12.568
2%	22.930	20.258	17.420	14.554	11.613
3%	19.874	17.857	15.622	13.274	10.774
4%	17.423	15.884	14.107	12.170	10.031
5%	15.436	14.248	12.822	11.212	9.373

Note: The columns represent the present value of a life annuity of one unit per year payable continuously to a male from the exact age given subject to the mortality experience of the S2PMA table, adjusted for use in 2019, allowing for future improvements in life expectancy based on the CMI_2017 Core Projections for males with a long-term rate of improvement of 1.5% p.a. and valued at the rates of interest shown.

FEMALE LIFE ANNUITIES ON S2PFA (Year of Use=2019) TABLE

With future improvements in life expectancy based on the CMI_2017 Core Projections for females with a long-term rate of improvement of 1.5% p.a.

Exact age:	55	60	65	70	75
Interest					
0%	33.864	28.924	24.096	19.496	15.117
1%	28.345	24.773	21.108	17.455	13.823
2%	24.073	21.461	18.654	15.730	12.699
3%	20.722	18.791	16.621	14.262	11.717
4%	18.059	16.617	14.923	13.006	10.855
5%	15.918	14.827	13.493	11.923	10.095

Note: The columns represent the present value of a life annuity of one unit per year payable continuously to a female from the exact age given subject to the mortality experience of the S2PFA table, adjusted for use in 2019, allowing for future improvements in life expectancy based on the CMI_2017 Core Projections for females with a long-term rate of improvement of 1.5% p.a. and valued at the rates of interest shown.

APPENDIX 5

USEFUL WEBSITES

This chapter shows the website addresses of the main sites likely to be of relevance to readers, together with brief description of some of the sites where content may not be familiar.

Government departments and organisations

Companies House Executive Agency	*www.gov.uk/government/organisations/companies-house*
Department for Work and Pensions	*www.gov.uk/government/organisations/department-for-work-pensions*
State Pensions	*www.gov.uk/browse/working/state-pension*
Welfare, including universal credit	*www.gov.uk/government/topics/welfare*
HM Treasury	*www.gov.uk/government/organisations/hm-treasury*
HM Revenue & Customs	*www.gov.uk/government/organisations/hm-revenue-customs*
National Insurance Services to Pensions Industry – scheme reconciliation	*www.gov.uk/guidance/nispi-pension-schemes-reconciliation-services*
Pension scheme administration including forms and information requirements	*www.gov.uk/topic/business-tax/pension-scheme-administration*
Government Actuary's Department	*www.gov.uk/government/organisations/government-actuarys-department*
UK Legislation	*www.legislation.gov.uk*

Regulators and ombudsmen

Financial Reporting Council regulates accounting, auditing and actuarial functions	*https://frc.org.uk*
Financial Conduct Authority regulates financial services industry	*www.fca.org.uk*
Find an Adviser	*www.fca.org.uk/consumers/finding- adviser*
Information Commissioner's Office data protection	*https://ico.org.uk*
Financial Ombudsman Service financial services complaints	*www.financial-ombudsman.org.uk*
Pensions Ombudsman pension complaints including PPF	*www.pensions-ombudsman.org.uk*
Pensions Regulator	*www.thepensionsregulator.gov.uk*
Prudential Regulation Authority supervises certain financial firms	*www.bankofengland.co.uk/pra/Pages/default.aspx*

Other Government sites

Parliament	*www.parliament.uk*
Pension Protection Fund including Financial Assistance Scheme	*www.pensionprotectionfund.org.uk/Pages/hompepage.aspx*

Financial Services Compensation Scheme	*www.fscs.org.uk*
Office for National Statistics economic statistics	*www.ons.gov.uk/economy*
Pension Wise (guidance on DC pensions options)	*www.pensionwise.gov.uk*

Industry and professional bodies

Association of British Insurers	*www.abi.org.uk*
Association of Consulting Actuaries	*www.aca.org.uk*
Association of Member-Directed Pension Schemes mainly represents SIPPS and SSAS	*www.ampsonline.co.uk*
Association of Pension Lawyers	*www.apl.org.uk*
Chartered Insurance Institute	*www.cii.co.uk*
Incentive Exercises Monitoring Board	*www.incentiveexercises.org.uk*
Institute and Faculty of Actuaries	*www.actuaries.org.uk*
Institute of Chartered Accountants in England and Wales	*www.icaew.com*
International Accounting Standards Board and IFRS Foundation	*www.ifrs.org*
Law Society	*www.lawsociety.org.uk*
Pensions Administration Standards Association	*www.pasa-uk.com*
Pensions and Lifetime Savings Association	*www.plsa.co.uk*
Pensions Management Institute	*www.pensions-pmi.org.uk/home*
Pensions Policy Institute comment on, and analysis of, public pensions policy	*www.pensionspolicyinstitute.org.uk*
Pensions Research Advisory Group principally reporting and accounting	*www.prag.org.uk*
Society of Pension Professionals	*http://the-spp.co.uk*

Other sources of information

British and Irish Legal Information Institute court judgments (including EU)	*www.bailii.org*
EU website	*https://europa.eu/index_en.htm*
The Pensions Advisory Service information and guidance on occupational/personal pensions	*www.pensionsadvisoryservice.org.uk*
Money Advice Service generic information on money issues	*www.moneyadviceservice.org.uk*

PENSIONS POCKET BOOK ONLINE

www.pensionspocketbook.com

The **Pensions Pocket Book Online** is a companion to the Pocket Book and provides additional data and information not included in the printed version. It is available exclusively to purchasers of the Pocket Book. Here you will find historical pensions information no longer included in the current edition, data that is too bulky for the pocket-size format, and some information not available when the publication went to press.

(NB – the website supplements the 2019 edition: a lot of information in the Pocket Book is not on the site, and vice versa.)

To access **Pensions Pocket Book Online** go to:

www.pensionspocketbook.com

Your username is:

PPB2019

Your password is:

BY92AHR

OFFICES IN THE UNITED KINGDOM

www.aon.com/unitedkingdom/

Belfast
1st floor, 65–67 Chichester Street
Belfast BT1 4JD
Northern Ireland

Tel: +44 (0) 28 9024 2771

Birmingham
Colmore Gate
2 Colmore Row
Birmingham B3 2QD

Tel: +44 (0) 121 262 5000

Bristol
25 Marsh Street
Bristol BS1 4AQ

Tel: +44 (0) 117 929 4001

Edinburgh
Atria One
144 Morrison Street
Edinburgh EH3 8EX

Tel: +44 (0) 131 456 6400

Epsom
Parkside House
Ashley Road
Epsom
Surrey KT18 5BS

Tel: +44 (0) 1372 733000

Farnborough
Briarcliff House
Kingsmead
Farnborough
Hampshire GU14 7TE

Tel: +44 (0) 1252 768000

Leeds
3 The Embankment
Sovereign Street
Leeds
West Yorkshire LS1 4BJ

Tel: +44 (0) 113 245 3366

London
The Aon Centre
The Leadenhall Building
122 Leadenhall Street
London EC3V 4AN

Tel: +44 (0) 207 086 5516

Manchester
40 Spring Gardens
Manchester M2 1EN

Tel: +44 (0) 161 687 2000

St Albans
Verulam Point
Station Way
St Albans
Hertfordshire AL1 5HE

Tel: +44 (0) 1727 888200

Sheffield
5th Floor
The Fountain Precinct
Balm Green
Sheffield S1 2JA

Tel: +44 (0) 114 275 5185